Alternative Agriculture
A HISTORY

Alternative Agriculture

A HISTORY

FROM THE BLACK DEATH TO THE PRESENT DAY

❧

Joan Thirsk

OXFORD UNIVERSITY PRESS
1997

Oxford University Press, Great Clarendon Street, Oxford OX2 6DP

Oxford New York

Athens Auckland Bangkok Bogota Bombay
Buenos Aires Calcutta Cape Town Dar es Salaam
Delhi Florence Hong Kong Istanbul Karachi
Kuala Lumpur Madras Madrid Melbourne
Mexico City Nairobi Paris Singapore
Taipei Tokyo Toronto Warsaw

and associated companies in
Berlin Ibadan

Oxford is a trade mark of Oxford University Press

Published in the United States
by Oxford University Press Inc., New York

British Library Cataloguing in Publication Data
Data available

Library of Congress Cataloging in Publication Data
Data available

ISBN 0–19–820662–3

Typeset by Jayvee, Trivandrum, India
Printed in Great Britain
on acid-free paper by
Biddles Ltd., Guildford and King's Lynn

PREFACE

LIKE a pilgrim at the end of a long journey, I look back with some nostalgia on my adventures along the way. My strongest feeling, however, is of gratitude to the many colleagues, friends, neighbours, and family members who have lent me a helping hand.

Lively interest, encouragement, and pieces of practical information were offered me in the early days of my work by Marion Stowell and the secretaries in the History Faculty Office at Oxford, when they read and typed some of my first manuscripts on alternative agriculture. Then, during my spell in the USA, at the National Humanities Center in North Carolina between 1986 and 1987, I entered another circle of interested people, with concern for the same subject, but having different insights into its problems; I am most grateful to the Center for the congenial environment in which I worked there, and especially to the librarians in Research Triangle Park and at Duke University, who made so much material available to me relating to the nineteenth and twentieth centuries. Living in Kent since 1985, I have again been continuously spurred on by neighbours and friends who kept a watch for me in current journals and newspapers, or offered their own current experience of experiments in alternative agriculture; among those I thank with special warmth are Margaret and Philip Lawrence, Jayne and Clive Semple, Joan Shaw, Jean Wallwork, and Mike Rodgers. My academic colleagues in agricultural history have time and again opened up fresh perspectives for me, whether wittingly or not; and among those who were more aware than others of what exactly I was doing, I thank Vivien Billington, Judy Gielgud, and Malcolm Thick. In my family, my brother-in-law, the late Arthur Blackburn, an argumentative Yorkshire farmer with wide literary interests, constantly illuminated my thinking; I wish he had lived to comment wisely on the present phase of farming fortunes. My sister-in-law, Betty Thirsk, was a keen-eyed reader of current news, and alerted me to significant new developments, including the start of a new phase in the herb-growing saga, beginning in her part of the world, in the Cotswolds. My librarian-husband regularly found answers to a great variety of bibliographical problems. And while I fixed my gaze ever more attentively on things in the past and the present that did not seem to change very much, my son, Martin, attended to the technical aspects of my word-processing procedures, and kept me abreast of a world which has changed beyond recognition in the last twenty years.

I thank those colleagues who read and improved my manuscript at the end.

First and foremost, I acknowledge my great debt to Paul Brassley, whose varied expertise and wide sympathies exactly met my needs at that time, and were most generously made available to me. For other most helpful and friendly criticism, I also thank Harold Fox, Alun Howkins, Brian Short, and Edith Whetham. When my book reached Oxford University Press, I received much encouragement and loyal support from the editors, Tony Morris and Anna Illingworth, to whom I express deep gratitude.

As I wrote my chapter on Alternative Agriculture Today, and attempted to summarize the present phase, I regretted my inability to visit personally all the brave pioneers experimenting with new ventures. I was greatly helped by Dr Louis J. M. van Soest, whom I visited in Wageningen in Holland, where I learned something of the far-ranging trials by scientists with potentially useful new crops. For their actual growers, however, I had to rely on the reports of journalists, and I apologize for inaccuracies or out-of-date information which have crept into my account as a result. I hope they will understand the constraints upon me: the references in my notes should indicate the practical difficulties, in one lifetime, of being both a historian and a journalist.

Now that I come to the end of my task, I feel more sympathetic than I could ever have expected towards those pilgrims in the Middle Ages who set out on their long journeys not knowing how and where they would end. I have undergone the same experience, and it is one that I would not have missed for the world.

JOAN THIRSK

Hadlow, Kent
April 1996

CONTENTS

LIST OF ILLUSTRATIONS

ABBREVIATIONS

AHEW	*Agrarian History of England and Wales*, General Editor, H. P. R. Finberg, later Joan Thirsk, 8 vols., Cambridge University Press, 1967– .
AHR	*Agricultural History Review.*
BAR	British Archaeological Reports, 122 Banbury Road, Oxford, OX2 7BP.
BL	British Library, London.
BPP	British Parliamentary Papers.
CJ	Journals of the House of Commons.
Courier	*Tonbridge Courier*, weekly newspaper, published in Tonbridge, Kent.
CSPD	*Calendar of State Papers, Domestic Series.*
CSPVen.	*Calendar of State Papers, Venetian Series.*
EcHR	*Economic History Review.*
GLRO	Greater London Record Office, 40 Northampton Road, London, EC1R 0HB.
HMC	Historical Manuscripts Commission.
IBG	Institute of British Geographers.
JRASE	*Journal of the Royal Agricultural Society of England.*
KAO	Kent Archives Office, now renamed Centre for Kentish Studies (CKS), County Hall, Maidstone, Kent.
n.d.	no date.
PRO	Public Record Office, Kew, Surrey.
VCH	Victoria County History of England.

❧ INTRODUCTION

SOME twenty years ago, when I announced my intention of writing this book, I had to explain what I meant by the term 'alternative agriculture'. That is no longer necessary. It recurs again and again in our newspapers, and at least two books have appeared bearing that title.[1] Moreover, the practicalities involved in the search for an alternative agriculture are conspicuous in the landscape. In my part of southern England huge machines have been tearing the fields apart to make golf courses; vineyards have become conspicuous, and invite visitors; goat's milk is advertised for sale along the roadsides. In widely separated counties, a sudden abundance of linseed (formerly known as flax) appeared in the fields in 1991 as an alternative crop. People gazed with puzzled faces at the brilliant blue flowers in bloom in July in Gloucestershire, and it gave great satisfaction to this historian to tell them that flax in the seventeenth century was a thoroughly familiar sight in that neighbourhood. Now it has returned. The same happened when rapeseed appeared in the late 1970s. It first arrived in England as a new crop in the 1560s, spread rapidly in the eastern half of the country in the mid-seventeenth century, and stayed for another three hundred years. But when it returned in the 1970s, all memory of its past had faded, and it was damned as an alien crop, more fit for the landscape of Van Gogh than of Turner.[2]

In the last fifty years, we have been so successful with the production of mainstream crops that in the 1980s we finally faced urgently a crisis of overproduction; we were storing more grain, dairy produce, and meat than we could possibly consume.[3] To some the crisis burst suddenly, like a bolt from the blue, posing a problem that seemed to be unknown in English experience before. In fact, to the agricultural historian, it was nothing new. Farmers have worked over this ground at least three times before in our documented history, and some of the parallels are remarkable.

The purpose of this book, then, is to survey our past experience of alternative agriculture, in order to place the present phase in better perspective. Santayana offered some wise words on this score in *The Life of Reason*, in a chapter on 'Flux and Constancy in Human Nature': 'those who cannot remember the past are condemned to repeat it.'[4] In this case, we have the chance to repeat some of our past without feeling any strong sense of being condemned to a sorry fate. Rather we can benefit from knowing more exactly how and where the past is being repeated. We have the chance to learn some lessons from hard-won experience, we may even be reminded of more alternative choices, and we can certainly be forewarned about the long-term consequences. The alternative would be to blunder into the unknown, and learn everything the hard way.

Finally, through knowing more of the past, we can learn to be more philosophical about our present state. As experience clearly demonstrates, finding an alternative agriculture is a painful, and for many a tragic personal experience. But those three earlier occasions in our history demonstrate convincingly that important new lessons are always learned which benefit humanity in the future. Moreover, no phase of alternative agriculture lasts for ever. This one may last more than one lifetime, and none of us perhaps will see the wheel turn again. But the wheel will turn, the circumstances will change, mainstream crops will return to the forefront of human needs, and those golf courses and race-cart tracks will be turned to another use. In an uncertain world we can handle our land with at least that one certainty in mind.

*

Our agricultural history has received much detailed study in the last forty years, and we are better informed than ever before on the cycles of prosperity and depression through which it has passed over the centuries.[5] The surveys of long-term development give the impression of movement steadily in one direction, achieving the production of an ever increasing volume of basic foodstuffs, while reducing the labour required. That onward and upward trend has, of course, been most conspicuous and dramatic in the nineteenth and twentieth centuries.[6] Deeper investigation into our agricultural history, however, coupled with the insights we now obtain from our experience of the present-day agricultural scene, suggest that we as yet understand only half the story. A different interpretation of long-term development is possible, which may be more successful in explaining how some of the advances have been made. The basic foodstuffs of Western peoples are cereals and meat, and the production of those essentials for life are fairly described as mainstream agriculture. But profitable production has not always gone smoothly, and, whenever circumstances have changed radically, farmers have been driven to seek alternatives. The interpretation of our agricultural history which is offered here stresses a sequence of movements from mainstream farming to alternatives, and then back again. Major disjunctures have recurred, obliging farmers to divert their energies from the primary pursuit of grain and meat, to investigate other activities. On each occasion, when diversification has been necessary, farmers' ingenuity has been taxed, but it has successfully produced solutions which enabled them to survive until the old order returned. The disjunctures have lasted for long periods, on two occasions for over a century, so they cannot be dismissed as minor setbacks. They have been accompanied by complex changes in the economy and in society, and these have sometimes positively prepared the way for, or at least assisted and then maintained, the reorientation of farming effort. In other words, a whole tapestry of changed circumstances has been woven into the background of every disjuncture in agriculture. But when all the disjunctures are studied in context and then in sequence, certain common features emerge. Our attention is directed at significant innovative elements, and then at a pattern, which could not have been recognized so long as we surveyed the scene conventionally, measuring only the output of grain and meat. The disjunctures, which required farmers to diversify, introduced them to new experiences, and the changes left a permanent mark. When the next disjuncture occurred, and farmers returned to the pursuit of mainstream foodstuffs, they followed some new procedures or specialities which stemmed directly from experience in the interval. Each phase, in other words, carried positive benefits onto the next.

How many disjunctures are considered here? Three phases of alternative agriculture can be documented in English history, set between periods of mainstream farming. The first occurred after the Black Death in the mid-fourteenth century, and lasted from 1350 until about 1500. The second occurred in the early modern period, and lasted between about 1650 and 1750, though the way was being paved for it from at least 1590 if not earlier. The third occurred in the later nineteenth century, from 1879, and lasted until 1939. We are now in the 1990s involved in the fourth phase, for which a path was being opened from the 1970s.

In the present-day case, a long-drawn-out prelude can be identified, which has notable features in common with the second phase from 1650 to 1750. Indeed, the two experiences have the very strongest similarities in several other respects as well. The first phase of alternative agriculture in the later Middle Ages has more in common with the third phase in the later nineteenth century, though events precipitating the two changes of direction were entirely different. In the first case, it was set in train by plague; in the second, by a dramatic widening of the world market in grain and meat. Thus all four occasions have been precipitated by different events, but all four express the same problem, a serious imbalance between supply and demand, and they all possess common features in their issue. Our vision and understanding is sharpened by examining them all, and allowing each one to illuminate the others.

Santayana again leads us forward by emphasizing the possibilities of learning from history: 'Progress, far from consisting in change, depends on retentiveness. When change is absolute, there remains no being to improve, and no direction is set for possible improvement: and when experience is not retained, as among savages, infancy is perpetual.' The bleak notion of futility if we do not retain any memory of our past explains Santayana's use of the verb 'condemn' to describe the experience of repeating it: 'those who cannot remember the past are condemned to repeat it.'[7] Yet it need not be seen in that negative way. It could instruct, encourage, even instil confidence; that is the hope of the author here.

PART I

꘠

THE FIRST EXPERIENCE
1350–1500

1 ❧ AGRICULTURE AFTER THE BLACK DEATH

THE dominant theme in our farming history is mainstream agriculture, which is primarily concerned with the production of cereals and meat. But when for some reason cereals are produced in excess of human needs, farmers have to find alternative uses for at least some of their land, choosing new enterprises which will yield a profit, and make up for the losses otherwise incurred through the slump in cereals. This search for new pursuits, termed in twentieth-century parlance an alternative agriculture, was urgently forced upon farmers in the later Middle Ages as a result of the Black Death. It may not have been the first such challenge in English experience; a plague in Justinian's reign in the sixth century is cited as a comparable event on the Continent of Europe, which possibly spread to England in the seventh century. But only in the fourteenth century are the documents sufficient to show the consequences.

The total population of England in the Middle Ages can be reckoned only in the most tentative terms, and all estimates are vigorously debated. But in the 200 years between 1100 and 1300 a rapid increase in the number of mouths to be fed is generally accepted, at least trebling, perhaps even quadrupling them, from about 1.25 million to about 5 million. Then disaster befell. Scattered outbreaks of epidemic disease and high mortality in the first half of the fourteenth century led to the worse disaster of 1348–9, when about a third, and in some places a half, of the population died in the Black Death. Not only was the demand for food dramatically reduced; so was the labour available to cultivate the land. Lesser epidemics followed, and in 1400 the population was only somewhere between 2.5 million and 3 million. That totally changed situation lasted for about a century and a half, for plague did not die away until the 1480s. Throughout the period between 1350 and 1480 the population remained at a low ebb.[1]

To meet the new situation, agricultural effort had to be reorganized. The dramatic fall of population resulted first of all in a redistribution of holdings which, on paper, at least, quickly filled vacant tenements.[2] But the reduced number of farmers could not, nor did they wish to, continue to cultivate as much land as before. English documents do not yield any words as poignant as the cry of French peasants in the vicinity of Aix-en-Provence, similarly afflicted by plague and economic slump, asking their landlord for permission to grow vines, since they could no longer earn a living from growing grain: 'it profits us nothing to grow grain,' they declared (*nihil valet ad bladandum*).[3] Vines, however, promised no relief to Englishmen. The first and readiest solution to the crisis in agriculture was to put former arable land down to grass. It was an expedient specially well documented in the accounts of manorial lords who had formerly depended heavily on hired labour, which now became expensive.[4]

Putting more land to grass was, in fact, a thoroughly rational choice for several reasons. Keeping sheep flocks was one venture with a hopeful future, for the textile industries of Europe in the thirteenth century had enjoyed a growing demand for their wares, and increasing sophistication was being shown by their customers when choosing between varieties and qualities. English wool ranked high in estimation, and so benefited from an assured demand, especially over-seas in Flanders. Later in the fifteenth century, the wool producers found more sales among English textile manufacturers. So despite the increasingly severe competition faced by English cloth workers, especially with respect to cheap cloth, the growers of wool found markets.[5]

Ewe flocks for cheese production also offered commercial opportunities. Indeed, as a farming venture and as a trade as well, wool and cheese probably prospered together. Certainly, for export, the two products were sometimes taken from monastic houses by the same buyers. The taste for ewes' milk cheese was well established in France, and it is mirrored in the traffic across the Channel of exports from English monastic estates. But whether sheep-dairying expanded generally in the fifteenth century, at a rate comparable with wool pro-duction, is less likely. Ewes have a shorter lactation period than cows, and this together with outbreaks of disease, taste preferences, and the high cost of labour after the Black Death probably gave wool-growing the edge. Nevertheless, ewes' milk cheese-making was an old-established branch of pasture farming in some areas, such as Canvey Island in Essex, and it is not unlikely that its scale was intensified in this favourable time. The possibility focuses attention on one question, waiting for a better answer.[6]

An alternative use for land under pasture was cattle-keeping, and because bad seasons caused so many sheep losses, it may in some places have sup-planted sheep. On one of John Hopton's Suffolk estates, for example, Colin Richmond speculates on a move from sheep to cattle-fattening from 1448 onwards. In coastal Sussex a shift to cattle also occurred around 1500.[7] Signs of more cattle and more beef, indeed, have led to the entirely reasonable sugges-tion that the peasantry, alongside the wealthy, were able to eat more meat in these days of alternative agriculture.[8] In some parts of England, however, signs of expanding cow-dairies also emerge in the later fifteenth century. As this was an activity more suited to family farmers than to large landowners, the documents are meagre and may disguise the scale of the change. The 'white meats' of the dairy were conventionally regarded as a mainstay of the poor, for peasant families, whatever else they lacked, always aspired to own a cow. So, while some may have exploited an opportunity here, our records tell us more about lords who kept dairies to serve their households than about peasant enterprise; in any case, the full market potential of dairying was far from being recognized as yet. So interest in its commercial possibilities may well have grown somewhat during the fifteenth century, while being masked in our meagre records by the fact that large estate owners chose to hire their cows to dairymaids and cowmen, and small farmers have left no accounts.[9] From Sibton, in east Suffolk, comes an unusual example from the end of the fifteenth century of a Cistercian abbey estate abandoning sheep-keeping, and itself maintaining a large dairy herd, despite the labour costs. Suffolk cows were crossed with a Northern steer, and 66 cows, shown in an account of 1507, had been increased by 1513 to 140.[10] This particular venture did not last long but, as the county of Suffolk subsequently developed a notable dairying speciality, this episode may count as a fleeting glimpse of wider interest and effort at the time, even though lordly undertakings did not ultimately succeed, and the activity found its more promising future among family farmers. All that can be added suggestively here is that, in every later phase of alternative agriculture, dairying took a substantial step forward, by improving or by varying its products and its marketing procedures. From hindsight, therefore, it may be possible to glimpse a moment in the fifteenth century when the first steps were taken in certain parts of the country to move cow-dairying onto a more commercial plane, and into a wider market.[11]

In later centuries signs of more dairying would immediately raise the expectation of more pig-keeping by using the whey. That association is not evident at this time, but it is worth asking whether pig-keeping, on legumes and grain, made new advances. In the grain-hungry years of the thirteenth century Walter of Henley, when advising manorial lords on farm management, expected them to rely on their woodlands to feed and fatten pigs, implying that few would be kept in sties and fed by hand. If that truly reflected lordly attitudes to pigs at that time, then this view seems to have changed by the first decade of the fourteenth century, at least on the estates of Peterborough abbey. The woodlands were now needed most of all for fuel and, instead of getting pannage, pigs were being generously fed on legumes and some grain. Was this, perhaps, the beginnings of a more intensive pig-keeping system? It would have fitted neatly and logically into the circumstances prevailing by the later fourteenth century, when beans, peas, and cereals could be more readily spared for alternative livestock. If so, did peasant farmers follow suit? The suggestion is a speculation only, but it deserves further investigation.[12]

A better-documented group of alternative strategies after the Black Death derived from the exploitation, and adaptation, of select innovations which had been introduced in the expansive years of the thirteenth century. It is a pattern of development which we shall see recurring in later centuries, to the point where it may almost be regarded as a rule: in a buoyant age of mainstream farming, luxuries arrive on the scene to serve a privileged few which then invite exploitation to serve a wider market in the succeeding phase of economic difficulty. Here we see the first occurrence of that sequence of events.

The crisis of the mid-fourteenth century followed a period of buoyant economic growth in the thirteenth century when population was rising, trade expanded at home and overseas, towns and their markets flourished, and every incentive was given to farmers to clear more land for cultivation. Even when the next fifty years, from about 1300 up to the Black Death, saw prosperity subdued by high taxation to pay for wars, and bad seasons in which crops failed and cattle disease was rife, contemporaries, who could not see the way ahead, treated them as temporary setbacks only. The general direction of farming remained unaltered, and the wealthy classes indulged in exotic and expensive fancies. Historians sum up the period as one of 'grandiose building', and 'ostentatious luxury'.[13] We need have no doubt, therefore, that the well-to-do fed and clothed themselves better than before. In short, while prosperity lasted, it created, within a limited circle, a specialized demand for luxury foods.

Throughout the Middle Ages the provision of luxuries required resources that were only at the disposal of gentlemen, rather than ordinary peasants; and some of their favoured indulgences required large amounts of land. An outstanding example of a modish food for the rich was the rabbit. Rabbits are first found in England in the late twelfth century, established on islands round the coast and on coastal marshlands. One of the first known cases of a rabbit warren being laid out deliberately to confine and breed them was at Guildford in Surrey, where the King owned one in 1241. At the same period lordly landowners, including bishops, the Earl of Chester, and the Earl of Derby began to set up cony warrens. Rabbit meat was becoming a fashionable delicacy of the wealthy. Was the fashion perhaps introduced by someone like Peter des Roches, bishop of Winchester, who had been accustomed to eating rabbit in his native Poitou? The question was put by Elspeth Veale, and it is certainly a likely possibility. But, from whatever part of France the currents flowed, a new fashion was clearly taking hold among the upper classes, and the right to set up a warren was claimed as a manorial privilege. Rabbits were destined for the tables of the well-to-do, they were carefully guarded in their warrens, and the meat was four or five times more expensive than chicken.[14]

After the Black Death, when landowners found themselves with idle grassland, or wished to put arable land to grass and make the best profit by the change, the idea of the rabbit warren lay to hand as an ideal solution. Warrens multiplied, and occupied ever larger acreages. In the Suffolk breckland Mark Bailey has shown how they were first set up on heathland, and then on converted arable. The rabbits had to be nurtured carefully, for they were tender animals, easily destroyed by bad weather and disease. But they hardened in course of time, increased in number, and eventually, of course, broke out of their warrens. Whereas the lord of Brandon received a negligible income from rabbit sales between 1300 and 1349, they represented 21 per cent of gross manorial receipts between 1350 and 1399, and 40 per cent in 1386–7. Methwold warren supplied 9,450 rabbits in 1390.[15]

As rabbit meat became more plentiful in the market in the fifteenth century, it fell in price and so ceased to be an expensive luxury of the rich alone. Poachers made it available even to the poor, and the task of guarding warrens called for the building of warreners' lodges. A surviving example of a lodge at Thetford stands two storeys high, and has flint walls 3 feet thick. Nor was meat the only source of income from rabbits. Their skins were another commodity, for which fashion obligingly created at the right moment yet another market.[16] Thus rabbits proved a most successful alternative enterprise for manorial lords.

Another alternative strategy for the same class, drawing again on considerable expanses of idle land, was the deer park. Its first purpose had been to allow gentlemen to indulge in the pleasures of hunting, and from the Norman conquest onwards park numbers increased, until at the Black Death they are said to have reached their zenith. Those of medieval origin have been counted at 1,900 by one author, and their total guessed at 3,000 by another. The licences to impark, which were awarded by the Crown, were numerous between 1200 and 1350, that is, in the period of mainstream agriculture. This is what we might expect, since a time of population growth was clearly more suitable than later for the creation of parks; they were labour-intensive in construction and in maintenance.[17]

But deer parks were not neglected after the Black Death. On the contrary, they were seen to have considerable merits of a different kind. They used vacant land to advantage: they could supply venison to gentlemen's households. Thus, in Shropshire after the Black Death, Ann Kettle writes of a 'flurry of park creations' between 1350 and 1370, when eleven new ones were laid out. It was also the period when many smaller deer parks were extended, until some single ones reached 3,000, even 4,600 acres. The work of enclosing them with high banks was now less thorough because of labour shortage. However, in some places the desertion of a whole village gave the golden opportunity to turn all the villagers' lands into a deer park. Thus some parks still show traces of ridge and furrow, indicating, as in Northamptonshire, that their land formerly lay under the plough.[18]

Is it possible to generalize, and say that parks were evaluated in a fresh light in the later Middle Ages, being used to serve somewhat different needs from those obtaining when they were originally introduced into the landscape? Without more household accounts, such an assertion cannot be confidently made. Different park owners, in any case, were likely to have different priorities. But the supply of venison from parks could well have taken a higher place in their owners' calculations in the fifteenth century, when mainstream agriculture stagnated. The notion of a park as an economic asset may be seen emerging somewhat more clearly if it is viewed in a longer perspective. When the grazing was not fully required for the deer, it was sometimes leased for the feeding of cows and oxen, or for the breeding of horses. The internal division of parks also became increasingly common in the later Middle Ages, again suggesting that the breeding and feeding of a variety of animals had become a more deliberate objective. That trend developed further after 1500, and along the same lines, when the economic circumstances changed. A larger population had to be fed once more, the pasturage of animals for food, and the breeding of better quality horses won still greater favour over the pleasures of hunting, and, in the words of Richard Carew, the deer were removed from parks 'to give bullocks place'. Some landowners went still further: when Lord Burghley acquired King's Cliffe park in Northamptonshire in 1593, he promptly cleared it to make a large grazing farm. So, if medieval records do not permit firm conclusions to be drawn, they at least hint at a gradual shift in the purposes of parkland, as management was adjusted to meet different opportunities and constraints after the Black Death. The interpretation that we place on fragmentary clues must be cautious and hesitant at this stage, but it will be strengthened by hindsight when account is taken of the development of deer parks in the next phase of alternative agriculture in the seventeenth century, and again in the twentieth.[19]

Another food resource which underwent heavier exploitation after the Black Death was the dovecote. Pigeons were a useful source of meat all the year round, as well as supplying much valued dung, but the right to keep a dovecote was deemed in the Middle Ages to be the prerogative of manorial lords. This restriction was doubtless a mercy as far as ordinary farmers were concerned, since the damage done by pigeons to their corn crops was much resented by poor men, and a monopoly confined to the lord at least reduced their numbers.

The first documentary evidence of dovecotes is found in the mid-twelfth century, and datable, surviving buildings begin in the late twelfth and early thirteenth centuries. This was the time when a rising population emphatically needed grain for bread and drink, rather than for meat.[20] The dovecotes do not appear to have been common features in the landscape, and it is likely that their rarity in the documents reflects rarity in reality. After the Black Death, however, the building of many more reveals a totally changed situation. The great mortality from plague reduced the pressure on grain supplies, more could be released for feeding birds, and dovecotes began to multiply. Considerate lords compensated tenants who suffered damage to their crops, either with money or with gifts. In their turn, lords took advantage of a not inconsiderable source of meat, by sending some of it to market. Since a dovecote at Blakemere in Shropshire yielded 1,222 pigeons to Lady Talbot in 1410, we can readily understand how she was induced to pay for an expensive new building for them in 1431–2.[21]

Yet another alternative enterprise was the breeding of fish in fish ponds. This was never claimed as a lordly monopoly, but the construction of ponds was expensive, and so the opportunities were restricted to the well-to-do with considerable reserves of land. Fish always played a prominent role in diet in Catholic countries, and throughout the Middle Ages the documents show large quantities of freshwater fish caught in rivers and in dikes in the fens. Seawater fish were, of course, available fresh near the coast, while inland, if fresh fish could not be had, then salted fish had to serve. The affluent chose the luxury of fish ponds, which allowed for a breeding programme and a ready supply of fresh fish on the doorstep at all times. Even then, the rare documents which reveal their existence in the late eleventh century show that such fish were reserved for 'great feasts' and 'great guests'.[22]

Most of our clues to the management of fish ponds relate to those belonging to the Crown, on which no expense was spared in the later twelfth and thirteenth centuries, when they were still luxuries.[23] Even when the first grants of ready-made fish ponds were made to new religious houses, it was not unusual to impose the condition that the fish, usually bream and pike, be reserved for special occasions, and not become an everyday food.[24] After the Black Death, however, fish ponds came to play a different role in food supply. Some wealthy lords continued to maintain them, but others leased them to peasants, who managed them as commercial undertakings. Pondwater fish, in short, ceased to be the tasty delicacies of the rich alone, and were more widely marketed. B. K. Roberts has illustrated this development most effectively in the Forest of Arden, Warwickshire. Ponds needed a retentive clay soil, and doubtless this region proved ideal. One great lord in the neighbourhood, the Earl of Warwick, had a fish pond in Arden from the early thirteenth century, but in the later fourteenth century numbers of peasants owned them. They assarted land under lordly encouragement, and enjoyed it by a free tenure which allowed some to build up considerable wealth. Land changed hands readily, and many sub-manors were created in the process. These free peasants then created, or renovated, numerous fish ponds in Arden. Fish stocks usually comprised pike, tench, and bream, but in one case in the fifteenth century included roach as well.[25]

The commercial advantages of fish ponds were further enhanced when they began to be stocked with carp. The carp was hardy and grew faster than bream or pike. It was a native fish of the Danube, which was enthusiastically taken up and bred in the Low Countries. It is fairly certain that carp arrived in England via the Netherlands; perhaps, indeed, they were brought by Flemish fishmongers setting up business in England. Certainly, a Fleming was lessee of some fish ponds in Southwark in 1381, and, although he did not name the fish which he lost in the peasants' rising of that year, carp were certainly known and eaten in England by that time. They are found in royal kitchen accounts in the fourteenth century; and, in another region which readily absorbed influences from the Low Countries, namely East Anglia, carp were stocked in ponds in 1462. An English treatise on fishing, stating that carp were 'but few in England', was published in 1496, and used to be thought to describe the situation at that time. It has now been found in an earlier manuscript version, dated *c*.1406–*c*.1450. We may reasonably conclude, then, that carp became more common in the course of the fifteenth century.[26]

The improved commercial opportunities for fish ponds in England match evidence of similar developments in France in the course of the fifteenth century. In the Sologne area, where medieval ponds abound, the dating of twenty-nine of them shows their construction to have been concentrated in the fifteenth century, especially in its second half. Many survive to this day, and the calculation that one hectare of pond now has the same value as ten hectares of good land in Beauce affords a glimpse of the incentives to build them 500 years ago.[27] Fish ponds, then, were transformed from a privilege of the rich to a commercial undertaking at a time when circumstances required farmers to find alternative pursuits. Since they were not the monopoly right of manorial lords, and, in any case, lords owning fish ponds frequently leased them to others after the Black Death, the fish pond gave a golden opportunity to farmers below the ranks of the large landowners.

Seen in this light, the use of moats by free peasants dwelling in moated farmhouses in the fifteenth century takes on a different complexion. English historians have long debated the purpose of moats, which were clearly a fashion, lasting from 1200 to 1500, without coming to one agreed conclusion. They are irregularly scattered over the countryside, but more than 5,000 have been found so far in England (including twelve in the single parish of Tanworth-in-Arden).[28] In the course of 300 years moats doubtless served more than one use. But whereas, in their beginnings, they are associated with the colonization of wasteland by farmers settling on isolated sites, who required moats to defend them against thieves and wild animals, and whereas a ready supply of water may subsequently have become another vital consideration against the hazards of fire and of drought (the sixteen years between 1284 and 1300 included ten dry years), it is likely by the fifteenth century that their use as fish stores loomed over the rest.[29] Fish ponds, and moats which were sometimes linked to a network of ponds, served an admirable commercial purpose at exactly the moment when agricultural conditions required them. The suggestion is presented tentatively here, but it will be strengthened by the parallels that come to light during the second experience of alternative agriculture, between 1650 and 1750.

The strategies so far enumerated and used in the crisis following the Black Death were available only to gentlemen farmers, who disposed of much land, or to the more prosperous peasants, who seized their chance to lease gentlemen's assets when the latter gave up direct farming. Lesser men required alternatives involving less capital outlay. Among possible choices the most practical ones were crops other than grain, which might be grown on the arable, possibly within the conventional rotations. What possibilities were available?

In searching for an alternative agriculture in the later Middle Ages, English farmers were not alone. The same calamity struck throughout Europe, so that the same restructuring was necessary. Hence ideas for alternative uses of land filtered into England from farmers on the Continent facing the same predicament. From the Mediterranean to the Baltic novelties began to appear. In Sicily, for example, the plague caused the population to be redistributed regionally, and to specialize in the export of a fresh range of agricultural commodities, including flax, silk, and sugar; sugar mills and presses were a timely introduction around 1350. From Russia buckwheat began its migration from eastern to western Europe. Majorca resourcefully found a market for its singing birds, and greatly exploited and expanded demand in Portugal, Spain, France, and the Low Countries. This in turn stimulated a demand for canary seed to be grown to feed them. The movement of woad across Europe from east to west seems to have quickened, though it did not start, in the fifteenth century.[30] This is not, of course, the place to discuss in detail the migration of all new crops and livestock across the Continent at that time. But some notion of their movement, and the expanding trade in these new commodities is a necessary background to the tentative experiments, seemingly frustrated yet discernible, in England at this period. They are not many or impressive, but they allow us to perceive an opportunity that was missed. As the long procession of alternatives moved across one country after another in Europe, England was at the end of the line. From the English point of view, the most arresting innovations were to be observed in the Low Countries and in northern France, for there the soils and climate were not dissimilar to those found in England. Not surprisingly, then, the few attempts to grow new crops are first found across the sea from those countries, in East Anglia and southern England, though they did not move far or fast.

We shall see more clearly below how foreign ideas have at all times been important in feeding debates, and encouraging trials, among farmers and landowners. What might have been significant at this time was that certain unusual industrial plants were already being grown in east Norfolk on monastic estates, but it happened before the Black Death. Being geographically well placed to draw ideas from the Continent, Norfolk monasteries were some of the best centres for the discussion of innovations. Did not one abbot lament the fact that 'when monks came together to talk, their tongues wagged not about the Songs of Sion, but about the progeny of bulls and the yield of fields'?[31]

Thus, among industrial crops on monastic estates in east Norfolk, rapeseed is found in *c.*1255, madder in 1274 and 1305–6, and flax and hemp are named in 1304.[32] In a later phase of alternative agriculture, these crops would show themselves to be notably successful in reviving some farmers' flagging fortunes. Whether they were further cultivated when they were more desperately needed in the fifteenth century is uncertain. Certainly, they did not spread widely. But then a likely reason is to hand, inasmuch as they made heavy demands on labour, and so were inappropriate after the Black Death when labour was short. From the same cause, but also because of an adverse climate, and a ready trade in wine from France, vineyards too faded from the scene. They had found a home on monastic estates and the principal home farms of great lords in the prosperous days of the thirteenth century, if not earlier, and some did, indeed survive in the fifteenth century. But by the sixteenth they were generally noticed only as decayed terraces. Some other industrial crops leave more positive traces, however: flax and hemp-growing seem to be more in evidence. Saffron found a niche in east Hertfordshire and Essex, even though it was a supremely labour-intensive crop; it managed to hold its own through the fifteenth century, and commanded a very high price at the market.[33] Other experimental ventures, if such there were, have yet to be found. But the possibility is not an idle notion, as the contemporaneous history of farming in the Low Countries demonstrates.

Some notable new crops, which failed to take hold in England, forged ahead in the Netherlands at this time, without setbacks. They were helped by the fact that plague mortality was much lower in the Netherlands; indeed, some areas went unscathed. So a plentiful labour supply helped these finicky, demanding crops to establish themselves firmly and, as better knowledge in cultivating plants like hops, rapeseed, madder, and woad accumulated in the fifteenth century, farmers in the broader Rhineland area all gained confidence in growing them. In consequence, historians write eloquently about the spread of intensive husbandry in the Low Countries, and more widely along the lower Rhine, in the fourteenth and fifteenth centuries. Rapeseed, madder, woad, flax, hemp, and hops are regularly found.[34] Other new crops were buckwheat by 1394–5, for feeding rabbits and fattening poultry; spurry, first mentioned in 1426 in Flanders, and much valued as a fodder for dairy cows; turnips as green fodder for livestock in 1404; and furze, cultivated for fodder (to feed rabbits *inter alia*) and for fuel by 1490.[35] All these crops would succeed in England at a later opportunity, when the circumstances as regards labour were more favourable. But in the fifteenth century, despite the tentative appearance of some of them in the thirteenth and early fourteenth centuries, they did not capture a secure place as alternatives. And when they returned in the next phase of alternative agriculture, all skill in cultivating them had been forgotten, and had to be relearned.

Saffron-growing, which plainly became a flourishing alternative crop in eastern England in the fifteenth century, uses small amounts of land and is highly labour-intensive at certain seasons of the year; it is better regarded as a branch of horticulture than as a field crop. This fact directs attention more generally to this branch of plant cultivation and its fortunes after the Black Death. Its labour requirements would at first sight suggest that it had little allure for the farmer. On the other hand, diversification was the watchword of the age, and, more significantly, every one of the three later phases of alternative agriculture to be examined below was accompanied by a flowering of horticultural endeavour. Moreover, since each such phase was preceded by a period of affluence for the rich, coincident with mainstream agriculture, the ground was laid for a new strategy by sparking the curiosity of the well-to-do, and allowing them to indulge in unusual foodstuffs. Thus a preliminary stimulus was given to horticulture, which opened up the prospect of further commercial development to benefit a wider circle of people during the next phase of alternative agriculture. The possibility that things happened in this way in the later Middle Ages deserves consideration, since the pattern recurs in later phases. Was horticulture, in effect, spurred on by rich men's tastes in the period of mainstream agriculture, and thus made ready to expand subsequently as an alternative pursuit? As a commercial venture, it was unlikely to appeal to lords of large estates, who were shedding their home farms because of the labour costs. Nor, among those farmers who were ambitiously seizing the many chances at this time to increase their acreages, were garden crops likely to make much appeal. But in the right places, around towns, and in the precincts of noblemen's houses, it had scope for development. And, although the documents are meagre in the period 1350–1500, and they cannot be pressed too far, such an interpretation of trends, mistily visible, is not beyond the bounds of logic.

It enables us to assimilate without surprise evidence of a fine orchard with wonderful fruits being laid out at Banwell in Somerset in 1443–65, and another at East Brent in the same county, about 1475, said to have had apples and pears of the finest sort, as well as elms and oaks.[36] John Harvey has produced far more persuasive evidence of horticultural progress. He writes of pottage—a vegetable stew, containing little more than onions, coleworts (cabbage-like leaves, plucked singly), leeks, garlic, and parsley—being a basic element in peasant diet, and accompanying bread and ale, throughout the Middle Ages. Even the poorest husbandman could grow these ingredients if he had a small patch of land. But monastic and noblemen's houses show more considerable vegetable gardens and orchards, and, since such food was regarded as the sustenance of the poor and meek, it featured prominently in the diet of the monks and nuns. Also, of course, most such plants had a medicinal use. Limited though the documents are, it is clear that after 1400 more variety in these foodstuffs entered the scene. References appear to scallions, chervil, chives, and rosemary. Most significant of all was the fact that root crops, such as skirrets, carrots, parsnips, and turnips, came to be eaten by the well-to-do as single items, and not mixed in a stew. The first very modest steps were being taken towards raising the status of horticulture.[37]

We have seen how some convenient alternatives in agriculture after the Black Death were those which used land extravagantly, rather than sparingly. They greatly helped large landowners, irked by labour shortages. Some estates, like that of the Berkeleys in Gloucestershire, even kept large herds of goats, a strategy that would have been unthinkable in the thirteenth century, when people pressed hard on food resources.[38] It is not surprising, therefore, that lordly solutions made some conspicuous changes in the landscape. Yet not all the changes suited their interests so well. Manorial lords with increasing frequency had to shed land, and even abandon direct farming altogether. Thus they conferred unexpected opportunities upon the peasantry to acquire land. Lords were prepared to lease out whole demesnes to groups of tenants, or to subdivide large units of land in order to rent out parcels severally. In this way large land aggregations were broken down. The net result cannot be quantified, since the beneficiaries frequently amalgamated their additional pieces with existing holdings, but we may guess from other evidence that the redistribution of land created many smaller units of cultivation than in the previous period of mainstream farming, even while it enabled the prosperous farmer to enlarge his holding. Peasant farmers in counties of the West Midlands, for example, were able individually to graze more livestock: those farming lands of Worcester cathedral priory after 1358 grazed well over 100 sheep, where before they would have had a maximum of 100. Where the usual size of herd was a dozen cattle in the hands of one peasant before the Black Death, herds of 40 beasts were not uncommon afterwards.

Thus the general trend was for land to be redistributed, removed from the hands of manorial lords with grand estates, or their single lessees, for the benefit of thrifty yeomen and husbandmen. In one remarkable intervention from Thomas Elys, the priest in charge at Quinton, Warwickshire, the social merits of such a devolution of land among many tenants rather than one 'strong man' was actually spelt out in 1493, in a bold letter to the landowner, Magdalen College, Oxford.[39] The net result of such redistribution cannot be measured, but the trend was strong and consistent in many parts of the country. It should be noticed now, for it will be found again in later phases of alternative agriculture when large estates were again broken up into smaller units. As it seems regularly to accompany phases of alternative agriculture, it carries a message for those dealing with the situation at the present day.

Alternative agriculture is a response to a crisis which is destined in due course to pass away, but while it lasts it prompts actions which furnish ideas for new strategies in the following age. Among peasants, one of the most important practical lessons learned after the Black Death seems to have been the advantage of leaving arable strips, not needed for cultivation, to rest unused for several years in the arable fields. Such leys, as they came to be called, produced a better harvest when ploughed again. The practice of leaving arable strips under grass in the common fields became noticeable in the fifteenth century. The expedient commended itself at this time since the demand for grain had slackened. Although peasants had more chance than before to serve the market with grain, as lords retreated from the farming business, they had to adopt flexible procedures to reduce risk. This was made possible by leaving leys in the arable fields, and the practice is reflected in village by-laws, where regulations governing the use of leys feature in the fifteenth century. It may, of course, be a mistake to think of ley-farming as the innovation, when it was the by-laws regulating it which may have been the novelty. But some mixture of both trends is probably a realistic verdict on the phenomenon. When once the practice was more widely adopted, it inevitably posed problems on a new scale for the grazing of livestock on commonable lands. Peasants who had more livestock than before would sometimes need more grazing and less grain; their animals breaking out onto neighbours' crops were likely to become a persistent source of strife. It is not

surprising, then, that village by-laws come to light in an attempt to accommodate the common field system to the practice of leaving strips in leys.

The benefits of leaving arable land for some years under grass were borne in
on farmers with a new intensity by their experiences after the Black Death. It
goes a long way to explain the vehemence with which they defended the putting
down of arable to pasture in the course of the sixteenth century, asserting that
the procedure enabled the land to regain heart. By that date, however, they were
contending with the prejudices induced by a different age. After about 1500,
when so many more mouths had again to be fed, conversion to pasture, in the
opinion of the government, denied grain to hungry stomachs. Yet the wisdom
of the practice for restoring tired arable to fertility *was* finally acknowledged: in
legislation in 1597, against enclosure and the conversion of arable to pasture,
farmers were officially allowed to practise ley-farming for the benefit of their
arable. The procedure became thoroughly commonplace in the next age of
mainstream agriculture.[40]

*

This account of alternative agriculture in the later Middle Ages contains more
than a little guesswork in interpreting slender evidence. But our documents at
this period never fully light up the whole scene. So the guesswork has been
phrased tentatively and seemingly bold assertions hedged about with many
cautionary words. It is hoped that the interpretation of the evidence will be seen
to be strengthened when parallel trends are illustrated by the later phases of
alternative agriculture. At a distance of more than five centuries, the context and
interrelationship of agricultural innovations in the later Middle Ages can only
dimly be perceived, and they certainly cannot be satisfactorily measured. But
when circumstances and sequences are repeated another three times over, some
of the debatable connections made here may be allowed to carry more conviction. A certain pattern of events which takes shape on more than one occasion
can illuminate some dark corners of the past. In the next chapters, in which features of the second experience of alternative agriculture are demonstrated
which bear a resemblance to those encountered in the late Middle Ages, more
light will be shed in these shadowy places.

PART II

❧

THE SECOND EXPERIENCE
1650–1750

2 ❧ ENTERING A NEW ERA

ALTERNATIVE agriculture dominated the rural economy until about 1500, when circumstances slowly began to change. Population started to rise again, the demand for grain increased beyond the level to which farmers had long become accustomed, and shortages threatened. Other factors then intervened, especially the arrival in Europe of considerable quantities of silver and gold from the New World, and the debasement of the English coinage, 1543–51. Food prices rose alarmingly. The government feared the outbreak of civil disturbances in years of extreme dearth, and many emergency measures had to be taken to provide cheap bread for the poor. Mainstream agriculture returned as the central objective, and it became a fundamental tenet of government policy to exalt the ploughman, and denounce and punish all who put arable land down to grass. Converting land to pasture was regarded as a 'turning of the earth to sloth and idleness', and was judged in 1597 'the greatest and most dangerous nuisance and damage to the common people'. In 1601 the Queen's principal secretary, William Cecil, delivered the weighty opinion in the Commons that 'whosoever doth not maintain the plough destroys this kingdom'.[1]

Deep prejudices against the life of soft, indolent shepherds and of casual herdsmen, sauntering after their cattle, became entrenched in the course of three generations after 1500. Pasture farmers could not hope to earn the nation's gratitude when the production of grain was the prime necessity. Cereal farmers were the most welcome figures on the agricultural scene, and constant exhortations to them to make greater effort gradually produced results. The grain harvest was much increased, partly through the ploughing up of land which had previously been under grass, partly through the use of more intensive rotations and more fertilizers, including industrial waste, and with the help of more laborious cultivation. By the early 1580s the age of grain shortages seemed to some to be nearing its end. More cautious politicians, however, were wary of this rosy view. In 1585 William Cecil expressed alarm at the amount of grain now being used to make starch for stiffening the highly fashionable ruffs, worn with such pride by himself and his peers and by their womenfolk too. Such extravagance was possible because England had enjoyed peace and plenty for twenty-seven years, but, in Cecil's view, the nation was being lulled into an unjustified sense of security about its food supplies.[2] His warning was uttered in a year when the government was alarmed by farmers' enthusiasm for growing woad. Since 1583 they had taken up the crop with alacrity, urged on by the high prices of this dyestuff at the market, and by the abysmally low prices of grain. In two years, 1583-4, prices had dropped by a quarter, and, since farmers were not allowed to export their surplus, they claimed that they had no way to pay their rents except by growing woad.[3]

Cecil's sober warning in 1585 that harvest failures had 'been many times, and such times may come again' proved to be prophetic. Poor harvests were gathered in 1586 and 1587, and the index of average prices for all grains shot up from 324 to 556 and then 684. Another run of bad harvests recurred in the 1590s, making a sharp impact not only on England but on other countries of western Europe also. The index of average grain prices, which stood at 350 in the harvest year 1593-4, moved up to 621 in 1594-5, 681 in 1595-6, and 1039 in 1596-7, before falling back slightly to 778 in 1597-8.[4] These traumatic years profoundly shook men's belief in a future of plentiful grain. Even so, within another three years prices had fallen again, and Parliament in 1601 was once more debating a proposal to allow enclosure and the conversion of arable to pasture. Grain was cheap; in fact, Sir Walter Ralegh affirmed that 'all nations abound with corn', and 'if [grain was] too cheap the husbandman is undone'.[5]

As it turned out, the first four decades of the seventeenth century brought an assortment of good and bad years, causing farmers and government policy to waver from one extreme view to the other. The overall trend, whether in favour of more grain-growing or more pasture-farming, can hardly be summed up in a sentence. Farmers who profited by woad in the 1580s, for example, did not necessarily abandon it in favour of wheat when prices returned to normal. In any case, woad was not a crop that was grown for long years in succession, but served best as a first crop when ploughing up land that had been under grass for some years, before it was sown with cereals. A single generalization which more accurately summarizes the trend from the 1580s to the 1650s would underline the new flexibility introduced into land use. Instead of retaining a relatively permanent distinction between arable and pasture, and a relatively strict arable rotation of winter grain, spring crops, and fallow, it became the common practice to lay down old ploughland to leys (or temporary pastures), lasting some four to eight, even twelve, years, and then plough again. At the same time, some unusual crops like woad were introduced into the conventional rotations. Specialist grain growers on the best soils, of course, persisted with cereals. Pasture farmers in the best grazing locations specialized more intently on livestock, and showed more interest in dairying. Other, less specialist, farmers selected between a diverse collection of alternative activities, now increasingly well publicized and available locally.

The years between the 1590s and the 1650s thus represented a prolonged transition from mainstream to alternative agriculture, even though contemporaries lacked the long view and were incapable of seeing it in that light. During this period clover, lucerne, and sainfoin made their first, modest appearance, sown in pastures for feeding horses and livestock generally, and then, after 1650, being introduced into arable rotations, where they helped to boost the productivity of grain.[6] Finally, during the 1640s the urgent need for large food supplies to feed the Parliamentary army in three theatres of war, Scotland, England, and Ireland, stimulated higher production all round, and encouraged further specialization. To read in the State Papers of the quantities of bread, beer, butter, and cheese ordered for the troops is to witness, indirectly, the pressure on farmers to satisfy a huge demand from wholesale merchants in many different areas of the country. Responses on the same scale help to explain the great surplus of foodstuffs that accumulated when once peace was restored.[7]

The second experience of alternative agriculture returned after an interlude of some 100 to 150 years. As a shorthand convenience its beginning can be given the precise date of 1656, but warning signs, as we have seen, had been accumulating for half a century and more. The year 1656 was the watershed, for Parliament finally recognized the serious plight of farmers, now producing a superabundance of food which they could not sell at home. Prices were falling calamitously, and farmers were threatened with bankruptcy unless they could find fresh outlets. At long last, Parliament agreed to an act which allowed farmers freely to export grain, cattle, horses, meat, and dairy produce, so long as domestic prices did not rise to levels denoting scarcity. Unlike the limits set in the sixteenth century which had allowed grain exports only in years of exceptional abundance, the new prices signified a general freedom to export, and excluded only years of extreme dearth.[8]

The Act of 1656 had waited four years while other more urgent Parliamentary business was concluded. It had been proposed as early as April 1652, and, in view of the fact that England had passed through almost a decade of civil war, and for some five years between 1646 and 1651 saw bad seasons and failed harvests follow one after another, it was remarkable that the excess of food production should so quickly manifest itself. Already in December 1653 Norfolk tenants were complaining that 'neither corn nor cattle nor butter nor cheese will give any price'. From Oxford in 1653 came news that a bushel of wheat which had fetched 10s. some years earlier was now priced at 2s. 6d. or 3s. In 1655 it was said that grain in Norfolk 'is so cheap as has not been known in late days'.[9]

The policy of allowing food to be freely sold overseas was a momentous inno-vation, and it continued after the Restoration. Indeed, exports were yet more positively encouraged, for it was deemed an urgent necessity to keep the farm-ing community solvent. If farmers could not pay their rents, then landlords could not pay the taxes laid upon them. An Act of 1663 not only encouraged food exports but imposed high duties on foreign imports of grains and pulses. In the next decade the government went further still to encourage grain sales wherever markets could be found. All ceiling prices governing grain exports were abolished in 1670, and in 1672 a new system was begun, of paying bounties on sales of grain achieved overseas. Bounties were promised for five years, but, in fact, were paid up to 1680–1, then lapsed, and were resumed in 1689. Other measures were taken to give preferential discounts to exporters of malt and liquors using grain. In this way, producers of inferior grains were also given a helping hand. 'Whatever would become of our corn injured by bad har-vests were it not for distilling?,' wrote a pamphleteer in 1736. Indirectly, spirit-drinking was thus much encouraged, while beer-drinkers too were persuaded to develop a taste for stronger beers which used more barley.[10]

Until the second half of the eighteenth century, interruptions in the payment of grain bounties were temporary, and few. High grain prices at home caused them to be suspended only in 1699, 1709, 1728, and 1740. In short, financial devices, introduced by the government, and the initiatives of farmers, maltsters, and brewers helped at least the larger grain-growers to survive nearly a century of adversity. Not everyone was so fortunate, however, for this is also the period which allegedly saw 'the disappearance of the small landowner'.[11]

The passing of the 1656 Act gave all farmers the first official glimpse of their long-term predicament, but it took decades more before it was clearly expressed, fully understood, and more widely acted upon. One pamphleteer, somewhat late in the day, expounded the problem clearly in 1677: 'Our lands fall for want of being improved *some other way* [my italics], besides planting corn, breeding for wool, etc., which are become so low a price as scarce to turn to account.'[12] In fact, ways of escaping from the dilemma were already being test-ed, and much discussed in scattered places around the kingdom. Eventually experience enabled the best of the innovations to spread widely and settle into a recognizable pattern. But the process of learning was slow: no one had the long-term view such as that given to us by hindsight.

What, then, were the strategies of alternative agriculture, which were chosen between 1650 and 1750, and how did they emerge from the bedrock of main-stream farming? Just as some of the ways ahead in the fourteenth century were pointed out by developments that had begun modestly in the buoyant period of mainstream agriculture in the thirteenth century, so various signposts were erected in the sixteenth century which were more seriously followed in the seventeenth. An alternative agriculture never emerges out of a cloudless sky; rather, ideas lie around waiting to be more fully developed when the time is ripe. By the mid-seventeenth century their time had come.[13]

Some of the first notions for an alternative agriculture were unwittingly introduced in the early decades of the sixteenth century, when mainstream farming was returning to favour, and the landowning gentry began to show a fresh enthusiasm for farming through their reading of the classical writers on husbandry. They had lost interest in their home farms in the fifteenth century, and had frequently leased them to others. But the coming of the printing press placed the classical authors in their hands, and with fresh eyes they read Xenophon, Cato, Varro, and Columella. Many gentry were thus persuaded anew of the intellectual satisfaction of farming, and this was at a time when food prices were beginning to rise again, and gentlemen faced unwonted practical problems in supplying their households with basic foodstuffs. Xenophon and Columella described the challenges of cultivating land to the highest standard, and affirmed the moral and religious duty of gentlemen to maintain their households in a state of peace and prosperity by their own efforts, feeding their members off their own land, and using that land in the most productive way. They challenged their readers to experiment, observe, and innovate. 'The most ancient farmers', wrote Varro, 'determined many of the practices by experiment, their descendants for the most part by imitation. We ought to do both—imitate others and attempt by experiment to do some things in a different way.' Such experience, it was argued, could lead them into quite different spheres of activity. Had not great men in government been summoned in the past from the plough to deliver the state?[14]

The message of the classical authors fell on fertile ground. The gentry embarked on a more professional management of their home farms, with the result that they made a considerable contribution to the market in basic foodstuffs. But in addition they seized on the classical suggestions for growing more luxury foods for their own private tables. The Scudamore and Beale families in Herefordshire began the study of apple varieties in their neighbourhood in an effort to improve the quality of the local cider.[15] It became a fashion among even the busiest statesmen and ambassadors of the realm to take a close interest not only in the management of their farmlands but in the construction of vegetable gardens and orchards, and in renovating fish ponds round their manor houses.

Another group of alternative crops was introduced into public discussion by government problems which touched upon commercial and defensive policies. As price inflation took hold throughout western Europe, and acute difficulties resulted when some foreign supplies were interrupted by war, Englishmen bewailed their dependence on increasingly expensive imports, and saw the sense of producing the same commodities at home. In 1540 among the most endangered goods were dyestuffs, linen, and canvas. This called for the domestic production of madder, woad, flax, and hemp. In 1549 woad and now oil were placed at the top of the list.[16] From Henry VIII's reign onwards, therefore, modest experiments with novel industrial crops began. They never amounted to a forceful programme, backed by government power or money, but items in the programme were coaxed along, some more effectively than others, through royal or ministerial endeavour. In some cases official invitations were issued to foreigners to settle in England and bring their skill in growing and processing the industrial crops. But in the context of this mercantilist age, the prodding by government ministers was sometimes enough to persuade gentlemen who came to Westminster and circulated at court to take action on their own. They returned to their estates, with more than an intellectual interest in innovations, resolved to implement official policy, especially if it was fortified by royal grants of land or licences that promised them personal gain. For example, when Henry VIII wished to improve the number and quality of English horses, which had proved so weak and few in comparison with the Dutch when waging war against France, some of the parks belonging to dissolved monastic houses were granted by the Crown to Gentlemen Pensioners. This was a new corps of servants in the royal household, furnishing riding horses on royal occasions. With grants of parks, such men could be relied upon to use them to promote the breeding of better horses.[17]

So politicians did not simply beat the air when they regularly reiterated the desirability of growing more flax and hemp, of finding an oil crop which would reduce expensive imports of olive oil, and of producing woad and madder for the dyeing industry, instead of importing woad from Toulouse in France and madder from Zealand in the Low Countries.[18] Some public men showed a willingness to foster trials. Many examples are given below, but one will suffice here: when Cranborne Chase came into the hands of the Cecil family, woad-growing became an early experimental venture.[19]

Thus courageous and far-sighted pioneers, others who were intellectually curious, and some eccentrics laid the foundations for alternative crops which, in more propitious circumstances some decades later, would come into their own. The dedication of the enthusiasts was intensified by the conviction of the classical authors, reiterated by English writers on husbandry, that all land could be made profitable if only one found the right crops.[20] Of course, only the gentry, among countrymen, had the money to experiment, take risks, and perhaps lose all, so their intellectual enthusiasm was a vital prerequisite if innovations in agriculture were to succeed. But they translated the enterprise into practical terms, adopting sometimes the less risky strategy to themselves of joining in partnerships with merchants who had journeyed overseas and had brought back ideas and information about new crops. Together they formed a powerful alliance, the gentry supplying the land and some of the cash, the merchant furnishing the technical expertise of cultivation and marketing. Thus risks were shared.[21]

By gentle prodding, propaganda, and grants of one sort and another, gentlemen, merchants, and, eventually, yeomen farmers were persuaded to become the agents of governmental scheming. Their undertakings might achieve immediate and lasting success, as was the growing of rapeseed as an oil crop in place of olive oil. Alternatively, after a bright beginning, some projects might fade into obscurity. Even then, they could return to the agenda when a sudden crisis jolted the matter to attention once more, and a fresh start, in more compelling circumstances, brought success the second time round. If not, then a third or fourth chance might be needed before the effort matched up to the opportunity or, alternatively, failure was ultimately accepted.[22] The final verdict on all these schemes was not ready to be passed until the later seventeenth century, when many efforts at substituting home-grown crops for imports had succeeded. Notable among these were hops, woad, rapeseed, flax, and hemp, all finding a secure place in farmers' cropping schedules, and contributing valuable items to the success of alternative agriculture now that it had become an urgent national necessity.

After industrial crops, the branch of alternative agriculture destined to help yet more farmers was horticulture, growing out of the revitalized interest of the gentry in vegetables, fruit, and herbs in the sixteenth century. It offered plants to be grown on several different scales, in small plots or in fields, and yielded good profits as cereal prices slumped. Farmers had to continue to grow bread-corn, but supplementary crops could make all the difference to the final profit which accrued from their land. The development of horticulture was long-drawn-out, but the seventeenth-century phase was significant in the sequence; it strengthened signs of growth which had emerged in the fifteenth century, and events at this time would have many parallels with the third experience of alternative agriculture in the later nineteenth century, and again now in the later twentieth century.

Gentlemen's fresh reading of the classical authors aroused curiosity in horticulture as well as agriculture. Columella devoted a whole book to horticulture, explaining his expansive mood by saying that it had been carried on half-heartedly in the past, but 'is now quite a popular pursuit'. There followed advice on many more vegetables than the usual onions, colewort, garlic, and leeks, grown in English gardens in the Middle Ages. A variety of lettuces, yellow,

1. Fruit-picking. This original drawing appears in Thomas Fella's *Book of Diveirs Devises and Sortes of Pictures, devised and made by T.F.*, 1585–98, 1622. The book is full of farming scenes and botanical drawings, suggesting the artist's lively interest in farming generally, and in some of the alternative plants and farming activities that were already conspicuous in eastern England. Within the book, a connection with Suffolk, and perhaps Essex, is indicated.

curly-leaved, purple, and dense were described, as well as cress, savory, cucumber, asparagus, and artichokes.[23]

Many gentlemen, on their first reading of Columella around 1500, must have felt themselves being introduced to a totally unfamiliar world. Greenstuff had been carefully tended in the gardens of monastic houses, and there, if nowhere else, a high, and probably rising, standard of cultivation had been maintained. But monastic houses were not ubiquitous, and their concerns did not exert much influence beyond their small local communities. A fashionable interest in some fruit, vegetables, and herbs is discernible in the fifteenth century among a minority of wealthy laymen—queens and noblemen—but generally these foodstuffs were regarded as the food of the poor and meek.[24]

Attitudes changed fundamentally in the early years of the sixteenth century, under the influence first and foremost of the foreign contacts made by Tudor kings and members of the court circle. Henry VIII was profoundly impressed by the fashions, manners, and, indeed, the whole culture of the French and Spanish courts. He introduced to his own court a multitude of practices observed in France at the court of Francis I. He then married Catharine of Aragon, who brought from Spain to England a taste for fine vegetables and fruits with which she had been familiar in her childhood in Granada. She had taken for granted the age-old horticultural skills of Moorish gardeners in Andalusia, and was thoroughly dismayed at the lack of salad lettuces in England. To satisfy her needs, they had to be imported from Holland. Nor is it irrelevant to this story that so-called 'Spanish lettuces' were described by Konrad Heresbach, a government official of Cleves, as 'the greatest esteemed' variety.[25]

By the 1520s or 1530s, then, the reading of classical descriptions of a great variety of vegetables known in the Roman world constituted an entirely different experience from the same reading in 1500; it now struck a chord of recognition and appreciation, for it had become the highest fashion at court to eat these exotic foods with relish. Henry VIII set up an orchard at Teynham in Kent in 1533, growing cherries and many different sorts of apples and pears.[26] When he was due to visit Calais in 1534, an order went forth to the Deputy Governor, Lord Lisle, to gather all the artichokes (globe artichokes) in the neighbourhood, and keep them for the king's pleasure. That was his 'special commandment'.[27] Despite the fact that artichokes (in Heresbach's words, in the mid-sixteenth century) were only 'a kind of thistle', they were by then 'in great estimation at noblemen's tables'.[28] Thirty years later it had become a convention for all gentlemen to have 'an artichoke garden'—not just a row or two of globe artichokes amid other vegetables, but a whole garden. At Paulerspury, in Northamptonshire, Arthur Throckmorton planted 229 artichokes when his new house was abuilding, and more artichoke gardens are found at Theobald's House, Hertfordshire,

Henry Oxinden's house at Great Maydeacon, Kent, in 1640, and at Queen Henri-etta Maria's Wimbledon House. All this is better understood when we also take account of the current belief that eating artichokes promoted the chances of pro-ducing male children—one of the strongest aspirations of gentry families.[29]

When vegetables and fruit ceased to be despised as the food of the poor, and became a fashionable food of the rich, a veritable revolution was slowly set in motion. 'Slowly' is the operative word, for the full story, as we shall see, shows phases of notable advance and notable regression, and its most dramatic phase has waited until the late twentieth century. But significant progress was made between the sixteenth and the mid-eighteenth century. First of all it was a fash-ion among the well-to-do. Then court fads captivated others, and Englishmen who travelled abroad were alert to new foods wherever they went.[30] Merchants, ambassadors, churchmen, and scholars ate fine foods at the tables of their Ital-ian, Spanish, Flemish, Dutch, and French hosts, and introduced more variety into England. The vegetables which pleased them were in some cases an entire-ly new experience, like globe and Jerusalem artichokes and asparagus, but in many other cases they were improved varieties of familiar foods. Colewort, or kale, became cabbage; then varied shapes and colours of cabbage were differen-tiated, and members of the same family, like savoy and cauliflower, became a familiar sight on English tables.[31] Different sizes and flavours were recognized in onions, and some finicky tastes were affected, so that even when improved cab-bages and onions were being grown in England by the end of the sixteenth century, the foreign varieties were still imported from Holland as well. Vessels entering the Port of London during November 1596 from Holland carried 12,600 cabbages, and onions in 65 barrels and 10,400 ropes. Spanish onions were prized then, as now, for their size, and perhaps for their sweet flavour, for, according to John Parkinson in *Paradisi in Sole* in 1629 some people ate them like apples. They were even singled out, on a list of desirable imports, in pro-posals for expanding overseas trade in 1595.[32]

Yet further fine distinctions were introduced by foreigners into the food sen-sibilities of the English upper classes, persuading them to differentiate varieties of the same vegetable. Some notion of this discrimination is gained from a sen-tence which Peter Erondell, a Huguenot refugee in London in Elizabeth's reign, set out in a textbook in dialogue form (in French and English on facing pages), to help his pupils learn French. Turnips lay on the table in the house of a gentle-woman. 'What manner of turnips are these?', asked Lady Beau-Séjour. 'They are our own growth,' replied her hostess. 'But the seed thereof was sent me from Caen in Normandy, where groweth the best turnips in France. They be not as our English turnips, which be big and round, but these are smaller and longer, and of much better taste.'[33]

By 1620 foreign visitors, moving in diplomatic circles in London, were giving high praise to improved English vegetables, though not yet to fruits. One of these Italian commentators, Busino, thought all the fruit, apart from apples, tasted insipid. But he also added the further significant observation that people did not generally put fruit on the table at mealtimes, but ate it between meals, munching it in the streets 'like so many goats'.[34] Many lessons about styles of eating had yet to be learned before the English could match the Spanish, French, and Italians in their appreciation of these foods. But while they learned to differentiate subtle flavours, a philosophical argument caught on to justify this turn of fashion's wheel. The simple food of the poor, so long despised, came to be praised for its simplicity. It was said to be a healthier diet, much superior to the rich foods hitherto eaten by the well-to-do. Moreover, it needed no fire to cook it, no mean consideration when fuel had become scarce and costly. Such arguments were more persuasive still when fortified by the comments of explorers in the New World, noticing the simple, vegetable diets of the Indians. The fact that the Indians lived to a ripe age was associated with their eating and drinking habits, which did not 'oppress nature'.[35]

The horticultural renaissance of the sixteenth century developed into one of the branches of alternative agriculture in the seventeenth century, and its more mature manifestations in the farming world will be examined in the next chapter. But beyond the cultivation of vegetables and fruits for the table, it had yet another dimension. The use of herbs as medicines entered a new phase. Of course, the apothecaries had always used herbs in profusion, and rich and poor alike had recourse to their own favoured medical remedies, many of which used plants that grew wild. But gentlemen took up a new viewpoint when they began to ask themselves why they should send to the east in search of expensive plants when every poor man had the right remedies in his garden.[36]

The incipient prejudice against imported medicines, seen in the mid-sixteenth century, may have sprung out of their rising cost, but it was also stimulated by the same mixture of fashionable influences which set vegetables and fruits on a new path to favour. A sufficient supply of herbs for all domestic uses, culinary and medicinal, was then secured by gentlemen who deliberately nurtured them in their gardens. Enthusiasm led to more purposeful cultivation, assisted by scientific advances in identifying the plants more exactly. This raised the status of herbal medicine in the course of the sixteenth and seventeenth centuries, and duly encouraged gardeners and market gardeners to meet the growing demand. Another factor enlarged these commercial opportunities when the art of distillation was made more accessible to people outside the small world of the apothecaries and the monastic houses. A landmark was the publication in 1500 in German of a treatise on distilling by Hieronymus von Braunschweig,

2. Culinary and medicinal plants. A page of botanical drawings from Thomas Fella's *Book of Diveirs Devises*, 1585–98, 1622 (see also above, p. 30), showing a hemp leaf, dill, mustard, mercury, elder, plantain, and burr. We cannot know why the artist chose these plants, but they were all useful crops in the seventeenth century. All had a medical use (see Grieve, 1985), and some were also much used in the kitchen. For example, the household account book of the Reynell family, of Forde, near Teignmouth, Devon, shows regular purchases of mustard seed every three months (2 quarts just before Christmas, 2½ quarts in September 1628), and sugared mustard was considered essential with venison (Gray, 1995: 7, 11, 16, 33). Dill was a common pot-herb, and oil was distilled from the seeds. It was also fed to ewes suckling their lambs. A photograph of 1933 shows dill being harvested in a field at Long Melford, Suffolk (H. S. Redgrove, *Spices and Condiments*, London, 1933, 214). Dog's mercury needs to be handled carefully, but the leaves of annual mercury, boiled, have been eaten as a vegetable in Germany.

compiled by this Strasburg physician to enable the poor to cure their illnesses without paying large fees to the doctors. Once the book was published in an English translation in 1527, some of the subsequent books on plants and farming by English authors gave unwonted space to distillation. Thus, one of the editions (in 1552) of Richard Banckes's *Herbal*, first published in 1525, contained extra chapters on 'the virtues of water stilled'. Better still, when John Fitzherbert's *Book of Husbandry* of 1523 was reissued in 1598, twenty-nine extra pages were filled with advice on distillation. Methods became better known, and the equipment may have become cheaper and more widely available. At all events, it became almost a rule at the end of the sixteenth century for every manor house to have its stillhouse, while storerooms were filled with scores, if not hundreds, of distillations for medicine and for cooking.[37]

The importance of these concurrent developments is best measured in the 1650s when William Coles, calling himself 'a good Commonwealthsman', published his little pocket book on *The Art of Simpling* (1656), that is, the art of gathering medicinal herbs; he wrote a larger work, *Adam in Eden* (1657), listing plants, and giving prominence to their medical uses, 'to promote the public good'. Judging by contemporary references, certain London markets had long been supplied with herbs at all times, doubtless serving the apothecaries first and foremost. But the accounts of country households afford occasional glimpses of the demand that came from local gentry, and was met by local growers. Thus the Cranfield household in 1604 paid for 'scrobegrass and other herbs to make a drink for Richard'. In the early decades of the seventeenth century Lord William Howard at Naworth Castle, Cumberland, showed himself an especially enthusiastic user of herbs, fruits, and vegetables. Delivered to his door were valerian roots, conserve of rosemary, of violets, and of primrose, 'roots of herbs', and purslane, while herbs were put into his drinks by his brewer. For all this Lord William depended on local people to send the herbs along with the seasonal cauliflowers, cherries, strawberries, pears, plums, quinces, and apples. Later in the seventeenth century Sir John Hobart of Blickling, Norfolk, is seen in his household accounts relying similarly on his tenants to supply him with 'herbs for diet drinks'. In short, a stronger demand for herbs gave the rural population another profitable use for their garden land.[38]

Thus the renaissance of mainstream agriculture in sixteenth-century England was accompanied by a subsidiary renaissance in innovative horticulture, which was at first confined to kings, nobility, and gentry, and which remained subdued so long as bread production was the prime necessity. But as William Coles later wisely remarked, benefiting from a historical perspective afforded within his own lifetime: 'we see that those fashions which sometimes seem ridiculous, if once taken up by the gentry, cease to be so.' That is what happened this time, but more quickly than might have been expected because the gentry found fresh allies. The immigration of middle-class refugees from the Netherlands and France, fleeing religious persecution at home, and bringing their dietary habits with them, spread the fashion for herb, vegetable, and fruit-eating to the towns. Foreign gardeners set up their market gardens in Sandwich, Kent, in London suburbs along the Thames, and in other towns, such as Norwich and Canterbury, where the foreign population congregated. John Parkinson's book, *Paradisi in Sole . . .*, published in 1629, showed keen observation of the way the French and Dutch, living in England, used herbs liberally in their stews or 'loblollies', as he called them. He also commented on the foreigners' liking for stronger herbs than the English, making it clear that the English had learned and adopted many of these unfamiliar food habits.[39]

Meanwhile, gentlemen at home in their country houses cajoled, or bullied, their tenants to supply them with novel luxuries they had enjoyed in London, with the result that many peasants grew them for sale at a surprisingly early date. Some of the new vegetables were even tithed, a sure sign that the garden produce of the parish was not simply for household use but for sale. Walnuts, filberts, pears, plums, damsons, and red roses (used for rose water) were tithed at Great Driffield, Yorkshire, in 1595; so were artichokes, parsnips, carrots, and turnips at Kirby Malzeard, Yorkshire, in 1614. Cabbages, onions, turnips, carrots, parsnips, apples, pears, and hops were tithed at Letwell in the West Riding in 1628; and, in the distinctly more favourable cultural climate which horticulture enjoyed in the later seventeenth century, tithes were levied in 1676 at Mappleton on the east Yorkshire coast, south of Hornsea, on apples, pears, crab apples, plums, cherries, parsnips, carrots, cabbages, rosemary, lavender, thyme, mint, sage, radishes, cucumbers, and roses.[40]

To cater for this demand, market gardeners, whose efforts were wholly dedicated to the growing of vegetables and soft fruits, made up an increasing body of men in London, who sought and successfully obtained incorporation in 1605 as the Gardeners' Company.[41] Thereafter, yet another breed of men appeared, best called farmer-gardeners, since they had a foot in both camps. They grew grain, but they had plots of land set aside for vegetables as well. At Fulham, near London, indeed, arable rotations had been devised to enable vegetables to be grown in the common fields.[42]

One of the conspicuous advantages of many of the new crops that won favour at this time was their demand for large amounts of labour. In this respect, England's second experience of an alternative agriculture dealt with markedly different conditions from those prevailing on the first occasion after the Black Death. The heavy death toll in the fourteenth century had made labour scarce and expensive, and farmers' best alternative enterprises had to be economical in labour. Under the circumstances prevailing by the end of the sixteenth century, however, the best solutions were those which used labour in abundance. The rapid growth of population, almost doubling numbers between 1541 (2.7 million) and 1656 (5.3 million), raised the critical problem of finding work in town and country alike. The new Poor Law under Elizabeth suggested one solution by obliging cities and towns, from 1576 onwards, to keep workstocks to employ the poor.[43] This work in towns mostly involved industrial tasks, preparing and weaving wool, hemp, and flax, knitting, lace-making, and so on. They seem to have been brought into operation in bad times only, rather than being a continuous regime. But any parish which grew a labour-demanding crop welcomed it as an equally constructive way of employing poor people. In the case of woad-growing, it was a veritable life-saver. An account of labour employed at Milcote in Warwickshire, when 41 acres of woad were grown in 1626, shows that between 150 and 250 people were employed daily in the months from May to September, in weeding the crop, and then picking the leaves as they ripened. In gardens laborious hand labour was even more necessary: enclosing the land first of all to shield plants from the wind (for which a bank of mud and straw was sometimes raised, and then thatched with eaves of ryestraw), removing stones, constructing raised beds, levelling the ground, and manuring, often with night soil brought from a distance, steeping seeds before sowing, sowing sparingly in rows, thinning, transplanting, weeding, erecting stakes as supports, using mattresses on top of the beds to keep out extremes of cold and heat, watering twice a day, in some cases even devising a filtering system, whereby water drained slowly from a pot through a cloth, deterring birds, worms, and infestations of all kinds—the toil was endless. Yet it was also rewarding. Fine-quality vegetables could be harvested early and yielded a premium price.[44]

Of a similar order to the toil required for vegetables, herbs, and fruits, were the labour demands of crops like madder, hemp, flax, rapeseed, saffron, and hops. In different places each was developed to exploit in the best way possible the local circumstances. Prejudices and fashions then bent themselves conveniently to assist the process. At first strong objections were raised against digging soils with the spade, as it was thought to damage the land. This viewpoint weakened gradually, and another argument supervened, pointing out that land sown and weeded by hand produced far more food per acre than under the old system.[45] This truth was demonstrated by one man in the famine years of the 1590s, when many hundreds of poor in Shrewsbury lacked bread, and were fed by Richard Gardiner for three weeks just before harvest on carrots, grown on less than four acres of ground, and 700 cabbages grown on another plot. Gardiner was a dyer and market gardener who publicized his achievement in a little book of *Profitable Instructions for the manuring, sowing, and planting of Kitchen*

Gardens. His desire was 'to provide sufficient victuals for the poor and greatest number of people', which he deemed preferable to picking 'dainty salads to provoke appetite to those that do live in excess'.[46] Gardiner's was a novel argument in the 1590s, but scepticism evaporated in the next generation. Many poor Londoners were seen at the end of the sixteenth century living on roots, including turnips, and on herbs which they grew on dung fields outside the capital. Their evident utility resulted in a policy that was officially recommended in Norwich by the Assize judges *c.*1620-1 urging that gardening for root crops be encouraged among the poor.[47]

From 1650 onwards, we can measure the success of alternative crops in the more deliberate efforts to advertise them as part of the campaign to improve agriculture. The republic newly created after the execution of Charles I in 1649 saw an unprecedented opportunity for change, and the debates in consequence showed not only intellectual excitement, but hard realism as well. Samuel Hartlib, a German-Polish immigrant to England and a staunch Commonwealth man, set himself up in London at this time as an information centre, for exchanging ideas, and promoting many educational and economic projects, Among these was agricultural improvement, and, with his encouragement and editorial help, literature in favour of a more diversified agriculture poured forth, reaching a larger circle of interested people than before. Much confiscated Crown, Church, and Royalist land was being put up for sale, and purchasers often needed fresh ideas for using it.[48] More encouraging still were the facts and figures, liberally offered on the profits to be earned. Walter Blith in his *English Improver Improved* (1651) gave many such details, and while the promises of gain may sound excessive, and they were certainly not calculated by professional economists counting every penny of the costs of cultivation, they can be accepted as a rough and ready guide to the returns from the best-managed crops in the most favourable market circumstances. They were not meant to be average prices, nor were readers unaware that the profits fell sharply when once rarities became commonplaces.[49]

Amplifying Walter Blith's advice in 1651 came another helpful handbook in 1659 commending alternative agricultures, and showing what ingenuity had been applied in one short decade. In *Adam out of Eden* Adolphus Speed, a gentleman in the circle of Samuel Hartlib, offered another catalogue of novel enterprises, including in his book considerable detail about some, though no more than throw-away remarks about others. His first proposal concerned the keeping of rabbits on an intensive system, not necessarily in large warrens, but at twenty to the acre, feeding them partly by hand in hutches, and giving shelter by the growing of French furze. Rabbits kept thus were twice the weight of those in warrens; the experience was that of two gentlemen who, with two pieces of land of five acres, had earned £10 an acre on this system. A poulterer would give 8*d*. apiece for rabbits till Michaelmas and 1*s*.–1*s*. 8*d*. thereafter. In addition, the breeder of the rabbits had the chance to sell the skins for 3*s*. 4*d*. each: caps of rabbit fur (called 'light demi-casters') were the vogue; some people were even spinning the fur into a thread for silk-like stockings; and the bare pelts were shredded for a fertilizer. Another recommended novelty was turnips, yielding both tops and roots to feed to all kinds of livestock, and proving especially successful when fed to dairy cows, or, when boiled, fed to lambs and poultry. Sowthistles were a crop recommended for feeding to milch cows and pigs, an idea which almost certainly came from the Continent, where this plant is still valued as a potherb and in salads, though it proved not to have a future in England. Good advice on clover was given, with a word of warning about sainfoin, all of it owing much to the experience of Sir Richard Weston, who had learned many lessons on this score when he sought exile as a Royalist in the Low Countries. Other proposed novelties were potatoes (as food for men and livestock), Jerusalem artichokes (for poultry and swine), pompions or pumpkins (to feed men and animals), fennel (to fatten cattle quickly), cabbages, Roman beans, liquorice (which one London gentleman had found more prolific if planted sideways on top of the ground instead of being dug deep), saffron, French peas, mustard seed (yielding £30 an acre), teasels, madder, osiers, willow (for fencing and shelter belts), French furze (superior to English furze for its prolific growth, and used not only for sheltering rabbits but for flash firing in ovens), woodland plantations, hops, flax, musk melons (to be grown only under walls in sheltered places), weld (the yellow dye crop well-known as a downland plant in Kent), coriander, aniseed, cumin, canary seed, asparagus, and, not so novel but seemingly neglected on a commercial scale, bees.[50] The variety of this list gives a glimpse of the range of alternatives being considered, and, although Speed vouchsafed meagre information about some, not one was a fanciful dream of the author; all can be shown to have occupied farmers in England somewhere or other.[51]

Other writers in the 1650s offered less spacious general surveys, preferring to make specialized recommendations, to which they brought more personal experience. Ralph Austen wrote on fruit trees, with much practical knowledge drawn from his Oxford orchards. On hops Reynolde Scot's sixteenth-century book still served admirably, and was reprinted in 1654. Hartlib issued a book on bees and silkworms, when hope for the silk industry was revived by the discovery in Virginia of another variety of mulberry tree, and the rumour spread (though it subsequently proved false) that silkworms could be successfully fed on lettuce. The monetary gains to be had from all these ventures loomed large in all discussions. William Coles commended the growing of fruit, flowers, and herbs, especially for their virtues in restoring health, but 'if this is not a melting inducement enough,' he was willing 'to descend to the great argument of the world, profit'.[52]

When surveying the comparatively long-drawn-out beginnings of England's second phase of alternative agriculture, from the first weak signals that were given in the early sixteenth century to its evolution as a prominent theme in agriculture in the second half of the seventeenth century, explanations for its slow progress are needed. Many of the innovations started as indulgences of the rich at a time when the prime necessity was to grow grain as the staple food. The prosperity of mainstream agriculture was maintained until the 1580s, and then ebbed and flowed until the 1650s. Until that later date there was no compelling reason for farmers in large numbers to accommodate alternative pursuits, and in any case the assumptions and prejudices of the age placed a brake on a switch to some other enterprises. Some landlords positively prohibited certain novel crops. Their need for gardening methods of cultivation, and deep digging, was thought to be harmful to the soil. But the chance to observe Dutch and Flemish gardeners around London broke down most prejudices by the 1650s, though ignorance was still said to prevail twenty miles outside London. Other deep suspicions centred on the medical efficacy and the culinary taste of herbs, vegetables, and fruits grown intensively outside their wild habitats, or grown in fields instead of in gardens. Plainly, they grew larger when tended and manured in gardens, but did this spoil their flavour? In John Parkinson's opinion it certainly did when horse manure was used; yet manure was essential in these intensively cultivated small plots. William Coles's remarks as late as 1657 on the superior quality of the mustard of Tewkesbury, picked wild from the roadsides, also implied a prejudice against mustard grown in gardens and orchards. By that time, however, the adverse opinion of spade cultivation was generally being overcome, though only to bring another prejudice into view, against growing greenstuff in fields. Again, it was held that their flavour and goodness deteriorated, whenever they were grown on a large scale. Such a view had been advanced in one of the earliest books on gardening by Thomas Hill, and, whether on the grounds of taste, yield, form, or for some other reason, Sir Richard Weston in the 1640s held strongly to the view that plants growing wild and in the garden were vastly different.[53]

Such doubts and hesitations inhibiting the commercial cultivation of new crops could be indulged in an age when grain-growing was still profitable, but, when once the declining profits from mainstream agriculture were sufficiently serious to prompt the Act of 1656 allowing food exports, and when decades passed without any return to prosperity for grain growers, the prejudices about the field cultivation of alternative crops had to disappear. Finally, the economics of the business prevailed triumphantly over finicky arguments about taste and efficacy. In the 1680s John Aubrey gave evidence of the carrots and cabbages growing in fields in Wiltshire, Somerset, and Dorset, while Oxfordshire yielded fields of caraway (home-grown seed being worth almost twice that of seed bought from London grocers), and one Huntingdonshire farmer at least was growing one ten-acre field of chervil in 1737.[54]

*

England's second experience of alternative agriculture underwent many subtle transformations as it emerged in the course of the sixteenth century and settled into a routine between 1650 and 1750. Delineating its clearer shape in the prime years after 1650 occupies the next chapter. But one sign of a changing viewpoint calls for mention here because it threaded its way modestly into the literature without mounting a loud or insistent argument. It will be heard again, more cogently expressed, during the third experience at the end of the nineteenth century, and it may well be heard again, as we undergo the fourth experience at the end of the twentieth century. As a result of practical observations of food crops harvested on small pieces of ground, some contemporaries spoke up in favour of smaller farms. The view was voiced in the 1640s and 1650s, first by Sir Richard Weston, a Royalist who had travelled observantly in the Low Countries. He recommended digging, claiming that one digging was as effective as three ploughings and not much more expensive. He then came to the conclusion that 'a little farm well tilled is to be preferred.' It would have less waste land, provide more work for the poor, and yield bigger crops. Gardening, he maintained, could support a family on two or three acres.[55] The Parliamentarians, devising policy from a different viewpoint, held high hopes of creating more holdings for husbandmen. But behind that dream lay the firm knowledge that husbandmen could live on smaller units of land, using gardening methods. So, although the argument was not vigorously pushed in open debate during the 1650s, it lurked in the background, and may have exerted influence on some purchasers when confiscated land was sold by Parliament. Large estates, at the first sale, were frequently divided between several, or many, new owners, and some purchasers divided them yet again when they resold. We do not know the exact acreages of the pieces that were finally cultivated by individuals, and cannot with any assurance describe them strictly as small farms or smallholdings.[56] But it is noticeable that some Parliamentarians demonstrated gardening methods when they acquired forfeited land, and grew special crops like onions.[57] Thoughts on the merits of small farms still circulated in the 1660s when Sir Thomas Culpeper's *Tract on Usury*, originally written in 1621, was reissued in 1668. Seeing the matter in purely practical terms, Culpeper maintained that the way to wealth lay in 'dividing of our lands into very small farms for the ease both of oversight and amendment'.[58] The logic of small farms, when a multitude of small crops was being advocated, was evident enough. Yet the debate died away, leaving doubts about the practical results of this phase of agriculture on the general size of farms, and posing a question for historians on which they have so far shed no light.

3 ⁓ SETTLING INTO A ROUTINE

ALTERNATIVE agriculture is a drab term for a richly innovative, slowly evolving process of agricultural change. It usually involves a fundamental transformation of attitudes towards foods and health, as well as a fresh appraisal of the land's potential, and it is difficult for people undergoing the experience to stand back and see it all objectively. Certainly no one in the seventeenth century used the term 'alternative agriculture', though they occasionally came close to describing it as agricultural diversification.

However, with hindsight, we can see that the process of change reached a watershed in the 1650s, when the scattered efforts of individuals were co-ordinated (notably by Samuel Hartlib acting as the centre of information), books gave better advice, and the government positively assisted by acknowledging that mainstream foodstuffs were being overproduced, and allowing them to be exported. The momentum was maintained after 1660, and, indeed, strengthened by another set of converging circumstances. First and foremost, the stagnation or fall of food prices persisted, and so the alternatives were better publicized, and convincingly shown to be profitable, either as main pursuits or, more often, as additional sidelines. The multitude of choices available was illustrated in more books, reflecting decades of hard experience. Purchasers and readers of the books are clearly seen, compiling notes in their own commonplace books, spreading more widely news of the merits of novelties, and recommending to their friends the best systems of cultivation, the sources of seeds and nursery plants, and the profits. Those with time on their hands regularly visited the growers to obtain first-hand guidance.

The alternative enterprises that were discussed and debated made a long list, and it would be a mistake to use hindsight to set them in one order of importance, when the ranking was regionally different and farmers were in the midst of more than a few new ventures. In the second half of the seventeenth century no one could tell which alternative crops and farming procedures would triumph and dominate the farming scene, and which would fade into obscurity. To see the situation through the eyes of contemporaries, therefore, we have to survey the most widely advertised choices in a wholly random order.

The serious attention given to horticulture is best exemplified in the books published. Blanche Henrey has drawn attention to their large number and the professional dedication that went into compiling them.[1] The newly formed Royal Society was responsible for urging authorship on its members, especially those belonging to the Georgical committee, or alternatively urging experiments. Consequently, the plea to increase the growing of potatoes coming from Mr Buckland, a Somerset gentleman, elicited promises of action by other Society members to plant them, distribute seed, and print growing instructions. Members also made sure that a scheme to compose a history of agriculture and gardening paid due attention to 'materials for kitchen garden . . . and winter greens' as well as new industrial crops, those named on this occasion being woad, hops, flax, hemp, madder, buckwheat, liquorice, and rapeseed.[2]

Pride of place in the literary effort to promote horticulture must go to John Evelyn, though he is more often associated with the campaign to stimulate woodland plantations. He exerted great influence over gardening, having been impressed, in his turn, by his travels in France and Italy between 1643 and 1647, when he diligently visited gardens.[3] His first book was a translation of a French work, *The French Gardiner*, 1658, and his second a horticultural calendar, *Kalendarium hortense*, appended to *Sylva* in the 1664 edition. Some years before 1664 Evelyn had embarked on a major work on horticulture entitled *Elysium Britannicum*, whose completion he expected, and announced, in 1669. But amendments and additions continued to be made to the manuscript, so that finally it was never completed. All that was published was one chapter on salads, *Acetaria. A Discourse of Sallets* (1699).[4]

Evelyn was a diligent gardener on his own estates, first of all at Deptford and later at Wotton, Surrey. Relatively late in life, he translated yet another French work, by Jean de La Quintinie, *The Compleat Gard'ner* (1693), which, while teaching gardening procedures which were followed in France at the highest social level (and, doubtless, at high cost for La Quintinie was gardener to Louis XIV), finally made them known in less exalted circles in England. Professional nurserymen in England already offered a wide range of plants to growers of all classes (the rise of commercial nurserymen and seedsmen was a notable phenomenon from the mid-sixteenth century onwards), and George London and Henry Wise at their Brompton Park nursery in London were sufficiently astute to see the commercial opportunities afforded by Evelyn's book. They reissued it in 1699 in an abridged and less expensive form, omitted Evelyn as author, and inserted an advertisement for their nurseries.[5]

3. Strawberries. This drawing by Marcellus Laroon of a strawberry seller in London (1687) shows a luxury fruit of the sixteenth century one hundred years later, when it was no longer a rich man's privilege, and might be bought by Londoners from street sellers. It shows the special baskets in which the fruit was placed to avoid damage (see Sean Shesgreen, *The Criers and Hawkers of London*, Stanford University Press, 1990).

Meanwhile another solid, sensible book on horticulture had appeared by John Worlidge, *Systema Horticulturae* (1677). Written by a well-informed Hampshire gentleman, it conveyed a message to gentry and working farmers alike: fruit and vegetables satisfied rich men 'with curious palates' but they also fed the common people, diversifying their diet, reducing the need for drink, and staving off hunger in years of grain scarcity. Worlidge even persuaded himself that horticultural advances had been so substantial that they were actually a cause of 'the deadness of the market for corn'.[6]

The promotion of fruit-growing had been strongly urged during the Interregnum in a book by Ralph Austen (1653, reissued 1657), who was a grower in Oxford, and by John Beale, an experimental parson, seeking better cider varieties in the West Country, and writing on *Herefordshire Orchards* (1657). After 1660 John Evelyn added his weight to the campaign with an appendix to *Sylva*, entitled *Pomona*. The constructive results of so much propaganda was visible in a notable increase in the numbers of orchards, especially in the West Midlands. Leases of land and surveys in Worcestershire, Herefordshire, Gloucestershire, and Shropshire frequently refer to orchards newly made out of pasture. The improved quality of West Country ciders after 1660 turned them into a successful article of commerce within the kingdom, with further hopes of success in exports overseas. A century later, in 1753, Batty Langley claimed that Hugh Stafford had restored a run-down farm partly with cider, and Stafford obliged with an essay in Langley's book giving instructions to others on making it. The advice continued to be relevant, for cider consumption remained high until the middle of the nineteenth century, when it declined.[7]

Along with fruit trees went an interest in nut trees which, while it did not generate much bookish literature, led to a fashion for planting them, and clear signs in the end of their commercial success in certain districts of the country. The evidence for this enterprise is discussed more fully below.[8] Woodland plantations for the supply of larger timber also moved into the limelight, for forests had been recklessly felled without adequate replanting throughout the sixteenth and early seventeenth centuries. Change was urgently needed, and it manifested itself after 1660 in much more professional management. This trend was not a little bolstered by the efforts of the Royal Society, which entrusted to John Evelyn the construction of a programme for regenerating woodlands. His *Sylva* (1664) was both a successful guide to action and influential in practice, although the most powerful spur to the landowner was, of course, rising prices. As Evelyn himself exclaimed, 'who would not preserve timber, when within so few years the price is almost quadrupled?'[9]

Industrial crops, like rapeseed, dye plants, hops, hemp, and flax had received official encouragement in the years between about 1540 and 1580 through a government-sponsored drive to curb foreign imports. Following from this, the immigration of foreign experts had established some of these new, or revived, crops firmly on the farming scene, and allowed another unanticipated benefit to emerge, namely, their ability to employ large numbers of the poor. Their advance after 1660 called for less publicity, though the task of fitting them into a rotation was a learning process, profiting from foreign experience, but involving trial and error, until a few satisfactory alternatives emerged. Hemp and flax, for example, had generally been grown on enclosed plots, but in the Isle of Axholme in Lincolnshire which specialized for the market, a four-course rotation, extolled in the mid-eighteenth century, comprised barley, hemp, flax, and wheat or rye, without any fallow. We are not told if this was used in common fields, but unusual rotations like this were certainly found possible in other places. Woad was grown when first breaking up old pasture before taking a cereal crop; rapeseed was sown when breaking up a ley before taking oats and then other cereals; it is unlikely, however, that either crop found a place in common fields. Their fortunes are followed in more detail in Chapters 4 and 5.[10]

Another distinct group of alternative plants for farmers to consider at this time were grass substitutes and turnips. Clover, lucerne, and sainfoin had made their first tentative appearance in the 1620s–1630s, but they had commended themselves to only a few enthusiasts, mostly gentlemen concerned with fodder for their best horses. None showed instant promise of their great future, but attention gradually centred on clover, and a more deliberate attempt was made in the 1650s in the Hartlib circle to assemble all men's experience, and arrive at a satisfactory set of rules for cultivation. This effort paid dividends after 1660, when clover was incorporated in the arable rotation and forged ahead, greatly helped in the West Midlands when a book was published by Andrew Yarranton specifically advising the best methods of establishing it on the ryelands in that area.[11]

Sainfoin, meanwhile, made steady but less spectacular progress. It proved to be a crop that flourished on chalky soils, and in the course of the later seventeenth century it found a congenial home on the Kentish downlands, in the Cotswolds, on the Lincolnshire wolds, and other similar shallow-soiled hillsides. Its spread was helped by a treatise on *Sainfoin Improved*, 1671, probably written by Nathaniel Fiennes, who plainly had practical experience. In places where it grew best, it was highly valued, lasting ten, or even fifteen to sixteen years on the better soils.[12]

Lucerne, on the other hand, suffered from the belief that preparation of the soil for this crop was laborious, and only gentlemen could afford it. Seed was usually bought in France in the early days, and even when the plant's needs were better understood seed still had to be imported, though now from Holland. In any case, lucerne required a rich soil, and natural grass was liable to overwhelm it after two or three years. In dealing with lucerne disagreements persisted about sowing the seed broadcast or drilling in rows, thus allowing the fields to be hoed. The harvest certainly made good hay for cattle, but it did not sell for so good a price at the market as sainfoin or clover, even though, in some weathers, it yielded a better crop. Lucerne therefore remained on the list of forage crops, but it was not generally put at the top, and it was liable to be jostled by other novelties.[13]

Turnips entered the farming scene as another livestock fodder, but by a different route. Foreign immigrants in the sixteenth century publicized them as food for the table, but the English affected at first to despise them.

> Our English nature cannot live by roots.
> By water, herbs, or such beggary baggage
> That may well serve for vile, outlandish coats,

wrote William Forrest in 1548. But the prejudices were worn down when these same roots proved invaluable in feeding the poor in lean times, and the varieties were improved to satisfy even the well-to-do. They then came to serve yet other purposes. Farmers in the Low Countries were familiar with the practice of feeding turnips to livestock, especially dairy cows and bullocks; that usage was being copied in East Anglia by the 1630s, and is well documented from the 1660s onwards. Turnips spread steadily on lighter soils, on loams, and on some flood plains, and, in Norfolk and Suffolk at least, the pace quickened from the 1680s.[14]

In the years after 1660 possible new forage crops were not seen to be confined to the four named above. A variety of others attracted experiment, and news from abroad, or the rereading of the classics, might at any moment start a fresh trial: spurry, burnet, and parsley were tried, and an interest was expressed in lupines, fenugreek, lentils, and millet. Later still, trials were made with timothy grass, and, at the end of the eighteenth century, with succory or chicory.[15] It was certainly not a foregone conclusion that clover and turnips, in a rotation incorporating both, would prevail, although the pace of their adoption separately was encouraging after the 1680s. Their great merit at this time, spurring the arable farmer on, was the chance they gave to achieve a different balance between grain-growing and livestock-keeping, thus avoiding the necessity to grow alternative crops which could not be assimilated into the conventional field rotation.

Where clover and/or turnips were chosen, they are often associated with a surge in commercial dairying, starting around the mid-seventeenth century. This, indeed, has to be seen as another alternative strategy, which brought increasing rewards to the farmer after 1660 in defined but scattered areas over the country. Clover and turnips were not the explanation for its success in all

cases, however. Some dairymen on the western side of the country still preferred to rely on natural grasses, and they were especially fortunate if they also
had water meadows, supplying them with lush grass in spring, weeks before
their competitors.

The first strong stimulus to dairying was given by the need to furnish large
quantities of cheese for the soldiery during the Civil War. The expanding market is indirectly made evident in wholly new legislation, in 1662–3, and 1692
(dealing with grievances, which were also aired in 1678) to curb the abuses of
cheese and butter wholesalers. But it is directly reflected in the probate inventories of farmers' livestock and produce at death, showing sometimes herds of
fifty and sixty cows and thousands of cheeses in store. In the first phase of alternative agriculture between 1350 and 1500, some weak signs of a new phase in
dairying enterprise were noted, though it was virtually concealed from sight by
the meagre documents concerning small family farmers. They were the class
most likely in the circumstances to have exploited the opportunity. In the later
seventeenth century a much brighter light is shed on such activities; in areas as
varied as north Shropshire, Cheshire, Derbyshire, Staffordshire, Dorset, the
Vale of Gloucester, cheese Wiltshire, around Newcastle, and in central Suffolk,
commercial dairying emerges as a notable success story.[16]

How far dairying increased pig-keeping at this time is a question which cannot yet be satisfactorily answered. In the Middle Ages, pigs were mainly woodland animals, and into the sixteenth century some continued to be fattened on
nuts in the autumn, giving their meat a fine flavour that was much esteemed in
London. But woodlands were diminishing steadily, and so it is reasonable to
guess that numbers may have been raised by more dairymen keeping pigs fed on
whey, and fattening them with peas and beans, while arable farmers who had
grain to spare also kept pigs in modest numbers. But the most conspicuous
publicity for pig-keeping, in fact, is found in towns where hundreds, nay thousands, were fed increasingly on industrial wastes, on the residues from London
breweries, distilleries, and starch-houses. The pork and bacon bought from
town and country sources came to be differentiated in price, as the flavour was
affected by the feeding, but encouragement to pig-producers generally must
surely be reflected in the fact that a 71 per cent rise in pig prices occurred
between 1640 and 1750. The pig, in short, offered an opportunity to the farmer
seeking alternatives. But farmers' inventories have yet to identify clearly the special districts, in woodland, in dairying or other pastoral country, or in towns,
where the chance was most vigorously exploited; and John Worlidge's observation, from Hampshire in 1675, suggests disappointment that, in his neighbourhood, at least, it was not taken: 'It is a great neglect that they are no more bred
and kept than they are.'[17]

Poultry-keeping, similarly, offered a golden alternative opportunity to small farmers, including women, but, since farmers' probate inventories usually refer to poultry in summary fashion, it is difficult to gauge the significance of the progress made at this time in stimulating a larger commercial market for meat and eggs. The largest numbers of poultry are found in probate inventories in East Anglia, and noticeably sometimes they occur in association with a French or Dutch surname. This fact is highly suggestive: a successful French book on poultry-keeping was translated into English in 1580; buckwheat, turnips, and carrots featured in East Anglia as new field crops from the Continent in the late sixteenth and seventeenth centuries, and all were valued as poultry feed. Foreigners may well have galvanized poultry production, and most of all in eastern England. But the inventory of William Dockray of Matterdale, Cumberland, in 1639, showing 160 head of poultry, hints at the initiative of a foreigner in a very different part of the country. By the 1670s John Worlidge was urging the business advantages of poultry-keeping on those who lived within a day's journey of London, and, at second-hand, he had heard of one farm 'wholly stocked with poultry'. It may also be significant that our evidence of turkeys and geese, walking in large flocks to London from East Anglia, pertains to this age of alternative agriculture. Imagination is fired when reading that in 1642 the common fen of Whaplode and Holbeach parishes in Lincolnshire was two miles in compass and the inhabitants had free common *without stint at all times* for geese, as well as cattle and swine. Defoe conjured up a vivid picture of 300 droves in a season, perhaps 150,000 birds altogether, crossing from Suffolk into Essex via the bridge over the River Stour. And, illustrating the dynamism of the metropolitan market, he described the four-storeyed carts, recently invented, to carry the birds non-stop to London in two days and a night. These were used not only for turkeys and geese but for live chickens 'in the dear seasons'.[18]

*

Nearly all the alternative farming activities noticed so far were strongly promoted by means of books and treatises. The literature flowed forth because the gentry interested themselves in all these possibilities, and deemed it their duty to publicize them. Recognizing the usefulness of these enterprises to all classes living off the land, authors gave extremely practical advice. But, whereas all classes needed an alternative agriculture at this time, their preferences were determined by different circumstances, and if a book on alternative agricultures had been written by labouring men, they would have commended each crop in different ways. However, since low grain prices persisted for almost a century, men had plenty of time to weigh the advantages and disadvantages of each alternative, and eventually their choices settled into a pattern. An almost embarrassing richness of choice was pruned down to a realistic shortlist, each appropriate to the circumstances of one class of farmers. One or two undertakings, like deer parks and fish ponds, offered themselves almost exclusively to one class only, in this case the gentry. Others could be exploited by several classes. Alternatives which used land sparingly appealed on a permanent basis to husbandmen, smallholders, and labourers who could take advantage of under-used family members. Other alternatives were less stoutly attached to one social class, and could shift their affiliations according to changing economic circumstances. Labour-intensive alternatives interested the gentry only so long as labour was cheap and plentiful, and took on a different aspect in the early eighteenth century. What was most noticeable about the period 1650 to 1750, when compared with the period after the Black Death, was the multifarious choices available. Some could be adopted as profitable sidelines without wholly overturning existing regimes; others more fundamentally reshaped the arable routine. Some called for long-term planning, patience, and capital, others for little. In sum they offered many chances to those with a readiness to be flexible.

The class-based affiliations of alternative farming strategies deserve further elaboration. Those which profitably employed large tracts of land with little labour plainly appealed to large landowners and large farmers. Hence, a trend towards more pasture farming was visible on some gentlemen's estates, and has been convincingly demonstrated by research in the south Midlands.[19]

Also favoured by the gentry were woodland plantations, using large acreages and promising in the long term considerable income. With obvious deliberation, some landowners sharply changed the direction of their policy in favour of woodland. Sir Henry Hobart at Blickling, Norfolk, for example, turned away from expenditure on farming improvements around 1683–96, to concentrate on timber, and during those years this became his largest source of income. The Craven family in Berkshire staked out new plantations across heathland at Ashdown House around 1700. Some thirty years earlier, in 1667, Charles Dormer, second Earl of Caernarvon, had neatly summed up his view of private woodland, by declaring to Pepys that it was 'created by God for the payment of debts'. For another generation at least after 1700 advice continued to flow in the same direction. Joseph Addison in the *Spectator* in 1712 reminded his readers that while woodland made a pretty landscape, it could also 'turn as much to the profit as the pleasure of the owner'.[20] In short, new timber plantations ranked high among the gentry's strategies for an alternative agriculture, and, as it turned out, time was on their side. In 1763 the Liverpool shipwright Roger Fisher noted the satisfaction of the second Earl of Warrington, seeing at Dunham Massey, Cheshire, in his own lifetime, the timber which he had planted worth more than double the land on which it grew. Favourable prices for timber persisted throughout the first half of the eighteenth century, and vindicated the gentry's choice. Not until the second half of the eighteenth century did the wheel of change turn again, and persuade landowners to grub up their woodlands to make more arable and pasture.[21]

Fish ponds represented another means of drawing profit from large areas on gentlemen's estates. The movement was evident from the 1670s onwards, and already in 1685 Lady Clarendon at Swallowfield in Berkshire was serving *at every meal* carp and pike of a size 'fit for the table of a prince'. John Evelyn looked on approvingly.[22] In this case, the books of guidance for those creating new, or improving neglected old, ponds was not abundant. But, in practice, old hammer ponds in Sussex are found transformed in this way, and by 1700 gentlemen who had slimy, smelly moats around their houses were being urged to use them for fish instead of draining them to make decorative gardens. Thus a feature in the landscape which had survived for centuries in decay was now seen capable of being restored to use, and profits were placed at the forefront of the recommendations. In a general textbook on agriculture in 1703, carp-breeding was commended by Sir Jonas Moore for its financial rewards, while Roger North followed ten years later with *A Discourse of Fish*, giving particular advice on pond construction to those living on clay soils, who lacked springs or rivers. Keeping carp, along with some pike, perch, and tench, the pond owner could count on a return of some £6 5s. per acre, a significant improvement on the standard return of £2 from meadow.[23]

Some enterprises, which had started as exclusively gentlemanly ventures, ceased to be their monopoly between 1650 and 1750, and spread their benefits in various ways to other classes in society. Such were the deer parks, rabbit warrens, and dovecotes which recovered the popularity they had enjoyed after the Black Death. In the boom years of grain-growing, many deer parks had been turned over to cattle-grazings. Even where deer remained, much damage was wrought during the Civil War, so that all parks had to be restocked and repaired at the Restoration. After some twenty years of war and deprivation, then, the gentry restored them, showing the strongest determination to enjoy hunting again, and reflecting that resolution in the increasing severity of the game laws, punishing poachers. But another consideration entered into the enthusiasm with which parks were rehabilitated: they showed increasing merits as a food-store, supplying venison to gentlemen's households and affording a 'gift currency' for paying friends. Indeed, the gifts of venison to kin and neighbours, together with the record of venison dispatched to gentlemen's kitchens, plus further hints of sales to the market, convey the impression that parks gradually came to be as much valued for their meat supplies as for the pleasures of the chase. The nuances involved in this interpretation of a contemporary viewpoint should not be over-confidently stated, lest it distort reality. Deer parks certainly continued to serve the huntsmen. But at the same time the number of parks refurbished after 1660 ensured that more venison was served at gentlemen's tables than had been possible for about a century; and, following from this, the marketing of venison and the poaching of deer undoubtedly brought more of the meat within the experience of other social classes.[24]

The renewed interest in rabbit warrens also spread economic benefits more generally through rural society. Warrens returned to prominence for the same reasons that favoured them after the Black Death. But in their case, it is far from certain in the intervening years, when grain-growing dominated the scene between 1500, and 1650, that rabbit warrens were neglected or reduced in number. Some decline might logically have been expected, for peasant farmers deeply resented the damage which rabbits did to their grain crops. When grain-growing was the first priority, it cannot have been easy for owners of rabbit warrens to live peaceably with their neighbours. However, both rabbit meat and rabbit skins continued to sell well at the markets, and many warrens are known to have flourished throughout the sixteenth century. This is apparent, for example, at West Dean warren, near Chichester in Sussex, where a tenant in 1583 had a breeding stock of 3,000 adults. In some cases, it is true, warrens were sacrificed for more alluring objectives: when woad-growing was in favour and earned large profits, warrens could not withstand the competition, and at least some segments of warrens were surrendered to woad.[25] Perhaps a halt was called to the making of new warrens, rather than any noticeable decline taking place in those already existing.

At all events, fresh ideas for regimes to keep rabbits duly surfaced in the mid-seventeenth century, and these are made evident in letters, and in the published literature of the 1650s. Plainly, a new look at the whole enterprise was being taken from several different angles. Experiments with the spinning of rabbit wool began, so that the present-day producers of angora wool can look back to the 1650s for the first pioneers in their endeavour. A Northamptonshire landowner discussed with Hartlib the importation of Dutch rabbits for his warren. Plans to keep rabbits on relatively small pieces of ground also circulated. Indeed, this may have been the idea that was being pursued by a correspondent of Hartlib when he reported his discovery of an old manuscript for keeping tame rabbits. It set him hunting through the books for further advice.[26]

In the later seventeenth and early eighteenth century, evidence accumulates of profitable warrens and of new ones being set up. When a purchaser was sought for Wrotham warren, Kent, he was assured that when skins sold at ½d. and 1d. apiece, the conies had always been sufficient to pay the rent, and now they sold at 10d. and 12d. A large new warren was established at Godalming,

Surrey in 1671–3 on a former sheep pasture of 260 acres, and another at Cran-well, Lincs., was laid out on heathland at around the same date, from which William Thorold expected an income of £20–30 per annum. More generally still, in the Ashdown Forest, Sussex, rabbit warrens had become by 1700 a favoured use for enclosed land, and such names as Hindleap warren and Press Ridge warren appear on the map accompanying the enclosure of 1693.[27] As more warrens were laid out at this time, an important organizational change seems to have taken place as well. In their beginnings warrens had been gentlemen's enterprises, and still in the sixteenth century the warrener was expected to be a manorial servant. But a petition from 'distressed warreners' to Parliament in 1710, lamenting their losses from thieves, implies that humble men had taken to leasing warrens from gentlemen, and were shouldering all the financial risks themselves. In other words, this alternative agricultural pursuit had been seized by countrymen below the gentry class. This may be part of the explanation for the notoriety of Mary Toft, the 'rabbit woman' of Godalming in 1727, com-manding attention half a century after the same warren had been laid out on a gentleman's initiative. As it turned out, though, no golden future lay ahead for warreners, for their warrens fell out of favour in the second half of the eight-eenth century, and many were dismantled to make way for more profitable grain-growing.[28]

If wider social participation in an economic opportunity is only hinted at in the case of the warrens, it is convincingly demonstrated in the case of pigeon-keeping. Dovecotes returned to favour among the gentry once grain could more readily be spared to feed birds and their presence caused less acrimony among neighbours. The meat added variety to diet in gentlemen's households, and pigeon dung was much prized in vegetable gardens, orchards, and fields.[29] Architectural historians have recently taken more interest in dovecotes, and have noticed the number newly built in the period 1640–1750. In short, a fresh phase of building precisely defined this phase of alternative agriculture.[30] Dove-cotes were recommended to the gentry by the fact that they brought 'a con-siderable yearly advantage with very little cost or trouble'. But such a commendation carried even stronger weight with ordinary farmers. So the privilege of keeping a dovecote, which had long been a manorial monopoly, was broken down in the mid- to late seventeenth century, with or without the assent of lords, and ordinary farmers kept pigeons just as effectively in simple lofts as in the architecturally decorative buildings which the gentry could afford.[31] Dovecotes thus became one of the many alternative pursuits in farming which the peasantry in this period shared with the gentry. A lively description of one beneficiary was of George Clements of Weston Subedge, Gloucestershire, whose sources of income were investigated in detail in 1682 because he refused

4. Pigeons. These illustrations of dovecotes show buildings newly constructed between 1650 and 1750, when pigeon-keeping was no longer a lord's monopoly. Samuel Hartlib in 1655 estimated that England's parishes on average had three dovecotes; some with only 50–60 households might have ten or twelve. He claimed that Judge Crook at the Assizes 'was of the opinion that it was neither fitting nor lawful for any man to have a dovehouse when so many poor people and their families may be maintained with the corn that the doves do eat, spoil, and devour'.—Hartlib, 1655a: 225–7. The dovecote at Barton in Fabis, Nottinghamshire (*top*), was built by William Sacheverell in 1677 (the date was found on the underside of the gypsum plaster nesting boxes), that at Proctor's Farm, Dry Drayton, Cambridgeshire (*bottom*), is of seventeenth-century date, and is said to be the only external loft in the county, built into the end wall of a red brick barn.

to pay tithes. He was a mixed farmer growing grain and keeping livestock. He also sold apples, beestocks, and poultry, including turkeys. But it is his dovecote which attracts our attention here, for he drew from it eight dozen pigeons in a flight, and four flights in a year. Fifteen hundred birds were sold at Chipping Campden market in four years, and this did not count the pigeon dung that fertilized his fields.[32]

The other alternative pursuits which commended themselves increasingly to ordinary farmers, both yeomen and husbandmen, were those which required moderate amounts of land, moderate amounts of extra, seasonal labour, and did not require radical alterations in the farmer's working routines. If possible, they had first been tried and tested by the gentry who could afford to take the risks. The grass substitutes fitted this description admirably, for they could be inserted into arable rotations, lengthening them and allowing more livestock to be kept, without overturning the basic system. Hop gardens and orchards had to be added alongside existing systems, yet they too proved to be notable successes. Only a small amount of land was required, and a moderate amount of extra labour.[33] Hops, of course, were more risky than fruit, but, despite the threat of losses in bad years, the gains in good years more than compensated. Hence the spread of hops on small acreages in Kent and Essex—Houghton in 1699 referred to massive production around Maidstone—while the expansion was quite remarkable in the second half of the seventeenth century in the counties of Worcestershire, Herefordshire, and Gloucestershire. In fact, Worcester became an influential hop market, competing uncomfortably with the London market where Kent hop growers had long reigned supreme.[34]

Orchard trees, similarly, found a more secure footing on farms of all sizes in different areas of the country. Apart from the commercial profits, arguments in favour dwelt on the usefulness of the timber to joiners, the health value of fruit and fruit drinks, and the merits of cider on long sea voyages. It was even suggested that cider-drinking on a large scale might result in smaller acreages of land needed to grow barley. The advocates of orchards could find reasons to suit all tastes, and by the second half of the seventeenth century their efforts wrought conspicuous results. Multitudes of new, modest-sized orchards were laid out in the West Midlands.[35]

Orchards in modern parlance suggest only fruit trees, but in the seventeenth century contemporaries would have expected to find nut trees as well, for they valued filberts, almonds, chestnuts, and walnuts, whether for dessert, pickled, or in cooked dishes. The most fashionable tree at this time was the walnut, grown during the Roman occupation, but by the Middle Ages tended only in monastic gardens and on the estates of great lords. Interest revived in the sixteenth century, as part of the fruit-growing fashion. But the trees were also cherished for their several medicinal uses, while walnut oil was used in joinery, and to mix white colours for which it was deemed superior to linseed oil. Documentary evidence shows walnut trees being carefully nurtured from about the 1560s.[36] And when the surveyor John Norden in 1607 recommended walnuts for 'mean land', he struck a chord that reverberated. As a strong movement was under way to find more rewarding uses for wasteland, walnut trees became a cliché on gentlemen's estates thereafter.[37]

In 1622 Richard Shanne, in his father's arms, watched the planting of walnut trees together with a chestnut tree at Methley, south-east of Leeds. Subsequently, the fashion was plain: the Earl of Northumberland in 1623 presented one thousand walnut trees as a gift to the Duke of Buckingham, for planting at Burley, in Rutland, where the duke was making large improvements to his park. In the 1640s a modest Kentish lady, widow of Basil Dixwell, planted at Broome a hundred walnut trees, and they remained high fashion during the Interregnum, when John Evelyn planted an elaborate grove with French walnuts at Sayes Court, Deptford, in 1652; he was then transforming the garden of the manor house.[38] The district where the walnut made most headway, however, was the Surrey heaths. Around Carshalton they were renowned by 1662, when Thomas Fuller praised their excellence. The walnut had found a congenial habitat and had consolidated its hold, furnishing both nuts and the increasingly fashionable wood for furniture and gunstocks. By 1791 a much larger area between Leatherhead and Mickleham boasted orchards containing 40,000 walnut trees, and the walnut fair of Croydon regularly drew throngs of Londoners.[39]

Since commercial fruit-tree-growing spread from the gentry to yeoman farmers during the seventeenth century, it is pertinent to ask whether walnut groves multiplied along the same social path. The long waiting time before walnut trees matured to bear nuts would suggest that the gentry were the foremost planters, and in Surrey perhaps they were.[40] But this was not the only place which became the celebrated home of the walnut. Many were planted in Gloucestershire (especially at Arlingham) and in Herefordshire, where they were still a valued crop in the early nineteenth century. Since nut trees were regularly coupled in discussion with fruit orchards, it is possible that they spread with varying success in all fruit-growing counties.[41] A sober legal document, giving a description of a demesne farm belonging to the Izard family of Beckley, Oxfordshire, in 1659, inadvertently illustrates something of the tyranny of convention in the seventeenth century: the estate included a rose garden, orchard, kitchen garden, plant nursery, hopyard, grove, and little nursery within it, hemp pens, artichoke garden, and 'all the walnut tree orchard'.[42]

The commercial crop which above all others claimed the efforts of every class of farmer, from the gentry down to smallholders and labourers, were vegetables.

5. Walnut-gathering. This engraving depicts the harvesting of walnuts at Bucklebury, Berkshire, c.1840. These trees may well have been 200 years old.

All the evidence shows them gaining ground after 1660. An upper-class view was expressed by Sir William Coventry, convinced in 1670 that he saw more fruits, herbs, and roots growing than before the Civil War, especially near the large towns. The gentry's belief in their commmercial advantages was explained by John Evelyn in the 1660s: many gentlemen, he claimed, had ploughed up part of their parks for gardening, while among humbler folk, we see the same trend in a tithe file from Chester (St Oswald) in 1671, relating to tithes at Broughton, and declaring that 'there is more gardening than before the late wars.'[43]

In general terms vegetables were being fostered by a range of arguments from which all classes drew comfort, whether it was their value to health, their productivity per acre, the profits they earned at the market, their ability to fill the empty stomachs of the penniless, or the work they gave to the poor.[44] Gardening skills ranged between two extremes, the most sophisticated at one end requiring cloches, bell frames, and considerable capital investment, while at the other the poor needed no more than sets, seed, and a rudimentary trowel to grow onions and roots on dung heaps outside town walls. John Worlidge, a gentlemanly observer if ever there was one, judged in 1675 that 'garden tillage is of late years become a more general food than formerly it was: scarce a table well furnished without some dishes of choice roots or herbs'. But in the same breath he also recognized practical considerations that weighed more with less affluent classes: they produced 'an extraordinary advantage', 'an incredible advantage' (presumably he meant financial), they were 'good for the poor labouring man', and some of them fed cattle and poultry as well.[45] Upper-class interest remained fifty years later when Richard Bradley in 1729 echoed the remarks of Worlidge: most of the quality in England, he said, took pleasure in the food of the garden.[46] To this we can add the signs of an intellectual zest, when the gentry went in search of yet more vegetables and new varieties. Mushrooms were being contemplated as a new food in the mid-seventeenth century, when they were viewed with misgiving by Sir R. Moray, but dubbed 'wholesome and toothsome' by John Beale. At the same time Beale was testing cauliflowers raised from seed that came from Cyprus.[47] Another gentleman reminded himself in his commonplace book in 1684 of the great Zealand (i.e. Holland) cabbage, as well as Spanish lettuces and Italian cauliflowers.[48] Nearly a century later (in 1741) John Cockburn procured, while in London, vegetable seeds which came from Turkey. They were promptly dispatched to his gardener near Edinburgh for trials.[49]

In market gardens around London some highly professional gardeners exhibited the best management. The inventory at the death of Robert Gascoine (note the French surname) in 1718 shows one of the most impressive plots in St Martin-in-the-Fields. In February Gascoine had already planted three rows of cauliflower plants, plus cabbage plants amounting to about a thousand altogether. Three further beds of cauliflower plants were under lights and in boxes, while other beds contained spinach, cauliflower, and cabbage, radish and carrot seed. More glass sheltered colewort and young lettuce, while the asparagus was classified into four categories: that of the first year's planting, cutting asparagus, young plants, and plants that were being forced under boxes and lights.[50] By 1745, if not earlier, some asparagus growers had a special trick of using the necks of broken glass bottles to encourage asparagus to grow through them in the sunshine.[51] The value of the asparagus crop to resourceful men may be gauged from two other inventories, one of Philip Luke in 1682 who had asparagus in mid-February valued at £32 out of total personal goods worth £124, and another of John Lea, taken in July when the season was over, but where the asparagus ground was worth £6 out of total personal goods worth £21.[52]

Less exotic vegetables found other niches. Potatoes finally began to establish themselves successfully in England after 1660, following many decades of failure. They had plainly flourished in Ireland from the moment that they were introduced there by voyagers from the New World at the end of the sixteenth century. Cromwellian soldiers in Ireland in the early 1650s were surprised to find whole fields of them, whereas in England they had failed to tuber successfully. The Royal Society pressed for more publicity after the Restoration, and gentlemen were active publicists. The fresh attempts now succeeded in Lancashire and Wales, and spread from there. But the process of acculturation was destined to be slow, as some landowners were prejudiced against potatoes and restricted cultivation in their leases. Nor was the best use for potatoes yet clear—a problem which vexed other vegetables as well. They were being treated variously as a flour mixed with wheat for bread, pastry, and cakes; for drinks; and for feeding poultry and livestock.[53] In the early eighteenth century, a significant qualitative change in the status of potatoes took place: a revealing glimpse of their success in Hackney was given in 1711 in the complaint of a surveyor when a turnpike road from Enfield to Shoreditch was under discussion. Small farms, he remarked, were being turned over to the growing of potatoes, which were then carried to market in panniers by horses. As a result, the number of horse teams available for mending the roads had shrunk in ten years from twenty-eight to fourteen. At the other end of the country, in 1729 in Lancashire, a gentleman who had recently introduced potatoes in his district, hoping they might be useful to the poor, congratulated himself when they relieved the threat of famine, *and* showed their value in rising prices, from 2*d.* per peck to 8*d.* and 9*d.*[54]

With a large market at hand, small farmers near London had a golden opportunity to grow vegetables profitably, doubtless using their families, and avoiding hired labour. But in other parts of the country too, farmers near towns all had

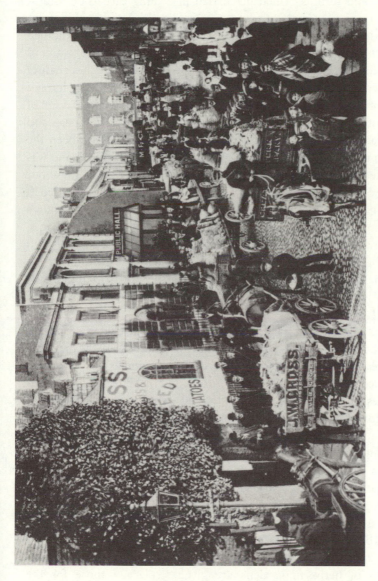

6. Potatoes. Carts of potatoes sometimes filled the main street of Wisbech, c.1906. They had by then become a major crop in some districts of England, and earlier uncertainty about how to use them, whether as a flour in pastry or as a vegetable, and landlords' prejudices against them, had disappeared. Edwin Pratt published this illustration in his *Transition in Agriculture*, 1906, when Wisbech, having once been a mainly wheat-producing area, had become a major centre of vegetable, fruit, and flower production by smallholders.

the same chances, though the full scale of their opportunism can never be measured. Only a chance glimpse is afforded here and there: one farmer, for example, is seen in 1713-14 when six acres of land were converted to orchard, growing apples and turnips, which he carried in a dung cart to be sold at Hagbourne, Berkshire;[55] carrots growing on a field scale were noted by John Aubrey at Beckington in Somerset in 1684-5, and in this case Aubrey claimed that men remembered their being introduced into the parish in 1668;[56] an acre of carrots were being grown in a field by Peter Cornelius (note the Dutch surname) at Hinton St George in Somerset in 1691, along with 2 acres of wheat, 3 acres of barley, 2 acres of beans, and 1 acre of hemp; a generation later Abraham Allan of Alcombe, Dunster, in 1731 had 12 acres of wheat, 5 acres of beans and peas, and two fields of carrots. In Sandy, Bedfordshire, carrots seem to have been the leading crop in the parish in the seventeenth century; in fact, arable land was sometimes called 'carrot land', and in 1730 three roods were bought for about three times the price paid for other open-field land.[57] Cabbages too appeared in field cultivation at the end of the seventeenth century: Sir Anthony Ashley's estate at Wimbourne St John's, Dorset, boasted great plantations of cabbages, almost certainly grown on the initiative of the Ashleys.[58] In a richly detailed exploration of farming in the Vale of White Horse between 1660 and 1760, many such initiatives caused Janie Cottis to underline the growth of this form of specialized farming, which was no longer to be rated just a minor element in arable or mixed agriculture.[58]

More difficult to document is the spread of herbs from the wild into gardens, and then into the fields. Apart from their culinary use, herbs were the mainstay of medicinal treatments, whether administered by professionals or, more often, self-administered. The recommended lists throughout the sixteenth and seventeenth centuries were long, and assumed that all well-organized households would have a store, annually renewed. Saffron, one of the sovereign remedies, is encountered in closes from an early date, but most herbs escape our gaze because, by convention, they were disregarded along with all garden produce whenever inventories of property were taken. Only slowly, after many disputes, did men recognize that times had changed, and, as commercial crops, they required to be counted and tithed. A burst of interest in herbs is proclaimed by the six books, all by different authors, published in the 1650s, when one book per decade had been usual earlier.[59] And the literature flowed on, though somewhat less abundantly, in the second half of the seventeenth century.[60] Whenever valuations of herbs in gardens are given, especially those for the apothecaries, high prices are indicated. The *bella donna* lily from Portugal, for example, seen in an apothecary's garden in Chelsea, sold at one guinea a root.[61] But a more illuminating general reference to 'herbs in the garden' belonging to

7. Kitchen herbs. This drawing by Marcellus Laroon shows a woman selling kitchen herbs in a London street, *c*.1687. Almost certainly, women gathered the herbs in the country and walked to London with them. Published in Shesgreen, 1990: 233, it is from an album of original drawings in the Duke of Marlborough's Collection, Blenheim Palace.

Henry Glouster of Croydon, Surrey, in September 1692 shows a value of £50 out of total goods worth £242 8s. 6d.[62]

Though never grown by large numbers or in massive quantities, herbs could be a considerable crop for single individuals, and even for whole communities with a reputation for one speciality, like the mustard of Tewkesbury. We have already noticed 10 acres of chervil being grown in 1737 by a Huntingdonshire farmer at Bury-cum-Hepmangrove.[63] Caraway was another speciality, at Clanfield, Oxford-shire, and in Essex caraway and coriander were known as profitable sidelines.[64] Nevertheless, one cannot always be sure of the use of such herbs. A writer on wild-fowling urged the feeding of pigeons, partridges, and pheasants with mixtures containing coriander, and fennel seeds that were first baked; and those who made a living trapping singing birds for sale—linnets, robins, goldfinches, and nightin-gales—were urged to breed their worms on herbs to snare them the better.[65]

Industrial crops were another large category of alternative plants, offering different advantages to various classes living off the land. The history of some of these, showing more precisely how they were disseminated geographically and personally, is given below, in Chapters 4 and 5. Others are dealt with more sum-marily here. They all showed a strong tendency after 1660 to cluster in one or more distinctive areas and become a locally renowned speciality. This was the case with hemp and flax. They were always common crops in small crofts on peasant holdings, but they were much more conspicuous in certain districts like the Lincolnshire fens, parts of Norfolk, and Suffolk, Dorset, Somerset, and Staffordshire, near Maidstone in Kent, and in Lancashire. From Henry VIII's reign onwards, intermittently but continuing into the second half of the seven-teenth century, government statutes tried to compel the growing of a small acreage everywhere—a quarter of an acre in every sixty acres was the propor-tion laid down in 1532. But specialized areas emerged and won a reputation for their ropes, sackcloth, sailcloth, canvas, or linen thread, and in such places no compulsion to grow was needed. A more localized crop, with an unusual his-tory, was canary seed. Without this food, caged birds will die, and in 1939–40, when canary seed could not be imported, the price reached £2,000 a ton. When once the keeping of caged birds became the fashion, after the arrival of the Dutch and Flemish refugees in the sixteenth century, canary seed was an essen-tial crop in England. It also made one of the whitest and best oils for limners. North-east Kent became the unique centre for growing the crop, and in the 1660s John Evelyn described seeing 'whole fields' near Sandwich and Deal. Indi-vidual growers did not devote large acreages to it, but its value may be judged from the care given to cultivation. They sowed the seed in rows from the spout of a teapot and weeded many times. Inventories show farmers holding seed in the early eighteenth century that was valued at large sums, like £30 and £50.[66]

8. Singing birds and canary seed. This engraving by Marcellus Laroon, *c.*1687 of a man selling singing birds from a couple of cages indirectly illustrates the demand for canary seed. It was a valuable alternative crop in Thanet, north-east Kent, feeding a fashion that had been introduced by Dutch settlers in the late sixteenth century of keeping caged singing birds in the home.

Teasels were another industrial crop, essential to the cloth industry, being used in the finishing processes to raise the nap. In the sixteenth century, they were imported from France, but, as contemporaries urged, they were perfectly capable of being grown in England. However, they needed growers who were willing to give them constant attention, and on those grounds, they were deemed by one writer in the later nineteenth century suitable only for labourers and smallholders. In a period when work was much needed, the crop plainly found a thoroughly congenial home in the later seventeenth century in north Somerset, around Cheddar, Winscombe, and Congresbury.

Expansion clearly took place after 1660, so that in the 1690s Congresbury grew eighty acres, and Winscombe in 1700 155 acres. Tithes worth £5 a year at Winscombe in 1640 were worth £30-40 p.a. in 1702. The full explanation for this labour-intensive enterprise plainly calls for a clearer view of the social structure of these Somerset parishes, but, significantly, they lay in dairying country, which was always the domain of small farmers.[67]

Yet another group of alternative crops was made up of those having a multiplicity of uses, or starting in one role and moving to another. Such were liquorice, later on rhubarb, and tobacco, all of which were first cultivated as medicinal plants. For some seventy years, between 1619 and 1690, tobacco continued to be grown by poor men in counties all over the kingdom, offering a lifeline to cultivators who were willing to give unstinting labour in return for adequate, and occasionally ample, rewards. It only faded from the scene after decades of government persecution. Its crime was to compete with the Virginia crop, which the government wished to protect, but, despite the sending of government troops to stamp out the crop every summer, it did not disappear until a cheapening of Virginia tobacco dealt the final deathblow in 1690.[68]

Saffron was a multi-purpose crop, always in demand in the kitchen, but also used in industry as a yellow dye, and, above all, as a medicine. Thomas Fuller called it 'a precious drug' which had saved his life when he was struck down by smallpox. It was much grown in Essex (hence Saffron Walden) and in Cambridgeshire and East Anglia generally, but small saffron closes could turn up anywhere, in the fenlands of Shropshire in 1549, for example, in Berkshire (where tithes were taken on saffron), or in Bethnal Green (though only the name survived there in 1671, the land then being under grass). It had a history going back into the Middle Ages, having probably been introduced into England in the mid-fourteenth century, but changing perceptions of its virtues (particularly, of its medicinal benefits) in the sixteenth century led to a noticeable spread in its cultivation, and then, during the seventeenth century, to a marked specialization in East Anglia.[69]

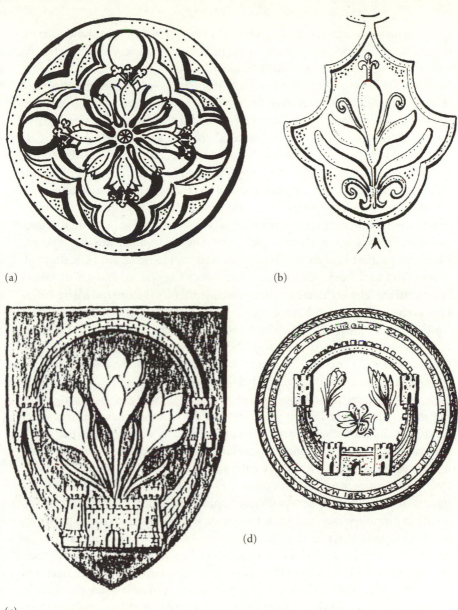

(a)

(b)

(d)

(c)

9. Saffron. Saffron was grown in many parts of England, including Devon and Cornwall, though it met with greatest commercial success in eastern England. It was at its height in the seventeenth and eighteenth centuries, yielding good, and sometimes outstanding, returns. It was most celebrated at Saffron Walden in Essex, where saffron was depicted on spandrels in the parish church (*a*), in pargetting on houses (*b*), in the town's coat of arms (*c*), and on the town seal (*d*). The emblems illustrated here are from Saffron Walden's Museum Leaflet 13.

The insurgents who joined Kett's rebellion in Norfolk in 1549 show what an impact saffron closes had already made in that county; they were protesting vehemently against enclosures in general, but were willing to allow existing saffron closes because of the expense of planting them, so long as no new ones were made. Wills and inventories from the parish of Sawston between 1531 and 1547 show how saffron had taken hold: seven out of thirteen wills made references to the plant, and showed great care in diffentiating the ages of the plantings. Saffron then found a secure home in Cambridgeshire and north-west Essex—in fact, on the direct route from Saffron Walden to Cambridge—and remained entrenched until the mid-eighteenth century, gradually fading thereafter. Of a sample of probate inventories from Cambridgeshire 7 per cent refer to saffron in 1665-90, 20 per cent in 1691-1710, and 24 per cent in 1711-30. Saffron was then conspicuous in Cherry Hinton and Great Shelford while, moving towards Essex, the greatest concentration (in 1732) was said to be around Chesterford, Linton, and Littlebury. Seemingly, saffron-growing was an expanding enterprise until the later eighteenth century, when other less labour-intensive enterprises returned to profit. Nevertheless, in some parishes of Cambridgeshire it continued to be grown into the nineteenth century.[70]

Saffron required large amounts of labour (a detailed estimate in 1732 showed three-quarters of the costs comprising labour), and so the acreages growing it appear small. But, as with similar alternative enterprises, the profits could be high, and all classes in rural society could be found growing, or labouring, on it. At Linton, Cambridgeshire, it was grown in the common fields in 1592, elsewhere in temporary enclosures in the common fields, and in numerous closes and gardens. Among the gentry, Nicholas Bacon at Stiffkey commands notice for the care he gave it on his own estate, as illustrated in his account books for 1587-98. When seen in a local context, payments for labour to individually named male and female setters vividly conjure up a picture of what this crop meant to humble villagers. Bacon, moreover, was buying the saffron grown by others in the vicinity, and dispatching it all to London. A generation later, the profits of saffron in good years were estimated by a member of the Royal Society (in 1678) at the large sum of £20 an acre in the first year, above all charges, but in 1732 at a more sober reckoning of £5 2s. 8d. per acre, if all labour was hired. If, on the other hand, family labour was used, then saffron fed and housed them all, as well as yielding a profit.[71]

*

Measuring the importance of an alternative crop by the national acreage which it occupied, or by the numbers engaged over the whole country in growing it, consigns many ventures like saffron-growing to oblivion, or at best bundles them into a miscellany of small items at the end of an account, where they can be quietly ignored. The fact that they could have life-saving value in whole villages vanishes from sight in this panoramic view. Yet the alternative crops were numerous, and can be shown conclusively to have found localized, specialist niches. Their scattered distribution and the absence of any market records, however, make it impossible to quantify them with any convincing statistics. The produce was frequently harvested without leaving a single record; it was delivered piecemeal at the doors of manor houses, carried on men's and women's shoulders walking to town, or transported to market in panniers on horseback. It was never measured in any toll-house.

Only indirectly does some weighty evidence of the economic significance of alternative crops come to light, namely, in the increasing numbers of tithe disputes after 1650. Many alternative crops had long been grown as food for the household, and had never been tithed. But when once they became a commercial item, regularly sold at the market, rectors or vicars claimed tithe payment. Some of the most incisive evidence of alternative agriculture, therefore, derives from the papers assembled to end such quarrels. In Staffordshire, for example, incumbents of different parishes showed tithe income from hemp and flax, potatoes, turnips, carrots, parsnips, peas, beans, hops, rapeseed, apples, pears, and plums. Some of this might be grown in gardens, even though it was destined for commercial sale, but increasingly it appeared in fields, as, for example, at Baswich, close to the town of Stafford, where in 1710 potatoes and carrots were both being grown in fields. By the end of the eighteenth century the vegetable markets of Liverpool and Birmingham were insistent customers for Staffordshire's vegetable production, and the tithe income was assessed by surveyors at something approaching 10s.–12s. an acre. Solving tithe disputes became imperative, therefore, and parishes often settled on a money sum in place of payment in kind. In the case of madder, as will be seen below, the wrangling was settled, not on a local basis, but by a Parliamentary statute fixing the amount paid per acre.[72]

The movement towards an alternative agriculture in the hundred years between 1650 and 1750 cannot be satisfactorily quantified, whether in figures of production, or, in the case of food, in consumption. Its impact was patchy, transforming some parishes, and sufficiently changing the appearance of the fields in some whole regions to draw the comments of travellers. But for a great many farmers in all ranks of rural society the alternatives were extras or sidelines. They contributed more than average profits to an income still drawn from farming in basic foodstuffs. This was not, of course, true for nurserymen and market gardeners, whose livelihoods were newly created by, and wholly dedicated to, the production of alternative crops. But the majority were less specialist, yet opportunist. The nearest approach to quantifying the movement was made by Gregory King in the 1690s when he estimated the contribution of industrial crops, fruit, vegetables, and garden stuff at 9 per cent of total agricultural production. It was a bold attempt at measurement, and we have no idea how he arrived at this figure. But, if true, it effectively substantiates the argument presented here, since none of these categories of farm production featured as significant commercial enterprises before the mid-sixteenth century.[73]

At the same time, reality slips from sight when an innovation is measured by its impact nation-wide. Innovations, by their very nature, make their influence felt in select places only; they are not spread thinly everywhere, but in a small locality they can transform the scene. Whole districts of England were untouched by the opportunities of an alternative agriculture throughout these hundred years, but elsewhere they could earn a third, a half, even two-thirds of the livelihood of those early birds who adopted a new crop. The penetration of alternatives into the economy is only perceived in briefly documented episodes, as a flashlight momentarily illuminates dark corners. In Thanet, Kent, in the 1680s, for example, an alternative agriculture was thrust into view by one defiant gesture: a claim for tithes from the lay impropriator provoked William and Elizabeth Payne of St Johns to fling a plum, an apple, a turnip, and a rosemary sprig at the tithe collectors. John Brewer of Lyng in the Somerset Levels had as his main livelihood in 1739 a herd of thirteen dairy cows, and some breeding mares, who had borne him thirteen colts that year. But when he was prosecuted for not paying tithe, his offence revealed another asset, in the harvest of his orchards, yielding 500 bushels of apples, pears, and plums, and deemed worth £25.[74]

The merits of an alternative agriculture shine through in yet other places. Garden flowers were regarded by Gervase Markham as a branch of English husbandry, and certainly that must have seemed a sound judgement to those who produced in the seventeenth century all the variety, including 'double' blossoms that were such a novelty, in the gardens of pleasure of rich men. As for fruit and greenstuff, food preferences at this period tell us that someone somewhere was engaged in growing these things to satisfy people's tastes. The botanist William Coles referred in 1657 to the gooseberries grown in great abundance around London because so many people ate gooseberry sauce in May and June with green geese, stewed them with mutton, or sugared them for tarts. Mustard seed was a crop because, among other uses, sugared mustard was deemed essential with venison. Edward Filewood of Reigate plainly derived profit in 1665 from keeping 200–300 fowl in a barn, feeding them with 'livers, lights and offells of dead beasts', to the annoyance of his neighbours. And, as for the numbers of people involved, in one parish alone, Farnham in Surrey, twenty-two persons were named in 1687 as hop growers, their hopyards being estimated at 250–300 acres, and that was not claimed to be a complete list.[75]

Arguments in favour of diversification were voiced as contemporaries observed the merits of innovative ventures.[76] The achievements were always discussed in relation to specialized regions; hops were associated with parts of Kent, Surrey, and the West Midland counties; vegetables with Evesham in Gloucestershire, Sandwich, Godalming, and the suburbs of London; rapeseed with East Anglia; walnuts with Surrey; liquorice with Pontefract in Yorkshire and Nottinghamshire; teasels with Somerset; asses' milk to restore the sick with Canterbury.[77] None of these ventures swept over the whole country, but wherever they were established, they had the potential to turn a farmers' modest competence, or loss, from mainstream arable farming to more satisfactory gain.

Specialization and success therein was helped by the gardeners and nurserymen who nurtured the best plant varieties and aspired to the best practices. Some of that experience was diffused by the gentry allowing gardeners on their own estates to sell surplus produce. Thus standards were raised, admittedly piecemeal but promising long-term benefits. The letters of John Cockburn, urging his gardener at Ormiston, near Edinburgh, to copy the professionalism of the London gardeners (most likely, those of Tottenham, since his gardener had trained there) is one of the most vivid illustrations of the way the best practices were transported far afield from centres of excellence. In long letters home Cockburn exhorted and then bullied his gardener; we catch a glimpse, in fact, of what many other gentlemen must have done to their gardeners face-to-face. And the economic arguments were monotonously reiterated: in 1675 Scottish farmers were told that 'the tenth part of an acre in gardening may yield more profit than ten acres of ordinary tillage in a cornfield'; in December 1734 Cockburn maintained that 'you may have a better return from kitchen garden than from corn'; and in June 1735 that raspberries 'will yield you more than wheat' and 'they'll require less husbandry than a crop of wheat'.[78]

The similarity in the circumstances to be seen in the striving for an alternative agriculture in the years 1650–1750, and in the movement that has now been under way for some two decades in the late twentieth century, prompts curiosity concerning the detailed processes by which successful solutions were found. Who were the first to make experiments? What urged them on? How soon was any success registered? Who benefited in the initial phases and in the long run? Those who are actively engaged nowadays in establishing an alternative agriculture move into an unknown future. The seventeenth-century experience offers information on the way it happened once before. In the next two chapters, some which were thoroughly successful and some which were failures are put under closer scrutiny.

4 ∾ ALTERNATIVE CROPS:
the successes

Rapeseed

THE first successful alternative crop to be discussed in detail in this chapter must be rapeseed, for its history mirrors many of the more general arguments of this book. Experiments had been made in the mid-thirteenth century, and it might have served as an alternative crop in the first phase of alternative agriculture after the Black Death, as it certainly did in places on the Continent of Europe, like the lower Rhine. In England, however, the venture seems to have faded from sight, not unreasonably perhaps in view of its labour demands, though it is not impossible that it survived quietly in some undiscovered corner of the kingdom in the fifteenth century. But, if so, it has left us no documents. When the task of reducing oil imports was thought imperative in the sixteenth century, rapeseed returned, and this time it established itself firmly in the course of the seventeenth century. It stayed until the mid-nineteenth century, when it disappeared, as oilseeds and mineral oils came to be imported from abroad. Then it returned in the late 1970s to serve once more as an alternative crop. Rapeseed thus affords a good example of a plant serving its turn more than once in phases of alternative agriculture, though the precise circumstances and uses of the crop were somewhat changed on each occasion. Between 1650 and 1750 it supplied an industrial oil; now it is used as a vegetable oil. Yet the idea of restoring its industrial use, to drive motor engines, is still under consideration, and its future remains to be seen.[1]

When once rapeseed spread in the 1980s, and became familiar from the Cheviots to the south coast, even colonizing the motorways, it was clear that its earlier cultivation had been entirely forgotten. Yet some of the circumstances that favoured its reappearance were recognizably similar to those that had brought it to England in the sixteenth century, notably the desire to reduce imports. So were the prejudices against it; its strident yellow colour was deemed alien in the 1970s, whereas in the seventeenth century it was criticized for its inferior performance in textile-finishing, breeding worms in the cloth when compared with olive oil.[2]

In the seventeenth century a conjuncture of favourable circumstances finally brought sustained success, but the initial stages of its introduction proceeded slowly. As we have noted already, rapeseed was not altogether new, having been grown experimentally on monastic estates in eastern England in the thirteenth century. It is found at Monk's Grange, Norfolk, for example, *c*.1255, but it did not leave any lasting impression.[3] Nevertheless, knowledge of the plant and its potential was maintained in East Anglia, through constant trade with the Low Countries. A fragment of evidence shows rape oil being landed at King's Lynn in 1450 to supply St Radegund's priory, Cambridge. This suggests a continuing familiarity with it in some circles, so that when changing circumstances prompted an active interest in import substitutes, the first site chosen for growing rapeseed was near King's Lynn, the port through which the oil had arrived from the Netherlands in the fifteenth century.[4]

The prime incentive now to revive the growing of rapeseed was a rise in the cost of olive oil from Spain; in 1549 it was said to cost one-third more than in 1542. Nor could supplies be guaranteed, even at that enhanced price. In 1553, when Spain stopped the sale of alum abroad except under licence, the prospect of her doing the same with olive oil immediately loomed. For two compelling reasons, then, alternative sources of oil came to the forefront of discussion in the sixteenth century. It was indispensable in the finishing processes of the textile industry, which constituted England's main export, and price inflation was making imported oil increasingly expensive. The reference in 1551 to rapeseed being grown around King's Lynn is perfectly credible, therefore, though it lacks circumstantial detail. Merchants were always alert to exploit new opportunities, as more examples below will show.[5]

A more active interest was signalled in the 1560s and 1570s by a patent issued in 1565 to two men, Armigil Wade and William Herle, almost certainly, judging by their names, from the Low Countries, to make sulphur and oil from seeds. Another device for making oils for English clothiers (by a method not explained) was proposed in 1571 by Giles Lambarde, and finally in 1572 a bill was introduced into Parliament to encourage the making of oils in England. All this coincided with the arrival of many religious refugees from Flanders, Holland, and France. They were familiar with the crop at home, understandably had ideas for growing it in England, and they did not debate the matter without practical experience.[6]

Matters still did not come to a head until the later 1570s, when political difficulties with Spain heightened uneasiness about oil supplies. Not only did the price rise again, but the quantities available for sale abroad were said to be falling. Spain was sending so much to the West Indies; the shortages were expected to be permanent. Furthermore, a body of more reliable information was now being assembled, both privately and officially, on the growing and milling of oil as practised in Flanders and France. Englishmen were acquiring a more exact understanding of how rapeseed was handled, and were increasingly struck by the large numbers of people employed on it overseas. These facts of life gave food for thought to Elizabeth's ministers, who were intent not only on reducing England's reliance on foreign imports, but wished to broaden her narrow industrial base and find more work for the poor. Dependence on the textile industry had proved a serious weakness when European trade depression struck hard in the 1550s. A report by William Herle, who already had an oil patent, and who became one of William Cecil's industrial informants on new projects in general, was therefore no casual commentary. Only about four or five people in the realm made oil from seeds 'in very imperfect or unprofitable manner', it was claimed. So the growing of more hemp and flax (both of which yielded oil) *and* rapeseed was urged. These crops, it was said, 'will be more gainful to the owners of land than any corn'.[7]

The 1570s saw a cluster of proposals put before the government for making oil. One request for a patent came from a Frenchman, another from an Italian, and another from a Dutchman called William Wade, possibly a kinsman of Armigil Wade, the earlier patentee. Other men were at work who did not wait on patents. Sir Thomas Gresham wrote in July 1579 to his son-in-law, Nathaniel Bacon, at Stiffkey in Norfolk, asking him to buy 100 quarters of rapeseed from the dealers in King's Lynn so that his mill at Osterley in Middlesex could have work in milling in three weeks' time. The rapeseed was to be sent by coastal vessel to London. When Bacon failed to conclude the deal, Gresham wrote again, two months later, to ask Bacon to send someone to the growers in the Lincolnshire fenland, this time to make a more permanent contract to buy 400–500 quarters a year. He understood that the growers there already shipped 2,000 quarters a year to Flanders from Boston and King's Lynn. In other words, he wished to intercept some of this for milling in London, but knew that he had to agree to take delivery from the growers at the port, for they would not make any contract that saddled them with the risks of the sea journey.[8]

The Bacon correspondence relates to the year 1579, when yet another oil milling project was producing substantial results. The soapmakers of the city of London were in dispute with Laurence Mellowes because they refused to pay him a fair price for oil that he had crushed from seed. Yet these two seed crushers, Thomas Gresham and Laurence Mellowes, were almost certainly not the only ones involved in the development of rape oil-milling at this time; others were already nursing further schemes. One which matured later was the brainchild of Benedict Webb, an energetic entrepreneur, born of a clothier family of Kingswood, Wiltshire, who learned something of the cloth trade under his father. He was bound apprentice in 1579, at 16 years of age, to a linen draper and French merchant, and was promptly sent to France. The next four or five years of his life were divided between Paris, Rouen, and Italy, after which he returned to England and established himself in Taunton, Somerset. There he developed the making of a multicoloured or medley cloth, which caught the public fancy because of its difference from cloth of one uniform colour; sometimes it was called Spanish cloth, sometimes Webb's cloth.[9]

The habit of studying the expertise of foreigners, and an admiration of French workmanship, 'far more curious and better than ours', had been instilled in Webb by his stay in France. During his first sojourn there, he had had two looms made and sent back to Exeter. Later on, he became a weighty figure in textile circles, and acted as the Crown's representative in France in 1605, negotiating better terms for English cloth merchants against the protectionist measures of the French. In the course of this diplomatic mission Webb learned enough of rapeseed-milling and cultivation to bring back a model of an oil mill. He erected one at Kingswood, took up land in the same place, acquired yet more in the Forest of Dean, and grew rapeseed.[10]

The perfecting of Webb's new enterprise took time and it was not until 1618 that production expanded sufficiently to make inroads on the local clothiers' usual purchases of Spanish olive oil (Seville oil, as it was often called) and rape oil from the Low Countries, bought in Bristol and London. By 1621 the production line at the mill was operating smoothly, and in 1626 20 gallons of oil were flowing daily. By that time land for rapeseed in the Forest of Dean amounted to 550 acres, and Webb was a substantial farmer, as well as clothier. If all 550 acres had been sown at one time (an unlikely event), it would have produced 1,650 bushels (3 bushels per acre) or 165 tons of oil. Webb reckoned his costs per 100 acres at £480 in rent, field labour, and milling, and expected receipts for the oil of £825, leaving him a net profit of £345, or £3 3s. 9d. per acre. This compares with a modern historian's estimate of about 9s. 8d. per acre from a mixed farm of 30 acres.[11]

Webb had to overcome deep prejudices among clothiers against his home-produced oil. But the price difference was a powerful solvent. Who could resist a price of 2s. a gallon when it was usual to pay 3s. 8d. for Spanish oil at Bristol? Gradually the West Country clothiers abandoned their misgivings, but it took some eight years. They mixed Seville oil with rape oil; they used it only on their cheaper cloth, not on the best quality; but between about 1618 and 1626 they came to rely on it. They finished up by praising it because of the small quantities needed, and the whiteness of the scoured cloth.[12]

Webb also faced competition from other oil millers. He was granted a patent in 1624 for the sole milling of rape oil, after his methods had been perfected by some twenty years of practice. But the monopoly was deeply resented by others in the business. Webb's toughest competition came from Richard Warner, a soapboiler of Bristol, using rape oil in soap manufacture. They became locked in lawsuits, Webb claiming that Warner bought his oil, pilfered some of his seeds, and lured away an apprentice and a mill carpenter, who then built Warner's mill. Warner set up one oil mill (in partnership with others) at Caerleon, in Monmouthshire, and sold his oil in Bristol. He thus became Webb's competitor in the same market.[13]

Warner contested Webb's claim to be the first inventor of oil-milling; it had been milled in sundry places for eighty years, he claimed, and this we know to have been the case. Warner claimed to have learned the business from John Pryce of Redriffe (Rotherhithe), near London, who had been making oil with others there for twenty years. Rotherhithe was a most likely place for an oil mill along Thames-side. Warner had also picked up the rudiments of oil-milling in the Low Countries, and when his mill was set up, it was on the lands of the Earl of Pembroke, Warner's 'honourable lord and master'. In other words, a courtier-projector was behind the scenes, promoting this oil enterprise. It is a familiar ingredient in the story of projects at this period. Warner then embarked on growing rapeseed in various places, not only in Wales but in Gloucestershire also. The family business was still in existence in the 1640s, milling oil and exporting cloth.[14]

One oil mill at Caerleon was not the only cause of Webb's anxiety. The truth was that by the 1620s oil millers were multiplying in other areas of the kingdom. The drainage of the fenland created new arable land which proved itself immediately receptive to the crop. Some of the lessees of fenland were Dutchmen and Frenchmen who knew a great deal about rapeseed and its management, and nourished no prejudices against it. It is not surprising, therefore, that the documentary evidence shows increasing acreages under rapeseed, focused mainly on East Anglia. Rapeseed was already being taken on board vessels sailing from Boston, Lincolnshire, in 1603. A small piece of one and a half acres in Gosberton, Lincolnshire, was growing rapeseed c.1625. A large expanse, of some 3,500 acres, was being cultivated at Long Sutton, Lincolnshire, in 1632.[15] When the fenlanders rioted and damaged the drainage works during the Civil War, jibes against coleseed featured among the insults hurled against the drainers; in their eyes, rapeseed was nothing but 'trash and trumpery' from Holland. Yet the crop spread, and in 1660 the government's Committee for Trade expressed concern at the quantities being exported.[16] In the fields it featured in large and small quantities from south to north of the kingdom, even growing at Whitwell, in Derbyshire, in April 1698, and in North Tynedale, in highland Northumberland, in 1709.[17] Eastern England, however, was its most congenial habitat. At

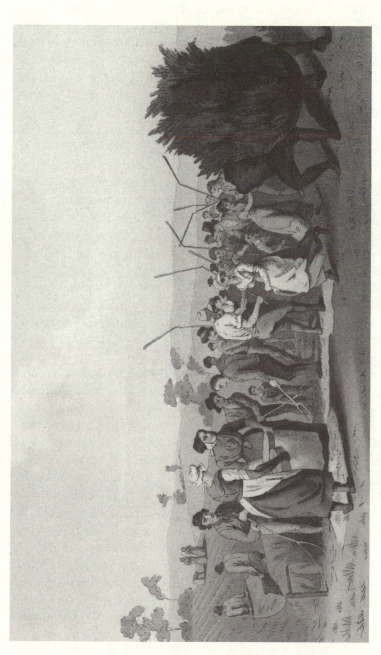

10. Rapeseed-threshing. Rapeseed, for industrial use, gradually spread from the fens of East Anglia, where it first found a congenial home in the seventeenth century, down the full length of eastern England, where it remained a familiar crop into the nineteenth century. This painting of rapeseed-threshing is taken from George Walker, *The Costume of Yorkshire*, originally published in 1814.

Winterton, Lincolnshire, William Burkitt had 116 acres of rapeseed in 1715, valued at £650; Yorkshire rapeseed prompted special notice from James Hart, travelling from Scotland to London in 1714, and seeing in Easingwold fields of 20 or 30 acres apiece, all supplying oil to the cloth industry. No hint of prejudices from the clothiers now held it back: farmers rejoiced in a crop which they used to feed cattle in autumn, and of which the seeds made a profit by this time of £10 per acre. This may be compared with something like £6 an acre for wheat, £2 7s. for barley, and between £3 6s. and £3 15s. for beans and peas.[18]

The agricultural textbooks after 1660 treated rapeseed as an ordinary crop in the English landscape. They recommended it for any flat land whether arable or pasture, but especially for marshland and fenland. That is why it appeared so often in areas like the Isle of Axholme, the Hatfield Levels, and in the East Anglian fens. According to John Worlidge, the seed was still brought from Holland, for English seed did not prosper.[19] Growers were warned to take care that too much seed was not shed when reaping—a warning that continues to be given to present-day growers.[20]

The inventory of David Goglar of Holbeach, Lincolnshire, in 1747 silently mirrors two of the merits of rapeseed. His 8-acre plot was called 'green coleseed' when the inventory was taken on 16 November, for it was pushing forth green shoots at a convenient time for feeding cattle and sheep. And it had been planted somewhere around midsummer, perhaps four to six weeks before the grain harvest, just when the poor needed work to fill an idle spell.[21] By the end of the seventeenth century rapeseed was visible all over the eastern half of England from Yorkshire to Essex and in certain parts of the West Midlands as well. Rapeseed and rape oil regularly travelled on river barges on the Severn between Gloucester, Chepstow, and Bristol. This implies some cultivation in Gloucestershire, while the lesser trade from Chepstow suggests that another growing area lay somewhere in Herefordshire and/ or Monmouthshire, perhaps the legacy of Warner's enterprise in Caerleon.[22] Nevertheless, the fens continued to be the main home of rapeseed, and that explains why Wisbech in Cambridgeshire was shipping 1,000 tons of oil annually in 1719, and why such a small town of only 2,000 people could have street lighting in 1700 when a much larger place like Leicester had to wait till 1761 for this amenity.[23] As an alternative crop, it was urged upon the Duke of Bedford in 1743 for some of his Devon land when 'hay and corn prices are very low'.[24] In the end, rapeseed was not displaced until cheaper industrial oils were made available in the mid-nineteenth century.

The story of rapeseed illustrates the long, but ultimately successful, establishment of a crop that was first envisaged as a substitute for oil imports, and then was found to be ideally suited to land newly made available for arable cultivation through drainage in the fens. Prejudices and obstacles beleaguered it, for not only methods of cultivation but the industrial processes of oil-milling had to be mastered. But instruction and experience were at hand on the Continent of Europe. Unanticipated merits of the crop gradually emerged, when it was seen to give valuable work to the poor, and to furnish an admirable fodder for livestock, whether eaten green or as cake after the extraction of the oil. Rapeseed's history followed a path that could never have been predicted at the outset.

Woad

The blue dye plant, woad, was another successful crop, whose history illuminates further aspects of the process by which alternative crops were introduced, and firmly established in this period. Among other things, we see more clearly than in the case of rapeseed the large debt which England owed to Continental countries for the stimulus and the expertise, since the cultivation of woad and the trade in this commodity was an old story in Europe. A fuller account of the foreign examples is, therefore, given here in order to place England's woad-growing history in a wider context. Light is also shed by woad on the way the risks in the experimental phase were shared, and on the role of government, vacillating between help and hindrance.

Although woad grew in scattered places in England in the Middle Ages, it evoked little or no interest as a commercial crop. English dyers relied on imported woad, and so the plant had to wait for its moment of glory until a period of disturbed European trade and mounting inflation directed attention to the possibilities of growing it at home. Then, when the economic interests of clothiers, dyers, and farmers coincided with the newly devised mercantilist policy of statesmen, woad was put on the agenda of projectors, of merchants, and of gentlemen who moved in court circles but who farmed at home as well. Gradually we pick up in documents clues to the lively conversations and schemes that were initiated in the 1540s, and were fired into more effective action at the end of the 1570s.

No new crop finds its niche immediately, and woad was like all the rest in its fumbling search for the right habitat. Cautious experiments were tried with an acre or two, and mistakes were made. At the same time, extravagant rumours circulated about the large fortunes in prospect. So the pioneers did not take long to find others with whom to share experience. They then went in search of kinsmen and friends with the same spirit of adventure, and with resources that they were prepared to risk in a gamble. A web of far-flung contacts was spun in a generation or two, and a body of knowledge assembled and exchanged which removed most of the uncertainties about the new crop in a matter of forty years.

Woad was then placed on the regular shopping list of alternative crops. It was grown widely until the mid-eighteenth century, then became restricted to more specialized areas, but continued in the Lincolnshire fens until 1932. It is found occasionally growing wild to this day, in the Welland valley, Leicestershire, for example, around Guildford in Surrey, and at Lavenham in Suffolk. As recently as June 1995, it has again been suggested for consideration as an alternative crop, for natural dyes have special qualities that are valued again by those working in textile crafts; and less reliance on chemical dyes could reduce energy consumption and pollution. A serious study of its economic possibilities is being made in Italy and England.[25] A neat bridge across 350 years of continuous woad cultivation in England is represented by a small sample of cloth dyed in the early seventeenth century with woad grown in the Dorset–Hampshire area. It lies amid correspondence in the Hampshire archives office, and storage has not in any way dulled its bright colour.[26]

Before indigo arrived on the scene in the later sixteenth century, woad was the essential plant for dyeing blues, purples, blacks, greens, and more subtle shades when mixed with other dyes. For purple, russet, and tawny colours woad was mixed with madder, and for greens with weld.[27] The fundamental importance of woad was underlined by an Elizabethan witness: 'no colour in broadcloth or kersey will well be made to endure without woad'.[28] Even when indigo became a strong competitor with woad from the later sixteenth century, woad continued to be used with indigo to aid fermentation in the dye vat.[29]

To obtain woad the English cloth industry before 1500 had looked overseas. Large quantities arrived in Southampton in Italian vessels from Genoa, carrying the woad of Tuscany and Piedmont. After the mid-fifteenth century the same ships also carried some woad from Toulouse, the town with which all French woad from the wide Garonne valley later came to be associated, although Toulouse did not wrest control of this trade from Bayonne till 1470.[30] Until the 1470s or 1480s Italian woad had the advantage in England, but when political disputes and war in Italy disrupted the transport of woad from Tuscany, they made room for the French to expand their trade with England.[31] A long-term decline in woad shipments from Italy to Southampton is conspicuous in that city's records from 1488 onwards, and may reflect the turmoil which gave Toulouse its opportunity.[32]

The glimpse given here of alternative sources of woad from Italy and southern France introduces us to the competition between two European centres of production. But more centres than these were engaged in woad-growing and the woad trade long before the English thought of entering the lists. Indeed, the magnitude of English ambitions only becomes apparent when account is taken of the longer, broader experience of others. The woad trade had already created many rich and influential men abroad.[33] Woad-growing had been a substantial enterprise in central and northern Italy since at least the early fourteenth century, and by the second half of the fifteenth century woad merchants belonged to the economic and political élite of their communities.[34] Another important centre with a web of trading links that extended much further north and eastward lay in South Germany, in Thüringia. The central towns involved there were Erfurt, Gotha, and Arnstadt, where woad had been a substantial source of livelihood to its growers and traders since at least the thirteenth century.[35] But there the merchants' sights were first set on cloth centres in the east, passing their woad through Görlitz for onward transmission to Oberlausitz and Silesia, even reaching as far as Bohemia and possibly Hungary. The Hussite wars in Oberlausitz between 1424 and 1434 disrupted trade for a while, and obliged the merchants to turn northwards to the Hanse towns, whence it is possible that some woad then reached England. But peace restored Görlitz to its position as the woad staple in the east and allowed it to maintain a virtual monopoly until it was challenged in 1490 by another entrepôt at Grossenhain. Thus the eastward trade remained paramount. Only half as great in the fifteenth century was another trade southward to Frankfurt-am-Main, Nördlingen, and Nuremberg. This carried the dye to another cluster of textile centres in Nuremberg itself, through Nuremberg and Nördlingen into Franconia, Swabia, and the Bavarian stretches of the Danube, and through Frankfurt-am-Main and Friedberg to the upper Main and middle Rhine rivers.

In still smaller quantities, South German woad reached further afield to France, the Netherlands, and Spain. It even came to England, for Erfurt woad was sufficiently familiar to be mentioned in public proposals in the sixteenth century for a tax to be levied on English woad growers.[36] In fact, it may be that Erfurt woad had regularly come to London while Italian woad went to Southampton. At all events, local investigation in every woad centre has revealed a fierce struggle between vested interests and new competitors for control of this vital article. The English entered the scene at a comparatively late stage.

Documents which shed much light on the woad trade say almost nothing about the woad growers in the fields. But the intensity of mercantile competition almost certainly reflects an increase in the number of woad growers in western Europe. Erfurt woad was sent to Holland by road, river, and sea, and this traffic westward intensified whenever troubles closed the eastward passages. Woad growers also appeared much nearer to England, around Cologne, in Picardy in northern France, in Brabant, and in Lüttich province on the banks of the Maas, all of these setting their hopes on sales in Flanders and Holland.[37]

In other words, the woad crop was moving into more westerly provinces of northern Europe, while it was not disappearing from its east European centres. Indeed, the woad of Thüringia provoked an unexpectedly vehement comment from Luther in his *Table Talk* at the end of 1531, implying that woad-growing was rapidly expanding. He deplored the exhaustion of the soil 'beyond all reason', caused by the rascality of the peasantry growing woad 'where good and noble grain used to be cultivated'. As markets had to be found for the larger crop, the network of trading connections was liable to change, sometimes spinning out much longer lines of communication—as, for example, when woad was carried from Ravensburg to Barcelona.[38] But while the number of woad-growing regions expanded, one fact emerges clearly. The plant was attracting widespread interest as an alternative crop, and was being grown in places that were far more accessible to England than Erfurt and Genoa. It would not be long before better information about growing woad, and the will to grow it, would make its way to England.

The trade in Italian woad from Genoa to Southampton, from which it passed inland mainly to Salisbury, Winchester, London, Coventry, Northampton, and places in Somerset, had begun to flag at the end of the 1480s just as Toulouse was energetically taking control of the market in the Garonne basin.[39] By the mid-sixteenth century Italian woad was hardly mentioned; the first name that sprang to men's lips was Toulouse woad, and if not Toulouse woad, then woad from the Portuguese islands of the Azores or the Canaries, though this was cheaper and considered to be of less good quality. It meant that yet another region of the western world was being drawn into the commerce of northern Europe. Then price inflation in England in the 1540s caused foreign woad to become unwontedly expensive and cries of complaint were heard.[40] In the 1560s the religious wars between Huguenot and Catholic made deliveries from France irregular and unreliable. The time was ripe for a serious attempt to grow woad in England.

The first recorded venture in the growing of woad in England had been made in 1542, when the rise in price spurred the government to encourage individuals to experiment. Two separate licences were issued to men 'to take ground and employ labour in woad-growing'. Of one of these intended ventures no further trace has been found, but the second emerged as a partnership of three gentlemen, two from Wiltshire, and one from Dorset, growing woad at Lymington, in Hampshire in 1548.[41] This was a significant choice of place and of people. Since foreign woad had long been arriving in Southampton, it was a reasonable centre in which to find information on the economics and techniques of growing it. Lymington lies to the west of Southampton Water, on the Hampshire coast, with plenty of flat, moist land around, and saline soils were regarded as eminently suitable for woad.[42] As for the people, one of the partners in the new venture was Henry Bretayne, who had already erected the necessary woadmills at Lymington; he was almost certainly a Frenchman with technical expertise. Another partner, Thomas Derby, was a government official, Secretary of the Council of the West, with an estate in Cranborne, Dorset. He was certainly aware of the government's aspirations concerning woad-growing, and may have been still more deeply involved in policy decisions than that simple statement suggests. Fifty years later woad-growing was well established at Cranborne; later still Robert Cecil, Elizabeth's and James I's Secretary of State, was lord of Cranborne, and when elevated to a viscountcy in 1604 took the title of Viscount Cranborne; throughout this time when Cranborne was associated with Westminster statesmen, the woad-growing continued.[43]

The Lymington enterprise may or may not have persisted, for it fades from sight. But, indirectly, it was plainly a considerable success, for in 1585 when a census of woad-growing was taken by the government, Hampshire had the largest acreage of any county, with 1,748 acres.[44] Two events spurred men on between 1548 and 1585: first a sharp rise in the price of foreign woad around 1579 (which set the Privy Council enquiring into indigo as a substitute); and then an unexpectedly sharp fall in the price of grain, which ran counter to all expectations. The harvests of 1583 and 1584 were so bountiful that grain prices dropped by a quarter. Farmers were forced to look for a more profitable crop to pay their rents, and woad-growing quickly spread. The government, fearing that grain shortages in the towns would surely follow if the process were not arrested, initiated a detailed investigation, that called for information on acreages since 1583.[45]

William Cooke, a merchant of Havant, on the eastern side of Southampton Water, was now said to be the pioneer grower in Hampshire, for men had evidently forgotten Henry Bretayne. But Hampshire was still the prime centre and Hampshire men were conspicuous in spreading the crop into Dorset and Wiltshire.[46] When the information from the census of woad is placed on the map, it is clear that it spread along the coast in search of saline soils and then moved inland along the river valleys. Thus from the Hampshire coast woad travelled along the Sussex coast, from Chichester to Littlehampton, to Shoreham, and Eastbourne. The rivers then pointed like fingers to the routes taken inland. The Itchen carried woad to Winchester, the Test carried it to Mottisfont, the Cuckmere carried it between the Downs, through Litlington, Alfriston, and Alciston to Salisbury. In north Hampshire, it spread from Petersfield along the River Rother into the Sussex Weald, and was taken up enthusiastically by many small growers in Midhurst. It reached the other end of the county, at Playden (but still in the vicinity of the River Rother), in time for a tithe dispute to have arisen by 1585.[47]

Since woad favoured the floors of river valleys, it competed for the same land as the dairy farmers. Thus in locating on the map woad-growing places mentioned between 1580 and 1660, we find woad at more than one place called Wickham, a place-name meaning 'homestead with a dairy farm'. It was at High Wycombe, Buckinghamshire, and at Wickham in Spalding parish, Lincolnshire. It could well have been growing at Wickham on the Sor brook in Oxfordshire, south-west of Banbury, for it was certainly growing at Broughton, next door to Wickham. And when one considers the men who conveyed the plant from one region to another, it may be no coincidence that the grower of woad in Wickham, Lincolnshire, was Anthony Cope, member of the gentry family, the Copes of Hanwell, who lived in the vicinity of the Oxfordshire Wickham.[48] Moreover, the proposition that new crops were frequently seen as the chance to turn a poor tract of land into something profitable places many of these examples in the midst of such possibilities. In one example, where the piece of woad land itself can be identified, the suspicions harden. In Steventon, Berkshire, land called Woad Piece in 1654 was later called Oatpiece Close, and appears then to have given its name to adjacent open-field furlongs. It lay on the boundary of the parish, between an enclosed meadow and common pasture. Such directions and field names thus locate this woad ground in a part of the parish where the land had not yet been brought into a state of high cultivation.[49]

The Lincolnshire example of woad-growing near Spalding gives proof of the crop spreading further afield in the second decade of the seventeenth century. But in its initial phase it moved unerringly from one textile centre to another in the southern counties, to Winchester and Salisbury, to Basingstoke and Reading in Berkshire, and westward to Wiltshire. It did not always appear in centres for the making of wool cloth, however. The wool for stocking-knitters, and thread for linen and hemp weavers, used woad. Abingdon, for example, became a woad market, and while this may simply be because it was a river port, in a low-lying vale with suitable land for woad, another reason might be its trade in sackcloth. A more refined investigation than this might even identify the household articles, the clothing, and the commercial sacks and wrappings that people expected to be blue in colour, for there were doubtless conventions in this matter. On one occasion, a gardener was described as a 'blue apron man'.[50] If blue aprons were needed for gardeners, were they also needed for butchers and barbers? And was the cloth also blue that was used to cover the sides of the woadcarts to hold the leaves in place in transport?[51]

Abingdon was considered to be a great centre for grain and malt which was transported along the Thames to London, and if any of this was packed into blue sacks, then it would add to the reasons why Abingdon was a considerable trading centre for woad.

The commercial links between woad growers and textile centres determined some of the directions taken when the crop moved further inland. Thus it found its way to the Vale of Evesham, to Evesham itself, and to Westbury and Chippenham in Wiltshire. But men also tried woad-growing on very different soils, though they were still near textile centres, for example, on chalk lands, around Marlborough and Salisbury. Success in such a very different situation is, at first sight, difficult to credit, but Robert Payne, the dyer-clothier-projector, who wrote a careful and informative treatise on woad in 1585, had recommended both rank, fat, sandy (*sic*) grounds, and chalky ground so long as the chalk had two feet in depth of good corn mould above it.[52] And the continuance for many years of woad-growing in Cranborne, Dorset, which lies mainly on chalk, suggests that woad could succeed in both habitats.[53]

When the government became concerned in 1585 at the large acreages of woad in cultivation, it appointed as its investigator Alexander King, an auditor in the Exchequer, to search the kingdom for woad between Easter and Michaelmas, and judge its extent, though on that occasion he did not go further north than Oxfordshire. A year later his exploration uncovered the crop in another eleven counties, as far north as Yorkshire, although only 20 acres were reported there, east as far as Suffolk with 32 acres, and west, as far as Devon with 186 acres. Even then King had not mapped all the woad then growing. If he had looked harder, he would have found it in Nottinghamshire and Lincolnshire.[54]

As for the people who promoted the crop, their network of personal connections gleams through the bare facts in the census taken in so many counties. Many gentlemen were growers of woad as well as being owners of the land. Sometimes they give signs of a partnership with others, in which the responsibility was equally shared. In others some kind of agreement is discernible between landlord and woad-growing tenant. Both circumstances help to explain how the crop was spread from one parish to another. For example, in Sussex, near Chichester, Mr Devenish, member of a gentry family established there since the fifteenth century, had 22 acres of woad land: 10 acres in Hampnett parish, 2 acres in Drayton tithing, 1 acre in Cockelayn tithing, and 9 acres in West Hampnett. In each place Peter Palmer was the tenant growing the woad, and so it is possible that Devenish and Palmer had a shared interest in promoting this new crop. Moreover, Devenish may have gone the rounds in this part of Sussex, picking up many pieces of land for this same purpose, for he also had 4 acres at Fishbourne, 6 acres in the liberty of Appledram, and 70 perches at Midlavant.[55] Elsewhere, landlords granted their land in various places to the same woad growers, who then made local arrangements for cultivating it. In yet other cases, gentlemen or merchants took the initiative, and remained in charge. A Salisbury clothier, George Bedford, took land in Cranborne and the next parish on which to grow woad. He had already had experience of growing woad (9 acres) in Salisbury in 1585; now he leased Blagdon Park, Dorset, and entered into a series of woad-growing agreements between 1597 and 1610, whereby local farmers living in the parish grew woad on his account. In 1597 William White undertook to grow 12 acres. In 1608 George Weekes, husbandman in the parish, made a similar agreement. Bedford undertook to pay specified rates for the carting of dung and the carrying of the woad to Salisbury, as well as for the cultivation.[56]

The cross-county connections also show how woad growers in distant parts formed a network of acquaintances and associates who were already, or became by marriage, kin. When George Bedford, the Salisbury clothier and woad grower, died, his widow married Henry Sherfield, also of Salisbury, who continued the woad business. Although Henry Sherfield was a lawyer by profession, his interest in woad was probably a good deal older than this marriage, for his previous wife had been the daughter of a north Wiltshire clothier, Christopher Baily of Southwick, and Southwick was a woad-growing parish in 1585. Moreover, before Mistress Bailey married Sherfield, she was the wife of Henry Long, clothier, of Whaddon in Buckinghamshire, another place in another county well suited to woad-growing.[57] Thus the woad areas of Hampshire, Dorset, north Wiltshire, and Buckinghamshire were linked by personal ties between clothiers, dyers, and cultivators. Another link tied Hampshire clothing interests with Farnham in Surrey, where woad found a suitable home, not least because Farnham was renowned for its smallholders and gardeners, and would certainly have been able to provide the necessary labour for careful cultivation. Thus John Michinall of Odiham, Hampshire, clothier, owned a small plot in Farnham which was being planted with woad by a Farnham buckmaker.[58]

The 1585 woad census showed a great many small cultivators with one or two, but not more than fifteen, acres, and very few large growers. If anyone had large acreages, it was made up of many small pieces. Thus the merchant John Haffard, of Lyme Regis, Dorset, with 38 acres, and Henry Williamson of Midhurst, Sussex, with 40 acres (rented from five different landlords) were unusual.[59] This, of course, was in the early days of the crop's history. It is also clear that growers were trying to wring some advantage from rough, furzy ground, mossy land, old rabbit warrens, and 'wild ground never broken up', even though some used much better land, even arable and garden ground.[60] Hopes of finding a crop that would turn derelict land into gold were the lure.

The very divergent views elicited by Alexander King on the merits and disadvantages of woad-growing left the government in a quandary. In the event, in October 1585, it stopped the breaking up of more land for woad, and banned cultivation within four miles of market towns, clothing towns, and cities, arguing that woad diverted labour from the cloth industry and appropriated pasture that was needed for the grazing of horses and cattle. It also prohibited woad within eight miles of royal palaces, because the fermenting of the woad leaves to make 'woad balls' which were then sold to the dyer, created an obnoxious smell that persisted for several weeks and annoyed Her Majesty.[61] The very bad harvests of 1585, 1586, and 1587 restored a sense of proportion to the farming scene by harsher means. A dearth of grain in July 1586 in Hampshire was sufficiently serious to cause outbreaks of violence against woad growers.[62] Men were reminded that woad, or the cash that it brought them, would not fill hungry stomachs.

For a while the government's unexpected restrictions on the doings of woad growers, plus two bad grain harvests, held back the advancing tide. The government then settled in 1587 on a system of licences to grow so many acres, which the Privy Council granted to individuals. No person could grow more than 20 acres, and no parish could have more than 40–60 acres.[63] This placed a heavy bureaucratic burden on the Privy Council and the system was revised in 1589; licences for so many acres per county were issued to individuals, who then let licences for smaller acreages to others.[64] If continued, this policy might well have had the effect of encouraging large growers, and discouraging the small ones. Mr Cope in Oxfordshire, for example, asked for a licence for 100 acres, and, judging by the family's interest in woad-growing in Oxfordshire and later in the Lincolnshire fenlands, he could very well have taken up the whole area for himself.[65] However, a Hampshire informer implied that the restrictions on acreage were wholly disregarded; he knew one man near Littleton (Lillington) growing 200 acres, and another in or near Pytt growing 140 acres.[66]

The system could not have worked for long. It was swept away in 1601, when a proclamation in November allowed woad to be grown freely again, except within three miles of London or any royal palace; the Queen begged the Commons that 'when she cometh in progress to see you in the country, she may not be driven out of your towns by suffering it [woad] to infect the air too near them'. This settlement was timely, for lawyers at any moment would have been muttering that it was against the law to forbid the sowing of any crop on a man's freehold.[67]

After 1601 woad-growing settled into the accepted routine of farming. It was especially conspicuous in all river valleys. Hence the Thames, the Severn, and the Trent valleys drew woad growers to Berkshire and Oxfordshire, Worcestershire and Gloucestershire, Northamptonshire and Nottinghamshire. The Ouse valley drew woad to Buckinghamshire, and it appeared regularly in some of the damp fenlands of Somerset, Lincolnshire, and East Anglia. It ceased to be considered as a suitable crop on permanent arable land and was unwanted on permanent pastures which served well for dairying or livestock feeding, but it had a well-defined use in old pastures that were ready to be ploughed for a few years before returning to grass.[68]

The statement frequently made in print that indigo from Asia drove out woad and woad-growing is not borne out by the facts. Certainly, foreign imports of woad dwindled but, while indigo was one substitute, home-produced woad was the other.[69] In fact, English growers found a market for their home-grown dye right through the seventeenth, eighteenth, and nineteenth centuries, though it was not, of course, every man's crop. Conservatism among the dyers may be part of the explanation for the continuing demand for woad, since indigo is said to contain the same colouring properties at almost ten times the concentration. But dyers favoured the use of woad to mix with indigo, and so help fermentation, and chemists now confirm the validity of that belief, which craftsmen arrived at without scientific knowledge but through practical experience.[70]

As for the prejudices of landowners and others against woad, these were allayed by better knowledge and practical good sense. It was agreed that the crop was exhausting, but when restraint was exercised, allowing at most three years of woad, and one or two years of wheat or barley, followed by seven or eight years under grass, woad proved itself an advantageous crop agriculturally and financially. The manuring, ploughing, stirring, and assiduous weeding of the land for woad was acknowledged to be thoroughly beneficial for it and succeeding crops.[71]

The unpleasant smell of fermenting woad never became agreeable, but experience quashed the allegation made in the early days that it spread an infection.[72] Some landowners, like the Isham family at Lamport, Northamptonshire, at various dates between 1727 and 1739 even allowed it to grow close to their manor house and were not averse to seeing mill and cabins erected on their land.[73] In other cases, the appearance of woad on the estate of a resident gentleman was likely to mean that he was not then living there. The woad found growing on the Cotton family estate at Conington in Huntingdonshire in 1751, for example, might occasion surprise because in certain generations this family had taken great care to adorn and improve both house and grounds. Sir Robert Cotton, the antiquary, built a new house there sometime before 1600, and Sir Thomas drained some of the land by installing a pump in 1639. But the puzzle is resolved when we discover that Sir John Cotton was not occupying the house in 1751, he had no male heir, and he was to die the following year, when the house passed to another family.[74]

One advantage of woad which none denied was its ability to employ large numbers of the poor for one-third of the year in weeding and picking the leaves. The common estimate of labour needs, which is confirmed in actual woad accounts, was four persons per acre. Since some gentlemen's ventures occupied 40 acres, they employed upwards of 160 people a day in the busy season from May to July.[75] Clothiers, of course, resented woad work because it deprived them seasonally of spinners. But in general, the large numbers employed made a powerful argument in favour of woad at the 1585 enquiry, when work for the poor was in the forefront of public discussion. It plainly influenced the some- what grudging decision of 1587 to allow woad-growing in moderation. The crop of 40 or 60 acres per parish, the official announcement conceded, would set to work '200 poor people wanting means for one third of the year'.[76] It was one of the motives of the larger woad growers themselves, who often mingled genuine concern for the public weal with their pursuit of private gain. Thus George Bed- ford, the Salisbury clothier, expressed warm appreciation to his labourers in the woad fields when he died in 1607; his bequests to the poor in the Dorset par- ishes around Cranborne were made 'in remembrance of my good will for their labours and work bestowed on my business'.[77] The same sentiments towards the poor may be seen in Henry Sherfield's continuing interest in woad-growing when he married George Bedford's widow. He was a notably zealous Puritan, conspicuously involved in a novel scheme of poor relief at Salisbury in the middle 1620s. Woad-growing was his private contribution to the same end.[78] But this is not the only case in which woad-growing is found in association with public-spirited gentry pursuing active measures to provide work.[79] Sometimes the congenial habitat of woad is known also as a distinctly Puritan area, as in Hampshire, where both features characterize the boroughs and townships in the river valleys along the Test from Southampton to Andover, and along the Itchen; one suspects a connection, though the conjuncture of such features should not be pressed without more investigation.[80] In the public mind by the early eighteenth century 'woad-growing' was almost a synonym for 'work for the poor', and some gentry, fearful of the rising cost of poor relief, fought shy of woad-growing for that very reason. It attracted too many poor, who posed problems when the work ended.[81]

It was inevitable that the growing of woad should become associated in the end with gentlemen farmers and yeomen, rather than with husbandmen and smallholders. The crop required substantial resources for the seasoning processes which had to be conducted on the spot. At the very beginning gentle- men were prominent among the growers, alongside dyers and clothiers and occasionally merchants, but this was to be expected in the experimental stage. All novel crops called for adventurers with capital. But woad imposed its own conditions which no amount of later experience could circumvent. A woadmill had to be near at hand, and to make this an economical proposition, woad had to be grown on a substantial scale in one place. Large farmers were the ones who could offer large acreages, and save the woadmillers the trouble of searching every year for many small plots. But eventually, it was the specialists who seasoned the woad who rose to the top as the organizers and masters of the business. From being employed as the servants of gentlemen farmers, as was Robert Payne, when engaged by Sir Francis Willoughby at Wollaton, Nottinghamshire, they moved into the prime entrepreneurial role.[82] They travelled around a district negotiating for land at the beginning of a season, and transported their woadmills to the site. The home bases of the woadmen then became sufficiently well known for occupiers of land to approach them, rather than the reverse. Thus we find a gentleman urging his brother in 1668 to negotiate with 'the woadmen at Coventry', with a view to their growing woad on his land in Rutland.[83] The phrasing of the letter makes it plain that the landowner was primarily interested in the high rent that woad would command.

In the course of the 350 years of woad-growing in England, brave attempts were made to settle the mill and the crop firmly in one place, rather than submit to the discipline of the plant which forced woadmen always to be moving on. An early example of some such scheme may lie behind details, given in a lawsuit in 1633, relating to a woad enterprise in Warwickshire, at Newton and Biggin, just north of Rugby. A mill was evidently already located there and may earlier have had other uses (mills often changed their function; woadmills were sometimes used to thresh grain, cider mills to thresh clover seed).[84] But the place was barely a hamlet, and certainly had no substantial dwelling house, though two small houses for shepherds had been built some twelve years before. However, barns, cabins, and woadhouses had been newly erected for woadmen, and woad was being grown on land that had hitherto been a rabbit warren, and thorny pasture. No one could remember a grain crop having been sown in living memory; so here was clearly a new venture in ploughing up old pasture for woad. The permanent buildings could only have been economically used if a sufficient amount of land made a long rotation possible.[85] Another such plan may have been in mind when woadmen negotiated to take a 21-year lease in Abbots Aston parish, Buckinghamshire, in the 1730s. Since a tithe at 2s. an acre was expected to bring £66 6s. to the rector, land extending to 663 acres was evidently in question.[86]

The continuance of the woad crop in one place for many years could, of course, be achieved by the co-operation of several farmers living as neighbours in one suitable tract of country. Such may explain the record in the parish register of Misterton parish, Leicestershire, where baptisms and burials of members of families 'working at the woad' occur in six different years between 1646 and 1665.[87] In the eighteenth century, however, explicit evidence is found of entrepreneurs trying to anchor the crop permanently in one place. Arthur Young's attention in 1813 was arrested by a thoroughly successful attempt by J. Cartwright, at Brothertoft Farm near Boston, Lincolnshire. His father had lived with movable woadmills, but he devised another system by taking 1,100 acres of land, of which he assigned 200 acres for three years at a time to woad. For twelve years the land was out of use for woad, but in that time it gave two years of oats, one of rapeseed, and another of oats before being put down to seven or eight years under grass. Two hundred acres of woad each year was expected to yield 200 tons of woad, which was as much as his mill could handle.[88] This enterprise, with its need for thirty labourers and a foreman, brought into existence a small hamlet called Isatica (the Latin name for woad being *Isatis tinctoria*), situated on the banks of the New Forty Foot Drain that flows through Boston.[89]

Since woad was widely grown for 200 years and by a devoted minority for another 150 years, it obviously paid its way. Its best days probably lasted from the 1580s, when French woad was pricing itself out of the market and indigo had not made its appearance in any quantity, until the mid-eighteenth century. In 1584, when the sudden craze for woad was starting to take hold, one reporter claimed that 1 acre of woad was more profitable than 6 acres of grain.[90] Alexander King, the government's thorough investigator of the matter in 1585, was bemused by all the varied estimates which he collected on his travels round the counties but, having set out the extremes at each end of the spectrum, he gave the middle range of figures as follows. Costs of cultivation averaged £5 6s. an acre, average yields at that date were 10–11cwt. per acre (though the average was soon doubled to 1 ton per acre and occasionally in the nineteenth century, with heavy manuring, yields of 2 and 3 tons were achieved). Woad in the 1580s sold for about 28s. a cwt. Net profit, per acre, therefore was of the order of £9 18s.[91] Others at this same period gave slightly different figures under each heading but arrived at a profit per acre of £8 16s. in one case, in another £10 14s. or more.[92] It could be a highly advantageous crop to farmers who normally expected a return of 9s. 8d. per acre from the average husbandman's 30-acre holding.[93]

Experience of woad in the next seventy years did not dull this favourable picture. Walter Blith in 1652 described woad in glowing terms, so long as the grower obeyed the rules: 'it hath been one of the greatest enrichments to the masters thereof until the midst of our late wars of any fruit the land did bear.'[94] John Worlidge, who farmed in Hampshire and certainly knew the crop, still called it in 1675 'a very rich commodity' and 'advantageous to the husbandman'; 'it more than doubleth the rent of his land, sometimes it quadruples it,' he wrote.[95] At much the same date, we catch a glimpse of a woad merchant and grower who was a living example of Blith's and Worlidge's claims. William Baldwyn of

Nether Eatington, Warwickshire, left at his death the large sum of £4,316 18s. 11d. Not all came from the profits of woad. Corn, cattle, and the leasing of land made their contribution. But woad was a conspicuous part of his business; among his debtors were dyers in Nailsworth and Tewkesbury, Gloucestershire, in Stratford on Avon, Warwickshire, in Kidderminster, Worcestershire, and in Oxfordshire. Baldwyn was growing some, if not all, of the woad himself, and some of it was sold for seed; he was manifestly well placed to find purchasers of the dye from among the many dyers distributed between Coventry, Oxford, Worcester, and Gloucester.[96] What is noticeable in this case, as in many other woad dealings from the 1580s onwards, was that home-grown woad went to a great many different clothing towns, many of which were of little or no renown in the international world—Newbury, Lacock, Andover, Mansfield, Chesterfield, Lichfield, and Grantham, as well as Salisbury, London, and Bradford. It suggests that English woad was used in a great variety of different types of cloth, some of which were in the cheaper ranges.[97]

Throughout the eighteenth century satisfactory gains were still found in woad, even though rents rose and the price at which the woad was sold fell. Woadland at Burley, Rutland, was rented at £2 10s. an acre in 1705, which still compared favourably with a rent of £1 10s. for land under oats, and £1 7s. for land after it had been woaded and had to be put under grass for several years.[98] Profits may be roughly calculated from one undertaking at Bristol at Happom's Court between 1738 and 1740. Three acres were being cultivated in 1738 and in the first year comparatively heavy expenditure was incurred on repairs and the thatching of the mill. Including these charges (of £11 2s.) with cultivation costs, the total expenditure came to £26 1s. 4d., which represented £8 13s. 9d. per acre, compared with an average of £5 6s. in the 1580s. In 1740, when it appears that 5 acres were being grown and the woadmill did not need expensive repair, the production costs including rent, tithe at 5s. an acre, plus cultivation and seasoning, worked out at £6 1s. 2½d. per acre. In all three years woad sold at 15s. a cwt. and the yield was 2½ tons. The clear profit per acre was £6 6s. 3d. in the first year and £8 18s. 9½d. in the second. This was a distinct improvement on the net profit suggested by a contemporary writer in 1739 of £6 0s. 9d. per acre for wheat, £2 7s. for barley, and £1 18s. for oats.[99]

That the market still expressed a positive demand for woad in the eighteenth century is reflected in two pieces of evidence at the beginning and end. A company of Manchester manufacturers and Yorkshire clothiers in the early eighteenth century set out to break what was claimed to be an oppressive monopoly by setting up a woad-growing enterprise at Tyringham in Buckinghamshire. This undertaking continued into the mid-nineteenth century. In 1797, the reporter on Somerset to the Board of Agriculture described woad-growing around Keynsham, and declared it so profitable that few farmers who tried the crop ever gave up growing it.[100]

Above all other regions woad suited the Midland counties, situated as they were on the frontier between the predominantly arable regime of the south and east and the predominantly pastoral regime of the north and west, just at the point where the boundary line was wavering and changing in the seventeenth century. On the pastoral side of this line more and more grassland was being ploughed for arable, if only on a temporary basis. If successful, a more regular system of alternate husbandry took hold, and local people rejoiced to find themselves less dependent on grain supplies brought in from outside. Thus was the dramatic transformation wrought in the Forest of Arden in Warwickshire by the clearing of woodland for crops.[101] In Northamptonshire also the large extent of forest on the eastern side of the county and the clay lands of the vale on the west gave ample scope for the practice of alternate husbandry. And when pasture was ready for ploughing, woad was the ideal first crop for it absorbed some of the excessive richness in the soil before wheat was sown. It is therefore no surprise that Walter Blith proclaimed his confidence in woad in his book of agricultural advice in 1652, for he was a native of Warwickshire, had lived in Leicestershire, and worked in Northamptonshire and Lincolnshire. He knew his Midland counties very well indeed.[102] The special place of woad in Northamptonshire farming was also asserted in 1712 by its county historian, John Morton. For him it was the county that 'either is, or has been, woaded most'.[103]

Throughout the Midlands the presence of woad continued to be generously documented in the eighteenth century. Less was written about it in some other counties, but it was plainly there since it was listed as a crop on which tithe was payable. Thus, it was in evidence in north-west Kent, and the tithe reference chimes with the observation of a traveller in 1801 passing through the same district who saw it 'in great abundance'.[104]

The other large region, apart from the Midlands, in which woad made a strong impact as an alternative crop was the fens. Drainage in the seventeenth century inaugurated a boisterous spell of ploughing and cropping with only a single year of fallowing. But experience taught greater wisdom, and on some land a longer rotation, involving seven or eight years under grass, was chosen as a better alternative. This made room for woad. A large crop of woad was record-ed in Conington fen, Huntingdonshire, in 1751, and when visiting the Lin-colnshire fen in 1813 Arthur Young wrote the fullest description of woad of any writer for the Board of Agriculture. Seeing it in the fenlands near Boston, he filled nine pages of text on its cultivation and seasoning, with engravings of woadhouses inside and out.[105] But while the specialist growers were impressive

11. Woad: seasoning and processing the leaves for the dyer. This blue dye plant was grown in England continuously from the sixteenth until the twentieth century, surviving longest of all in the fens of Lincolnshire. The top photograph, *c.*1921, shows woadmen balling the pulped leaves near Wisbech, Cambridgeshire. The bottom photograph shows the sheds at another site, Skirbeck, Lincolnshire, where the woad mill closed in 1932. The woad balls were laid on planks, to dry for several weeks. Both photographs, together with personal reminiscences of the woad workers, are contained in Wills, 1979.

professionals, the demand for woad was becoming restricted to a small circle, and Arthur Young cautioned newcomers against considering it. Mainstream agriculture was returning to dominate the scene, and woad was passing out of the common farmer's everyday catalogue of possible crops. Yet it would remain for more than another hundred years in the Lincolnshire fens, attracting notice from time to time because of the unusual requirements of the seasoning process and the persistence of ancient methods of cultivation. In 1896 Francis Darwin, scientist son of Charles Darwin, wrote with R. Meldola an account of woad-growing for the scientific journal *Nature*. They had seen it at Parson Drove, and knew of it in three other centres in Lincolnshire, at Algarkirk (which had started in 1843), at Skirbeck, and at Wyberton.[106] The market was then relentlessly shrinking, and yet woad-dyed cloth was still in demand in Bradford and Leeds in Yorkshire, in Lancashire, and at Buckfastleigh in Devon. In the United States army and police treasured woad for their uniforms the longest of all.[107]

One of the last users of woad in Leeds boasted a century-old connection with both the cloth industry and woad-growing. This was George Nussey, manager of the woadmill at Algarkirk, and the son of an earlier George Nussey, who had been a Leeds dyer, had taken out a patent in 1838 for a vegetable dye in blue and other colours, and had then bought land in Algarkirk on which he grew woad. Was he conversant with the long history of woad in the past? Possibly not. Yet it served his family for a hundred years. The Parson Drove Mill was demolished in 1914; his at Algarkirk lasted until the end of 1927. The Skirbeck mill survived until the 1932 crop was harvested.[108]

*

Woad-growing offers some varied insights into the way a new crop finds and holds its place through several centuries of changing circumstances. The political and economic situation encouraged it at the beginning, and growers were in a mood to take risks, for the sixteenth century was an age of projectors. As trials proceeded, the projectors cleverly devised partnerships to spread the risks, and alighted on different systems of collaboration, involving gentry, merchants, farmers who took responsibility for the whole programme of cultivation, and casual labourers. But in the end, it was the group of skilled woadmen who rose to the top, and held the whip hand, for they were the vital intermediaries between growers and dyers.[109]

Government policy wavered, starting with exhortations at the beginning, switching to damaging and insensitive interference a generation later (even though ministers showed a serious desire to conduct research before they acted), and finally leaving farmers to decide matters for themselves. Fortunately, when official intervention caused a storm of protest, Queen Elizabeth's government listened more carefully to reasonable argument than did some that came later.[110]

As a labour-intensive crop, woad made a timely appearance by giving much work to the unemployed. Indeed, that virtue stands out above all others in the pages of Lionel Cranfield's account book, recording the wages of 249 men, women, and young people working on 41 acres of woad at Milcote, Warwickshire, in the month of June 1626.[111] Its demand for labour made woad much less attractive once mainstream agriculture returned in the later eighteenth century, and more hands were needed to man expanding industries. But the scene at Milcote was not wholly unrecognizable some 350 years later, when this author saw labourers hoeing cabbages in the same place.

Hops

Hops rank high on the list of alternative crops between 1650 and 1750; indeed, they may be said to have passed through a period of excessive popularity in that hundred years, verging on a craze. But the craze mounted to its height only after a long period of slow familiarization, for hops were the earliest of the new plants to attract interest at the beginning of the sixteenth century. And they have stayed with us longest, despite fluctuating fortunes in the present century.

Like woad, hops were not, strictly speaking, a new crop in the sixteenth century, but were entering upon a new phase of development.[112] They were grown in Anglo-Saxon England, and one place-name in Worcestershire, Himbleton, testifies to that fact. Himbleton stands for Hymel-tun, meaning 'a hopyard'. Moreover, the use of the hop in beer is explained in the Anglo-Saxon version of the *Herbarium* of Apuleius. From the *hymele* or hop, it explained, a 'wort' was produced which was considered 'that degree laudable that men mix it with their usual drinks'. But, except in monasteries, the use of the hop in England seems to have been neglected in the Middle Ages until the fifteenth century. Then the Englishman's interest revived, doubtless under the influence of agricultural innovations in the Netherlands and North Germany, where the search for alternative crops after the Black Death resulted in the cultivation of a number of other new (or revived) plants, like woad, madder, and buckwheat.[113] When Flemings came to settle in England in the fifteenth century, they naturally brought their taste for hopped beer with them, and encouraged beer brewers also to come and settle. Beer brewers in London in the fifteenth century included many Flemish and Dutch, and hops were imported in quantity from Flanders.

The legend that associates the introduction of hops into England with the year 1524—'Hops, Reformation, bays, and beer, came into England in one year'—gives, therefore, a wholly false impression of their history. But the date may not be wholly irrelevant. In that year Sir Edward Guildford of Kent obtained a licence to export hops and madder. The role of the gentry in promoting the domestic production of essential imports has already been noticed. That, and the fact that the Guildford family was constantly present at Henry VIII's court, and much involved with the management of the royal household, makes it entirely possible that this grant was intended to fulfil government aspirations. In other words, it was made in anticipation of efforts by the Guildfords to set up hop- and madder-growing in Kent.[114] It is a not unreasonable guess that Flemish hop growers were settled in Kent at this time, at the invitation of the Guildford family, just as ironworkers from France can be identified in the 1520s in Sussex and Kent. If not in the 1520s, then certainly in the 1540s, steps were taken in official quarters to the same end. Government action is made known to us when the Privy Council authorized payment of £140 'for charges in bringing over certain hopsetters'. In other words, a deliberate policy was being implemented, which brought Peter de Woolfe into Kent, possibly, it has been suggested, to the Maidstone area, where he was paid for hiring workmen and advancing the planting of hops.[115]

The first English writer on husbandry, Fitzherbert in 1523, did not refer to hops, though this is not surprising since, in his native county of Derbyshire, he is unlikely to have had any familiarity with it. But in 1557 Thomas Tusser, living in Essex where hops were more at home, compressed good advice on their cultivation into twenty stanzas of his verse. Then, in 1574 an admirable practical textbook on hop-growing was published, which plainly met a need, for two further editions appeared in quick succession, in 1576 and 1578. It was the work of a Kentish gentleman, Reynolde Scot, of Scott Hall in the parish of Smeeth, near Ashford, who was a practising farmer with expert knowledge of his subject. Among other things, his text shows how seriously he followed the advice of the classical writers—in taking pains, and sparing no effort to attain high standards of cultivation. 'The covetous man', he wrote, 'that lyeth in wait to spare his halfpenny, the sluggard that sleepeth away opportunity, and the unskilful that refuseth to learn the right order, may happily relish the bitterness of the hop but shall never savour the sweetness thereof.'[116] Authors of agricultural textbooks, as this passage shows, could write graphically as well as crisply.

The eastern counties lying closest to Flanders took up hops readily in the later sixteenth century. They were grown in Norfolk, Suffolk, and Essex, as well as in Kent; indeed, as Sturbridge in Cambridgeshire became a chief market for the commodity, and Suffolk, Essex, and Surrey were singled out by the surveyor John Norden as hop country, these counties may well have had more hop grounds than Kent in the early days. It is impossible to measure their extent, however. They were grown in gardens and yards rather than in fields, and

If you laye softe grœne Rushes abroade in the dewe and the Sunne, within twoo or three dayes, they will be lythie, tough, and handsome for this purpose of tying, which may not be fore=

slowed, for it is most certaine that the Hoppe that lyeth long vpon the grounde before he be tyed to the Poale, prospereth nothing so wel as it, which sooner attayneth therevnto.

12. Hops. Reynolde Scot, a gentleman's younger son of Smeeth, Kent, wrote the first book of instruction on growing hops in 1574, when they were still a relatively unfamiliar crop. He had learned hop-growing at Poperinge in Flanders, and his work was dedicated to William Lovelace, who lived at Bethersden, Kent, and wanted to plant a hop garden. But Scot also wrote for those 'placed in the frontiers of poverty', 'whose hope is in their hands'. These two illustrations, showing the training of the hops on poles, are taken from Scot's book.

almost always the acreages were small; one or two roods of land were said to be enough for the ordinary family.[117] Moreover, the appraisers of a dead man's goods were not legally obliged to record hops; grass, fruit, and hops on bines were considered to have come from the soil 'without the industry or manurance of man'. So references to hops, which we seek in probate inventories, are infrequent. A veritable conspiracy was afoot to ignore the spread of alternative agriculture.[118]

The incentive to grow hops was maintained and even strengthened through the second half of the sixteenth century because hop prices rose, and the demand could not be met by any substitutes. Hence, merchants were engaged in what Gervase Markham called 'daily traffic to France and Holland' for them. In 1559 the value of imported hops was reckoned at nearly £17,000, the same as flax, and only a little less than iron. In 1571, when Duke Alva imposed restrictions on exports from the Low Countries to England, hops that had cost 14s. and 16s. per cwt. in 1568 rose in price to 45s. and 50s.[119]

By 1600 comments on hop-growing make it clear that farmers had passed through several sobering decades of trial and error, and one wave of hop-growing had come and gone, leaving some growers sadder and wiser men. It was a risky crop that could easily fail if bad weather struck. On the other hand, a successful crop, carefully handled in the kiln, was extremely profitable. Robert Reyce, from experience in Suffolk, and writing in the first two decades of the seventeenth century, spoke of some years of grievous failure, which had persuaded many to give up hops and turn to other things. Alternatively, they consigned the hops to their poorest land.

Nevertheless, the plant was gradually finding a settled home, wherever farmers were willing to accept the terms which it imposed. It had to be set apart, in a close, garden, or yard, carefully prepared with surrounding windbreaks. The full cost of cultivation could be daunting, for many poles were needed (which, incidentally, placed fresh, but welcome, demands on coppiced woodlands nearby), plus intensive labour at certain seasons. Every rood of land accommodated 250 hills, and one man, growing for the market, could attend to no more than 2,500 hills. So 2½ acres was the maximum size of a hop garden for one man to manage alone.[120] Furthermore, good weather and skill in kiln-drying were essential. In the course of the seventeenth century, then, the dilettantes fell away, leaving certain regions and certain classes of farmers dominant in the business. The middle years of the seventeenth century suggest something of a new mood developing. Scot's book on hop-growing was reissued in 1640 and 1654; John Beale in Herefordshire remarked on a new burst of hop-growing in the last three years; and in 1655 a return of the acreage of hops was called for, as legislation was contemplated (perhaps to regulate the quantity being grown). This showed fourteen counties growing them, but one-third of the acreage lay in Kent, more than a quarter in Essex, and one-tenth in Sussex. In other words, two-thirds were grown in the south-east of England.[121]

In Kent, which became a prime hop county, hops were most conspicuous between 1600 and 1630 on the ragstone soils around Maidstone, and these were described in 1639 as 'a great country for hops'. After 1660 urban hop gardeners came to prominence, especially at Canterbury, where so many Frenchmen settled, mainly working in the silk-weaving industry. They set aside half an acre or less of land in the town, and employed hop specialists to plant their hills for them, tie up the bines, and harvest the crop.[122]

Another noted hop area lay on the Surrey–Hampshire border, where Farnham hops were celebrated. Indeed, the Farnham hop (like the Canterbury hop) was a named variety, its special features being that it generally ripened a week or ten days later than others, and was used in the brewing of fine ales rather than porter. It was also recognized as superior in quality because it was picked fastidiously, and the buyer could be sure that no leaves were mixed with the hop. As this was a market gardening area of some note, the hop growers were probably gardeners, rather than farmer-gardeners.[123]

The third specialized hop region was Worcestershire and Herefordshire in the West Midlands, gradually turning Worcester into a major market for the area. The timing of this development is not altogether clear, and it may have started around 1600, gathering momentum after the 1650s. Worcestershire had an ancient gardening tradition, as we have already noticed, and the county had some important monastic houses which cultivated gardens in the Middle Ages. True, it was the eastern side of England which claimed the limelight, because foreign hop gardeners first arrived there. But it is not unlikely that foreigners were responsible for raising standards in the West Midlands also. At all events, by 1670 competition from this part of the country was an uncomfortable, and seemingly recent, fact of life for Kent growers.[124]

In general, the momentum of hop cultivation built up in the second half of the seventeenth century. This is evident in the comments of John Worlidge in 1675, despite his prejudices against the plant itself—'an unwholesome herb or flower for the use it is usually put unto', he sniffed. Yet he had to admit that 'of all other plants, it advanceth land to the highest improvement, usually to £40 or £50; sometimes to an £100 per acre.' Moreover, demand exceeded the home-grown supply, and so Flemish hops still had to be imported, though they were 'nothing near so good as our own'. His warnings to growers centred on two considerations: first, the great labour needed to cultivate them properly, since, carelessly handled, they yielded scarcely one-fourth of the possible profit; secondly, they were very sensitive to excessively wet or dry weather, mildew sometimes destroying the crop altogether. In consequence, the harvest was uncertain, and farmers were discouraged. But Worlidge thought hops so substantial a business that he placed them first in his chapter on 'Garden Crops', and devoted twelve long pages to instructions on growing and drying them. As he lived at Petersfield in Hampshire, and Farnham's hops were growing only fifteen miles away, he had advice near at hand, even if he did not grow them himself. In fact, the guidance given suggests that he had the benefit of close observation and perhaps some personal experience as well. His instructions were precise enough to extend hop cultivation among yet more growers.[125]

According to Worlidge, rich land was needed for hops, but other soils would serve, so long as they were not stony, rocky, or very stiff clay. Preparation could be done with the plough or the spade, and when the bines needed tying in during April and May 'you must be daily amongst the hops.' Throughout his account, Worlidge laid emphasis on the care and diligence required of the toiler in the field, and, after that, for the drying and bagging as well. But at the end of it all, no hop grower needed to complain of the rewards. 'An acre or two of ground so managed by one or two persons shall redound one year with another to more advantage than 50 acres of arable land, where there is much more time, cost and experience bestowed on it.' Farmers' probate inventories match these observations, by showing some high valuations when farmers died: a yeoman in Kent in 1692 had seven bags of hops worth £80, and Lady Margaret Culpeper at Leeds Castle, in 1710, had 21 bags worth £262.[126]

Dennis Baker's careful study of hop-growing in Kent leaves no doubt of the scale on which hops were grown in certain areas of the country by the second half of the seventeenth century. A correspondent claimed that the Maidstone district received £200,000 for hops which it dispatched to market in one year, c.1697. Among gentlemen who made them a substantial business was Sir John Banks, with some 20–30 acres of hop ground in Aylesford between 1680 and 1700. But beyond the farmers' enterprises, another mode of production developed in the city of Canterbury, beginning modestly in the 1660s, and expanding in sixty years into what Defoe called 'the greatest plantation of hops in the whole island' by the 1720s. Oast houses were set up in the city centre, serving the hop gardens of saddlers, grocers, flaxdressers, silkweavers, and widows in the suburbs. Hops were the town dweller's sideline; or as Dr Baker puts it, hop-growing was 'a gamble played for high stakes'. But 'in the long run it was a reasonably safe undertaking where it was subordinate to a more stable and solvent enterprise.' In the countryside, that other enterprise was a gentleman's landed estate or a farmer's mixed farm, while in Canterbury it might be a malthouse, brewhouse, or retail shop, these last all benefiting greatly from the plenty of horse manure and other town waste. Silkwinders and weavers in the city became the hop pick-ers, ever ready to turn to this work in the season.[127]

For a few years in the second quarter of the eighteenth century, between 1725 and 1732, hops sustained a serious setback through bad weather at critical seasons, but it was temporary and confidence returned, prompting a comment in 1736 from an observer in Brightling in Sussex that 'everybody is now in the humour of planting hops.' In Canterbury in the 1770s they were still reckoned a major enter-prise, keeping 2,000 acres of land in continual cultivation. In short, hops consti-tuted an alternative crop which did not recede into the background when cereal cultivation returned to profit in the second half of the eighteenth century. Domestic and overseas demand together maintained cultivation at a reasonably stable level. In the specialist counties, hops were no longer regarded as a wild gam-ble, even though weather and disease resulted in a fluctuating harvest from year to year. The routine nature of the Kentish crop was implied by John Banister in 1799, when he said that farms of 100 acres usually had 8-10 acres of hop ground. Growers took the bad and good years in their stride, and did not hire special labour for this one crop, as did the Canterbury growers. The years between 1767 and 1781, in fact, produced alternating good and bad harvests with such regular-ity that the hop merchants fixed their prices on the assumption that the rhythm would continue. They were badly caught thereafter by the American war, which reduced overseas demand sharply, and discouraged growers to such an extent that in 1780 some Canterbury hop planters grubbed up their plantations.[128]

The later history of hops can be anticipated here, since it allows some gen-eral observations to be made on alternative agricultural pursuits when once a new phase of mainstream agriculture returns; alternatives may, or may not, persist with the same vigour and success under the new regime. We have seen above, in the case of coleseed and woad, and we shall see in more examples below, illustrations of their varied fortunes. Having started as 'new ventures', 'minor pursuits', or 'luxuries', some alternatives do not manage to compete any longer when mainstream farming returns, and they fade from sight. Others survive but lose their dynamism, though they still have the chance to regain ground, and, indeed, make fresh advances when the wheel turns again. Yet other alternatives come to be regarded as essentials; as food and drink habits change, and living standards rise, the new farm produce finds a secure place on the land, and is not readily dislodged by changing circumstances.[129]

Hops were one of the successful survivors from the seventeenth century, into the next age of mainstream agriculture, when the total acreage under hops actually increased. It is not absolutely clear when the hopyards of Canterbury finally left the scene, though doubtless urban-building pressures played a large role alongside the hazards and discouragements of fluctuating harvests. But on mixed farms hops settled in as a specialized pursuit in certain areas, dovetailed with other activities, and through to the nineteenth century acreages in some places increased boisterously. The figures for England and Wales rose from 32,218 acres in 1807 (when the figures start) to 51,014 acres in 1819, while in 1850 they stood at 43,125 acres. In Herefordshire and Worcestershire, they rose remarkably from 6,000 acres in 1840 to 10,000 acres in 1890. In the kingdom as a whole, the years 1869–75 were deemed especially prosperous, while the return of alternative agriculture after 1879 was called a depression.[130] Since then hop acreages have fallen as a result of mixed causes, higher productivity per acre, changing tastes in beer which require less hops, and the setting up of a Hop Marketing Board in 1932 to regulate output. It is no longer a small farmer's speciality; individual farmers grow larger acreages, 15 acres being an average venture with hops in 1930, and 23 acres in 1957. Local labour is no longer essential at harvest time: until the 1950s–1960s, in Kent at least, it was supplied by Londoners and gypsies, whereas now harvesting is carried out by machines. Yet hops may still return as a large crop in the present phase of alternative agriculture. English ale is now beginning to win favour away from lager, thus raising the demand for English hop varieties; new strains are being developed which resist disease and produce dwarf-sized plants (only eight feet high), and these can be harvested more quickly than ever by machine. A new era for hops may be dawning.[131]

Every alternative crop has a different history in the long term. Hops had the distinction of an especially early introduction in the sixteenth century, arriving well before an alternative agriculture was economically necessary, and they have enjoyed a more continuous career than some others to the present day.[132] In the next chapter, we turn to some of the less successful seventeenth-century ventures.

5 ∾ ALTERNATIVE CROPS:
the near-failures and failures

Madder

AN alternative crop, with a record of intermittent, rather than lasting, success in England at this period, was the dye plant madder. It produces a red dye which was essential in the textile industries, and was used by the apothecaries in their medicines. The crop offers a uniquely intimate insight into the risks taken by individual innovators when they competed with foreign growers who already had a secure footing in the market. Some of the tribulations of the early planters, described here, must also lie behind the story of rapeseed, woad, and hops but that evidence has not survived.

During the first experience of alternative agriculture in the later Middle Ages, madder made its appearance in the Netherlands; it is found growing in Zealand, in Holland in 1326, and in Flanders at much the same time, though its origins almost certainly go back earlier than this.[1] The vigorous trade links between the Netherlands and King's Lynn probably explain why madder is also found growing in Norfolk earlier still, at Catton in 1274, and Monk's Grange in 1305–6.[2] This interest—on monastic lands—was almost certainly for medicinal purposes, and it did not swell into a larger enterprise. In Holland, on the other hand, madder forged ahead and Zealand became its acknowledged centre in northern Europe.

When madder-growing returned to the agenda in the mid-sixteenth century, it is likely that some early experiments had been tried of which we have no record. In 1524, for example, Sir Edward Guildford, an influential Kentish gentleman, was given a licence to import wine, woad, and canvas, and to export madder and hops. It is possible that at that early date he had it in mind to grow both madder and hops, thus endeavouring to satisfy the aspirations of Henry VIII's ministers and reduce imports. Both crops were certainly grown in Kent later on; indeed, madder was grown in the vicinity of Guildford's own home near Romney Marsh, and, although the Guildford family had no personal hand in this coincidence, the idea of madder-growing in this area may well have persisted through the generations.[3] Other examples recur in this book of a tradition persisting in one place, and being revived whenever one economic phase ended and another began.

Madder featured with woad in occasional debate throughout the sixteenth century, for its price and sporadic shortages made home production desirable. No botanical reasons prevented its cultivation in England, but strong economic stimuli were needed, for the dye comes from the roots, and these have to be in the ground for three years before they are sizeable enough to yield a decent crop. Hence, a three-year investment of money, labour, and hope was required. In 1559 the need to grow madder (and woad) in the realm was affirmed, and publicity was given to a patent in 1568 allowing a Dutchman from Brabant to collect wild madder in Ireland.[4] Matters did not come to a head, however, until the early 1620s, and the choice of that particular moment for a sustained effort at growing madder must be closely linked with an order to the Commission on Trade in 1622 to 'inquire into the causes how dyeing stuffs [have] become dear'. The government was prodding people into action.[5]

Before madder was grown in fields, it had been grown in gardens. London market gardeners disposed madder plants between their rows of vegetables, thus distributing the risks of a three-year investment. They almost certainly supplied the apothecaries first and foremost, though they could have supplied the dyers too with small quantities. When the government urged madder-growing, however, it had larger-scale cultivation in mind, and the best places to turn to for support in this direction were textile centres with a market gardening tradition as well. Thus it is no surprise to find the botanist William Turner recording in his *New Herball* in 1568 seeing his 'fairest and greatest' specimens of *Rubia tinctorum* on the road from Winchester to Southampton. These may, of course, have been rogue plants from consignments that passed along the road from the port to the clothiers inland. On the other hand, Winchester had had an abbey, and many gardeners lived in the town in the later sixteenth century, and cultivated vegetables and less usual plants.[6]

When earnest trials with madder started in 1621, governmental urgings were firmly in the background. The pioneer was George Mynne, variously described as a draper and a dyer, and allegedly an aggressive, and possibly ruthless, wheeler and dealer on the London scene. He had many irons in the fire, and their number mounted as a result of his contacts in court circles, for he was the brother-in-law of George Calvert, James I's Secretary of State. He launched a madder-growing project by sending his brother and cousin on several trips to Holland in March 1621 to get madder slips, followed by an expensive trip of his own, costing £117 7s. 7d.[7] Thereafter he engaged George Bedford, son of the Salisbury clothier who had promoted woad-growing in Hampshire and Dorset in Elizabeth's reign, to study the subject systematically, and conduct trials.

George Bedford began a series of visits to Holland in July 1622 where he sought out the expert madder growers of Zealand.

The letters of George Bedford to his stepfather in London show more effectively than anything else the hazards of growing a new crop, and the accidents that at one moment could delay, or entirely halt progress, while giving new life to it at another. Personal misfortunes could distract the pioneers, who were in any case few and battled against odds; they could emanate from the government mishandling a delicate situation, or miraculously choosing the right means at the right time; or they could derive from a sudden change in the economic climate, which abruptly switched attention from one enterprise to another. All classes in society were ready to pick up and drop occupational projects at a moment's notice. So, whereas we expect continuity of effort, they were more alert to the opportunities of a passing moment: these were seized on an instant, but just as promptly abandoned, in favour of something better. If several opportunities presented themselves at the same time, then so much the better; adventurers grasped them all, alerted their family and friends, and borrowed on a shoestring to make the most of a fleeting chance.

Through George Bedford's experiences with madder we glimpse a whole range of current projects entering into view, embarked upon, and equally summarily thrust into the background. To learn the secrets of growing and drying madder Bedford went to Holland seven times in sixteen months, staying for periods of from two weeks to two months. Thus he observed cultivation procedures at different seasons, negotiated for plants, and fetched some back. He constantly had to pay out money to persuade the Dutch to reveal their secrets, when and if they did not prove totally hostile and obstructive.

George Bedford's first letters home do not survive, but, at the rendering of an account of monies spent, it appears that his first visit lasted two months from 17 July 1622 until 14 September. He lived modestly, and spent less than £17. He returned on 8 November 1622 to watch the digging up of the madder roots and to buy a stock of madder dye. This latter transaction doubtless gave him the pretext for being there, as well as ensuring some profit from the journey. On 3 February 1623 he returned again to learn how madder was dried in the stove and prepared for the dyers' use. A letter to his stepfather soon after he landed on his third visit between 3 and 4 a.m. on a wintry morning spoke of such extreme cold that his feet were swollen and he could not immediately continue his journey. He expected that his mission on this occasion would tax all his powers, and would cost George Mynne far more than he anticipated. Subsequently we learn why. The plan had now been formulated to set up a madder plantation in southern England, and to combine in one project the growing of madder and rapeseed. The idea was to grow rapeseed at Sandwich in Kent, while setting the madder first of all on Sir William Paulet's land near Weymouth, in Dorset, from which it would be removed to Sandwich. A madder plantation of 20 acres was the original scheme, but Bedford thought 8 or 10 acres, or better still, 3 or 4 acres, a more reasonably sized operation, for which he could be sure of finding sufficient labour when transplanting the plants to Sandwich.[8]

Obtaining madder plants from Holland and securing their arrival in good condition at the right season in England called for careful planning. At first Bedford expected to buy a load of madder slips, that would be detached from the roots in May, after some early spring growth. But slips had to be speedily planted in the ground—certainly within eight days of being separated from the parent stock. Ships' skippers could guarantee to get them across the sea in forty-eight hours even without a wind, but Bedford envisaged delays in finding labourers to plant them promptly in England, and knew that considerable losses could ensue. He was advised instead to buy madder roots which he could plant in autumn, thus giving them time to put forth shoots which could be detached in May. In the event, his later correspondence indicates that he bought some roots and some slips.[9]

A measure of madder roots, called a mett, cost Bedford about £14 and was enough to plant up two acres. When the roots sent forth shoots in the spring, the slips would be enough to plant up another four acres. The most delicate, if not the most dangerous task, however, lay in acquiring the first mett of roots, since it was not the usual time for digging, and the authorities would be curious to know the why and wherefore. Moreover, the stoveman had only half a mett of roots to hand; he would have to buy another mett to fill his stove, and a high price would be asked.[10]

At this point Bedford's account of his negotiations with the madder growers affords an unusual glimpse of the ingenuity and intrigue needed to embark on a new agricultural venture. The Dutch were much admired by the English for the freedom which they allowed to foreign traders. English merchants frequently pointed out the lesson to their own government. One measure by which in Zealand the authorities ensured fair and honest treatment of foreigners was described by Bedford thus: on the occasion of his first agreement to buy madder from the growers, Bedford had to pay half the cost and he took the Dutchmen's bond for good performance of the final deal. If when he returned to Holland they let him down, he had the right, by way of compensation for the injuries received, to become a free citizen of any Dutch town he wished. Presumably this was a sharp inducement to Dutchmen to keep their word, otherwise they would have been swamped by foreign intruders. So long as things did not come to this pass, he expected to carry his madder to the ship one evening and the boat would leave for England that night. If some calamity befell, and he was challenged about his doings in Holland, he intended to say that he was disillusioned with England and had resolved to spend his days in Holland; he would choose to become a free citizen of Kampveere (the old name for Veere), and claim to be trying his fortune in Zealand.[11]

Obviously, it required great fortitude to battle on against all obstacles, and suppress the worst apprehensions. George Bedford was not always cheerful in the face of discouragement. To procure the information he needed on madder-growing and drying cost him some days 5s., some days 10s. in bribes and tips, and when money was short this meant going without some of his meals, and walking from town to town. On his February visit he took the portentous step of bargaining for madder slips which he would collect on his next visit. The difficulties in procuring them may be gauged from the high costs incurred—just under £46. On a fourth journey on 3 April 1623 to collect the madder slips, the cost was higher still—£65, and it was on this visit that Bedford lured Adrian Cornellis to come to England and oversee the planting. A fifth journey to Holland on 10 May 1623 to fetch more madder slips lasted almost a month until 2 June, cost Bedford £76 17s. 5d., and was followed by two more in October 1623.[12]

Mounting expenses reflected the increasing delicacy of the negotiations, as the Dutch madder merchants realized what Bedford was up to—he was not just buying madder for the English dyers, he was planning to grow madder in England, was learning the Dutchmen's expertise, and had already hired a skilled planter. A letter sent to his stepfather in Lincoln's Inn during the October visit conjures up the atmosphere of lurking danger. On arrival, Bedford had visited the skipper of a vessel plying between Middleburg and London who was to take delivery of some of the madder slips he had ordered. In Bedford's absence the skipper had suffered harsh treatment when news of the deal reached the madder merchants. They had angrily pursued him, had had him clapped in prison for four days, and, but for his having wife and children, would not, he thought, have spared his life. They were intent on discovering the identity of the principal negotiator—in other words, George Bedford. When Bedford next faced the Dutchman with whom he had made the deal, he found him unwilling to go back on his promise to Bedford, but he lectured him severely on the enormity of his doings, and advised him to conceal himself from the madder merchants at all costs. He ordered the stovemaster in charge of drying the madder to deliver the madder roots to Bedford, but, since Bedford had not arrived at the right time for digging them up, Bedford was left to do it himself, but was still made to pay as if the digging had been done by the Dutch. He was also charged more than anyone else for drying it in the stove. Bedford began to wish he had never got involved in the business.[13]

Throughout these months Bedford lived from hand to mouth, constantly appealing to his stepfather for a little more money to tide him over. As he set off on his sixth journey, and waited at Gravesend for the boat to Flushing, money was delivered to him from his stepfather, but within ten days of his arrival in Holland he needed another £25 and was writing to ask that his cousin seal up an envelope and give it to the skipper of the next boat to Flushing. Alternatively Mynne should arrange a letter of exchange with a Dutchman in London—a 'Whislebreefe' as he called it (in German a *Wechselbrief*). But he must be paid, he insisted, in English silver guineas, certainly not in gold, nor in Dutch guilders, for in that way he would incur a loss. A month later he wrote again, for no money had arrived; he had seen four ships arrive in Flushing from London and on each occasion was disappointed of his expected package. He had managed to get most of the remaining madder dug up, but his labourers demanded money first, he was spent up, and had nothing to pawn but the madder, which he dared not surrender. He was in a quandary: 'the least courtesy here must be paid for before it be enjoyed, and then what shall I do in this business, with never a sliver in my purse?' Should he come home to collect the money? He dared not leave his business in midstream 'in regard they are ready to wrong me before my face'. Still he hoped for a profit at the end since he had heard that the market price for madder in England was £3 10s. a cwt., and in Zealand it cost half that.[14]

Bedford's main objective in Holland that October was to see the madder he had ordered dug up and dried. But because twenty-seven other men were ahead of him in the queue for the stove, he could not expect his batch to be dried until Christmas week. Meanwhile, in the earlier part of the year George Mynne had found other land in Kent for his plantation, and Bedford had been making journeys there from September 1623 onwards. Some of the land may have been in Rye, for payments at Rye appear in the account, including one for the decking of the madder there, that is, the banking up of earth to cover the roots. George Mynne had been paying rent for 4 acres of land in Kent at 4 nobles per acre (26s. 8d.) since Michaelmas 1622, but he was not bearing the whole cost. A partnership had been formed between Mynne, Henry Sherfield (Bedford's stepfather), and George Bedford whereby they shared the costs and the profits between them. All the expenses were added together and then divided by three, but it is clear that George Bedford felt himself constantly under criticism from Mynne for spending too much, and until he rendered an account, he depended on his stepfather to produce the ready cash he needed. The partners' plan anticipated the grant of a patent, presumably for the exclusive growing of madder in England, and the fact that Secretary Calvert lurked in the background, to whom Bedford looked eventually for 'other requital of my pains' beyond his mere expenses, gave foundation to such hopes.[15]

During 1624 Bedford lived at Appledore in Kent, where the madder ground was now located (perhaps the earlier reference to land at Rye had been a loose reference to Appledore). In other words, the land was on the edge of Romney Marsh, where the damp atmosphere bred malaria and laid all but the strongest natives low. Bedford fell victim, and the illness lingered despite much kindness from Sir Thomas Culpeper, owner of the land, who urged him a dozen times to move into his house for a change of air and a quicker convalescence. Bedford wrote miserably to his stepfather from his sick-bed, for he was now at odds with Mynne and wanted to go to London to patch up their differences. Adrian Cornellis, the skilled Dutchman, had been in charge of the plantation for a year and by early October 1624 the madder was in its third year and was ready to be dug up. It was patchily distributed in the field, but the size of the roots gave great satisfaction. Bedford was sure that the land had been wisely chosen. Nevertheless, others were already prying into the business, and he feared 'we shall not be masters of it long unless our patent be passed'.[16]

The anxieties were endless. The madder of more recent planting suffered from the attention of the neighbours' rooting pigs, and Bedford had to hire someone to guard his field. He intended to sue two men for trespass, for which he asked his lawyer-stepfather to send the appropriate writs. The next letter was a much more emotional outburst against the ingratitude and false dealing of George Mynne towards him. In it Bedford referred to the rough handling that Benedict Webb, the substantial West Country clothier who also grew rapeseed, had received at Mynne's hands, and from other sources we have evidence that bears this out. Benedict Webb went to law against Mynne and Secretary Calvert in connection with some dealings in cloth, and claimed heavy losses as a result of Mynne's ruthless business procedures. Bedford's bitterness was sharpened by the fact that his stepfather seemed to believe Mynne's story rather than his own.[17]

The difficulties with madder steadily mounted higher than the hopes, but other plans were maturing which promised alternative sources of revenue to the three partners. The Dutch routine of madder-growing involved a rotation of rapeseed, madder, rapeseed, madder, followed by two or three years of wheat. Apart from the convenience of the rotation itself, an oil crop could bring a regular flow of cash, in contrast with the madder which yielded only once in three years. Bedford expected in two years' time to plant 60–80 acres with madder, but in the mean time he proposed sowing 100 acres of rapeseed that would keep an oil mill busy for eight to nine months. The money was to be borrowed in Salisbury, where his family lived.[18]

In January 1625, however, Adrian Cornellis discharged himself from the Appledore plantation, and left amid recriminations. Bedford suppressed some of his anger, knowing that, if he did not, word would get back to Holland, and his problems would be that much greater when he had to recruit Dutchmen for both the oil-milling and madder-grinding. Then in June 1625 the three partners learned that their application for a patent to grow madder had failed. The grant had gone to Mr Shipman, Charles I's gardener, whose plantation was along the Thames at Barn Elms, and who, judging by his surname, was a Dutchman. This was the turning-point for Mynne, who withdrew from the enterprise, although he undertook to help in further negotiations, already under way, to share in some way in Shipman's patent. The plan was to sell the Appledore madder to Shipman.[19]

In March 1627 the fear of prying eyes was so great in the fields of Appledore that Bedford was obliged to dig up his madder at night and did not trust others to do it for him. But he was also very ill with pleurisy and anticipated death. A long gap in Bedford's correspondence leaves us in doubt about the way this crisis passed, but Bedford recovered and must have decided that the marshland climate would be the death of him, for in 1628 he was in London trying to persuade the Lord President of the Privy Council to grant him the office of inspector of madder. Now he undertook to weigh and assess the amount of sand and earth that was mixed with the madder imported from Holland; sometimes, he alleged, it amounted to between 2 and 30 pounds per hundredweight. To obtain this office Bedford loitered for weeks and months in anterooms at Westminster and other royal palaces, receiving encouraging words and an occasional more serious interview, always hoping that these would be translated in the end into a remunerative office.[20] The dyers were up in arms at his proposal, claiming, no doubt correctly, that they were accustomed to dealing with the sand and had a perfectly good arrangement with the Dutch when arriving at a price.[21]

Bedford's pleading and waiting went on through 1629 and 1630 while he turned in all directions to borrow money. In September 1630 he found himself in the King's Bench prison for debt but somehow got his release. At some time in the past he had contemplated throwing everything up and going to Virginia or the West Indies, but he was nothing if not long-suffering, and in June 1631 he reached his goal—he was appointed to the official post of inspector and sealer of imported madder. Still the dyers fulminated and conspired against his 'impertinent surcharge'. Finally to resolve their dispute with him, Bedford was summoned to a meeting with the Warden and members of the Dyers Company, attended by the Earl of Bridgewater, at which he demonstrated the amount of sand in single bales of madder and emerged triumphant. By 1633 Bedford's affairs seemed to be on an even keel for he was lodged in London, was going to Sussex to bring his wife back, and was paying off his debts.[22] He had dissociated himself from the growing of madder, but others had now moved in on the project and were concocting even grander schemes.

The idea of a madder growers' corporation was now being floated by Philip Burlamachi and the Dutch drainer, Cornelius Vermuyden, that would be supported by a prohibition on madder imports. Vermuyden had bought Malvern Chase from the Crown, giving an undertaking to plant madder there. But he sold the Malvern land to Sir Robert Heath, who in turn wanted to sell the land to another but found the clause about madder-growing made the deal impossible, and asked for it to be withdrawn. Vermuyden had passed his responsibility for growing madder to William Shipman and a Mr Corsellis. Shipman, as we have seen, had received the royal patent for madder-growing. Was this Mr Corsellis, who was now named in partnership with him, the same Adrian Cornellis who had been in charge of Bedford's plantation at Appledore? It seems likely. The plan for a corporation duly passed to William Shipman. It allowed him the right of sole planting of madder for four years, but it did not prohibit imports. Instead an extra duty on imported madder was to be charged (£10 per ton for the better quality, £8 for the poorer). The finer details were still being argued over in June 1636, but the agreement to incorporate a company had been achieved.[23] Plainly, the government was still actively promoting madder-growing; this shows in Secretary Windebank's notes of matters under consideration in the same year (1637) by the Committee of Trade; it listed madder.[24]

In the event, the Civil War spelt the end of the madder corporation, and even without the war it is unlikely that the scheme would have succeeded. Later references to it suggest that it failed because William Shipman was a poor man without sufficient capital, and the war finally broke him. When new agricultural crops and techniques came up for discussion again in the 1650s Walter Blith knew only of madder cultivation in gardens, where it was grown with great profit. He also knew that Shipman's madder had been successfully sold to London dyers. He believed that if madder in fields grew as satisfactorily as in gardens, it 'would prove the richest commodity that I know sowed in England'. But these glowing words were moderated in the 1653 edition to read that 'it is like to prove a staple commodity'.[25]

Madder was certainly not forgotten, but a fresh impetus was needed. Englishmen in Ireland at the same period were still speculating on the possibility of developing the wild madder found there; Charles Worsley had poor people gathering some for him, and had assembled a small nursery of roots. A petition and remonstrance of Charles Webb concerning madder was heard by the Council of State in 1656 and some time between that date and 1660 Nicholas Crisp set up a large plantation at Deptford along the Thames. Again the choice fell on damp marshland, not unlike that at Appledore, and, significantly, Crisp was a salter, a member of the London Company which had earlier showed active interest and business acumen in all dealings concerning new raw materials for industry and alternative agriculture.[26]

When Cornelius Vermuyden withdrew from Malvern Chase and his undertaking to grow madder there, he had moved to the fens of eastern England to engage in large drainage operations; doubtless, he took his ideas for madder to the new location. These came to fruition at the Restoration in the Wisbech area of the fens when madder-growing started *c.*1661, and continued for some eighteen years, if not longer. The project received publicity in a patent granted to James Smith, merchant of London, in 1670, allowing him the privilege of planting and making madder for fourteen years. Smith was said to have learned 'the mystery' abroad, had imported skilled foreigners, erected mills and stoves in England, and prepared land for the purpose. Smith's expenditure was deemed to have been £10,000.[27] A tithe dispute in the Isle of Ely in 1679 sheds further light on the venture. The planters were James Smith with John Lilburne, William Hills, and Francis Hacker. Hacker sounds like one of the Dutch experts mentioned in the patent. John Lilburne was a druggist of London. Their partnership had been formed in 1671, the madder had been growing in Walsoken and Leverington, and in 1673 an agreement had been reached with the incumbents of these parishes, promising 4*s.* per acre in tithe.[28] The collapse of the market seems to have occurred in 1676, when the sales price did not meet the costs of production. The explanation almost certainly lay principally with a fall of madder prices in Holland, brought about by a plentiful crop. A second reason was poor seasons in England.

So long as high prices for madder lasted, it was a profitable operation for the English growers. The costs of cultivation were reckoned at £12 per acre, plus £2 for stoving and drying (others quoted higher costs of £15 and £3, respectively). But a good crop produced 10 cwt. per acre, which could earn £32 (just over £3 per cwt.). This would have yielded a clear profit per acre of between £14 and £17. Since a total area of 150 acres was mentioned under madder in 1677–8, a clear profit of £2,100 or even £2,550 from such an enterprise would have lived up to Walter Blith's highest hopes. Before 1676, it is likely that the profits, about which the growers guarded silence, had, indeed, been of that order. Some even named higher prices for madder of £40 per acre of 10 cwt. But then the price of £32 for 10 cwt. had fallen to £16; the bubble had burst.[29]

Some of the details given in the tithe dispute reveal a well-organized and well-established operation. The grower/dealers had taken up pieces of land from many different landholders, making 208 acres in all; sixteen landholders were mentioned in 1677 and 1678 as having madder of two, three, or four years' growth. The largest landholder offered 75 acres, others yielded pieces of 10 to 25 acres, others 2 acres upwards. One witness believed that Curtgate Marsh in

Walsoken was the best ground for madder—thus confirming once again the suitability of marshland.[30]

Madder in the Isle of Ely faded from sight after 1680; it seems to have come and gone in a matter of twenty years. But scattered references to madder in other places leave the lingering suspicion that shrewd market gardeners continued for a long time to grow it alongside other crops. It may have been growing at Forthampton, in Gloucestershire, in 1637, for example; it was certainly grown at Godalming, in Surrey, at the end of the seventeenth century. Yet in 1698 John Houghton thought madder-growing had ceased because Dutch prices undercut the English. He may have been wrong about the complete cessation of madder cultivation, but he correctly alighted on the reason why madder did not spread more widely.[31]

Yet madder did return again. In the 1760s it enjoyed a remarkably successful revival, assisted by several different developments occurring together. In the first place patterned cottons became high-fashion goods in the eighteenth century all over western Europe; their manufacture imitated the calicoes that had originally come from India in the seventeenth century and proved so popular. Calico-printing, using the oriental patterns, began in Britain, France, Germany, and Switzerland before the end of the seventeenth century, and in the eighteenth spread to Spain, Scandinavia, and eastern Europe. It became a major industry, and as madder was the most satisfactory, economical, and effective red colouring agent, the new surge in demand totally outran the supply. Apart from some madder of inferior quality grown in Silesia, Holland was the only supplier. This explains why in the mid-eighteenth century not only the English but the French also started to grow madder, in Provence and Alsace, and then in Normandy and Poitou. The Danes and Swedes followed suit, so did the Swiss; indeed, the educationalist Pestalozzi employed orphan children to experiment with the growing of madder on his own estate. In the second place, a Turkish method of dyeing a variety of Turkey red shades was introduced by Greek workers into Rouen, in France, in 1747. The shades were colour-fast and yet bright, and the process spread to England; it may have been in use there by the 1760s.[32]

Together, the success of calico prints and Turkey red dyeing increased the European demand for madder, and caused Dutch madder prices to soar. In 1765 a pamphleteer wrote of a 100 per cent price increase since 1758 in Dutch madder of the cheaper quality and a 40 per cent increase in the best.[33] The expense doubtless explains why imports of madder into England fell from 20,000 cwt. in 1760 to 13,000 in 1765.[34] Englishmen saw good reason to grow their own.

The means by which madder-growing was publicized and assisted during this new phase of interest in the mid-eighteenth century illuminates the more favourable environment for advertising and promoting new agricultural

ventures after 1750. Disagreements about the tithe payable on madder had fes-
tered since the seventeenth century, for a tithe in kind was difficult to collect
when madder slips had to be planted within a few days of being taken out of
the ground. In 1757 this obstacle was removed by a statute fixing the tithe at
5s. an acre for the next fourteen years.[35] A year later Philip Miller published an
exemplary treatise on the way madder was cultivated in Zealand (an account
for which Dutch historians are nowadays supremely grateful, for nowhere do
they have a better description) in which he referred to the increasing demand
for the dye, the raising of the price, and the adulteration it suffered in Holland.
Standards had evidently fallen since the 1620s. 'It ought to be more grown in
England,' he wrote; the Dutch found that even on their worst land madder was
more profitable than anything else.[36] Miller wrote with thirty years' experience
of growing madder in England, apart from having seen it in Zealand on a
number of visits between 1723 and 1730; also he was the gardener at the physic
garden in Chelsea.[37] Miller's knowledge of the earlier history of madder in England, however, went back no further than to Sir Hans Sloane (who was only one
generation older than Miller) who had taken delivery of some wild plants
gathered between Scanderoon and Aleppo; it was generally understood at this
time that madder from the eastern Mediterranean was the best, although Miller
knew that a variety grew naturally in England on St Vincent's Rock, Bristol, and
on rocks near Bideford, Devon.[38] Past English expertise in growing madder for
the dyers had almost been forgotten—but not quite. Miller had discovered that
people in Godalming, Surrey, remembered its having been grown there, and
another pamphleteer a few years later talked with a Mr Hutchins at Barn Elms
who had grown it. (This was significant because William Shipman, Charles I's
gardener, had also grown madder in Barn Elms in the 1630s.) Miller himself
might have been expected to know of Nicholas Crisp's plantation at Deptford a
hundred years earlier, since Miller's own father had been a market gardener at
Deptford, but for some reason he seemed not to know of it.[39] His advice to English growers was encouraging, and included the observation that they might
adapt malt or hop kilns to dry the madder. This may well have been a remark
that helped to rekindle interest in the crop in Kent, since so many hop kilns were
distributed across the Kentish landscape.[40]

Following on Miller's treatise on madder, the Royal Society of Arts between
1761 and 1766 encouraged growers by offering a subsidy of £5 for every acre
grown at home. The subsidy attracted attention and seventy-eight claims were
submitted, for plantations amounting to nearly 300 acres in all. They included
two from Arthur Young for one acre grown in 1765 and 1767. The supreme prize,
however, went to John Crow at Faversham, Kent, who achieved a yield of 18 cwt.
2 qrs. 18 lb. from one acre of ground in 1777 and received a prize of £10. The tithe

dispute in 1680 in the Isle of Ely had shown that men then considered something nearer half that amount—10 cwt.—as a good yield.[41]

John Crow had evidently brought the cultivation of madder to perfection in Faversham, as well as erecting a mill for grinding the roots. A generous tribute was paid to him, and others in the same place, by the historian of Faversham, Edward Jacob, writing in 1774. By then, however, the terms of trade had turned against the English growers (had the Dutch meanwhile made a successful effort to increase production?), and poor summers in England had further reduced the crop. The high hopes entertained for madder in 1760, and which continued high until 1771, were fading. During the eleven or so years when demand boomed, madder had fitted admirably into the local scene, and given much needed work at times in the year when other jobs were few. When hop-picking finished, digging up the madder roots had employed men, women, and children for another two months.[42]

Madder-growing may quietly have lingered beyond the 1770s. A traveller to London in 1773 remarked on the madder ovens he saw at Mitcham in Surrey and Stratford in East London, and ovens cannot have survived without madder growers to use them.[43] Both locations bespeak the continuing activities of market gardeners in the London suburbs. But beyond that madder failed to hold its ground.

The enactment of the tithe modus in 1757 had helped madder growers to overcome the difficulties of paying their parish dues on a special crop, but they continued aggrieved at the grudging attitude of the government in assisting their efforts. Resentment was exacerbated by the generally accepted view that French growers received active government help. Publicity in France had been achieved in much the same way as in England. Duhamel du Monceau wrote fifty-four pages of instruction on growing and drying madder in his *Elements of Agriculture* (four years after the treatise written by Philip Miller), and the French government allowed concessions to growers, so that in due course France succeeded in becoming a leading producer. It may well be that English producers could have benefited from similar help in the critical early stages of development.[44]

Writers on madder always emphasized the intensive labour required in cultivation, and with good reason. It was the principal element in costs of production. When George Bedford described his patchy field of madder in Appledore, in the 1620s, for example, he admitted that in Holland the growers would have gone over the ground six, seven, or eight times, if necessary, planting up the vacant spaces so that no land was wasted.[45] This was only one of many laborious operations; frequent weedings were another and the digging up of the roots another. Yet Miller in 1758 saw the possibility of using a hoeing plough to reduce some of this hand labour—in other words, a future for wheeled implements entered into his calculations when he recommended madder-growing, and he expected that with this advantage the labour costs might be cut below the level of the Dutch, who were said to buy labour more cheaply than in England.[46] A more precise calculation of costs was offered in an anonymous pamphlet published in 1765, explicitly designed to encourage madder-growing, and to persuade Parliament to extend the act allowing a fixed money tithe. It argued that madder was really better suited to England than Holland, since the English frosts were less severe, and the land was not threatened by so much flooding. But the growers needed encouragement because of their heavy outlay on buildings to dry and grind the root as well as on the labour costs, which were prolonged over three years. Admittedly, the capital costs were daunting, but so long as madder fetched £50 (or even £60) a ton the profit per acre was expected to be £50 gross, £25 16s. net, a handsome reward if men would take the risks, and wait for their deserts.[47]

If production costs had been lowered by the use of machines, madder-growing might well have continued for another hundred years in England. In Ireland, where wild madder had been regularly collected, and where in the 1650s it was said that people in Dublin would like to grow it, if they knew how to use it, the Dublin Society published in 1800 a ten-page booklet on the culture and curing of madder; the hopes of growing it there persisted much longer.[48] The prime cause of its failure in England was that the opportunity came too late. The urge to grow a labour-intensive industrial crop in the 1760s was out of tune with the time. It could not withstand the much stronger pressures encouraging a return to traditional cereal-growing. If the dramatic explosion of demand for madder, and the consequent incentive of price, had been present in 1700 rather than in 1760, it might have captured the imagination of more growers with capital resources. They could then have exploited the newly appearing wheeled implements and developed production on a larger scale. Only with this longer period of trial and error could they have reached the position of competing with the Dutch when prices returned to a more stable level.

Madder cannot be described as a successful crop on the English scene, but it might have been if the circumstances in detail had worked out differently. Even though the Dutch commanded the European market for some two or three centuries, French growers, with government help, managed to break into it, whereas the English did not. The madder story vividly illustrates the truth that new crops had to be introduced at the right moment, and needed plenty of time to find a secure niche, if they were to survive competition when mainstream agriculture returned. Its beginnings in the early seventeenth century were promising; it enlisted the interest of professional growers and serious projectors as well as light-hearted, unreliable speculators. It followed the correct path in seeking out small pieces of land in unfashionable places, and found a comfortable niche, as regards soil, labour, and local attitudes to newfangled crops, in market gardening countryside, first in Wisbech and then in Faversham. It showed that it could reward its growers handsomely. But to embark most energetically on madder growing in the 1760s was to choose the wrong time.

The chemical ingredient in madder, called *alizarin*, was isolated in 1826, but not until a generation later, in 1869, was a method devised for producing the dye artificially. In Holland, therefore, madder-growing fell away sharply after 1874; no grower could then survive the arrival of a standardized colouring agent to assist factory production and achieve uniformity of product. But fashion's wheel has now turned again, and a non-standardized, faded colour is appreciated by some for its individuality. Will madder have a chance to return to satisfy special, if not mass, tastes?

Mulberries for Silk

Keeping silkworms on mulberries to make silk was one of the failed schemes of this period, but it was pursued in a serious and professional manner, was not lightly abandoned, and its progress has left a surprising amount of information in documents. These shed light on a dream that might have made a contribution to alternative agriculture. That it did not succeed is best understood against the background of circumstances in Europe and the New World, with which the English experience was closely entwined. Some of the ramifications in establishing new crops were quite different in this case from those making up the history of rapeseed, woad, hops, and madder. Yet the inevitability of failure was as sure as with madder. It survived on the Continent and in the New World until the nineteenth century, but in England the precocious industrial revolution killed it. Labour shortages loomed much earlier.

All this prompts reflection on the long-term future for silk production, for while Far Eastern countries industrialize, and their silk production diminishes, Europe is plagued with problems of unemployment, and could certainly produce silk if it wished. Meanwhile, silk remains as highly valued a fabric as ever, and is still produced at Compton House, Dorset, though for royal use only. Thus is maintained a silk farm which Lady Hart Dyke set up from nothing in the 1930s at Lullingstone Castle, Kent, and which continued till her death. In the twentieth, as in the seventeenth century, the success of silk production is not impossible, but it is determined by a multitude of factors, of which the weather and the production of mulberry leaves are only two.[49]

Textiles made in England in the sixteenth century were woollen cloth, linen, and canvas. For all these fabrics much of the raw material was home-grown. The wool was produced on English pastures, and woollen cloth production was so important that it constituted three-quarters of all English commodities traded overseas. When a severe depression struck in 1550 and revealed how heavily the economy relied on one article for its foreign trade, the government strove to broaden the economic base of the nation's wealth.

Among the first opportunities seized was the chance to extend the variety of cloths manufactured. More lighter-weight fabrics were already entering the home market from abroad. New Draperies, as they were called, mixed different fibres—for example, linen with wool—and achieved more varied finishes. Cloths with more mixed fibres began to be made at home. As for English-made linen and canvas, these did not compete favourably with the quality of foreign manufacturers, and so a great deal continued to be imported from France, the Netherlands, and Germany. In the new mood of economic nationalism, home producers were now put on their mettle to achieve something that was equally marketable.

Statutes were passed to encourage more hemp- and flax-growing, which thus became a useful branch of alternative agriculture. It was far from being a new venture, for flax and hemp were commonplace crops on peasant farms, but it was launched on a new lease of life. To improve the standard of weaving, the government encouraged town authorities to invite foreign weavers to settle in England. This policy, inaugurated in the 1560s, resulted in a denser concentration of linen and hemp manufacture in certain parts of the country, notably in Norfolk, in Suffolk, and in Somerset, around Bridport, and much closer attention paid to standards of workmanship. As a result, the English, while continuing to produce rough canvas for sacks and aprons, also produced finer thread for lace and shirts.[50]

The urge to set up silk production and a silk industry came from a somewhat different quarter. Silk was manufactured in Sicily with Arab skills by the end of the fifteenth century, and thence transferred into Italy and Spain. In the next hundred years the industry was carried into France. In England silk clothing and silk embroidery were still a rich man's luxury in Henry VIII's reign, while knitted silk stockings were the privilege of monarchs alone. But the tyranny of fashion made silk more and more desirable, the enterprise of traders carried it to more markets, and travellers and merchants gradually made it more familiar and available. In particular, the success of the Italian silk industry in overseas trade drew the attention of all west European countries to possibilities they had hitherto neglected, and at a comparatively early date in Henry VIII's reign one project for introducing the weaving of silk to Southampton proceeded beyond the idly speculative stage to practical action. But the scheme was ahead of its time.[51]

Some thirty years later, in the 1560s, London's silk-weaving industry took a leap forward when Huguenot refugees arriving from France included silk weavers, who instinctively moved to London as the most promising centre for the pursuit of their trade. Spitalfields became their principal home; Shakespeare himself at one period lodged with one of them. At the same time, increasing numbers of French craftsmen were setting up other luxury trades in London, as tailors, embroiderers, makers of gold and silver lace, and button makers; and, since each stimulated the demand for the other's wares among the upper classes, all encouraged the establishment of their industries in this one centre. Nor did the wearing of silk continue for long the rich man's monopoly. If one could not afford silk stockings or a silk waistcoat, then a silk fringe on a jacket or silk buttons could make a satisfactory substitute. Silk in some form or other was finding buyers among the middle as well as the upper classes.

When once the silk-weaving industry found a secure home in London, the flow of raw silk thread at the right price became a matter of some concern. The sources were various: from Antwerp came Spanish silk, Bruges silk, and Genoa silk; from Bruges came Paris silk. Sometimes it was already dyed, sometimes not. The merchant had considerable choice, but quantities could fluctuate sharply. In 1600 bad weather in Italy delayed the coming of spring; the mulberry leaves did not open in time for the hatching of the silkworms, the silkworms were starved of food, and word reached England that silk was likely to be in short supply and very expensive that season. The idea was born of producing silk in England.[52]

In the early seventeenth century the possibilities did not appear unrealistic, principally in view of French success. Olivier de Serres, a gentleman farmer and influential writer on agriculture in France, had publicly pressed the possibilities of silk production there and had found in the King a willing listener. Although ministers in the French government like Sully were not so well disposed, what counted was the King's enthusiasm. He gave Serres every encouragement and facility, and accepted his advice. Serres urged that every useless tree be banished from the royal gardens to make way for mulberry trees, and evidently something akin to this recommended large-scale uprooting did occur. Fourteen thousand mulberry trees and a large quantity of seed were ordered from Italy to fill the vacant spaces, leaving some over to be distributed to others who followed the royal example. Sufficient mulberry trees were planted in Paris for the King to rear silkworms in the Tuileries palace. Trees, silkworm eggs, and printed instructions were distributed free, and Parisians were encouraged by letters patent, even by titles of nobility, to set up silk production on their country estates. Other cultivators of mulberry trees were offered 3 *livres* for every tree found in a thriving condition three years after being planted. This had the desired effect and established many plantations in Provence, Languedoc, Dauphiné, Vivarais, the Lyonnais, Gascony, and Saintonges. An Italian silk weaver was subsequently invited to France and given an extensive plantation of mulberry trees and a castle on the river, near Nîmes; silk production was successfully established there. Altogether the King was said to have spent one million *livres* on the project, and, although success did not come immediately, it was secured in the end when still more concessions were given by Colbert in the reign of Louis XIV, and a silk industry was securely set up.[53]

James I followed this example with almost slavish exactitude. As soon as he was installed on the throne of England in 1603, he proceeded to follow the example of Henry IV of France. As for the moving spirit behind the new project, it is tempting to guess at the role of Esmé Stuart, the Seigneur d'Aubigny, brother of the Duke of Lennox, James's cousin and a royal favourite. He was but newly arrived from France, was an authority on all things French, and used his considerable influence over James I to introduce many French conceits, possibly including horse-racing. If the speculation about his role in silk-making seems fanciful, it is not entirely without basis since a grant on the patent roll of 1618 to Anthony Barbatier of Languedoc, allowing him to plant and sell mulberry trees in England 'to his best advantage', so 'it be not prejudicial to grants formerly made to other men', was procured for him through the efforts of the Lord d'Aubigny.[54]

While it may seem to us to have been a vain hope to set up an industry in England that was associated with the Far East and the Mediterranean, English aspirations should not be judged unfairly, with the benefit of hindsight. Given the right conjuncture of circumstances, namely, an assemblage of raw materials, sufficient skill, and sufficient labour at the right price to compete with Continental producers, it might have found a niche. The French, after all, succeeded in competition with the Italians. The Germans persisted with their experiments into the nineteenth century. In England, however, the right conjuncture was not achieved. Even if the mulberry trees had produced sufficient leaves at the right season, almost certainly the cost of labour would have been too high to compete against French costs.[55]

Royal support for silk production gave the venture a remarkable start, and for some fifteen years no expense or ingenuity was spared. First came a textbook on the subject. William Stallenge received a licence from the King in January 1607 to print a book of instructions on the cultivation of the trees and the keeping of silkworms. Prepared and printed that same year, it was a translation of the French work by Olivier de Serres, who had played so large a part in promoting the enterprise in France. It appeared as a two-page pamphlet, illustrated with clear engravings and entitled *Instructions for the Increasing and Planting of Mulberrie Trees and the Breeding of Silke-wormes, for the making of Silke in this Kingdome*. At the same time Stallenge was licensed to import mulberry seeds and grow them anywhere in the kingdom.[56]

Royal instructions were issued in 1609 making it plain that the French king's example was prominently in mind. James urged his subjects to go and do likewise, for 'we have conceived, as well by the discourse of our own reason as by information gathered from others, that the making of silk might as well be effected here as it is in the kingdom of France, where the same hath of late years been put in practise'. With these words James I issued instructions to lord-lieutenants of the counties to exhort men of means and goodwill at the Quarter Sessions, or on some other public occasion, to buy and distribute 10,000 mulberry plants. James undertook to supply mulberry seed in March or April the following year (1610).[57] Deputy lieutenants and justices of the peace were expected to set a good example by distributing plants and seed on their own lands. James I hoped, he declared, to achieve the same success as 'our brother, the French King . . . whereby he hath won to himself honour, and to his subjects a marvellous increase of wealth'. This glowing description of the French industry was premature, for in fact it had made a halting start. The industry was not securely established until the reign of Louis XIV. The optimism of James I's message, however, was mingled with practical good sense, for his exhortations were accompanied by sound instructions on the planting of mulberry seeds, even though they did not draw attention to the length of time that would be needed before the trees would reach their full height of 6 feet. Instructions for keeping the silkworms were also given, with illustrations of the racks in which the worms were to be housed and fed. The author of the printed details, William Stallenge, confessed his inability to describe adequately the winding of silk onto a wheel, but made the promise that a man with a wheel would be sent to each county to demonstrate the method.[58]

It was already known before this date (1609) that the best mulberry leaves for feeding silkworms came from the white mulberry (*Morus alba*) and not the black. This is made clear in a draft patent, dated 1606, lying among the papers of the Cecil family at Hatfield, in which some aspiring patentees hoped to become the sole importers of white mulberry plants, 'and not slips of others, and of one year's growth'.[59] But the simultaneous discovery of red mulberry trees (*Morus rubra*) as native trees growing in abundance in Virginia seems to have diverted attention after 1609 from the significant difference between the two varieties. That they did not have the same capacity to feed silkworms satisfactorily was not fully understood for some years. Even when Frenchmen, who were

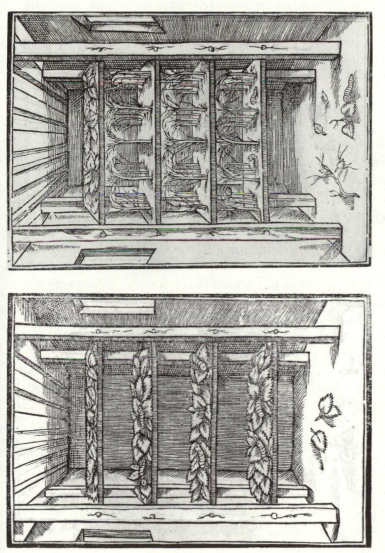

13. Silkworms feeding on mulberry leaves. Strenuous efforts by King James I to encourage silk production in England included the distribution of young mulberry trees to gentry in every county, and the publication of a leaflet of instruction. This was written by John Bonoeil, Keeper of the King's Silkworms at Oatlands Palace, Surrey. These two engravings are taken from the 1622 edition of Bonoeil's work (first edition, 1620). They show the worms handsomely housed in this instance, whereas peasants carried them around in their clothing to keep them warm. The original caption to the figure (*right*), showing arches on the shelves, explained that 'it shewed the manner to place the rods between the tables for the worms to climb up and spin their silk'.

accustomed to the white mulberry, went to Virginia to teach the skills of silk production, they at first expressed themselves entirely satisfied with the leaves of the Virginian trees. It was not until 1639–42 that official instructions from the governors of Virginia insisted on the white mulberry being planted.[60]

In England the patentees who successfully secured the sole right to supply the mulberry trees were William Stallenge and the Seigneur de La Forêt, and both subsequently feature prominently in the efforts to spread knowledge, plants, and silkworms. A list of thirteen southern counties was drawn up, and the main town was denoted in each, to which William Stallenge was to send 10,000 plants. A new contract was appended under which Stallenge and Mr Forrest yielded up their patent and accepted in lieu thereof a grant in somewhat different terms; they were to supply worms and instructions, and, if any of the great decayed towns of the kingdom planted the trees and set up work projects for silk production, then they undertook to assist and to buy such silk, unwrought, at a fair price. In other words, the patentees shifted, or enlarged, their responsibilities by promising to promote the silk industry in towns that needed more work for their citizens. They may at the same time have reduced their heavy obligation to supply all the trees that were needed throughout England.[61]

The letters to all the English counties from James I were quickly followed up by a personal messenger going the rounds of the county towns and country gentlemen's seats, persuading all men of ability to buy trees and induce others to do so. The messenger, the partner of William Stallenge, was the Seigneur de La Forêt, otherwise known as François de Verton. The trees were to be drawn from a nursery in Languedoc, and a demonstration by silk spinners at work was planned to follow at a later date. On his first journey, Verton was canvassing orders for trees that would be delivered between Michaelmas and Christmas, though bad weather delayed the fulfilment of this promise.[62] A careful report presented to the Earl of Salisbury in August 1609 shows the method used to engage the interest of county notabilities.[63]

Verton first visited Hertfordshire, where the royal letters had already been publicized by Sir Henry Coke and others, but he did not manage to distribute many trees there. He distributed a little more than half the number he hoped in Norwich, staying there eight days at the invitation of Sir Arthur Heveningham. He met a fair response in Bury St Edmunds, where he stayed four days, but had a rather less warm reception in Cambridge, although Lord Bath took 600 from him. The Earls of Southampton and Essex, Lord Brooke, and the Earl of Montgomery were staying nearby and they took almost 1,000 between them. In Huntingdon, he did not arouse much interest, and so went to visit Lord St John of Clifton, who was found at home. He distributed a certain number at Bedford, but was more cheered when he visited the Earl of Exeter and two deputy lieutenants in Northampton, who took a large number of trees from him, and distributed most of them in the county.

In Buckinghamshire the deputy lieutenant would not open the King's letter since it was addressed to Lord Chauncy, and so it was passed on to other lords, though its effect Verton passed over in silence. On his next journey to Coventry, he saw the Earl of Huntingdon in Leicestershire, who took 3,000 and ordered the rest to be taken to Leicester; Sir Henry Pierrepont, who took 1,000 at Nottingham for distribution in his county; and the Duke of Rutland at Belvoir Castle, who refused to have anything to do with the scheme. Lord Burghley at Newark took a few; Lord Shrewsbury took a good number, and tried to urge the JPs of Derbyshire 'to perform their duty', but they would not. Lord Cavendish took some, but barons Darcy and Paget, whom he visited at some expense at home, would take none. At Quarter Sessions at Stafford the Sheriff and JPs were obstructive, but Lord Garat (probably Lord Gerard of Gerard's Bromley [64]) was more favourably disposed. At the Assizes at Chester Verton was pleased with the response of Sir Thomas Holcroft and Sir Wrain Leigh, who took a good number of trees for themselves. Going north he penetrated as far as Lancashire, where Lord Derby at Knowsley took many trees off his hands and urged the Sheriff and JPs to do likewise. Altogether Verton claimed to have distributed 100,000 trees great and small and travelled 1,100 miles. The number of trees sounds inflated, but the report has the ring of truth when describing the author's mixed success with the county magnates and gentry. The project had been launched in a practical way, and could only advance past the experimental stage with the help of gentlemen of means.

James I set the first example. At the end of 1609 he paid £935 to enclose some ground near Westminster Palace for the planting of mulberry trees (one tree in the grounds of Buckingham Palace is believed to be one of these, or its scion).[65] William Stallenge received payment of £435 for the necessary trees. A pump was sunk in the mulberry garden of St James's Palace to ensure that they were kept well-watered in accordance with the advice given in the manuals. Another Frenchman, John Bonoeil, also from Languedoc, was engaged to keep the King's private collection of silkworms at his palace of Oatlands, in Surrey. A fine silkworm house was built—a two-storey brick building, with three or four rooms on the ground floor, and one large room above (presumably for the silkworms). Somewhere in this substantial edifice was wainscoting, a stove chimney piece, and in one window a representation of the Queen's arms painted on glass, for James had granted Oatlands Palace to his queen in 1611.[66]

At the royal palace at Theobalds, in Hertfordshire £50 was paid in 1618 to the Keeper of the Gardens there 'for making a place for the King's silkworms and providing mulberry leaves'.[67] This seems to be the time when renewed activity enlivened the silkworm project. At Greenwich Palace a mulberry-tree garden already existed in Elizabeth's reign, for a 'fair standing seat', probably surrounding the trunk, was constructed for it in 1598–9. But a more formal phase was inaugurated in 1614 when John and Francis Bonoeil were granted the office of Keepers of the Silkworms at Greenwich as well as Whitehall,[68] and revived enthusiasm may explain the stove built in 1617–18, placed in a fairly ornate building of two or three rooms.[69] All the manuals insisted on the need for warmth when silkworms were hatching, and while French peasants managed this by carrying the worms inside their clothing, kings could afford to fuel stoves in elegant houses.[70]

Tensions soon developed between François de Verton and John Bonoeil in their competing efforts to further silk production under royal auspices.[71] But Bonoeil had a considerable career ahead of him, particularly in giving assistance to the silk-making scheme in Virginia. In January 1617 he received letters of denization, along with another silkworm expert from France, John Laurien.[72] He then wrote his own treatise on mulberry trees and silkworms, which was translated from the French and became the main handbook used by the planters in Virginia.[73] This project went hand in hand with the English one; silkmen and wormseed had been dispatched at an early stage in the colony's history, either with the first supply vessel in January 1608 or more probably with the second in the autumn. In the winter or spring of 1608–9 buildings were erected for the worms which hatched in March–April and were fed on the indigenous mulberry trees. Virginia's first colonists set such great hopes on the silk project that they fully expected to fill the role previously played by the Italians in the European silk trade.[74]

The quantity of mature mulberry trees growing in Virginia—'as many mulberry trees as in Persia or in any other part of the world besides', according to John Pory, secretary to the governor of Virginia—fostered high hopes for the future.[75] More wormseed was sent to Virginia in autumn 1613; more skilled advice was carried by a servant of John Bonoeil who went there c.1615 and stayed at least six years; the King sent more seed from his own silkworms in 1619, 'being the best to be had'. Some of the resulting silk was sent back to England to be wound in Sir Thomas Smith's Hall, and in heavy tones the King expressed the hope that more energy would be devoted to silk-making—'this rich and solid commodity'—than to the growing of tobacco.[76]

The story of Virginia's experience with silk-making has been fully told by Charles E. Hatch and does not need repetition here.[77] The efforts to establish a silk industry continued in the New World right through the seventeenth century, and were resumed at intervals during the next two hundred years. In the eighteenth century individual states of America took their own promotional measures. At the plantation of the new colony of Georgia in 1725, German Protestant immigrants took land grants on condition that they planted one hundred white mulberry trees on every ten acres of land. In the nineteenth century the discovery in 1821 of another species of mulberry tree by a French botanist in Manila, in the Philippines, gave a fresh impetus to silk production in the United States. *Morus multicaulis*, as it was called, was easily propagated by cuttings and layers, gave abundant foliage, and allowed close planting and low pruning. Moreover, it was well adapted to the climatic conditions in most, or all, areas of America. It arrived about 1827, certainly by 1831, and many states encouraged a revived interest in silk, with bounties and other inducements; Virginia proposed using worn-out tobacco land for mulberry trees and communicated its interest to North and South Carolina.[78] Yet hopes of making silk a staple crop alongside cotton were disappointed. The cultivation and labour requirements of mulberries and silkworms at this point in the nineteenth century could not compete with existing crops and industries that were already thriving and profitable.

The same explanation must be given for the blighting of the enterprise in England in the seventeenth century. Silkweavers, using foreign silk, spread themselves thinly around England, and were not unsuccessful. Canterbury was noted for its substantial nucleus of silkweavers, originally from France. Others moved into Cheshire, Derbyshire, and Nottinghamshire. Some men schemed to set up an urban industry to revive decaying towns. Citizens of Abingdon, in Berkshire, almost certainly hoped to establish silkworking as an occupation for the poor when a Frenchman from St Omer arrived there in 1630, for he received a loan from a fund set up by a local benefactor, Katharine Hyde, and took a lease of the town's new workhouse sometime before 1634. At least four silkweavers in Abingdon were recipients of poor relief in the second half of the seventeenth century.[79] In general, however, silk production remained the hobby of men of means, even though John Bonoeil's handbook had given sensible advice to poor men, knowing that they had all the labour that was needed, and, if they could not afford to build houses with stoves, then some very simple alternatives were entirely effective.

James I's enthusiasm for silkworms did not pass to Charles I, but in the 1650s Samuel Hartlib's letters and books showed a fresh flurry of interest, stimulated by an exchange of experience with Virginia which spurred American planters in their turn into fresh action. Hartlib published *The Reformed Virginian Silkworm* in 1655, publicizing all the latest information that came his way. The Oxford gardener Ralph Austen wrote of his trials with silkworms in 1654. Having grasped the essential point that easier ways were needed for propagating mulberry trees, he was comparing three methods of propagation, by seeds, by innoculations, and by grafts. Hartlib also received news of other practical

efforts in progress. Major General Lambert, that calm and tolerant Parliamentarian soldier, was 'a huge undertaker about the design of silkworms, intending
to raise a great estate by it'.[80] Doubtless his worms found a home somewhere in
his house in Wimbledon, a one-time Crown property that was forfeited and
sold to him by Parliament. Yet another enthusiast, reported to Hartlib, was a
Mr Middleton, who had an abundance of mulberry trees and made very good
silk.[81] John Beale, the parson who wrote of fruit-growing in Herefordshire, had
correspondents as far north as Cheshire, and eastwards into Huntingdonshire,
who described their success with mulberries and silkworms at the same period,
1651–5. Some painstaking individuals produced enough silk to knit themselves
gloves, stockings, and waistcoats. But the most colourful anecdote, recorded by
Hartlib, describes Mr Castel's eldest daughter, on her wedding day, giving to
each of six or seven bachelors a pair of silk stockings, made from the silkworms
which she had bred herself. Incidentally, Mr Castel was almost certainly Colonel
Castle, a taker of newly drained fen in Lincolnshire who promptly set about
growing onions, peas, and hemp.[82]

All this effort, however, was the work of individuals for domestic use. John
Worlidge in his *Systema Agriculturae* summed up the current situation in 1687.
Interested people managed to produce 'great quantities of silk'. But the supply of
mulberry leaves was insufficient to sustain anything but a hobby, and no one
was prepared to embark on a larger enterprise, when the land could be put to
more profitable use by growing other fruit trees.[83] No substitute was found for
mulberry leaves, though it was not for want of trying; dandelions, lettuce, and
poplar leaves at different times were thought to serve equally well, but failed to
do so.[84] Worlidge lamely suggested that the King should allot a piece of a forest
or chase for growing a mulberry-tree wood.[85] The very suggestion was an
admission of the economic reasons why men, after nearly three-quarters of a
century, were losing interest in domestic silk production.

As a private hobby, silkworms continued to be kept into the eighteenth century. In June 1724 the Verney family sent silkworms (presumably, with their silk
ready and waiting to be wound off) from Claydon to London.[86] This home-
produced thread was probably going to be wound and woven into garments for
the Verney family itself. Was the silk by any chance destined to be handled in the
silk mills of the Lombe brothers in London, one of whom at this very period
(c.1718) was in Italy stealing from the Italians the secrets of the new silk-
throwing machinery that would be successfully set up in Derby? In the
event, silk-throwing and weaving made thoroughly successful industries in
Derbyshire and Nottinghamshire throughout the eighteenth and nineteenth
centuries.[87] Only in the production of the raw silk did England fail to curb
reliance on imports from Bengal, China, Italy, and Turkey.

The failure of the mulberry tree–silkworm project in England was inescapable at this period, given the unreliable supply of mulberry leaves in the English climate, and the growing of the wrong variety of tree. Worlidge attributed it to 'our insuperable sloth', but it should also be seen alongside the much longer persistence of other north European countries.[88] The explanation for England abandoning its silkworms must surely be the early onset of the agricultural and industrial revolutions which made grain so profitable by the later eighteenth century that it was unnecessary to look further afield for alternative crops. On the Continent of Europe the industrial revolution started later, and allowed another intensive effort to produce silk to be initiated in Germany, Russia, and Sweden in the second half of the eighteenth century. The German experience was especially instructive for it followed two earlier attempts around 1598 and 1669 that had failed. Yet the style of the third attempt followed the same pattern. The pioneer was the ruler of Prussia, Frederick the Great, who learned on a visit to Saxony that French silkworkers had migrated to Berlin, and so resolved to sponsor a revival of silk in his kingdom. Using exactly the same methods as European monarchs before him, he promised bounties, ordered the planting of trees, issued printed instructions, and erected buildings. Similar measures were taken in Saxony, where between 1744 and 1755 35,678 mulberry trees were planted, as well as in Württemberg, Anspach, Bayreuth, and most of all in the Palatinate. In certain towns like Munich, Landshut, Engelkofen, and Arnsdorf, city promenades and ramparts were ornamented with mulberry trees. Unfortunately, they reached maturity on the eve of the French Revolution, and the wars which ensued turned the nursing of an infant silk industry into an irrelevance.[89]

When the Napoleonic wars ended, the purposes of the mulberry trees had been forgotten, and avenues of trees were cut down for fuel. In one district, the Regenskreis, it was said that 100,000 mulberry trees were cut down in ignorance. But the total destruction of an asset that would take years to replace was arrested by the intervention of Leeb Straubing, a noble German lady, recalling the past, and arousing the interest of several German states yet again in the possibilities of silk production.[90] But her efforts came too late to contend successfully for labour and capital with the advancing industrialization of well-established manufactures, and the more urgent task of farmers was now to produce mainstream foodstuffs for a rapidly increasing population. Novel alternatives were not required.

Experience of mulberry-growing for silk, both in England and elsewhere, reveals inordinate sums of money having been spent on this new branch of farming and industry. It was a fad of kings, it promised to yield a luxury for the rich, and it could be justified by the work it held out to the poor. Its progress reveals how well organized could be a royal project, harnessing some of the most efficient resources of the administration when it also inspired the enthusiasm of the gentry. Nothing else of its kind was attempted on the same scale, and so it is a singular story. It has also left to this day a singular legacy. It is generally thought that some of the mulberry trees that still survive in our countryside date from this period and this project; when they are found in the vicinity of gentlemen's estates or in palace grounds, this guess gains further credibility.[91]

Two More Dye Crops: Safflower and Weld

Two more potentially good crops, dye plants again, shed further light on commercial ventures in this age of alternative agriculture, though they have left us much less information than madder and mulberries. As we have seen, the times were generally propitious for the success of novel crops, yet the particular circumstances in which these two plants were developed failed to ensure their long-term survival. One of them, namely, safflower, has found a future in the USA in the entirely different circumstances of the late twentieth century. In the 1930s it was being tried as an industrial oil for use in the manufacture of paints and of linoleum. The variety now under cultivation, because it is high in linoleic acid, sells as an edible oil, and is recommended to those with heart problems. Its earlier history in Europe and England deserves to be recalled.[92]

SAFFLOWER

Safflower, or *Carthamus tinctorius* L., is an annual, of the thistle family, hardy, but requiring a moist soil at planting, and through the flowering period. In the later phase of growth it needs a dry atmosphere for the best results, but a reasonable summer in England could produce those conditions. It should not be grown for more than one year at a time, but generally it does well on land that will grow cereals, and fits well into a grain rotation as a break crop. It is usually planted in spring, but cannot compete on weed-infested land, and several decades of experience in the USA has produced the further verdict that 'diseases are partly responsible for the restricted culture and environment under which safflower is grown'.[93]

Safflower was grown extensively in the seventeenth century in Germany, in the Strasburg region of Alsace, where madder also found a congenial home. Thus local growers of safflower already had firm links with the dyeing trade. It yielded a rosy-pink dye which was claimed to have special virtues when used on silk. This explains the interest in cultivating it in England, at the moment when the silk industry was finding its feet in the second half of the seventeenth century. We have noticed already how the search for home-grown dye plants to reduce the costs and uncertainties of imports had led to pronounced success with woad, and some encouragement for madder. The search for other plants continued: Dr Theodore Mayerne, physician to the Stuart kings, was reported in 1639 to be experimenting with dyeing, without using cochineal (which was imported), but using herbs grown in England. Doubtless, other anonymous people were following the same quest.[94]

One solution, that of growing safflower, was first suggested in a State Paper in 1663–4; Eustace Burnaby proposed to plant it in England, having learned the method in Alsace. He was promptly granted a patent allowing him the sole right to grow it for fourteen years. That he pursued his plan is made clear ten years later, in March 1673, when he joined in another debate. A depression in trade was taxing the politicians and economic theorists, and those who saw merit in protectionist policies promoted a bill at Westminster to encourage English manufacturing industries at the expense of the foreign. Eustace Burnaby seized the opportunity to inform the committee of the progress he had made in growing safflower in England. He explained that it was essential to the silk dyers for dyeing scarlets, carnation, rose, and pink colours, and already he had 200–300 acres planted with it; the resulting dye was 'better than foreign'. He wished to see safflower imports prohibited so that its growth in England might be further encouraged. He even conjured up a vision of the future when English safflower might be exported abroad.[95]

The bill before Parliament, into which Burnaby's clause was to be inserted, came to nothing; the committee's tangled discussion on it showed how difficult it would have been to enforce such an Act. But Burnaby's enterprise opened up the prospect, as did so many other alternative crops, of employing many poor, as well as yielding profits to the growers. Burnaby claimed a value of £14 a cwt for English safflower, compared with £11 for the foreign.[96]

When Burnaby's special pleading is discounted, the proposal to grow safflower in England can be judged opportunist, but not unrealistic. Carew Reynel, who wrote in optimistic vein in 1673 of many other inventive and novel industrial schemes afoot, all promising more employment for the poor, cited safflower-growing as one of them. His informants had spoken of £20–30 p.a. net profit.[97]

Where was safflower grown? One of the sites comes to light in Robert Plot's *Natural History of Oxfordshire* (1677), and his remarks can be amplified from Plot's notes for his book, which came into the possession of Thomas Hearne. In 1674 in North Aston, south of Banbury, Oxfordshire, Plot met 'with a new improvement of land by sowing the herb *Carthamus* or bastard saffron, but commonly called the scarlet flower, by Colonel Vernon'.[98] Colonel Vernon was Edward Vernon, son of Sir Edward Vernon of Sudbury, Derbyshire. He did not own the manor of North Aston, but he was an agricultural improver with more than one interest, since he was said to have been instrumental in spreading the 'Nonpareil' apple, brought from Normandy to North Aston *c.*1600. In 1680 he was a JP in Staffordshire.[99] Another site for safflower-growing mentioned later still by John Mortimer was at Norton, presumably Chipping Norton, in Oxfordshire.[100] Two isolated references like this are tantalizingly meagre, and almost certainly do not tell half the story. It is likely that safflower occupied land in other counties as well, for the importers felt the situation sufficiently threatening to issue a printed leaflet opposing the idea of a duty on foreign imports. The duty was the obvious second-best proposal from the growers if a total ban on foreign imports did not succeed. The growers of madder had followed the same line of reasoning.[101]

In the broadsheet the importers of safflower laid emphasis on the importance of the English ribbon industry, which used safflower to dye ribbons red and pink, and dispatched great quantities to the countries of western Europe (Germany, Holland, France, Spain, and Italy). Obstructing the imports of dye would have upset the industry, which was in keen competition with Lyons, and so do far more damage to the job opportunities of the poor. In any case, they argued, safflower was gathered in Germany for 1*d.* or 2*d.* a day, whereas in England no one would work for less than 8*d.* Not above 2,000 lb. was then being produced in England; whereas 600 cwt. was imported from Germany. English safflower could never achieve a lower price than imports.[102]

Who was Eustace Burnaby, the principal grower of safflower at this time? He was probably the son of Northamptonshire gentry, for a Eustace Burnaby of that county, perhaps the very same man, matriculated at Oxford in 1621.[103] At his death in 1684 he was a gentleman of Coventry, a city whose dependence on the textile industry, on dyeing, and on threadmaking went back to the Middle Ages. His will gave no indication of his business interests, but because he had to arrange for the repayment of a debt, owed him by his son, he referred to another of his enterprises, namely a half-interest in 'the making of French barley'.[104] French barley is a species of barley—*tritico-speltum*—which shares some of the characteristics of wheat and some of barley, and produces unusually high yields. It was being canvassed at this period as an ideal crop for poor farmers. Immediately before Burnaby made his request in 1663 for a patent to grow safflower, he had asked for a patent to grow French barley, 'at present imported at dear rates', and when he planned to grow safflower he also wanted to plant rice. Eustace Burnaby was plainly an experimenter with more than one alternative crop.[105]

Whether or not Eustace Burnaby persisted with safflower is unknown, but the interest of others was maintained, certainly into the 1680s. John Houghton printed a report in 1683 from a Henry Hall, describing how a gentleman friend had obtained safflower seed to be grown not far from London, and had recommended his sister to sow some at Evesham, Worcestershire. Evesham was an appropriate place for such a trial, since it was the home of market gardens and had a tradition of care for unusual plants. His sister accordingly leased 'to an adventurer' 25 acres of land, charging the extremely high rent of £25 an acre, because safflower was thought to impoverish the soil. He grew the safflower but was disappointed by the price of £10 per pound which he got for the dye in London. Hall disbelieved his informant, maintaining that the grower must have made 30s. an acre, above all charges.[106] But adventurers, as we have seen, always had high expectations of profit from a pioneering venture of this kind.

The complaints levelled at safflower at this date showed up problems that could not have been foreseen, and these condemned it to final failure. The English seed proved not to be as good as the German, and continual imports were expensive. It ripened at the same time as wheat and so created labour problems. Nevertheless, for a long time safflower remained on the agenda. In 1694–5 an attempt was made to grow it in Ireland, and in the eighteenth century the Royal Society of Arts offered premiums encouraging more trials. But the only venture reported to the Society seems to have been an experiment at St Vincent, on the Windward Islands.[107]

WELD

The second dye crop, which neither failed entirely nor markedly succeeded, was weld, sometimes called woold, or dyer's weed. Its botanical name is *Reseda luteola*. It produces a yellow dye, and was used also to make green colours. It grows well on chalky, barren hillsides that are warm and dry, and so found a congenial habitat on downlands. It is likely that the quantities grown in England, some wild, and some cultivated, were sufficient to meet domestic needs, with only small imports, since no official action was ever taken, and no official word uttered, to augment the supply. Pehr Kalm, on a visit to England in 1748, saw weld growing everywhere outside London on earth walls, and, since market gardens frequently had earth walls round them, we may assume that the gardeners gathered it for sale. Despite its easy growth, some imports had been necessary in the fifteenth century, as is evident in a scale of duties for commodities arriving at Southampton which included weld. At that time the weld probably came from Italy, but in the sixteenth century and later it certainly came from Flanders. But small needs are implied in John Houghton's remark that 80 cwt. of weld was imported in the year 1694–5.[108]

The principal centre for weld was on the North Downs in Kent, around Canterbury and Wye. But it also grew wild in Gloucestershire, probably on the Cotswold hills, where country people continued to collect it in the early nineteenth century (*c.*1820) to sell to the dyers at Bristol. Still further afield, it turned up in June 1996 in the grounds of Mount Grace Priory at Northallerton, Yorkshire, having lain dormant for several centuries until disturbed by the digging of the archaeologists.[109] Books of husbandry in the seventeenth century regularly mentioned it, and affirmed that it was a profitable crop, and not difficult to grow. In an arable rotation, it was planted after barley or oats had been sown (sometimes after buckwheat), and harrowed in, but no crop was gathered that summer. The grain was harvested and the weld crop followed the next year, when it was pulled up by the roots, dried, and stored. The seed was then threshed out in readiness for the following year, and the roots and stalks were offered to the dyer.[110]

Walter Blith in 1653 gave an adequate account of the cultivation of weld, and encouraging information on the profits: a fourfold gain could be expected after rent and the costs of cultivation had been deducted (at 15*s.* per acre). The grower could expect profit of between 40*s.* and £12 an acre. Another writer in the same decade, Adolphus Speed, whose book was designed to encourage experiments in husbandry, also wrote enthusiastically about weld, and probably with slightly better information. He cited the experience of a Kentish grower who undersowed weld on a crop of barley, used the field for grazing that autumn, and sold the seed the following summer far more advantageously than wheat.[111]

Yet such remarks failed to stir farmers into growing larger quantities. Weld retained a secure, but modest, niche in Kent, especially in the north-east, on the downland margin. It is found in farmers' inventories and other documents between 1680 and 1770 growing south of Canterbury at Patrixbourne, at Boughton under Blean, and at Rainham, Newington, Lynsted, Tunstall, and Milstead, all near Sittingbourne. It found a modest home in places in Sussex and Norfolk too, but did not spread there as widely as in north-east Kent.[112] Two reasons for its modest career are suggested. It was never as well publicized as woad and madder. When Walter Blith wrote his description of it, he seized this moment to lament the secrecy of gentlemen growing all novel crops. They had grown weld 'this many years . . . but not discovered [it] for public practice . . . I fear men's spirits are strangely private that have made excellent experiments, and yet will not communicate'.[113] Weld, in short, furnished a good example of a crop with a secure niche in distinct localities, which remained relatively unknown further afield. The most circumstantial advice on growing weld was given by a Kent farmer, John Banister, in 1799, but by then bread grains had returned to profit, and men had little reason for bothering further with weld. Bannister mentioned inordinately high prices in exceptional years like 1780 and 1791, which persuaded local farmers to grow weld in large quantities, but this forced the price down the following year. It could, indeed, be undersown on a cereal crop, but it throve best on its own. It was still a 'ticklish vegetable', for disease in May could ruin all and leave the farmer with nothing.[114] A further reason for its modest role in alternative agriculture was that yellow was not a specially fashionable colour, and no one succeeded in making it so. Dyers were far more interested in blues and reds. Woad and madder were in higher demand, for a greater variety of colours; so woad and madder attracted most farming interest, while weld quietly held its own but made no great advances.

Vines

Finally, an alternative enterprise which ended in failure at this time, but which has returned in the late twentieth century with hopes for its future, is vines. Vineyards have increased in number and size since the 1970s, thus conferring a fresh interest on the history of their cultivation between the sixteenth and eighteenth centuries. It is worth stressing also the age-old wisdom, which has recognized the role of vines in serving as an alternative crop, and in providing much-needed work. The first viewpoint was visible in Italy in the first century AD when the Roman emperor Domitian curbed the spread of vineyards by edict, believing that they led to the neglect of corn and could cause food shortages. The second viewpoint was evident in the seventeenth century, when the French minister Colbert, wishing to spread the knitting industry into the countryside, recognized the difficulty of getting adequate labour wherever vines were planted.[115] Vines in England were reasonably obedient to the rules of alternative agriculture, by returning to favour in propitious times and fading from sight in phases of mainstream agriculture. But when in favour they never threatened to reduce grain growing significantly, so that edicts never had to be issued against them, as occurred in the case of woad in the late sixteenth century.

Vines had been cultivated in England, possibly by the Belgae, but certainly since Roman times. They were neglected by the Anglo-Saxons, who preferred ale, but, not surprisingly, interest recovered again with the coming of the French at the Norman Conquest. When Domesday Book was prepared in 1086 vineyards are seen to be associated with the head manors of great lords, like the 'good vineyard' at Wilcot, belonging to the sheriff of Wiltshire.[116] Thereafter, vineyards were a class-based interest of rich and powerful lay lords, and of churchmen who, until 1281, needed considerable quantities of wine to administer to all members of their congregations at communion.[117] As for any possible rise and decline of vineyards in the course of the Middle Ages, such fluctuations are usually measured by historians alongside the changing fortunes of trade with France, and not alongside the rise and fall of mainstream agriculture.

But, whether coincidentally or not, English vineyards declined when the demand for grain was at its height in the thirteenth century. Whether they revived in the later fourteenth and fifteenth centuries is not clear but, as they were labour-intensive undertakings, the times were not propitious after the Black Death. In Continental countries, on the other hand, the rise of vineyards at this time is an accepted feature of the agricultural scene.[118]

We may reasonably assume that some monastic houses and great lords pre-served a vineyard here and there throughout the fifteenth century. But by the middle of the sixteenth, observers commented on the decayed vine terraces seen in the landscape. When Barnaby Googe translated the *Foure Bookes of Husbandry* by the German diplomat and landowner Konrad Heresbach, in 1577, he noted 'a number of places in this realm that keeps [*sic*] still the names of vine-yards and upon many cliffs and hills are yet to be seen the roots and old remains of vines'. He attributed their decline to civil discord (the Wars of the Roses) and men's slothfulness, but this last accusation might be turned around and attrib-uted to a shortage of labour. At the moment of his writing, however, the readi-est explanation was the need to grow more breadcorn.[119]

The interest of gentlemen had not entirely evaporated at this time, and Googe drew attention to the lady of the manor at Chilwell, Nottinghamshire, who still made wine from her vine there, and treasured a stained glass window in the manor house, depicting all the tasks in the vineyard from planting to pressing. He also commended Lord Cobham's vines and those of Lord Williams of Thame, being 'as good vines as are in many places in France'.[120] As Googe was an adventurous, new owner of dissolved monastic land himself, he included in his translation of Heresbach the passages on vines, deeming them 'worth the trial'. He pointed out that Germany lay on the same latitudes as England, and grew vines successfully, words which were echoed by George Ordish, a vine grower of experience in southern England, in his book in 1977: 'It is not as diffi-cult as might be imagined to grow grapes in England and Wales and to make good wine from them.'[121]

Vines are not infrequently encountered in late sixteenth-century documents in descriptions of gentlemen's manor house gardens. Some, of course, pro-duced dessert, rather than wine, grapes. Indeed, Gervase Markham assumed this to be so in all cases, and recommended the building of a round house with windows, so that the vine could be planted outside, and the grapes grown under glass inside. Some vines were routinely grown against a wall, and so could be protected in winter. Where vineyard sites were chosen, they might be encircled by brick walls, like the vineyard at the royal palace of Oatlands, having a brick wall eleven feet high and 700 feet long.[122]

Plainly, vineyards were a rich man's hobby in the sixteenth century, requiring larger expenditure and more care than their fruit and vegetable gardens. They remained a gentleman's interest throughout the seventeenth century, but by the 1650s were not seen to be quite such outlandish ventures, appealing only to rich men. Hartlib and his associates exchanged information in the 1650s and encouraged each other with level-headed, practical advice, gathered from knowledgeable people. Often first-hand news came from Europe, especially France, but some came from English growers too. When Hartlib lamented the neglect of vines in his *Legacie*, published in 1652, he named Sir Peter Ricard of Great Chart, in the Kentish Weald, producing yearly six to eight hogsheads of good wine, and a successful Surrey woman, making a 'fine, brisk wine'. Hartlib's 1655 edition altered the second reference, robbing the Surrey lady of her claim to fame, and transferring it to Captain Tucker (or was it Tuck?). We may tentatively restore the lady to the record by noting a further entry in Hartlib's diary, given him by Sir Cheney Culpeper, and stating that Captain Tuck married Lord Winchilsea's sister from Kent, and 'is the likeliest gent. who hath so many tuns of wine out of English grapes'. As for the spur to grow grapes at this time, Hartlib made a significant reference to French prices: 'French wine is so dear here, and I suppose is likely to be dearer'.[123]

In 1658 John Beale was writing some passages for Hartlib to publish, encouraging the planting of vines, and had the idea of editing a Latin treatise which Hartlib had given him.[124] A number of Parliamentarians were tending vines and gaining experience all the time. Some had acquired established vineyards when they bought forfeited land, confiscated from Royalists. Thus, a purchaser of Theobalds palace, surveyed in 1650, came into possession of 2 vines in the Pheasant Garden, 4 in the Laundry Garden, 28 on various walls, and 14 muscadine vines on the walls of the house, these last bearing sweet table fruit.[125]

Since the love of horticulture ignored political boundaries, Parliamentarians and Royalists shared much experience of vines with each other. The much-respected horticulturist and royalist Sir Thomas Hanmer of Bettisfield, Flintshire, wrote out instructions for vines in his *Garden Book*, started in 1659. He had travelled in Europe, offered some observations from Italy, and then, under the date 1665, described the newly planted vineyard of the Parliamentarian Colonel Blount at Blackheath and the tips he had picked up from him. Hanmer was also a good friend of Colonel Lambert, another Parliamentarian, who gardened contentedly at Wimbledon after the Civil War. Hanmer's note, dated 1669, about the Wimbledon grape implies that he had recently paid another visit there.[126]

Publications after 1660 continued to spur on those who were already sympathetic to the idea of keeping vines. William Hughes published *The Compleat Vineyard* in 1665. In 1666 appeared *The English Vineyard*, allegedly by John Rose, then gardener to Charles II at St James's Palace. The text was written up by John Evelyn from information given him by Rose when Rose was gardener to the Duchess of Somerset at Essex House. He was deemed 'the best of his profession' at that time, and had studied vine-growing at Versailles. Blanche Henrey's bibliography of books on vines shows lively interest reflected in publications until 1750, after which the subject, up to her concluding date of 1800, was sustained by one author only, John Speechly. And when he arrived as gardener to the third Duke of Portland at Welbeck Abbey (and stayed from 1767 till 1804), he 'found everything wrong . . . all the gardens, the nurseries, the heating apparatus, all were out of order.'[127]

In other words, judging by the books about growing vines, this activity remained a specialized, local, yet never totally forgotten, interest of the gentry through to the mid-eighteenth century. George Ordish, writing a history of vineyards in 1977, counted at least fifteen books written in whole or in part on vines in the seventeenth century, but then passed briefly over more than a hundred years, until 1875, when he found the Marquis of Bute planting a new vineyard in Glamorgan. Interest was then about to revive, as the third phase of alternative agriculture dawned, but, in the event, it was not vineyards which caught the enthusiasm of growers, but the production of hothouse table grapes, grown in heated greenhouses. Glasshouse cultivation spread rapidly in favoured places, with dramatic results: by 1906 daily consignments of grapes 'more or less throughout the year' were being dispatched from Worthing in Sussex; and on Jersey and Guernsey nine-tenths of the population were said to be occupied in some way or other in greenhouse produce, and the value of grapes exported to England rose in value from £104, 304 in 1900 to £156, 312 in 1904. A splendid photograph of grapes dripping from vines in the Hangleton nurseries of Mr G. Bullen of Goring in Sussex adorned Edwin Pratt's book on *The Transition in Agriculture* (1906), accompanied by the statement that the average housewife could now buy English grapes at 6d.–1s. 6d. a pound, whereas some years before, they had been reserved for rich men's tables, and cost 5s.–10s. a pound.[128]

The late seventeenth century, in contrast, was the age of vineyards for wine, rather than grapes for the table, and vines were regularly mentioned by topographers and writers on local horticulture and agriculture. John Aubrey in 1684–5 knew of Sir William Bassett's successful vineyards at Claverton, Somerset, using the Navarre grape, another of John Ash at Teffont Evias, and yet another in progress near Devizes.[129] At Over Arley, Staffordshire, Robert Plot praised Sir Henry Littleton's improved vines, and reported his making good wine which was indistinguishable from the best French wines. Like many a sceptical Englishman, Plot could not then resist adding a cold douche of realism, saying he thought it likely that Littleton's success was 'done only in some favourable over-hot summer'. But an indignant reader of one copy of this book, now in the Bodleian Library, protested with a marginal comment: 'I have made most years a considerable quantity of good wine of my grapes at Derby. D.'[130]

Kent was one of the counties recognized as a good centre for vine stocks: Arthur Throckmorton had bought his vines from there when establishing his garden at Paulerspury, Northamptonshire, in 1611.[131] But Herefordshire, Gloucestershire, Worcestershire, Essex, and Dorset, indeed, most southern counties, had fine vineyards receiving mention at some time or another. Early in the eighteenth century the vineyard at Painshill Park, Cobham, in Surrey came to prominence, planted by the Hon. Charles Hamilton, son of the Earl of Abercorn.[132] After the Revocation of the Edict of Nantes, when a fresh wave of Huguenot refugees came to England, the Painshill vineyard benefited from the skilled management of David Geneste and the French workers and tools he brought with him. The sales of the 1753 vintage, at 60 guineas a barrel, gave much satisfaction, as some letters of 1748–55 testify.[133] At much the same time, 1750–1, another visitor to Lord Cobham's vineyard, Thomas Pococke, reinforced the story, remarking on the champagne and burgundy, selling at 7s. 6d. a bottle at the local inns.[134]

A search for the most suitable vine varieties, as well as methods of cultivation, lay at the heart of all discussions in the seventeenth and eighteenth centuries, and as a central problem for viticulturists it has waited till the late twentieth century to find a more satisfactory solution. During the present-day phase of alternative agriculture, vines have returned once more to the agenda, and are now recording some notable successes in wine-tasting competitions. But in the second phase the hopes of a dedicated minority of enthusiasts did not blossom into a larger farming venture, and vines must count as one of the failures.

Conclusion

Examples of a variety of alternative crops, tried and tested between the sixteenth and eighteenth centuries, teach some similar lessons about the circumstances of success and failure, enough, in fact, to allow for some general rules to be enunciated. Ideas for an alternative agriculture were rarely entirely new in the sixteenth and seventeenth centuries. Sometimes they had already been tried once, in the fourteenth and fifteenth centuries in England, and been forgotten. Sometimes plants were involved which had long been grown, or had grown wild, in scattered places, but their commercial value had gone unrecognized. In a period of changed economic conditions, however, they were seen through fresh eyes. Their current commercial possibilities were revealed especially when experience was brought from abroad by curious and observant English travellers or by foreigners who settled in England and brought with them thoroughly practical skills and the most up-to-date knowledge of their potential.

The successful commercialization of a new venture depended on the stimulus being given at exactly the right moment, allowing the pioneers sufficient time to experiment, make mistakes, overcome them, and finally launch a serious enterprise while the economic conditions were still favourable. That stimulus was more effective still if, after a lull, enthusiasm was fanned into a brighter flame by a sharp crisis of shortages and high prices. In the interval, a few anonymous pioneers had usually persisted, quietly nurturing expertise, though exercising no great influence, nor attracting attention. But when the stimulus mounted to new heights, the renewed efforts could well emerge conspicuously at the old sites, showing that memories of seemingly forgotten aspirations had survived.

Prejudices against alternative enterprises always surfaced, like those shown against rapeseed oil when compared with olive oil, and against home-grown woad when compared with foreign. But advantageous prices ultimately overcame prejudices, and unforeseen advantages usually emerged as well. No one saw at the beginning the advantages of alternative crops in employing the poor, in revealing the merits of row cultivation, or in demonstrating how the condition of the land was improved for future crops by the meticulous weeding which the novelties demanded. While rapeseed was recognized from the outset as a useful industrial oil in the cloth industry and for lamps and paints, it was not seen as a useful cattle feed, which it later became, nor could anyone have anticipated that it would make possible the cheap street-lighting of towns.

No one at the outset could fully assess the practical difficulties of innovations as they would appear to different classes of farmers. They had to fit reasonably into an existing rotation; if not, then specially reserved pieces of land had to be found for continuous cultivation. They were often thought to be exhausting crops, and landowners either prohibited them or demanded high rents. Cultivation involved matters which, to the superficial observer, might appear to be trivial detail, whereas in the end these matters assumed major significance, and determined success or failure. Yet they could not emerge clearly until the innovators were thoroughly embroiled. The historian, therefore, should proceed cautiously in passing judgement on farmers' resistance to innovations, for sound practical reasons often lay behind the prejudices.[135] In some cases, tithe quarrels, or the heavy demands for labour at an inconvenient season, were strong deterrents. In the case of woad the requirements of a mill nearby to handle the leaves from woad fields meant that large acreages were needed within a small area, unlike the milling needs of rapeseed, which could be carried considerable distances and await processing for long periods without damage.

The financial risks of pioneering ventures had to be met realistically. Many first ventures shared risks prudently among partners, but it is rare for documents to uncover the full extent of the divided risks.[136] In an unusual case, the risks can be seen divided into eighths and sixteenths. But in the case of madder it was shared between three people, a London dyer, who launched the project at the outset, the younger son of a gentleman seeking to make his way, and a third partner who was the younger son's stepfather, a lawyer with the financial means to speculate in a new venture. Often the documents show a new crop growing on many small pieces of land, each in the hands of different landowners and lessees, and it is possible that at least some of the many willing partners to the venture in these cases offered labour in return for a share in the profits.

The land chosen for new crops was likely to be neglected pasture or waste, not highly cultivated, and so, although this did not always mean that it was rented cheaply, it was at least readily available for new ventures, though it was not necessarily on the most appropriate soil. The land is often found to belong to the Crown or to the nobility and notable gentry, and the landlords' permission usually had to be sought for new crops; here the suspicion lurks that rich men were supporting the venture for a mixture of public-spirited and private speculative motives. Yet again, in a number of new ventures, members of the Salters' Company are seen to be involved. Since they had experience in a multitude of new trading commodities at home and overseas, and so had access to more knowledge than most Englishmen about novel commodities and innovations, they were prepared to take more than usual risks. But not enough of the records of the Salters' Company survive to shed further light on their special contribution to an alternative agriculture.[137]

For yet other reasons, a tradition of deep interest in agriculture and horticulture developed at this period among English nobility and gentry, with the result that they initiated many ventures on their own estates and at their own expense. This gave several experimental crops a good start, and the interest survived into the eighteenth century. It explains why nobility and gentry were prominent in the next phase of agricultural revolution, which involved a return to mainstream crops and pastoral products with the benefits of a new technology.[138]

Information about new ventures flowed across Europe without much official let or hindrance, and, indeed, religious persecution and governmental encouragement for new enterprises accelerated the flow by sending refugees and skilled artisans to settle in new lands. But those who went abroad from England in search of new information were usually well aware that they were engaged in economic espionage. Indeed, they sometimes met with a wall of secrecy, which they surmounted only at a price. When they returned to England to cultivate their new crop, they too guarded their secrets jealously. But their need to hire many labourers on these labour-intensive crops meant that information quickly spread.

The practical requirements of every innovation determined how quickly it found the appropriate farming classes to exploit it. Vines always remained a gentleman's concern—fortunately, for it had no great future at this time. Tobacco found poor men to cultivate it on their own behalf with remarkable speed. In the case of fruit and hops, ordinary farmers more slowly, but steadily, managed to incorporate them into their business alongside an existing routine. Thus they supplemented their living from a conventional arable regime, while diversifying their crops and shielding themselves from excessive risks.

As information about alternative agricultures spread more widely, different projects were assembled in a veritable shopping list which reappeared time and time again in private discussions and official proposals. Thus Robert Payne, promoting Irish settlement at the end of the sixteenth century, commended the soils of Ireland for their suitability in growing madder, woad, rapeseed, hops, hemp, and flax. When George Bedford grew madder at Appledore, he was following in the footsteps of his father who had grown woad in Dorset, and of his stepfather, Henry Sherfield, who grew rapeseed. In short, three members of one family had a hand in three novel ventures. Instructions from the Privy Council to the Governor of Virginia in 1628, when Virginia tobacco was falling in price, urged the colonists to consider hemp, flax, rapeseed, madder, orchards and gardens, vines, and mulberry trees for silk. Walter Blith in 1652 recommended to his farming readers a similar list of crops, to add to the more conventional ideas which he had urged in his less well researched book in 1649. These were clover, sainfoin, lucerne, woad, weld, madder, hops, saffron, liquorice, rapeseed, hemp, flax, orchard and garden fruits. Thereafter, the shopping list featured regularly in the literature of husbandry until new conditions after 1750 restored the prosperity of mainstream farming for grain and meat.[139] Then the alternatives receded gradually into the background, except for certain successes like potatoes, which were by then being absorbed into the mainstream regime.[140]

Nevertheless, the alternatives had left behind a strong belief in the virtues of row cultivation and thorough cleansing of the land by hoeing and weeding, for these had been an essential requirement of nearly every alternative crop in the previous phase. The lesson was well learned, and led to the invention of wheeled implements in the arable fields. This made regular row cultivation and thorough weeding an economic proposition on farms, as they had long been taken for granted in gardens. The last word may be left to Arthur Gregory, writing from Kent to George Lucy in July 1779, at a transitional moment in agricultural affairs when mainstream farming was returning to prosperity. He wrote from a county which had embraced a remarkable number of alternative crops in the previous two hundred years, and had learned some fundamental lessons in the course of that experience.

This is the best cultivated part of England I ever saw. They make great use of the hoe plough, plant all their grain by drilling seed, and leave large openings between . . . The land [is] kept the clearest from weeds I ever saw any. I much admire their good husbandry and mode of agriculture, as they make more of their land and have a greater produce at less expense than any farmer I ever saw.[141]

PART III

❧

THE THIRD EXPERIENCE
1879–1939

6 ∿ *FAMILIAR STRATEGIES*

Introduction

A century or more of alternative agriculture began to fade in the 1740s and 1750s, and a fresh wave of mainstream agriculture supervened which would last for well over a hundred years. In many respects a familiar pattern from the past was being re-enacted, although only a few historically-minded commentators in the 1880s and 1890s recognized any similarities, and they focused entirely on monetary influences on agricultural prices.[1] The change of direction in 1750 was set in motion by the same agency as had been at work in the early sixteenth century. The population began to increase markedly after long years of stability. The rise steadily gathered momentum, raising the demand for grain, increasing its price, and so encouraging farmers once again to concentrate on growing mainstream produce. Grain and meat returned to the top of their agenda.

The pressure on farmers to change direction can be measured indirectly in population figures. A total population of 6.2 million in England and Wales in 1751 rose to 6.6 million ten years later (1761), and reached 7.6 million twenty years later still (1781). After 1791 the rate of growth per decade accelerated although at varying rates (fastest of all around 1821), until in 1851 numbers had more than doubled in the intervening sixty years, and stood at 17.9 million.[2] In these circumstances it is not surprising that the demand for cereals reached a height which farmers could not meet at sufficiently low prices to suit the needs of the burgeoning industrial population. A hard-hitting, fevered debate began in the 1820s against the corn laws which protected farmers from the competition of foreign imports. The battle reached its climax in 1846 with their repeal, though farmers' fears that they would then be ruined by low prices did not immediately materialize.[3]

The accelerating drive after 1750 to grow cereals above all else had consequences similar to those already described in the thirteenth and sixteenth centuries. Grassland and heaths were brought into cultivation in order to enlarge the arable acreage,[4] and small farms were amalgamated wherever the opportunity existed to make larger units. As mainstream agriculture moved into the ascendant, alternative agriculture retreated into comparative neglect. It did not, of course, entirely disappear. In some areas certain specialities had become sufficiently well established in a favourable location to hold their markets. This was notably true in market gardening areas that were serving large hungry towns. Quarrels over potato tithes in Cheshire, for example, shed light on some entrenched gardeners in the vicinity of Liverpool who did not need to turn to new endeavours.[5] But in some way or other the alternatives in general lost momentum, while some faded into obscurity. Rabbit warrens often disappeared entirely, being ploughed up to make way for arable crops.[6] Elsewhere the scale on which alternative crops were grown was reduced, or they did not expand and diversify any further. A telling description of the Lincolnshire fens, cited in 1881, showed how the varied crops of the past, including flax, mustard, carrots, and poppies had left the scene, and a more exhausting rotation of wheat and potatoes supplanted them, even though that rotation actually reduced the yield of the potatoes.[7] Where alternatives did not disappear altogether, the enterprise lost dynamism. From the West Midlands, the south-west, and Kent came descriptions of neglected orchards. Many were eventually grubbed up, because the trees were allowed to grow old without fresh plantings. Yields then diminished and a fall in fruit prices (sometimes brought about by foreign competition) was enough to persuade growers to abandon their orchards entirely.[8] Plainly, the demand for fruit gradually shrank as supplies shrank. By 1867 contemporaries thought that the poor, if they ate fruit at all, only ate the poorest quality, or only in periods of glut.[9] Vegetables were said to be eaten by working people no more than once a week, though in this case a different explanation was offered: greengrocers concentrated on the more expensive and exotic vegetables like asparagus, because the profit from cabbages was too small in relation to the cost of transport.[10]

The retreat of alternative produce from the farming scene was the negative side of the agricultural revolution, and since historians concentrate on its positive aspects, giving them the central place in our textbooks, the losses are neither discussed nor measured. A more balanced picture filters through in scattered documents and comments. A comparison of the 1801 crop returns nation-wide with the tithe files of 1836, for example, shows the acreage of woad, caraway, and liquorice diminishing, while hemp, flax, and hops became concentrated in a few specialized areas.[11] Rider Haggard in 1901 cheerfully reported on the time 'when grain was profitable, [and] it knocked out hemp'.[12] Another, later observer remarked on how interest in dairying had receded when mainstream farming flourished; it had resulted in more foreign imports of butter and cheese, until 1876 when a noticeable revival of English dairying began.[13]

The intervening age of mainstream agriculture, lasting from about 1750 to 1880, was not, of course, an altogether smooth and continuous period of prosperity for grain/livestock farmers. Rather, it should be broken down into three phases, the first lasting from 1750 to 1815 when cereal prices rose, the second showing lower prices from 1815 to 1850, and the third embracing a 'golden age' between 1853 and 1863 and more moderate years of contentment mingled with some anxiety about the future, lasting until the late 1870s.[14] Within every over-arching main trend of an economy, fluctuations occur; but mainstream agriculture remains an accurate description of the main goal of the farming sector as a whole. The fluctuations may well reward closer study in the future, since the sources of information are more abundant at this time, and they could well show a minority of enterprising and far-sighted farmers experimenting at an early date with different regimes of alternative agriculture which would later reap a richer reward. We have already noticed in the sixteenth century precocious developments, which subsequently launched themselves on a grander path of progress when the time was ripe. In fact, they prepared the way for larger successes in the seventeenth century, and it is likely that the same pattern will be found in the nineteenth century. Such an enquiry, however, must not hold up the narrative here, which strives to uncover the larger, longer cycles of repeated experience. The fluctuations between 1750 and 1880 were minor disturbances when compared with the dramatic 'agricultural depression' which struck after 1879. Until that moment arrived, farmers in general adhered to a regime of mainstream agriculture, and were not seriously jolted by extreme adversity. Only after 1879 was the fall in grain prices so steep that minor adjustments could not possibly save many farmers from ruin. More radical solutions were needed.

The changed circumstances which inaugurated the new phase of alternative agriculture dawned suddenly in the late 1870s. A dramatic collapse of grain prices occurred in 1879, and continued in 1880, 1881, and 1882. Wet and cold seasons ruined one harvest after another, without bringing the usual compensation to farmers in higher prices. Instead, cheap grain flooded in from North America, and farmers were warned that if the American supply fell short, then Australia could send much more. A sense of doom hung over the farming world, and some of the most pessimistic thought that the British farmer's occupation had gone for ever.[15] At the same time, it was perfectly possible for many to hope that the collapse of grain prices was no more than a temporary aberration. Many farmers resorted to short-term stopgap measures. After a brief respite in the later 1880s, however, bad seasons, due this time to heat and drought, resumed between 1892 and 1895. When the government renewed its enquiries into the fortunes of agriculture in the 1890s, some farmers counted 1875, others 1879 as the beginning of their misfortunes. By 1894–5 they had lived through twelve to fifteen years of deep depression and no end was in sight. In the next decade 1900–1910, as the depression persisted, reporters could take a longer view when gauging the success or failure of the varied measures taken by farmers to survive. But they still could not see the whole picture, for the phase was far from reaching its end. It was to be interrupted by the 1914–18 war, but that constituted only a brief interlude.[16]

At the outbreak of war in 1914, and partly because of its abrupt beginning, politicians did not expect it to disturb the existing agricultural regime, and that viewpoint held sway for more than two years. Such optimism was made possible by continuing food imports. When these did not flow smoothly, and shortages raised prices, some farmers of their own volition ploughed up grasslands, found the necessary labour by employing more women, and so initiated their own move back to mainstream farming. But in 1916 the poor harvest of that year, plus the loss of ships bringing in food supplies, impelled the government to take the lead in encouraging more land to be ploughed. This was followed by the Corn Production Act of 1917 which guaranteed farmers a remunerative price for two of their cereals, wheat and oats, and so changed the economic scene. 'Back to the 1870s' became the slogan for the 1918 harvest, and by the time of the peace-making policymakers had accepted the changed priorities, and expected a continuation of the *mainstream* trend. It was not that they anticipated a greatly enlarged demand for arable crops henceforward, but the war had underlined the lesson that it was unwise to become too dependent on food from abroad. In the expectation that mainstream farming would prosper, therefore, the Agriculture Bill of 1920 promised that price guarantees for cereals would continue, and that four years' advance notice would be given to farmers before terminating those promises.[17]

In the event, the period from about 1920 to 1939 resumed the characteristics of a phase of alternative agriculture, though some of the dynamism that might have surged again after the peace, and allowed a more vigorous and innovative resumption of alternative strategies, was leached away by economic problems pervading both the industrial and the agricultural sectors of the economy. High unemployment cut purchasing power severely throughout the 1920s and 1930s, and this affected the market for basic foodstuffs, let alone extra luxuries. A more varied diet was put further out of reach when the economic crisis deepened between 1929 and 1933, and farmers' prices for staple foods fell by 50 per cent or more.[18] Nevertheless, it was the alternative agricultural enterprises which showed the greatest resilience in these years, as the following account will show, and it was not until 1939 that the Second World War forced the country again to rely as far as possible on home-grown supplies of grain and meat, and mainstream agriculture returned to dominate the scene until the 1980s.

Pastures as a Remedy

The first expedient chosen by farmers for survival after 1879 was to lay large acreages of arable land down to grass. In short, the first action taken was exactly the same as that taken after the Black Death. But whereas a discussion of its practical problems is totally missing from the surviving literature of the later fourteenth and fifteenth centuries, the printing revolution that had taken place in the mean time allowed abundant space to be given to it in books and journals of the late nineteenth century.

Farmers bitterly regretted their folly in assuming that the boisterous phase of mainstream agriculture between 1750 and 1880 would last for ever. To increase the cultivation of grain, a strong drive had been made to plough up old pastures regardless of the destruction of ancient sward of high quality; forests had been cut down, and fens and marshlands drained. The campaign had gone far beyond sound sense. Even grassy downlands which had once produced the finest wools had been ploughed. Looking backwards, one discerning farmer described it as 'simply suicidal'. 'All history shows that that was a dangerous thing to have done', and it would take half a century for similar quality grassland to be recovered. Others concurred: it was not going to be easy to restore pastures to their former quality, and some deemed it impossible.[19]

The incentive to put arable to grass lay in the reduced costs in the long term. But in the short term the expense was high, in preparing the land, buying the best seeds, and selecting the best procedures for different soils.[20] A choice had to be made between the costs of permanent pasture or the cheaper alternative of temporary leys.[21] The best procedures were highly debatable. In eastern England it seemed better to sow the seeds along with a thin grain crop; in the west seeds were sown alone or with a small quantity of rapeseed. Not all farmers had the right skills for managing pastures. In the end most success was achieved in northern England, where the pastoral tradition was of longest standing.[22]

Much ingenuity was exercised everywhere as farmers relearned some of the lessons that they might have learned from the past.[23] J. B. Lawes carried out research into the quickest methods of conversion, and advised feeding cattle and sheep on cake, to transform a pasture of couch grass into good grass; the expense of 'fancy' seeds was, in his view, a waste of money for the native vegetation always triumphed.[24] A resourceful Yorkshire farmer reported his method of paring off fine old grassland into 9-inch square pieces, which he laid at 9-inch intervals on former arable fields. These had been prepared with a thin sowing of seeds in the last grain crop, and the new turf was rolled in. The method was called innoculation, and was copied by others.[25] The *Journal of the Royal Agricultural Society* devoted much space to the differing methods used by farmers, who could learn only by doing. Some spent much money only to see their efforts wasted as the grassland deteriorated. To help them, laborious analyses were made of grasslands seeded under different conditions. Farmers came to accept the fact that the process of restoring pastures was long and slow; no one had a magic formula for success in all situations, although later on Sir George Stapledon's work yielded wise advice when he urged farmers to spend more on good seed.[26]

In every district of England a large-scale conversion of arable to pasture proceeded, and in the course of ten years between 1877 and 1887 2 million acres were added to permanent grassland—an increase of 14 per cent.[27] In single counties, the increase was much more dramatic. Dorset registered an increase of 61 per cent in acres of permanent pasture between 1879/80 and 1894. Measured over a longer span of time, the acreage of permanent pasture in England rose from 10.5 million to 13.5 million acres between 1875 and 1895, and to 14 million acres by 1914.[28]

If grassland was not made permanent, then leys were extended from one to two years, or much longer; Lord Leicester at Holkham was thoroughly satisfied with leys lasting as much as sixteen years, though other Norfolk farmers settled for six to eight years, and Northamptonshire farmers for four years. On some downlands disheartened farmers did not even try to make the best of a difficult job, but left the land to tumble down to grass.[29]

The task of restoring grassland in these years seemed to contemporaries a hard struggle with a fresh problem, on which the past could teach no lessons. In fact, they were repeating the efforts of their forebears after the Black Death when large acreages of arable were put under grass in the same circumstances—after a long spell under the plough accompanying a phase of rapid population growth. Viewing both occasions in long perspective, we can see parallels which shed fresh light on the medieval scene. Historians have long known that farmers in the fifteenth century started to make increasing use of temporary leys in the common arable fields, and this became familiar practice in the sixteenth century. In the light of experiences after 1880, those leys can be seen as lessons in the difficulties of creating good permanent pastures. Ultimately they revealed their additional merit in improving the fertility of the arable, so that, when mainstream agriculture was restored in the sixteenth century, the use of leys spread widely. Indeed, in common arable fields in the sixteenth and seventeenth centuries, their value as grazing and at the same time enhancing the fertility of the arable postponed the need to enclose land.[30] This is but one example of the insights made possible when our vision is sharpened by repetitions of historical experience.

After the changes wrought by war between 1914 and 1918, when grassland laid down after 1879 was ploughed up, farmers faced the practicalities of laying it down yet again. Some measure of the task can be gauged from the statement that by 1923 the acreage of pasture had returned to its 1914 level. In the next two decades plant scientists laid out a firmer base of knowledge than before when they carefully analysed the performance of different grasses and legumes in the short and long term. In the course of that time, Sir George Stapledon became the leading publicist for the system of ley farming. Some of his work greatly helped small farmers on poor upland grazings to improve the feeding/fattening capacity of their lean hillsides, for his work at Aberystwyth was inevitably much concerned with Welsh conditions. (He favoured indigenous plants in his mixtures rather than those of foreign origin.) Valuable work in this regard was also done at the Cockle Park Experimental Farm by research scientists based in Northumberland. But for mixed farmers the result of Stapledon's work was better mixtures for laying down temporary leys on arable land, and this much assisted those farmers whose survival still depended on producing the mainstream crops. In due course, the lessons of those years were yet more highly valued during the war of 1939–45, when they enabled mainstream cropping to return with a more efficacious, self-sustaining crop rotation.[31]

Preserving an Arable Rotation

Amid lively discussion lasting three decades on the need for change, a surprising number of farmers in the 1880s and 1890s made no changes at all. At the beginning this conservatism was not perhaps surprising (commissions of investigation were first appointed in August 1879 to examine the depression of 1877–9); in so short a time after the onset of new circumstances, no one could tell how long it would last.[32] But in 1896 some north Lincolnshire farmers were still adamant that only one system of farming was possible. On the chalk wolds of Lincolnshire and Yorkshire, and on the limestone heath and cliff of Lincolnshire, farmers still practised the old four-course, only extending the grass leys a little. Some farmers in Norfolk likewise made no changes, despite the economic gloom everywhere.[33]

Another of the strategies chosen by those who contemplated the minimum of change was to grow more grain, or grow it more economically, in order to offset falling incomes. It was an expedient which was recognized also in the century 1650–1750, and then it hastened the incorporation of clover, sainfoin, and lucerne into the arable rotation, as well as stimulating the use of lime on acid soils.[34] In the late nineteenth century the policy was seen again, employing different tactics. Renewed attention was given to the more efficient use of fertilizers, both natural and artificial. Cattle yards were covered, to preserve the nutrients in natural manures. Dr Augustus Voelcker, professor of chemistry at Cirencester, who became consulting chemist to the Royal Agricultural Society, attracted support for a scheme of using artificial fertilizers more economically, arguing that this was cheaper than converting arable to pasture. He wrote regularly in the Society's *Journal*, reporting on his experiments with the continuous growing of grain at Woburn, Bedfordshire.[35] One of his followers was John Prout of Blount's Farm, near Sawbridgeworth, Hertfordshire, who stoutly favoured continuous cultivation without fallows, relying entirely on artificial fertilizers. Significantly, perhaps, Prout had had ten years' farming experience in Canada, but he revised his views later, finding the need for a fallow every eight to ten years.[36]

Another scheme was propounded for increasing yields by deep cultivation, combined with complete pulverization and aeration of the soil. General Sir Arthur Cotton, who had been employed in irrigation works in Madras, favoured this idea, and experimented at Tunbridge Wells, Kent, and in Surrey. Deep cultivation was done with the spade, but he expected to repeat his remarkable yields of 150 bushels of wheat per acre (compared with the usual 40 bushels) by using a steam plough instead of a spade. Lord Tweeddale had already experimented on the same lines, and another trial was in progress on the chalklands of Salisbury Plain, ploughing 10 inches deep, and subsoiling another 10 inches. Such experiments compare with the no-tillage system of the present day, though the latter lies at the opposite end of the spectrum in its labour requirements.[37]

Despite the advocacy of profitable grain-growing by new means, grain was so much out of favour by the mid-1890s that a wheat bounty was actually suggested in 1896 to prevent it going out of cultivation altogether.[38] Those who urged it feared the country's vulnerable situation, if it came to depend wholly on foreign supplies to feed the population. Yet no one seemed to remember the grain bounties introduced in 1672, which had been paid out for at least two-thirds of the eighteenth century, and which had been introduced for exactly the same reason.[39] Although the flight from cereal-growing had fundamentally changed the farming scene, most people saw their problems as entirely new, and without precedent; their attention was focused on novel ventures that might brighten the future, and no one turned for ideas or consolation to the experiences of the past.

After the 1914–18 war, among farmers who clung to their mainstream routines despite deteriorating terms, there remained a few who still held faith with Mr Prout and his regime of continuous cereal-growing, and that strategy already pointed towards a much heavier dependence on chemical fertilizers, which would take stronger hold after 1939.[40] But it was ley farming which triumphed and held back that tide.

Industrial and Other Cash Crops

When bounties were suggested on cereals in 1896, and when ley farming was much canvassed and scientifically improved, notable similarities could be seen with the strategies taken in the second phase of alternative agriculture between 1650 and 1750. In two other respects, yet more precedents from the past can be recognized.

One of these was the revival of interest in industrial crops, or, to give the enlarged group a more accurate description, we may call them cash crops since they now came to include a food crop, sugar. All phases of alternative agriculture magnify the attractions of cash crops, and we are justified in suspecting that some ventures along these lines were undertaken in England after the Black Death, even though our documents so far have not revealed them. As we have noticed, such innovations were conspicuous and enduring on the Continent of Europe at that time, whereas in England the seventeenth to eighteenth centuries saw more success, with rapeseed, woad, hops, flax, and hemp, while experiments, which had a chequered career or were a failure, were tried with madder, tobacco, safflower, vines, and silk. Now industrial crops came under scrutiny again.

The first noticeable difference on this occasion was the absence of interest in dye plants like woad, madder, saffron, and safflower. Chemical dyes were now firmly established as substitutes. They were more reliable colour-wise, and dyers welcomed, and fashion at this time demanded, consistent, uniform colours.

A crop which was inherited from the past, and which was more assiduously tested was tobacco. It had shown itself capable of being grown all over England in the seventeenth century, and fresh hopes for it were awakened in the 1880s and 1890s. It was discussed by one writer as early as 1881, only to be promptly dismissed as unlikely to succeed. But this was not the brisk verdict of all.[41] Some of the commissioners investigating agriculture in 1881 asked for opinions on its possibilities. A passage from Lewis's *Topographical Dictionary* about tobacco-growing at Winchcombe, Gloucestershire, in the seventeenth century was read out to the owner of an estate at Glynde, in Sussex, in the hope of yielding further information or provoking a spark of interest. It did not; the witness, the Right Honourable H. B. Brand (Speaker of the House of Commons, and later first Viscount Hampden) declared himself totally ignorant on the subject.[42] But the experimental urge was not quenched everywhere by ignorance or pessimism, and a long article in the *Journal of the Royal Agricultural Society* explained in 1886 how tobacco was cultivated in north-west Europe. It was intended to inform and encourage trials, for the government had agreed to allow experimental cultivation under licence. But it was still extremely grudging in its concessions, and excise officers kept a sharp eye on the tobacco fields; when Messrs Carter, seed merchants, conducted a trial on three-quarters of an acre near

Bromley, Kent, in 1886, and grew a lush crop with which they were supremely satisfied, the excise officers visited the field six times between 8 July and 13 September![43]

Apart from Carter's venture, some larger landowners and farmers carried out careful trials, and a number of books on tobacco-growing were published.[44] The High Sheriff of Kent, C. de L. Faunce de Laune, wrote about his experiments at Lynsted, near Sittingbourne, while two other Kentish farmers tested tobacco at East Malling and Faversham. Having seen tobacco-growing in America, de Laune returned home to consult a sixteenth-century book showing that tobacco had, indeed, been grown in England in the past. He pushed on with his experiments in the conviction that all crops should be tried 'in the present extraordinary depression', and he had his leaves chemically tested by J. B. Lawes at Rothamsted. Meanwhile Mr Bateman grew tobacco in Essex, Lord Walsingham at Merton, and Sir E. Birkbeck at Horstead, both in Norfolk, while others unnamed experimented in Berkshire, Worcestershire, Devon, and Westmorland.[45] The flavour of de Laune's tobacco was different from the Virginian, and seemed to resemble that produced in Smyrna, and smoked by poor Arabs.[46] Clearly, to smoke English tobacco the public would have to get used to a different taste. But such a verdict on the English product carried distinct echoes from the past, and would have been well understood by seventeenth-century smokers. When tobacco was widely cultivated in England at that time, it was grown and smoked by poor men, or was mixed with Virginian and sold at a higher price. The poor accepted its flavour, and it sold readily; it was not until the price of Virginian tobacco fell in the last decade of the seventeenth century that the government's continuous battle to destroy the crop succeeded, and poor men forsook their native crop.[47]

In another significant respect the seventeenth-century experience of tobacco cultivation was rehearsed in the 1880s, for at least some of the landowners who carried out trials openly recognized the crop as being, on their part, a 'philanthropic' as well as a commercial venture. It employed large amounts of labour, and spade cultivation was still recommended as superior to the plough when preparing the ground. For a smallholder having his own land it was recognized that tobacco gave independence because it yielded a good profit from a small acreage.[48] For these, as well as agricultural reasons, writers urged the government to relax its restrictions on cultivation, since they were irksome and discouraging. Farmers continued into the mid-1890s hankering for the chance to give tobacco a fairer trial. In Kent, particularly, the owners of oasthouses saw their buildings well suited to drying tobacco leaves.[49] The government, however, turned a deaf ear, the licence system was left in place, and the chance to grow tobacco freely was denied.

14. A tobacco field in 1886 in Bromley, Kent. Tobacco flourished as a poor man's crop in the seventeenth century, and was again proposed as an alternative crop in the late nineteenth century. The government had banned it in the seventeenth century, to protect the exports of tobacco from the new colony of Virginia, but now it allowed some trials, though the excise officers kept a close eye on proceedings. This lush crop was grown by James Carter & Co., the seed firm, at Holloway Farm, Bromley, Kent.

Two fibre crops which had been much grown in the past, and had been strongly urged on farmers, to good effect, in the seventeenth century were flax and hemp. Official prodding had been markedly successful in Scotland and Ireland, but it also made an impact in England, though the results can only be guessed at, and occasionally glimpsed, in the legislation to increase the acreages grown, the bounties paid thereon, and the penalties on imports. The outstanding flax-growing counties come to light in 1782-5 as Somerset, Dorset, the fens of Lincolnshire, and West Yorkshire; and the same counties, plus perhaps Staffordshire, would probably have been distinguished if hemp-growing had been measured. But the two crops were by then at odds with their time, and, if East Anglia is representative of the other areas, the crop was killed by high cereal prices in the French and Napoleonic wars. Certainly, it faded from eastern England between 1780 and 1810.[50] In the 1880s it might well have flourished again if the factories processing the fibres had still existed, and if the rail freight costs had been lower. In 1881 detailed procedures for growing flax in Ireland and the Netherlands were publicized, and a Welsh farmer from Newport, Monmouth, reported success with flax for paper-making. He supplied a paper mill in Cardiff, and found that his customer gave him far less trouble than when he was producing the fibre for linen.[51] Some of the commissioners investigating the agricultural depression questioned their informants about a future for flax, and found them at a loss to explain why the crop had been discontinued.[52] The most satisfactory answers to this question came from two of the counties where it had once been a routine crop, Dorset and Norfolk. In Dorset, where some 250 acres were devoted to it in 1881-2, this acreage fell further, to 25 acres only, by 1894; the county had preferred to increase its permanent grassland, the acreage of which rose by 61 per cent between 1879/80 and 1894.[53]

In Norfolk the memory of past flax-growing was still alive around Diss at this time, for a courageous enterprise had been launched in the 1850s with an eye to creating employment in an impoverished area. A factory to handle flax was built at Scole in 1854 and another at Eye; flax was being grown locally (250 acres at Debenham) in 1863, and twine, rope, and sacking were being made. But the undertaking had started at an inauspicious time, and everything had been brought to an end some thirty years before fresh efforts were made to grow flax in 1896. The scutching factory at Eye—the largest in England, so it was said—had continued until the 1860s, but two years of failed crops, when the flax was attacked by pests, and a simultaneous rise in the price of barley, had persuaded farmers to abandon flax-growing, and the factory had closed.[54] The chances of reviving flax in the 1890s had thus been killed in the previous generation.

Hemp, similarly, might have had a new future, for it had been grown in many counties in the past for making canvas and rope, and English hemp was considered to be of excellent quality. The Secretary of the Hemp and Tow Spinners' Association, William R. Storey, was questioned by Rider Haggard *circa* 1900, but he told a sorry story. The profits of grain in earlier decades had knocked out hemp, and, although he would have favoured English hemp before any foreign imports, it was now brought from Russia and Italy, and the freight costs gave no encouragement to English growers. To transport hemp to Ripon from St Petersburg cost 28*s*. a ton, compared with a cost of 31*s*. 6*d*. a ton from Hilgay in Norfolk.[55] Hemp-growing had no future in such circumstances.

A newcomer on the scene at this time, which eventually showed its great potential as an alternative crop after a reluctant start, was sugar beet. It had established itself on the Continent of Europe long before English farmers would consider it, partly because it had benefited there from state bounties supporting the new venture, first in France, then in Belgium, the Netherlands, Russia, and Austria. Factories were a necessity, and these called for capital and confidence in the future. Britain, in contrast, was wedded to free trade and the import of sugar cane. Thus, Germany had 176 factories in 1890, whereas England had none. It had had one much earlier near Mabledon, Essex, set up in 1832 by a singular and courageous individual, and another appeared in Lavenham, Suffolk, in 1868–9, but both had failed for lack of support from farmers. A third pioneering effort was the factory at Cantley in Norfolk, opened in 1913, but even that had to close in 1915. Nevertheless, it was reopened in 1920 and, joining forces with another at Kelham, Nottinghamshire, battled until 1922 against excise duties on sugar. Then in 1924 the crop at last received subsidies for ten years to help the early stages of development. By the late 1920s eighteen factories were operating, and the years of ever deepening depression revealed the whole venture in a different light. Both the reduced imports of sugar from abroad, and the new work which it created for large numbers of people unemployed at home, were now warmly welcomed. It was certainly a labour-intensive crop, for whereas an acre of wheat required 6½ man-days per acre, sugar beet needed nearly five times more—at its highest, 34½ man-days. For the farmer, however, its merits lay in three other advantages: the assured payment of cash for the harvest, guaranteed by the contract with the factory; the fact that it cleaned the ground and left benefits from the manuring of the beet which improved the next cereal crop; and the fodder which it supplied to livestock from the tops, leaves, and factory residues, equivalent in nutritive value to what had formerly been gained from turnips, swedes, and mangolds. Sugar beet became a common sight in eastern England, and then, with the encouragement of the subsidy and the setting up of more factories, it spread into the West Midlands, Yorkshire, and further afield. In fact, it served much the same role as turnips had played in the second phase of alternative agriculture, though, in the light of our present, fourth experience, historians nowadays may well recognize more clearly the value of the work which it created.[56]

The most immediately successful of all the industrial/cash crops in the late nineteenth century, however, were hops. To some extent hops had defied the general trend of events in the period of mainstream agriculture between 1750 and 1880. They had remained an essential ingredient in beer-making, and sustained demand had saved them from being displaced in the fields. Nevertheless, hops retreated from many areas of the country where they had flourished in the seventeenth-century phase of alternative agriculture. At that time, as we have seen, hops had spread noticeably, out of the south-east into Worcestershire and Herefordshire, so much so that in 1724 a government estimate showed a full 36 per cent of England's hop acreage located in the West Midlands, compared with 51 per cent in the south-east, and 13 per cent elsewhere.[57] Subsequently, hops withdrew from many scattered strongholds, in Essex, Suffolk, and Nottinghamshire in the eighteenth century, and from the West Midlands in the nineteenth century. The result was that the south-east dominated the scene in 1878. The Southwark market had become the main sales centre, and hops survived and prospered best in the neighbouring counties, especially Kent, while keeping a moderate and steady acreage in the kingdom overall, allowing, of course, for severe annual fluctuations. The regional concentration is revealed in the fact that only 12 per cent of English hops were grown in the West Midlands in 1878, even though the quality of Worcester hops was high. Kent grew 64 per cent of all hops in England, and the south-east 86 per cent.[58]

In the new circumstances prevailing after 1880 hops might reasonably have been expected to return to the West Midlands, but, as it turned out, fruit and vegetables proved a safer venture. Hops were always recognized as a gambler's crop, highly profitable sometimes (returning £100 an acre according to the rector of Staplehurst, Kent, in 1881), but in other years they were a ruinous failure.[59] In the 1840s the seeming certainty of profit from hops had caused some cherry and apple orchards in Kent to be grubbed up, while the removal in 1861 of the duty on hops had prompted another surge of interest. Looking back later, hop growers thought they had never seen better years than those between 1865 and 1877. But in different parts of one county experiences in the same year could vary greatly, and some spoke of low prices and poor yields after 1874.[60] Moreover, English hops stood in a constantly shifting relationship with Continental hops, and latterly with American hops. In the later 1870s possible competition from American hops was a laughing matter; but by 1881, when the Americans had mastered the curing process, Farnham, the centre of hop-growing in Surrey, was much alarmed by the competition.[61]

With the remarkable rise of fruit-farming after 1880, which is further elaborated below, the relative merits of hops oscillated. In a general summing up in 1893 Charles Whitehead considered that hop growers had fared well in recent years. In 1896 hop-growing was said to have paid enough in the last seven years to make up for losses in other branches of farming.[62] For certain classes of farmers it was worth the risk. A hop enterprise did not have to be large: 40–50 acres were said to afford a living, and in 1895 one report on the crop was optimistic. The harvest was judged excellent, imported hops were declining, and English hops were being exported to Germany.[63] But when assessing other alternatives, which were successful in the very same regions as hops, we can see that the relative advantages of fruit often outweighed those of hops because of the smaller risk.

Among industrial/cash crops only hops and sugar beet materially assisted farmers who were seeking alternative enterprises at this time with a view to reconstructing their systems and securing a decent livelihood, Mild hopes were raised for industrial crops from the past, but they were not realized. As it turned out the greatest success with alternative farming pursuits were achieved with three different activities, all of which women had nurtured for centuries, but which had been conducted on a domestic and local scale, without aspiring to create a wider national market. These were dairying, horticulture, and poultry production. But before we turn to these activities, which expanded agricultural effort in fresh directions and brought good results for many farmers working modest acreages, it is convenient to summarize the expedients of a numerically much smaller group of people in a different situation. These were the owners of great estates, looking for ways of using large acreages. They found them in gamekeeping for sport, in developing rabbit warrens, and, to a lesser extent, by improving their management of woodlands.

Game Reserves, Warrens, Woodlands

Great landowners in the late nineteenth century, in fact, chose the same pursuits as had served their ancestors well during the two earlier phases of alternative agriculture. On thin chalky soils on downlands, and on sandy heaths, game and rabbits took over increasing acreages, and more land was regularly recommended for this use.[64] In Norfolk, a county so hard hit by the collapse of grain that it was in a 'deplorable situation' in 1896, the partridge was described as the salvation of farming.[65] Suffolk was in the same state, farmers bitterly regretting the damage done to great tracts of grassland by ploughing in the era of high grain prices, and now lying derelict and incapable of being restored to the same quality. Around Thetford, where brecklands lay wholly uncultivated, some were taken over by game without any deliberate intervention by their owners.[66]

In exploiting the value of land for sport the gentry were helped by a fashion which had taken hold noticeably in the 1860s, when game reserves for the pleasures of shooting became the rage among large landowners. New designs for sporting guns allowed for more accurate and faster shooting, and gave the recreation greater appeal. The adversity confronting mainstream farming pointed to a way of turning a leisure pursuit into a source of cash (golf courses are the late twentieth-century equivalent). Landowners could charge shooting rents that well exceeded the basic farm rent: a Norfolk farm with a rent of £500 p.a. brought in £2,000 from shooting leases, and hard-pressed farmers were certainly not averse to seeing 'town millionaires' bringing trade as well as guns into their district. Shooting rents, in short, could subsidize arable farming, while the arable crops themselves were often chosen to serve the needs of the game. One farmer indulged his imagination further with the suggestion that game might be kept, not for sport, but on a poultry system to satisfy a larger circle of consumers. He was told that this had, in fact, been tried and had failed.[67]

Along with the pheasants, partridges, and other flying game, rabbits returned to occupy again a respected place in the countryside. Landowners showed greater esteem for rabbits from about the 1860s onwards, seeing their virtue in adding variety to the game already established in their reserves, and in increasing the number of foxes in the district for the benefit of their fox-hunting. The rabbit warrens now multiplied. Extensive areas of derelict chalk downland in Hampshire, Berkshire, and Wiltshire, and of heathland in East Anglia, were given over to them, and new warrens were laid out in fresh districts. In his book on *Rabbits and their History* John Sheail printed a plan of 1896 for a proposed new warren in hitherto rabbit-free country, occupying 67 acres of field and woodland at Burton Agnes on the North Yorkshire moors. Such warrens, being no longer enclosed by high, stout, and expensive banks, as in the seventeenth century, allowed the rabbits ever more freely to feed on farmers' grain, so they did not promote friendly relations between tenants and landowners. Nevertheless, this was a less controversial development than the sale of one depressed agricultural estate at Netheravon on the perimeter of Salisbury Plain. It too might have ended up as another rabbit warren; but it belonged to the Chancellor of the Exchequer, and he managed to sell it to the War Department at a fancy price, for military use.[68]

Elveden in the Norfolk breckland makes an excellent example of countryside which became a virtual game estate by 1900, half the land comprising warrens, while the arable was planted with buckwheat and kidney vetch to feed them. Thirty warreners were employed in the Game Department. In Hampshire, the sales particulars in 1900 of Glebe Farm at Ovington inadvertently summarized three different phases of farming fortune which had affected much downland country in the nineteenth century. Some 130 acres of land had once been a rabbit warren; these were now used as sheep pasture; but the land was again being recommended to the new buyer for game or rabbits.[69]

Not all the benefits from rabbits necessarily accrued to landowners alone. As in the seventeenth century, rabbit-farming in hutches (which were sometimes movable, like Major Morant's, which he supplied from Dulverton, Devon), was a practical scheme for small farmers and market gardeners, and was publicized in the literature. But how many breeders followed this system it is impossible to know, for the statisticians did not pay any attention to such lowly pursuits.[70] Others were able to take a share in the sale of wild rabbits after 1880 when the Ground Game Act of that year dealt with grievances about the damage to crops, which had accumulated noticeably since the 1860s. It granted to tenant farmers shared ownership with their landlords in the rabbits on their land. This had the effect of encouraging farmers to catch rabbits and sell them profitably, or to lease the land to professional rabbit catchers. From as far apart as Devon and Northumberland came news of these practices. Three groups now gathered some advantage from the spread of the wild rabbit, and it was not until the inter-war years that attitudes changed and they came to be viewed as more of a pest than an asset.[71]

We have already seen how the planting up of fresh woodland and the more professional management of old woods featured prominently in the second phase of alternative agriculture, 1650–1750. The stimulus was the demand for timber for the navy and its high price generally. Now another renaissance was urgently needed. A careful survey of English woodland in 1903 revealed decades of neglect, both in plantations designed for highwood, which was regarded as a capital asset, and those managed as coppice to provide regular income.[72] A few individuals won publicity for their strenuous efforts and seeming success on both counts. Rider Haggard remarked on the dedication of Mr Sutton Nelthorpe of Scawby Hall, Lincolnshire, who planted up woods, especially with larch and ash, and managed them on a system, justified in his eyes by his anticipating a timber famine in the near future.[73] Elsewhere, on the brecklands of East Anglia and on the Bagshot sands of Surrey and in east Berkshire, some conifer plantations were laid out. Noticeable, at least in southern England, was the deliberate attention to coppicing, which had never wholly lapsed in the years of mainstream farming. The Assistant Commissioner who investigated the agricultural depression in that part of the country in 1880–2 was evidently surprised to discover the large acreages of woodland so used in Hampshire, Kent, Surrey, and Sussex; they represented in 1881 between 8 and 12 per cent of the gross area of each county.[74] Experience on the Cowdray estate in Sussex, published in the *Journal of the Royal Agricultural Society* in 1880, also demonstrated how profitable was coppicing, while Lord Leconfield at Petworth, Sussex, explained how the business worked on his estate, leading him to conclude that 'underwoods pay very well where properly planted and well managed'. The wood was separated for hop poles, barrel hoops, sheep hurdles, brooms, and walking sticks, each purpose having its own price. The Commissioner observed finally how many fields in the Weald were surrounded by copses which 'were said to pay as much as the land would let for if it were cleared'.[75]

The tide of opinion moved in favour of coppicing in the 1880s, and the success of a few individuals in the Weald was well publicized. But in the next twenty years drawbacks were seen in the rising cost of labour, low timber prices generally, and a declining demand for such wood products as barrels (replaced by packing cases), sheep hurdles (as sheep-keeping declined), and hop poles (as wire was used). These trends stifled many possible initiatives in woodland. Moreover, foreign competitors were able to invade the English market with such timber products as barrel hoops which otherwise might have been supplied from home.[76] In consequence, copses proved a more profitable asset as covert for game than as coppice for staves, hurdles, and palings, since shooting now flourished as a sport.[77] When attention shifted to the development of high-woods, the future there could only be described as hopeful, rather than certain. It depended on some emergency arising in the future when imports might cease. When the policy was urged in 1903, no such eventuality was in sight. So the planting of fresh woods as a third alternative use for land on large estates was not then widely judged to be practical or realistic.[78]

The war of 1914-18 changed all that. The Selborne committee had urged a forestry policy as early as 1917, and action was taken immediately after the war to set up a state-financed Forestry Commission. It was empowered to buy and plant trees, and by 1929 it was managing in various ways 3¼ million acres. The Forestry Commission held its ground thereafter, and survived through the next phase of mainstream agriculture, though passing through many vicissitudes. But in the new search for alternatives in the use of land in the 1990s, we are seeing a strategy that lifts the plans for woodlands onto an entirely new plane. It extends even to the notion of a new Midland Forest.[79]

7 ∾ DIVERSIFICATION AND INNOVATION

THREE activities which had begun to expand noticeably in the second phase of alternative agriculture, 1650–1750, entered on a markedly new phase of enterprise in the years after 1879. Horticulture and poultry-keeping had been given a strong stimulus in the sixteenth century when, for various reasons already explained, contacts were strengthened with the food and farming traditions of Continental Europe. Dairying showed signs of more commercial ambition a little later, around 1650. In all three branches of agricultural endeavour, substantial progress was made up to about 1750. Thereafter, the momentum was gradually lost, though fading effort is not easily measured so long as attention is directed at more positive achievements elsewhere. While the profits of grain and meat production were satisfactory, other branches of farming effort were not closely scrutinized. Only when the prices of mainstream products collapsed in the late nineteenth century did observers recognize their poor performance in other sectors. Fresh efforts were then launched to recover the lost ground.

Dairying

As a result, dairying was a farming speciality which saved the livelihoods of many pasture farmers at this time, and some arable farmers as well. It had signalled its potential during both of the two earlier phases of alternative agriculture, and, with hindsight, this can be seen to have been portentous. Its progress was confined to certain regions only. Nevertheless, it paved the way for the leap forward in the 1880s and 1890s, with the result that some dairy farmers hardly recognized the meaning of the term 'The Great Depression'. For them it proved to be a period of unprecedented opportunities, leaving them comparatively prosperous. In the words of one contemporary, Professor John Wrightson, summarizing 'the agricultural lessons of the eighties', 'it is scarcely too much to say that modern dairying arose during the eighties'.[1]

Being originally an enterprise of small family farms, where women commanded the skills in making cheese and butter, commercial operations were an elusive, self-effacing business before this surge of success occurred. Dairying has left no abundant records of its early history, and even in the twentieth century no major surveys have been attempted until recently, notably in the years 1966–76.[2] Especially obscure is its history in the Middle Ages, though David Farmer's recent survey of marketing yields many suggestive pointers. In the period of strenuous grain and meat production in the thirteenth century, dairying for a commercial market is best documented in the making of ewes' milk cheese, which was associated with the keeping of sheep for their wool. Such cheese sales as reached the market, therefore, were linked with wool sales. This association, of course, simply reflects the bias of the documents, and gives us a record of the business activities of monastic houses and large lay landowners who were the managers of much the largest sheep flocks. But it may not tell the full story. The cow-dairying of small farms could have expanded alongside the dairying of larger landowners, but since small dairymen would undoubtedly have sold directly to local consumers, mostly in small quantities, their contribution has left no trace in the records. After the Black Death, the conversion of many acres from arable to pasture permits a guess that dairying expanded, and that is certainly implied in Professor Farmer's perceptive analysis. Sales of cows' milk cheeses were now more commonly referred to in documents than those of ewes' milk cheese, and some large landowners consigned the dairying business to cowkeepers and dairymaids who leased dairy herds from them. Thus a significant transformation of the dairying business seems to have occurred in the fourteenth century, having a social as well as economic dimension. The subsequent fall in prices of dairy produce may well be explained by the higher production of small but resourceful family farms, tending small herds, and giving their womenfolk full rein in the dairy to make the most of cows' milk.[3] A momentary glimpse of a monastic house at Sibton, Suffolk, establishing a dairy herd, on a seemingly commercial scale, suggests a venture that would have been more wisely devised for domestic needs only, since this farming speciality flourished best in the hands of small cow-keepers.[4]

With the return to mainstream farming pursuits after 1500, dairying faded from the record once more, emerging to prominence again only in the mid-seventeenth century, when another phase of alternative agriculture dawned. The evidence is still meagre, but reverberations of the expanding opportunities in dairying are clearly heard, when for the first time in Parliamentary debates, in 1650, legislation was called for to control the abuses of middlemen in the butter and cheese trades. The result was a statute to regulate weights and packing, the first statute to concern itself with dairying for a hundred years. It was followed by another in 1662–3, yet more complaints against cheesemongers in the 1670s, and another statute in 1692.[5] By then a far more diversified internal trade in dairy produce existed alongside a modest export trade, and evidence accumulates of some bold, larger-scale dairy farm enterprises in select areas, such as the Cheshire and north Shropshire plains.[6]

The favourable circumstances for dairying lasted until about 1750, when mainstream agriculture resumed momentum. After that, dairying failed to improve its standards or to enlarge its horizons, and in the view of a later commentator, William Bear, it was the passivity of dairymen which allowed importers to invade the market, and secure a firm place for their foreign butter and cheese. Only when the next crisis called for an alternative agriculture did dairying stimulate revived interest. Its potential for growth at that date might then have been thought to lie primarily in the expansion of cheese and butter production—the direction in which it developed on the Continent of Europe. But in England rapid industrialization in towns opened up the greatest opportunities for the sale of liquid milk to city dwellers. Since this was accompanied by the steady spread of railways, giving more and more dairy farmers access to hitherto inaccessible markets, dairying expanded mainly to satisfy the demand for milk. The result was that foreign competitors in the 1870s invaded the English market for butter, margarine, and cheese, and in 1897 it was said that 50 per cent of English consumption was supplied from abroad.[7]

The demand for milk in towns, and some highly favourable milk prices for farmers, had already made their impression on the dairymen in the 1860s and 1870s, before the grain market collapsed. One writer calls these 'the heady years', for they were responsible for launching dairying into new growth.[8] The British Dairy Farmers' Association was founded in 1876, and a journal and an annual show in London were started. Thereafter, events encouraged still higher production; milk prices tended to fall in the 1880s, but a fall in costs occurred at the same time and kept the business profitable. Overall, the period from the 1880s until 1914 saw an expansion of dairying, despite short-term doubts and lapses.[9] A study of one county—Lancashire—shows the stimulus of demand: an increase of population of about 50 per cent between 1867/71 and 1894/8, led to a per capita rise in milk consumption of about 25 per cent.[10]

In short, the need for alternative farming pursuits after 1879 gave dairying a new lease of life, but it put milk sales at the head of the list of saleable products. James Long of Graveley manor, near Stevenage, in Hertfordshire, wrote farsightedly about the many tasty cheeses which were becoming popular with the English, but which were imported from abroad. Soft cheeses, Camembert, Brie, Gorgonzola, skimmed-milk cheese—all offered scope to the English dairy farmer if only he was willing to learn a lesson from the foreigner.[11] If Long's view had prevailed, butter- and cheese-making might have returned to the path on which it had been launched with considerable promise between 1650 and 1750. But, despite exhortations and foreign examples, this did not happen. Positive efforts in that direction were certainly made. H. M. Jenkins, Secretary of the Royal Agricultural Society and editor of its *Journal*, made a study of dairying in the Netherlands and published his findings in the *Journal* in 1882. He also went to Denmark, reporting his experiences to the Royal Commission on Agriculture, and giving his account wider publicity in the *Journal* in 1883.[12]

As the lessons from abroad were absorbed, critics viewed the dairying business at home, and directed their most cogent demands not at increasing the variety of produce, but at standardizing its quality, so that it could compete with imports. This plainly required a shift to factory production, and to that end the first steps were taken by Lord Vernon in Derbyshire, who set up a factory at Sudbury with American expertise. In 1894 it was said to be the largest in the kingdom.[13] His example persuaded others to follow suit, so that at least six factories were in operation by 1874, and more still by 1894. Twenty-seven factories were at work in Derbyshire and north Staffordshire alone at that date, and large landowning noblemen set up more elsewhere, the Duke of Westminster in Cheshire, Lord Hampden at Glynde in Sussex, and Lord Spencer in Northamptonshire. In the course of this transformation, women lost their prime place in dairying, and it became a scientific operation, standardizing output and directed by men.[14]

Some forms of co-operation in dairying were urged upon small farmers at this time, in order to give them a more secure future, even if it did not help the dairywomen.[15] But milk held most attraction for producers. Where railways gave reasonable access to large towns, the demand for liquid milk was sufficiently assured, and at a rewarding price, to prevail financially over all arguments in favour of expanding the making of English cheese and butter. Profits were cited in 1865 of £18 per cow for liquid milk, £16 for cheese, and £15 for butter.[16] Moreover, the English dairy farmer faced stiff and ever increasing competition from foreign cheese and butter, whereas he had no foreign competitors for his fresh milk.[17] In consequence, dairying for the sale of liquid milk expanded in step with the opening up of more branch railway lines; indeed, some arable parishes west of Salisbury Plain were wholly transformed into pastoral parishes when rail transport arrived. Migrant farmers from Scotland who took up vacant farms in the Midlands and Essex also brought dairying to places where it was not hitherto a speciality.[18] Only the dairying areas with less easy access to railway transport, such as parts of Lancashire, the Lake District, Dorset, Devon, and Cornwall, continued to make farmhouse cheese and butter, adapting their recipes to suit changing market tastes and holding the loyalty of a discriminating clientele for their local specialities.[19]

Contemporaries living through these years recognized a dramatic transformation of the dairying industry. John Prince Sheldon in 1908 marvelled at 'the exalted position which dairy farming fills today as compared with forty years ago'. People who drank nine gallons of milk in a year in 1861 were drinking fifteen gallons in 1900.[20] Even fashion lent a hand, when soda and milk became a fashionable drink, while the form of milk consumption was varied further by the addition of condensed milk from 1881 onwards.[21]

The war years, 1914–18, set back this growth, but did not halt it entirely for, although much grassland was ploughed up, the nutritional value of milk was now emphasized, large numbers of men having been rejected as unfit for the army. This drew public attention to the quality of the English diet: more milk was urged for children, while judicious price-fixing assisted the new regime.[22] After the war dairying continued to expand in old, and into new, areas of the country. The need for rapid transport no longer confined it to areas near railway lines, for it could be carried by road. By 1925 milk and dairy production was 16 per cent higher than in 1908, and by 1930 milk alone represented roughly one-quarter of all agricultural production. Viscount Astor and Seebohm Rowntree in 1938 dramatically proclaimed milk to be 'the most important product of British agriculture . . . far more truly the cornerstone of our agriculture than wheat'.[23] This branch of alternative agriculture had come a long way since 1880. In the long term, however, seen from the viewpoint of the late twentieth century when multitudinous varieties of cheese are so boisterously successful in the market, it is perhaps regrettable that the success of liquid milk diverted the English farmer from any vigorous efforts to revive and expand cheese (and butter) production.[24]

Horticulture

If dairying became the notable success story for pasture farmers in old grassland areas, and in some that were far from old, the comparably successful alternative in traditional arable areas was horticulture. It was a spectacular development, far surpassing the dreams of those who had first fostered it in the seventeenth century, and revolutionizing perceptions of its role in the economy. The word 'horticulture' was not at first used to describe it, for that was a word inherited from the past, and signified the growing of vegetables and fruit in gardens. The land so used was of garden size, and commercial operations were therefore distinguished as 'market gardens'. Developments in the period 1880–1914, however, set the business on a much broader path, until it emerged eventually on the same scale as mainstream farming. The biggest enterprises began to use glasshouses, and large storehouses for produce, until they finally called for as much capital investment as any corn/livestock farm. In the light of such expansion, the word 'horticulture' eventually acquired a different meaning, and nowadays has all but lost its association with gardens. It is a specialist branch of farming, having, it is true, a different structure and routine from mainstream agriculture, but carried on on a scale that resembles farming more than gardening.[25]

In the 1880s, when the business began to be transformed, and before it became a confident, independent branch of agriculture, fruit and vegetable production was likely to be described as 'Garden Farming', or 'Market Garden Farming', and to be recommended to cereal farmers as a supplement to their existing enterprises.[26] A review of various books on horticulture, published in the *Quarterly Review* in April 1888, was given the running headline in that journal of 'Garden Farming', and Charles Whitehead, one of its most eloquent advocates, writing 'Hints on Vegetable and Fruit Farming' for the *Journal of the Royal Agricultural Society* in 1882 addressed his remarks to farmers, not gardeners. He did not wish them to overturn their existing routines; rather he urged them to incorporate some vegetables into their conventional rotations or add a few acres of fruit.[27] At another time, Whitehead urged the business as something more than a sideline, on what he called 'peasant proprietors'; it had become clear by then that *lessees* of garden land could not be sure, when surrendering their land, of securing compensation for all the money invested in improving its soils. Experience on the Continent had also shown that horticulture was ideally suited to peasants who were owners. Other writers, however, recommended fruit- and vegetable-growing to a far wider circle: John Wright wrote *Profitable Fruit Growing for Cottagers and Small Holders of Land* in 1890, and Brian Wynne expected more readers still for *Our Hardy Fruits: A Practical Guide to their Cultivation for Landowners, Tenant Farmers, Cottagers, and Allotment Holders.* In other words, horticulture was taking the first steps towards its total transformation, and was reckoning to accommodate the smallest growers alongside the large.[28]

Writers advocating vegetables and fruit as an alternative agriculture saw its potential for growth in several different directions, provided that certain essential conditions were met. Growers needed land near large towns, or easy transport to them. The spread of the railways was quickly enlarging those opportunities, but freight charges were high, and provoked constant complaint. Reductions in cost were being fought for, while, at the same time, the introduction of new transport links changed the economic landscape every year: it enabled the Isle of Axholme, for example, to achieve remarkable success when once it could send its celery to Sheffield.[29]

It no longer appeared essential for horticulture to be confined to a few naturally suited market-garden soils. These plainly helped, and in the seventeenth century they had been deemed an essential condition for success, but now they no longer dictated the location of gardeners. The excellent soils in use around London were recognized as being man-made, and so long as town manure was available to maintain fertility, more such soils could continue to be manufactured. On Rixton Moss, Lancashire, indeed, the making of its garden soils is remembered to this day by descendants of the original families. Their forebears laboured for twelve years around 1879, adding marl and night soil from Manchester before they turned oozy bogland into a fertile condition for vegetables. Similarly, in the Tamar valley between Devon and Cornwall, smallholders striving for early soft fruits pulled up soil from the valley bottom, using pulleys and sledges, to clothe the thin-soiled slopes; and around Mount's Bay in Cornwall, where they layered composted haulm with sand and seaweed, 'there were always farmers down on the beach loading seaweed on to carts.' John Hargreaves, who recently recorded these heroic efforts, reckons that 3–4 feet of soil were thus added.[30]

Most remarkable and singular of all, perhaps, in making their own soils were the mushroom farmers, growing their produce out of doors on banks composed almost entirely of horse manure. They spent nothing on costly structures; only canvas sheeting was sometimes draped across the banks to conserve heat. They gathered their crops continuously for nine months of the year, from September to the following June. Theirs was agreed to be the greatest success story in all the horticultural ventures of this age, and it was publicized by John Wright in a book of which the first edition sold out in weeks, the second edition within a year, and the third, fourth, and fifth editions had appeared by 1887. The master of the art was J. F. Barter, living at Portland House, Lancefield Street, off the Harrow Road in London, working with a little over one acre of ground. He paid generously for fresh horse manure, specially collected for him from London stables by a trusted man who rejected all supplies where the grooms gave their horses much medicine, or where carrots were consumed. Barter earned his entire living from the mushrooms and the making of spawn, and in one year sent over two tons to Covent Garden market; he even anticipated the day when he would send five tons. Fervently believing that mushrooms should not remain the luxury of the affluent, he generously gave detailed information on his procedures, showing his extreme care in handling the manure, maintaining the right temperature, and selling it on when exhausted to London parks and square gardens. His advice was thoroughly down-to-earth: 'you must start small', he urged, as he had done seven years earlier. The profits from such enterprises were startling. Whereas the value of one acre of potatoes was reckoned at

15. Mushroom-growing with manure from London stables. The expert on mushroom growing in the 1880s was Mr J. F. Barter, living at Portland House, Lancefield Street, off the Harrow Road in London, and working on little more than one acre of land nearby. He earned his entire living from this one crop, grown out of doors, without any costly buildings. He picked a crop steadily from September to June, and only missed picking for one week during one severe winter. He had originally been a carpenter, but thought he could improve on the system which one of his relatives used in a small way. He thought his method far superior to the French method of growing mushrooms in caves, and after seven years was supplying Covent Garden with two tons a year, intending to increase that quantity to five tons. His method was explained in J. Wright, *Mushrooms for the Million*, 4th edn., 1886, from which these illustrations are drawn.

£100, of onions £192, of blackcurrants £168, of filberts £200, and of tomatoes in a good season £300, the clear profit of one acre of mushrooms with half an acre of ground for storing the manure was given as £950. Better still, Mr Dunn, a gardener to Colonel Gascoigne of Parlington Hall, Leeds, calculated his profit at £1,600 an acre. Wright's book encouraged many more growers with modest amounts of land, keen enthusiasm, and an eye for detail. Three tons of home-grown mushrooms were said to be sold at Covent Garden every week; and doubtless they had an excellent flavour.[31]

Many contemporaries quickly recognized their opportunities at this time for widening the demand for vegetables and fruit by bringing them to more people socially and geographically, and by reducing their price. Working people ate very little in the way of fruit or whole vegetables except in times of glut. A vivid glimpse of the limited purchase of vegetables by working-class families was given from Lancashire, where the peat of Chatmoss was being turned into extremely fertile market-garden land. Its sprouts were cut up with shabby cabbages, leeks, and parsley, and sold in a mixture for making vegetable pottage or soup.[32] In other words, the pottage of the medieval peasant was still recognizably a mainstay of poor men's diet. Although many improved vegetables had been introduced in the early modern period, and they survived and passed into the new age, they were still reaching the tables of working people in a traditional stewed form.

As journalists urged the sound economics of more horticulture, existing market gardeners of the old style feared the prospect of more intense competition from farmers, and were not persuaded by the argument that supply positively created demand. They could not, however, deny that the bulk of existing produce went only to large centres of population, and never reached small towns in any quantity; a large untapped market lay in wait there. Also fruit was still a mainly middle-class luxury, which the working class would share if only the price were right. A noted market gardener at Woodlands Farm, near Putney, William John Lobjoit, of French origin and, therefore, we may assume, conversant with French tastes in these matters, saw no reason why consumption could not increase fivefold, allowing households to eat vegetables not once, but five days a week.[33]

The basis of commercial fruit- and vegetable-growing had been laid in the second phase of alternative agriculture, in the seventeenth century, and from that base the first promising fresh green shoots now appeared. With a few notable exceptions, as at Evesham in Worcestershire, horticulture had been concentrated in southern, and indeed, south-eastern England. Now it expanded from that centre, spreading outward from the familiar sites around London, invigorating some modest but long-standing traditions in areas like the south-west of England, and, as the commercial prospects brightened, moving into wholly new territory. The total increase cannot be gauged statistically, for it was never reliably measured at the time. As always, observers woke up too late to the importance of these activities, and did not adequately record all aspects of an endeavour in which all classes working the land were making different contributions. But all the figures that were produced suggested growth—rather too slow for the propagandists in the 1880s—but gathering pace in the 1890s and in the first decade of the twentieth century.[34] More convincingly, all visitors to market-gardening areas saw with their own eyes impressive evidence of expansion. In the seventeenth century, market gardens of 2-3 acres were common, and 15 acres unusually large; the London Gardeners' Company had laid down a maximum size of 10 acres per gardener in 1649, though members evaded the restriction. Now, although some gardeners still made a satisfactory living from 15 acres, and 25-30 acres was cited as the usual size in Cambridgeshire, others were cultivating 120, 140, over 200 acres, and a few far more still.[35] A fruit farm in the Teme valley in Herefordshire was a 500-acre enterprise around 1900, Mr Wilkin at Tiptree Farm in Essex had 300 acres, and at Orpington and St Mary Cray, Kent, Messrs William and Edward Vinson had 1,000 acres of strawberries and raspberries.[36]

At the beginning of the agricultural depression, the total acreage of market gardens in 1881 was reckoned at 440,000, though this was an underestimate since it did not include the considerable acreages already cultivated with fruit and vegetables by farmers; cabbages, broccoli, kidney beans, carrots, and peas were already field crops. Between 1872/3 and 1880/1 the increase of market gardens was greater outside southern England than inside, and only 21 per cent were located in the south-east. Orchards, which in 1872 were only 156,007 acres, had risen by 1909 to 245,657 acres. Soft fruit was so little regarded as a commercial proposition that no figures at all were collected before 1887 (though other agricultural statistics had been gathered since 1866). After that, a rise was measured from 32,776 acres in 1888 to 69,610 acres in 1896.[37] Such acreage increases, presented officially henceforward, looked impressive enough, but they could not gauge the full achievement, which had to be judged as well by the quality of the produce, the density of cultivation, and the higher yields.

The local history of the many market-garden areas developing in scattered but rationally chosen areas round England at this time deserves a study to itself, for each had its individual history. While the whole business expanded in a mood of enthusiasm, ingenuity, and willingness to undertake novel ventures, each district underwent its own pattern of change as new influences and new opportunities arose. Sometimes change was forced by external competition, sometimes improved procedures were adopted by examples set within the region. Different regions learned to dovetail their efforts to exploit their seasonal advantages.[38] The busy, sometimes exhilarating, but sometimes disappointing, scene can only summarily be described.

Fruit-growing was inextricably mixed with vegetable-growing, in the same areas, and frequently on the same farms. A mixture was positively recommended in the end, which was called in 1899 'the Kent system'.[39] Rows of fruit trees in orchards were separated by rows of vegetables, so that no land was left idle which could accommodate a crop. At Evesham, for example, Rider Haggard described broad beans, lettuces, parsley, potatoes, cabbages, and radishes growing between fruit trees. At Ledbury, Herefordshire, soft fruits were grown between standard fruit trees on a farm of 40 acres. Vegetable growing, however, was not always mixed with fruit. In the fens of Lincolnshire vegetables were sometimes cultivated alone, like the celery grown in every fourth row of potatoes.[40] A multitude of alternative regimes were being tried and tested in different districts.

When journalists described the heroic scene they selected the outstanding instances. A district around Penzance, Cornwall, drew their attention in the south-west, furnishing markets with fruit and vegetables like early broccoli and cauliflowers.[41] The Evesham–Pershore area had a continuous history of market gardens since the Middle Ages and was again forging ahead with hard and soft fruits and vegetables. In 1889 its fruit land had increased by a quarter since 1845; its asparagus was a noted speciality until disease struck.[42] Round London the counties of Surrey, Middlesex, Kent, Essex, and Hertfordshire received many visits from journalists, and were given the maximum publicity.[43] Then came Bedfordshire, noted for its onions; at one time a train-load per day was dispatched to Manchester until foreign growers by the late 1890s mounted stiff competition. They did not, however, oust from favour the silver-skinned onion of Biggleswade. Bedfordshire cucumbers were also welcomed in Manchester until locally grown hothouse cucumbers stole some of the market.[44] In parts of Cambridgeshire, especially round Wisbech, market gardens brought unaccustomed prosperity to local populations. The Isle of Axholme proved to be another area ideally endowed, having an old tradition of small farmers, and seizing the chance to use its fine soils and good transport to feed the industrial north with potatoes and celery.[45] The newly drained mosses of Lancashire presented severe competition when their cultivators concentrated on garden crops, but Lincolnshire's celery growers managed to avoid a collision of interests by their different seasonal pattern of production.[46]

One of the supreme advantages, which horticulture eventually enjoyed as this phase of development moved on, was something that could not have been predicted at the outset; it benefited from scientific advances in food preservation, refrigeration, and improved transport. Without these its expansion would have been cut short; with them, a marketing revolution was set in motion which spurred further endeavours to increase production. In the seventeenth and early eighteenth centuries most fruit and greenstuff had had to be eaten fresh, despite much effort put into devising ways of storing it through the winter. The storage problem partly explains why so many different varieties of the same fruit were cultivated; they overcame some of the difficulty by ripening at different times. One or two books of advice on this score were published, and it is likely that some skill lingered long in manor houses which had the room to store produce in cool cellars, in barrels and straw, and had the servants to make syrups, and distil essences.[47] But it could not be a routine activity among classes below the gentry. Now mounting success on the side of production intensified the pressure to solve long-term storage problems.

Making cider and perry, of course, was one way of storing apples and pears, and in orchard districts, after long neglect, very considerable improvements were made to the quality of these two liquors. Something of their commercial potential had been glimpsed in the second phase of alternative agriculture between 1650 and 1750, but the project had then fallen into the background again. In 1888, when interest revived, the past history of cider was described by D. R. Chapman thus: neglect had set in in the 1740s, when farmers concentrated on cereals and cattle because they fetched high prices. Now the fruit trees needed to be either regrafted or uprooted.

In an unexpected move in 1876-85, the present made contact with the past, through an edition of *Herefordshire Pomona*. Its title recalled John Evelyn's *Pomona*, originally printed with his *Sylva*, as 'an appendix concerning fruit trees in relation to cider'. In fact, this was something different, inspired by members of the Woolhope Naturalists' Field Club, tramping the fields in search of fungi, and dismayed by the neglected condition of the orchards. According to Chapman, it was their book which sparked a fresh interest in fruit and its potential in that county.[48] Rider Haggard in 1902 took no rosy view of Herefordshire's fruit drinks then on sale, describing some family cider as tasting of steel filings mixed with vinegar and mud. But thoughtful and well-informed remarks by Charles W. Radcliffe Cooke, owner of a cider works, chairman of the National Association of Cidermakers, and MP for Hereford, revealed the renewed attention that the professionals were giving to cleanliness and selecting the best fruit varieties. The medicinal properties of cider were also underlined, while one writer urged a new product, the distillation of perry to make a brandy, as practised in Germany. At Rampton, Cambridgeshire, yet another liquor was being made, using gooseberries to make so-called champagne, a venture which nowadays would doubtless provoke a European lawsuit.[49]

Some contemporaries made passing references to crystallizing fruits and fruit-bottling, but neither processes developed in Britain on any scale.[50] The one fruit enterprise which forged ahead rapidly was jam-making. It had been held back by high sugar prices, but in the 1850s and 1860s sugar fell in price, and in the early 1870s jam ceased to be a luxury in rich men's diet, and could be eaten by all. Lord Sudeley set up a jam factory at Toddington, Gloucestershire as an annexe to his fruit farm, and his example was followed elsewhere; factories multiplied, for the demand seemed almost limitless.[51] Exports overseas increased also for England was now said to enjoy 'the cheapest sugar in the world'. For cheap jams apples were used to add bulk to other fruits, thus using up some of the apple harvest. But plum and damson jams were the favourites in the market, and this explains the enthusiasm for the new planting of so many damson and plum trees, and why the celebrated yellow plum of Evesham scored such success at this time.[52]

Preserving fruit and vegetables by drying them was a new method which was introduced from America and Canada in 1888, where the same agricultural depression had likewise boosted horticulture and posed the same storage problems. It seemed at first sight to hold out possibilities in England too. The first evaporator, the Ryder machine, a simple piece of farm equipment, was shown at Nottingham, and 2,000 such machines were already said to be in use in America by 1888 in western New York state alone. Apples, peaches, plums, and raspberries were all being dried.[53] The dryer was next manufactured under licence in Germany, and in 1896 Augustus Voelcker demonstrated it at Leicester. But the reason for the Englishman's reluctance to take it up then became clearer: a total absence of fresh garden produce in Germany between November and April made drying the greatest attraction in that country, whereas it had fewer merits in England; fresh fruit and vegetables, said Voelcker, were available in England all the year round.[54]

Voelcker had urged the cause of vegetable-drying most vehemently when the English had to buy dried onions from Germany to feed the soldiers they sent to quell disturbances in Ashanti, West Africa, in 1895–6; it was deemed a humiliating experience. But a single emergency of that kind was hardly a strong enough incentive to start a new industry.[55] Nevertheless, fruit-drying trials were held by Lord Sudeley at Toddington, and in Kent at Tunbridge Wells and Maidstone. But English fruit was found to have a much higher water content than that of hotter climates, and drying did not seem an economic proposition in competition with other countries. In any case, English fruit and vegetables were generally sold fresh, and found a satisfactory market. Only in scattered places were methods of preserving purposefully pursued, as, for example, in the Biggleswade area of Bedfordshire, where pickling flourished.[56]

When fruit-farming is discussed nowadays, nut trees are not usually auto-matically included as part of the same endeavour. In the seventeenth century, however, they were taken for granted in the orchard, and, as we have seen already, walnuts spread so widely in parts of Surrey that the walnut fair in Croy-don in the autumn was a celebrated event for Londoners.[57] The tradition of growing nut trees was still alive at the end of the nineteenth century, and George Bunyard in his book on *Fruit Farming for Profit*, 1899, devoted a whole chapter to walnuts and chestnuts. Small chestnuts were used as cattle fodder, while the larger ones were marketed. Walnuts were pickled or sold ripe, and were singled out by Bunyard as the most generally appreciated of table fruits. In addition, walnut wood was prized for furniture and for making gunstocks.[58]

Two other promising nuts, which entered the discussion in these years were the filbert and the cobnut, always named when the orchards of the Greensand escarpment overlooking the Weald of Kent were described. The tradition of nut-growing in this area went back centuries, since pig-keeping in the woods was evident in Domesday Book, and nuts were a basic foodstuff for autumn fat-tening. If they included filbert trees, as Charles Whitehead who lived in the area (at Barming, near Maidstone) thought, then some change of variety must have begun around 1870, replacing the filbert with the cobnut because it was a larger nut yielding better crops and selling better. In some years the harvest was said to be 'very remunerative', and hopes of a possible new market for cobnuts loomed in America when an adventurous salesman saw them well received by the epi-cures of New York. Owners of land on long lease were therefore urged to plant more, and, judging by the survival of considerable plantations of cobnuts to this day in the same area (and now attracting renewed commercial interest), the statement by Whitehead that nut cultivation in the 1880s was increasing may be deemed true for parts of the Kentish Weald.[59] The nut harvest was precarious, being easily damaged by early frosts and caterpillars, but the growers of this spe-cialized produce in Plaxtol and Ightham parishes and thereabouts could be cheerful about the future, for their nut trees were 'amazingly' well suited to the loams of the Lower Greensand and Atherstone clay overlying ragstone, as these occurred near Maidstone. Elsewhere, apart from a scattered reference here and there to singular individuals like Mr Cooper of Calcot Gardens, near Reading, growing improved varieties of filberts, nut trees in the orchard did not find the followers they had attracted in the period 1650-1750. The waiting time for returns was too long, and orchard owners saw more promise in hard fruit, being lured on by the quick-fruiting varieties and dwarf trees that were now being developed.[60]

The geographical and social expansion of horticulture, bringing fresh vege-tables to more people, as well as fruit, either fresh or in jam, was not the sum of the achievement at this time. The enterprise expanded in still another direction, adding the wholly new branch of flower and decorative plant-growing, which in turn enlarged in a revolutionary way the use of glasshouses, not only for flowers and plants but for vegetables and fruit also.

From time to time horticulturists expressed fears of overproducing fruit and vegetables as more growers entered the field. In the event, overproduction did not threaten, because the horticulturists found these other options. They constructed another branch of business, serving the market with flowers, cut flowers, pot plants, bulbs, and bedding plants. Near London, this meant that flower growers took over much vegetable land, driving the vegetable growers further from the centre.[61]

The miraculous growth of commercial flower-growing seemed to contemporaries like a revolution swirling in from nowhere. In fact, of course, it had a long-drawn-out earlier history, having started in the nurseries of gentlemen's manor houses, and established solid foundations in the seventeenth century with the emergence of seed merchants and professional nurserymen.[62] The 1880s and 1890s saw spectacular new growth, because a long-neglected opportunity was seized at an opportune economic moment. The flower and plant business became another branch of alternative agriculture, this time supplying the consumer market with a luxury, rather than a necessity. Amid the rapidly growing population at this time were people with surplus income to spend. One of the best-informed observers of the phenomenon was Mr Assbee, the superintendant of Covent Garden market, who watched the innovation gaining ground under his eyes daily. For him it was a sign of the material progress of the working and middle classes in improved taste and refinement.[63] Thus the indulgences of the gentry were being put within the reach of the classes below. Even the working class could buy, when costermongers called on the market gardeners in the Thames valley, and bought their plants, buying also sometimes from local cottagers who seized their opportunities on the fringe of the new developments. The barrow boys then sold their wares in central London streets and suburbs.[64]

The flower market was at a transitional stage in these years, still attached in some areas of the country to its seventeenth-century roots. Around Leeds the gardeners of the gentry still played a considerable part in supplying flowers to townsmen, while a more revealing appraisal still was made of the flower market at Carlisle: no great demand lay there, it was said, for the population consisted only of the labouring and artisan classes.[65] Clearly, the flower market had more worlds to conquer in the future. But around London, and in select places further afield, its growth was remarkable.

A great concentration of flower growers was found in the vicinity of Twickenham, Richmond, Cranford, and Mitcham, another in north London in the

Enfield, Edmonton, and Cheshunt area, while another, celebrated for orchids, developed in Belvedere and Erith on the Kent marshes.[66] Bulb-farming and the spring flower trade had invaded the fens around the Wash since 1878, notably around Spalding, Lincolnshire, and in the Wisbech area of Cambridgeshire; in Rider Haggard's words in 1902 it was 'of gigantic proportions'. In the southwest, the Penzance area and the Isles of Scilly ranked foremost, and more flowers came from the Channel Islands.[67]

Success brought rapid change in management systems, and especially a great increase in the use of glasshouses. Roses and lily of the valley were made available all the year round. But other popular plants, whether for bedding or as cut flowers, made a long list, including chrysanthemums, asters, stocks, wallflowers, violas, pansies, Iceland poppies, and carnations. Fashion played a commanding role, keeping the florists on their toes and keeping the customers buying afresh. In 1898 stiff, bunchy flowers were said to have fallen out of favour, to be replaced by long-stalked marguerites, lilies, narcissi, and chrysanthemums. But new items in the list of modish plant decorations were grotesque cacti. Among bulbs the prize for fashion was won by narcissi (a term including daffodils), of which 600 varieties were known in 1898, and 120 were worth cultivating. For this author, it was a revelation to discover from all this why the daffodil was chosen as the flower to wear on Founder's Day at Frances Mary Buss's school, the Camden School for Girls. Miss Buss died in 1894 just when the daffodil was reaching the peak of its popularity.[68]

As usual the agricultural statistics offered no clue to the acreage of land absorbed into flower cultivation. But progress was generally agreed to have started *circa* 1868 and to have accelerated greatly after 1888. The supply of cut flowers increased fivefold in ten years, and Mr Assbee measured its effects in the layout of Covent Garden. The covered market was now filled to overflowing with flowers and foliage plants, while supplies from the Channel Islands and Scilly were removed to the Foreign Market, which had been enlarged by a half in 1897.[69]

Glasshouse cultivation constituted a new dimension of horticulture in this period, making great strides forward beyond the boundaries which it had reached in its previous phase of expansion, 1650-1750. The use of glass had begun by being a luxury in private gardens only, and was then taken up by commercial gardeners. Its use after 1650 is described by Malcolm Thick as 'the most important technical innovation in market gardening in the seventeenth century'. Bell glasses were being placed over single plants or groups of seedlings, and flat panes (called 'lights') were formed into cloches and raked towards the sun. A London gardener in 1718 in the Neathouse Gardens in Westminster had 1,240 bell glasses and some lights worth £30-40, while in smaller towns like Canterbury or Banbury the use of glass was modest and spread slowly.[70]

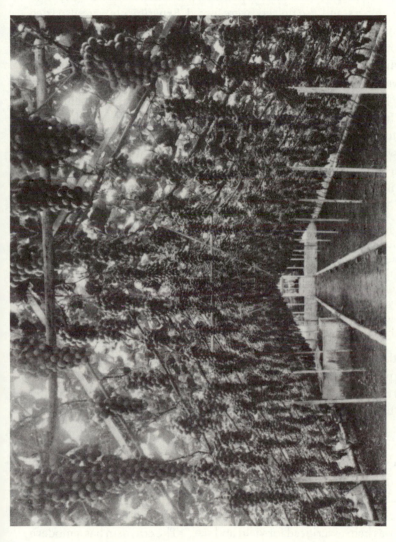

16. Greenhouse grapes. When the use of greenhouses spread in the late nineteenth century, indoor grapes became one of the successful commercial crops. A conference in London in 1905 deplored the quantities of imported fruit that might have been grown at home: £827,000 was spent on foreign grapes in 1904, though the scene was already changing, and 1,500 tons were said to have been produced in 1905. This photograph, published in Pratt, 1906, focuses attention on the notable expansion of horticultural activity on the Sussex coast at Worthing. Chrysanthemums were said to be brought into the greenhouses from the open when once the grapes had been cut.

A great leap forward was made possible in the late nineteenth century by the removal of duty on window glass and the invention (1835 and 1839) of boilers allowing hot-water pipes to be used to heat glasshouses. The cheaper glass was used first to cover outside walls and make orchard houses for early or exotic fruit.[71] In this way, grapes, strawberries, peaches, nectarines, melons, figs, tomatoes, and cucumbers, and also flowers, were forced. Experiments were also tried with mushrooms, seakale, and asparagus but not with conspicuous success: so ran the report in 1897.[72] But it was not long before glasshouses were used for seeds and bringing on early plants before planting outdoors. In the Lea valley the expansion was dramatic: Edmonton had 10 acres of glass in 1870 and 100 acres in 1890. In 1897 J. Assbee thought that 32 million square feet of glass was being used for growing fruit and flowers in the United Kingdom, and if the houses had been placed end to end they would have covered 735 acres. In the Lea valley, where much glass was concentrated, 200 growers with 900 acres of glass were found in 1913 between Tottenham and Broxbourne, Hertfordshire. Could any more vivid description be found of the seething human activity daily found in such places than that of Alfred Palmer, describing Edmonton's main street around 1882?

One of the sights of Edmonton was the long line of piled-up market wagons from about 11 p.m. on Mondays, Wednesdays, and Fridays, conveying market produce—mostly vegetables and fruit—from Hertfordshire and Essex to London, the same vehicles returning on the following afternoons, loaded with manure for use on the land. Often the drivers, going to and fro, were asleep (rumour said they never had their clothes off except Sundays!), and their intelligent horses threaded their way unguided through the traffic. Occasionally a tramcar conductor had to get off and gently remind the horses they were on his track, or ruthlessly rouse the driver from his peaceful slumbers![73]

Along with glasshouses went another aspect of horticultural improvement in these years, picking up threads of development that were first woven into the fabric of horticulture in the seventeenth century. This was the growing of better varieties, either by importing them or by selection and hybridization. J. Assbee thought the greatest progress had been made in fruit varieties, but a more informed grower of vegetables, Arthur Sutton, enumerated impressive achievements in the vegetable sector too. In 1897 when everyone was celebrating sixty glorious years of Queen Victoria's reign, a congratulatory review of horticulture was undertaken. In every vegetable named, Sutton found improvements of yield, size, or flavour, though he did not go unchallenged by those who thought that flavour was being sacrificed for yield and size.[74] The criticism has a modern ring. Nevertheless, he showed convincingly that every single vegetable had been transformed in some way or other. Potatoes were improved in yield, flavour, and disease resistance. Celery was improved in solidity and flavour. Broccoli and cauliflower were now available throughout the year.[75]

Many varieties of fruit and vegetables from abroad were tested, and, while some failed in the English climate, others settled successfully. Argenteuil asparagus from France came to be considered the best variety; Continental turnips and cabbages which were less susceptible to bolting took hold, as did French carrots, and Spanish and Tripoli onions. To a very modest extent people's tastes were educated to enjoy more salads, and to eat a larger number of edible plants—sugar peas (mangetout), celeriac, chicory, endive, cardoons, and aubergines. But far and away the greatest success was achieved with tomatoes. In 1837 they were considered poisonous. In 1852 a seed catalogue offered only one variety. But by 1897 they were being eaten by everybody, and plants were found in almost every garden from the cottager's upwards. Even so, the startling statement was made by one salesman, that nearly all the tomatoes he sold were eaten in salad or as a fruit.[76]

By the first decade of the twentieth century, horticulture in general could be viewed in longer perspective. Many more growers had entered the field, and profits were no longer as spectacular as in the recent past. Returns from narcissi, once reckoned at £100 an acre, had fallen dramatically in 1897. Cut flowers were said to be 'pretty nearly overdone' in 1898. The profit from bulbs had fallen likewise but not as much as from fruit.[77] Foreign competition was steadily intensifying since the agricultural depression afflicted other European countries besides England, and they too were devising an ever more professional system of garden cultivation. Lobjoit spoke in 1881 of asparagus growers in Fulham ruined by imports from France and Spain, with more expected from Algiers.[78] Nevertheless, as the years passed, growers found themselves able to dovetail their harvesting with that of foreign imports, and by 1920 John Wright, editing a revised edition of his father's book on fruit-growing of 1889, mentioned a refrigeration plant in Kent which would be able to store fruit and eliminate growers' fears of glut.[79]

High transport charges remained a constant source of complaint in the 1880s and 1890s, and it was a long time before railway companies gave the gardeners cheaper contracts. The market-garden area at Mount's Bay, near Penzance in Cornwall, where the equable climate allowed two vegetable crops to be grown in a year, found their markets in the Midlands and north of England, but paid freight costs twice as high as their competitors from Jersey. Cheshire growers made the same complaints in relation to produce from France and the Channel Islands. It was not until 1900/1 that the Evesham growers boasted a better deal recently concluded with the new Great Western Railway.[80]

Horticulture was a successful and optimistic branch of alternative agriculture, but it was not without its current problems and fears for the future. Much room for improvement was seen in the sorting, grading, and packing of fruit and vegetables, and at least one combination of growers at Hereford set itself this objective, although it was considerably later, in the inter-war years, that most progress was made on this score.[81] In periods of depressed prices, evasive action became more urgent, but co-operation did not elicit great enthusiasm. Instead, growers set their sights on more efficient routes to market; both small and large growers resented the comparatively large profits of the middleman. So some small growers in the north (Cumberland was cited) chose the solutions of individualists, carrying their produce to market themselves twice a week, while others became their own retailers. Those who had once sent their produce to London for onward dispatch to the north sent direct to northern markets. Growers large and small also sought more retail outlets locally.[82]

Considerable interest was shown up to 1914 (though less, perhaps, afterwards) in the ways of foreign horticulturists, and the reports from visitors abroad were highly instructive. The greatest impact was made by the so-called 'French garden', which became the model for what was thought to be a wholly new style of market gardening on small acreages. In fact, it was the seventeenth-century system revived and further modernized. It was introduced to the English by C. M. McKay, a Fellow of the Royal Horticultural Society, who knew the gardens round Paris, and led a party of Evesham gardeners to visit them in 1905. There they saw a highly intensive procedure, using hotbeds, frames, bell glasses, and many specially designed tools and equipment; manure, for example, was carried in baskets on men's backs as paths between the rows were too narrow for a wheelbarrow. Labour-intensive it was, most emphatically; yet it had outstanding merit in calling for far less capital investment in glasshouses and heating systems, and the high productivity of small plots was barely credible. Delicate green vegetables were grown in winter, including a most successful cabbage lettuce; cauliflowers sown under frames, and then moved under bell glasses at the end of February, were ready for market in six weeks; mustard and cress (for which there was a great demand in London) was grown on bass mats and so cut clean. Elated by this view of market gardening, seen with their own eyes, the Evesham men brought back a Frenchman to work with them, and copied the method. By 1908 other 'French gardens' existed in Essex, Surrey, and Berkshire, and in 1910 Captain A. B. S. Fraser (mayor of Hove) wrote and illustrated a splendid account of his French garden at Withdean, Patcham, in Sussex. Fraser had a Frenchman as gardener in charge (with a working wife, not mentioned, but seen in a photograph attending to the radishes), and although he had to continue buying some of his equipment from France, a French Clôche (*sic*) Company now existed in Evesham, sending out cases containing 200–300 cloches apiece. The *Daily Mail* reissued McKay's book on the French garden in a sixpenny edition, and further detailed accounts of French market gardens

17. Salad crops on the French system. The French method of intensive horticulture was studied, publicized, and copied in England, notably at Evesham and in the neighbourhood of Worthing. The necessary equipment, including bell-glasses, and portable manure baskets, was imported. The row upon row of bell-glasses shown above were in the French Garden of Captain A. B. S. Fraser, mayor of Hove, situated at Withdean, Patcham, Sussex, in 1910. The King's gardener was one visitor. (Reproduced from Fraser, in *The Country Home*, Feb. 1910.) A still more detailed account of the labour-intensive practicalities of the system was given in Helen Nussey and O. J. Cockerell, *A French Garden in England: A Record of the Successes and Failures of a First Year of Intensive Culture*, London, 1909. The specially designed basket (*left*) enabled the carrier to walk, pause, and distribute manure between the rows. It was illustrated in McKay, 1909.

were published in the *Journal of the Royal Agricultural Society*. One item of procedure which stood out from the account of the Paris area, namely the use of
sewage to fertilize the soils, was an obviously successful practice, but in this matter the Englishman refused to model himself on the French gardener.[83]

Further Continental influences infiltrated by other means, and were highly
influential in the long term. Foreigners came to live in England and set up some
outstanding enterprises. The surnames Lobjoit, Poupart, and Mizen identify
three families of great distinction. Mr Mizen (or Mizzen) of the first generation
grew vegetables at Mitcham in 1867, and in the second generation, by 1899, his
two sons, while still noted for the many cucumbers they produced, turned also
to flowers and mushrooms.[84] Among other 'new' methods of cultivation,
imported from abroad, were the use of dwarf fruit trees—a French innovation,
though the name of the 'pioneer' at this time is unknown. The use of dwarf trees
had become widespread in France before being reintroduced into England, but
reintroduction is the correct term, for the English had made acquaintance with
dwarfs between 1650 and 1750. Even now when the practice made new headway,
dwarf trees were only recommended for planting interspersed with standards.
It was recognized that they came into bearing more quickly, were easily pruned,
and yielded a heavier crop. But deep-rooted traditions still persuaded English
gardeners that dwarf trees should be grown for six or seven years only, and when
the standards had matured the dwarfs should be discarded.[85]

With all this in mind, it becomes necessary to underline the debt owed to foreign experts and to recognize repetitions of the seventeenth-century experience. In some details, such as the use of hotbeds and glass, gardeners were
simply returning to methods which had been practised once before but which
most people had forgotten during the decades of mainstream agriculture.
Arguments in favour of intensive labour on small acreages were also a repetition
from the past. Captain Fraser had started his Sussex garden as a hobby that must
pay its way, and it had proved 'a great success financially'. Mr McKay considered
that a French garden made a comfortable living for middle-class people with
education, energy, and small capital, and, as well, the work of 'keeping more
people on the land has become an urgent national obligation'.[86]

At the same time, differences between the nineteenth and seventeenth centuries were considerable. Whereas many new vegetables and fruits, as well as
new varieties of familiar ones, had been introduced in the seventeenth century,
totally novel foods were not a conspicuous feature in the late nineteenth century. Unfamiliar foods were doubtless tested, but they were not discussed
prominently in the literature. Root chicory *was* tried, but failed to live up to
early hopes for its use in a mixture with coffee. It was being grown in 1849 in
Yorkshire, Northamptonshire, Lincolnshire, and Cambridgeshire, and had

come to be centred on York by 1904, but because of an excise duty it was unable to compete with Belgian chicory. The bulk of the fruits and vegetables now being developed had long been familiar in the diet of a privileged minority. Time and familiarity had made them acceptable to more people, and so they could be expected to find a larger market when more abundantly and cheaply supplied. Thus tomatoes surged ahead; they were an entirely new crop in the Vale of Evesham in 1887, but they were certainly not a new introduction to England. The one new vegetable mentioned in the literature was turnip tops, accidentally discovered by Hampshire men in March 1880 when growing turnips on a field scale, and finding that the roots were worthless that year but the green leaves sold successfully to domestic consumers.[87]

The commercial development of produce reaching more classes forged ahead at this time, and yet it left many possibilities unexplored. George Bunyard, commending fruit-growing in 1899, attempted to lengthen the list of fruits by naming mulberries, quinces, medlars, bilberries, and cranberries, but he made no impression. A more remarkable article still appeared, far ahead of its time, in 1892 by G. L. Goodale, suggesting 'Cultivated Plants of the Future'. The author recognized how many more plants might be developed for food, and asked why trials were not made. His suggestions included cardoons, celeriac, salsify, seakale, spinach beet, custard apples, and plants with a medicinal or aromatic use. A Professor Georgeson, with personal knowledge of Japan and its foods, named yet more possibilities, including the soya bean, gingko nuts, seaweeds, and daikon (the large radish or turnip). But Goodale's article appeared a century too soon; such suggestions elicit far more interest in the 1990s than they aroused in the 1890s.[88]

After the 1914–18 war, through the 1920s and 1930s, horticulture continued to yield 'a fair living', the words used in a report on fruit-growing in 1921. Sir Henry Rew in 1927 conceded the importance of what not long ago had been considered to be 'the minor products' of farming, and while his figures of gross production showed that livestock afforded much the largest slice (35% of the whole), his point was validated by his figures of other produce, 26% comprising milk and dairy goods, and 11% comprising fruit, vegetables, and flowers. Significantly, this last item came not far behind cereals and potatoes which yielded 16%. When 7% was added for poultry and eggs, the three most successful items in 'alternative agriculture' in this phase represented 43% of all home-grown foodstuffs. In 1929 farmers who were losing money from livestock, cereals, and potatoes were addressed yet again with advice on how to move to market-garden crops. Admittedly, they had to watch for the dangers of overproduction, but, they were told, as standards of living rose, more such foods would be needed. Strawberries and cauliflowers were especially noted on this occasion as being in short supply, while all soft fruits were described as 'real money crops'.[89]

Structurally, a significant change took place in the inter-war years. By 1937 more mixed farms had learned to accommodate fruit and vegetables, and this diversification had produced some remarkable regional specializations. The acreage of vegetables as a whole had increased by 62 per cent between 1926 and 1935, but, seen regionally, an eightfold increase was recorded in the quantities of Brussels sprouts grown in Norfolk, a tenfold increase in peas picked green there, and somewhere between a two- and threefold increase in cabbages from Bedfordshire and Norfolk. Celery, cauliflowers, Christmas cabbage, broccoli, and savoys, as well as strawberries and rhubarb, were only some of the many other items which found their appropriate local niches on mixed farms. The remark that a small acreage of celery in the Black Fens of the Isle of Ely 'contributed substantially to gross income' stood as one illustration for many other single items. Changing circumstances in the mid-1930s led to a further spurt in horticultural production, which was attributed partly to the surplus of milk, which was making dairying less profitable, and partly to a more favourable market for home-grown vegetables now that import duties restricted supplies from Europe and the Canary Islands. Farmers were switching direction with some agility in these lean years. At the same time the canning industry offered another market for fruit and vegetables, while one author in 1937 wrote of 'propaganda' by doctors and dieticians in favour of more fruit and vegetables in diet, using words which suggested that he suspected a plot.[90]

Advances achieved in horticulture in the late nineteenth and first third of the twentieth centuries (up to 1939) went so far, but not as far as they might have done. Visitors to France remarked with some admiration on the discrimination of the French, when choosing their fruit and vegetables at the market, and the wide range of their greenstuffs. Lettuces were divided, and subdivided, into innumerable varieties, each having their own proper season, distinctive virtues, and use. The field cultivation of dandelions was introduced in France, to provide salads midwinter, and the French chose between five different varieties. All this presented the strongest contrast with England, where dandelions were only allowed a place for modest medicinal use. Sorrel was noticed as another salad plant in Paris, whereas it was totally neglected in England. French markets routinely supplied savory and scent-bearing herbs such as peppermint, absinthe, and angelica, of which the quality was excellent.[91] Herbs were urged upon English growers particularly strongly during the 1914–18 war, when imports, on which food and drug manufacturers normally relied, were halted. It was perfectly well known that many of the imports could be equally successfully, or even better, grown in Britain. But such hints mostly passed unheeded, though women herbalists held their ground as leading specialists, and like Mrs M. Grieve, Principal of the Whins Medicinal Herb School at Chalfont St Peter, Buckinghamshire, and Mrs C. F. (Hilda) Leyel (founder of the House of Culpeper, and of the Society of Herbalists) were renowned in their circle. Only now, a hundred years since the last onset of a crisis in mainstream agriculture, do we see herb-growing evoking a fresh wave of stronger practical interest.[92]

England's horticultural revolution which started at the end of the nineteenth century radically changed methods of cultivation, and business management, and developed a scale of production which brought fruit, vegetables, flowers, and garden plants generally to far larger numbers of people. But there it stopped; it did not greatly add to the number of foodstuffs offered, nor did it yet broaden English perceptions of fruit and vegetables in diet to match those of the French.

Poultry-Keeping

A third alternative strategy which began to show something of its full potential in the late nineteenth century was poultry-keeping. It was specially suited to the circumstances of small farmers, and gave scope to some notably successful women. Its development at this time not only paved a more solid way into the future: it also sheds a brighter light on the poultry-keeping of the seventeenth century. Although the subject is poorly documented at that time, faint signs of some significant advances are visible, which can now be seen to conform to an expected pattern: they represented a preparatory phase which would lead to another spurt of progress at the opportune moment, which returned in the 1880s.

In the seventeenth century French, Flemish, and Dutch influences on farming were conspicuous in East Anglia, and significance may be read into the fact that some immigrants at death plainly possessed larger than usual numbers of poultry. Indirectly, the renewed growing of buckwheat in East Anglia, and also perhaps the interest in clover (though the benefits of clover are not usually discussed in connection with poultry) may signify improvements in their feeding. By the time of Defoe great flocks of turkeys and geese walked from East Anglia to London, and his description is among his best-remembered passages. Three hundred droves of turkeys (roughly reckoned at 150,000 birds in all) had been counted in one season passing over Stratford bridge between Suffolk and Essex, yet this was only one of several routes that were used from East Anglia to London. Nor did this count geese, numbering between 1,000 and 2,000 in a drove, which also walked to London between August and the end of October, though these were beginning to enjoy a journey in four-storeyed carts.[93] Defoe's account was vivid and memorable; most of his contemporaries passed over poultry in a brief reference or in total silence, and a true measure of the advances made at that time eludes us. By comparison, the literature in the 1880s–1890s is voluminous.

If we guess at some decline in the commercial dynamism of the poultry business in the period 1750–1880, hard evidence to support that guess is not lacking. Charles Whitehead, a diligent and knowledgeable writer on Kentish affairs, chose the year 1879 as the date before which, he said, poultry in Kent were commercially neglected, whereas the business thereafter greatly expanded. Over a much longer period, we know that the feeding grounds for geese, on open commons, were being destroyed by enclosure, and this occurred most rapidly in the period of mainstream agriculture between 1750 and 1880. Some idea of the numbers that might be kept where commons still existed in those years may be gathered from William Cobbett, claiming to have seen 10,000 geese on his rides in the 1820s on one common, six miles long, in Surrey. In contrast, a descriptive account of the poultry market before 1880 in northern England conjures up a dispiriting picture: birds were always sold at so much each, and not by the pound weight; they were likely to be scraggy and sometimes tough; and the most discerning purchasers sent to London for well-fattened specimens.[94]

But already in 1882 poultry were foreseen as having a bright future on a mixed farm, for, echoing the perceptive words of the French writers Estienne and Liebault, already cited in connection with the sixteenth century, the parson of Godmanstone, Dorchester, also saw that 'in these trying times . . . we cannot afford to despise small things'. His article for the *Journal of the Royal Agricultural Society* gave advice on the best breeds and management of all manner of poultry, including ducks, turkeys, geese, and guinea fowl. These activities suited small men above all, for small units of production were recognized as reducing the risk of disease.[95]

The virtue of small enterprises was already well understood in France, and H. M. Jenkins did much to bring Continental experience to the attention of English farmers.[96] Larger enterprises were encouraged to pay heed also: a mixed farm could use its greater acres to give larger numbers of poultry fresh and varied grazing. An example was cited from Svendborg, in Denmark, where 600 birds were kept along with fruit-growing, and they grazed over orchard and forest land.[97] Such larger enterprises began to appear in England too, first as experiments, and later because success led some modest beginners to expand their business. A grain farmer of 500–600 acres at Kimbolton, Huntingdonshire, made a trial in hard times by reducing his land to 100 acres and turning to poultry-keeping. He had 1,500–1,800 birds in 1882, kept them in movable houses in the fields during the day, and recorded a profit of 5–10 per cent. He did not recommend this large scale to others, however. A better system, he thought, was for farmers and also cottagers to keep small numbers, and, although the large enterprises emerged more confidently in course of time, poultry-keeping remained a markedly successful venture for 'small under-capitalized farmers and labourers to weather severe economic fluctuations'.[98]

Specialized poultry-keeping did not, except in a few instances, move into entirely fresh areas of the country, but it did expand noticeably from bases that were already identifying themselves in the seventeenth century.[99] This is consonant with the fact that the occupation suited small men, and found its best chances wherever they clustered in large groups; such concentrations were not found everywhere. Where it was a characteristic of the local social structure, co-operation was possible, and this facilitated day-to-day operations. At the same time, another vital necessity was good transport to towns.[100]

Because these features were all present in the Heathfield district of the Sussex Weald, a poultry-cramming speciality became notably successful. Poultry-keeping was already known in 1673 at Horsham, and a good trade link was established with London. Thereafter, a poultry trade persisted in the Weald, and quietly diversified, though without attracting much notice. Cramming—the forcing of food from something like a sausage-making machine down the throats of birds—began to be practised in the 1830s, and expanded to a point in the 1860s when it was plainly a routine among many smallholders. The cramming itself was not an innovation, for the method was described by Leonard Mascall in a book in 1581, but doubtless the machine was new. Such intensive production may have been encouraged by a shift from cattle-fattening to dairying, which yielded skimmed milk for feeding to the poultry. But it depended also on the ground oats 'of the district', and hence presumably took advantage of a crop that was traditionally favoured in the Weald. This was mixed with fat as well as sour skimmed milk to make a paste which put on flesh fast and made it white and delicate.[101] Nevertheless, it was only when alternative agricultures were urgently needed in the 1880s that publicists sought out the Wealden poultry business, now recognizably centred on Heathfield. Rearing formed one branch—and Kentish Wealden parishes bred many of the young chickens, selling them on at 10–12 weeks—while fattening formed the other. Even then the rearing did not fully meet local demand, and large numbers of young birds were imported for cramming from Ireland.[102] Many poultry keepers were mixed farmers with 70, 100, even 200 acres, but cottagers and what were called 'big men' with 15–20 acres also made a large contribution. It was the joint achievement of both groups that dead poultry valued at £140,000 left Heathfield in 1895, compared with £60,000 in 1885. The whole effort in filling the 'chicken trains' to London was further served by higglers (that is, traders) who linked rearers to crammers, and crammers to the railhead.[103]

Other celebrated poultry centres mixed and managed their poultry enterprises differently. The Vale of Aylesbury had a reputation for its ducks, some being sold from mixed farms, some being kept by labourers and smallholders. A well-informed account in 1894 centred the business by that date at Leighton Buzzard, and identified egg producers on the one hand, rearers and fatteners on the other. Close attention to detail, and untiring care and cleanliness, were the hallmark of the successful fatteners. Often a cottager with little ground and no expensive accommodation could work wonders; one in 1893 sent 1,900 fat ducklings to the London market in the course of one year. And early birds in February earned 16s. a couple, compared with 5–6s. in July.[104]

The origins of the occupation almost certainly have to be associated, as in the Weald of Sussex, with the favourable social structure of the area. Defoe had seen the Vale of Aylesbury as cattle-grazing country above all else, but he may not have noticed what a comparatively small number of humbler men were doing at that time. When Scotsmen moved into the district in the late nineteenth century, dairying increased, and this could have greatly helped duck-keeping by mixed farmers. In business flair and innovation, however, the Vale of Aylesbury did not win the same acclaim as the crammers in Sussex. Only the latter merited a detailed investigation, resulting in a Parliamentary report which now serves the historian so well. One commentator in 1911 criticized the Aylesbury 'duckers' for old-fashioned methods which exposed them to considerable competition from newer centres.[105] Elsewhere ducks were sometimes bred in very large numbers, indeed. Hunter Pringle, reporting on the agriculture of Bedfordshire, Huntingdonshire, and Northamptonshire, knew a farm with 6,000–7,000 ducks.[106] In the specialist counties of Norfolk and Suffolk, which had entered the poultry business much earlier in the seventeenth century, Rider Haggard selected for notice a Suffolk farmer at Cockfield who grazed thousands of turkeys, geese, ducks, and fowls on stubbles hired from his neighbours. Young turkeys and geese were imported from Ireland, ducks and fowls from Norfolk.[107] In another part of the country entirely, near Fleetwood, Lancashire, duck-rearing was also being developed, though only a close study of local conditions would explain what made the circumstances so favourable. Geese were urged for revival in Northumberland and Cumberland, where an older tradition was known from a century before. Cumberland, however, was already claimed as a notable egg-producing county as well as south Lincolnshire.[108]

When observers surveyed the poultry scene in the mid-1890s, their accounts were thoroughly optimistic. Egg consumption in England was thought to have doubled in fifteen years, and home supplies still did not meet the demand, as increasing imports bore witness. The obvious success of the foreigner, indeed, prompted English producers to visit Sofia to study egg production in Bulgaria.

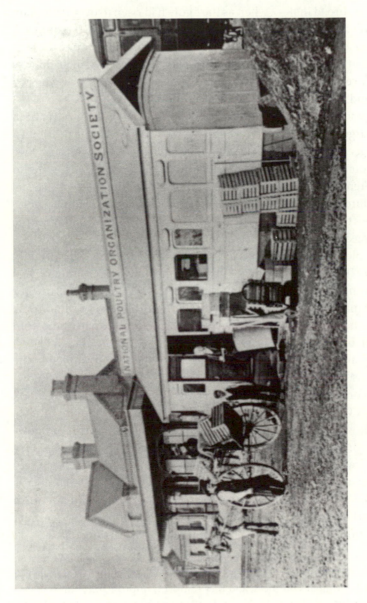

18. Egg-collecting at Stoke Ferry, Norfolk. The cost of imported eggs increased more than eight times in forty years between 1864 and 1904. Home production was promoted by the National Poultry Organisation Society, setting up, by 1904, forty depots to facilitate transport to the markets. Edward Brown was the Secretary of the Society, and he had a Model Poultry Farm, which gave instruction to women farmers attending two-year courses in agriculture at Reading College, Berks. He visited the Balkans and described the massive scale on which eggs were produced there. This photograph of a Norfolk depot was published in Pratt, 1906, in which long passages from Brown's foreign experience were cited.

As usual with new ventures, no official recognition was given to poultry-keeping at this time, and no statistics were gathered to measure progress. But egg imports showed the increasing role of eggs in diet: less than half a million were brought in from abroad in 1870, whereas the figure had risen to over 1½ million by 1896 and over 2 million by 1900. This encouraged, rather than discouraged, the home producer: Edward Brown reckoned in 1902 that one-third of the estimated home output of 1,241.5 million eggs was supplied by small poultry keepers. Moreover, a rising demand for British 'new-laid' eggs was reported between 1875 and 1911, and prices rewarded the effort.[109]

Contemporaries fully recognized that many opportunities had not yet been grasped. The larger production of ducks and geese was seen as one possibility, but hopes for geese faded somewhat when they fell from favour, because they had less meat on them than turkeys. Poultrymen were urged by one writer to consider the French practice of cutting up geese and selling the joints separately, a procedure which any visitor to Hungary nowadays can appreciate.[110] Now in the 1990s the latent potential of geese-keeping may surge again, since the flavour of the meat is much appreciated.

A more feasible objective at this period was the improvement of egg production in winter. It was easily achieved by one impressive professional, Mrs Feather of Soham, Cambridgeshire, who was exceptional. Her personal care for every detail of management, insisting on absolute cleanliness, good housing, and warmth for her birds, feeding them herself (every one and a half hours from 6 a.m. to 6 p.m. in order to fatten spring chickens for early sale at high prices) was exemplary, and gives an all too brief glimpse of the role of women in the poultry business.[111] Elsewhere the work of women was only briefly acknowledged, if not contemptuously dismissed. A highly significant exchange took place between a Commissioner, investigating the state of agriculture in 1896, and Edward Brown, FLS, their informant on poultry-farming with a knowledge of French practices. He attributed the superior quality of eggs and poultry production in France to the women whose care it was, and where 'there is a very marked difference in one respect, and that is that the men there do not hinder as in some cases here.' By this he meant that the menfolk in France did not brush their wives' work aside as unprofitable. To the commissioner's next question, 'Then an alteration in the social habit here is needed?', Mr Brown replied

we do not want an alteration so much in the social habit as in the prejudice. We have in many parts of this country a very strong prejudice on the part of the farmers against poultry. . . . It is the women's business, and they think it is unprofitable; but in France they look upon poultry as being profitable, and give proper attention to it, but in France there is no doubt that the women are most skilful poultry keepers.

Foreign success with egg production provoked further questions, since Britain imported 35 per cent of its eggs. Did Mr Brown 'regard the social habit of the people and the prejudice against women's labour in that direction as a material factor in the present situation?' Mr Brown most certainly did.[112] But when Lewis Wright wrote on poultry-farming in 1911, his language was positive and his descriptions glowing. A 'remarkable development of what was termed "utility" poultry-breeding' had been seen since 1890; duck-rearing was 'a very profitable industry, very high prices being paid for ducklings in the early months of the year'; and, finally, 'poultry pay best of any branch upon a farm'.[113]

The 1914–18 war had the effect of directing more attention at egg than meat production, and this preference persisted throughout the inter-war years to 1939, causing reporters to dub table fowls 'quite subsidiary'. Egg production rose 36 per cent between 1908 and 1925; in other words, a million more fowls were being bred each year, 500 million more hens' eggs were laid, and the new venture with duck eggs registered 25 million of them in 1925. Between 1924 and 1934 poultry numbers doubled again, and the work was said to occupy more people than any other branch of agriculture, including many working on a small scale. The poultry business became one of the outstanding achievements of small farmers in Lancashire, and while the official statistics showed an impressive rise in poultry numbers in that county from 1.8 million in 1913 to 5.1 million in 1929, we should also heed the words of a knowledgeable local observer that those figures ignored 'the vast numbers' of birds that were kept on holdings of less than one acre.[114]

Still brighter marketing possibilities were seen ahead because Great Britain was importing eggs costing £18 million in 1929. Confidence spurred innovation, and several different experiments were under way in the 1930s in keeping poultry in movable pens on a folding system, thus allowing them to be moved regularly onto clean grass to avoid disease.[115] A general summary in 1938 reiterated the 'immense room for expansion', though the writers of it were still thinking of eggs and took it for granted that poultry meat would continue to be the privilege only of the well-to-do. While poultry-keeping was now plainly launched on a broader path than before, none could have predicted in 1880 how things would look a hundred years later.[116]

Pigs

The most successful enterprises in the third phase of alternative agriculture were dairying, horticulture, and poultry-keeping, and all were enterprises which had once been described as 'small things'. They had occupied poor men or their wives, or were the sole responsibility of the womenfolk on larger farms where they were still deemed minor sidelines. They had started to move up in the world in the seventeenth century, and they moved up further still in the late nineteenth century. Since they proved to be lifelines in distress, they grew into major branches of food production, and lost their image as lowly, womanly pursuits.

Pigs might have been expected to feature in the same list, but, surprisingly, they did not become a specialized occupation at this time, remaining instead a subsidiary occupation everywhere. They were an adjunct of dairy farms, eating the unwanted by-products; they could be well fed on fruit farms and in market gardens, as consumers of waste; they were a subordinate branch of mixed farming, for which some meal might be bought in; and some were still woodland animals, as in the New Forest. They *supplemented* the living of farmers from all classes, without achieving any identity as a special branch of farming in their own right. Nevertheless, a reading of Louisa Jebb's detailed account in 1907 of the way smallholders and small farmers got their living, leaves no doubt about the value of pigs in the varied routines which they pursued in different parts of the country. One writer in 1910 assured his readers that nothing was more profitable on a small farm than rearing and fattening pigs.[117]

It is puzzling that pork and bacon did not receive the attention that was proving eminently worth while in Denmark at this time. Up to 1914 total pig numbers in the official figures for England showed no tendency to rise noticeably, though everyone admitted that the pigs in backyards and outhouses could never be counted. A writer who did his best to promote the pig was James Long, already mentioned for his books on dairying. Writing in 1886 and again in 1918, he gives us a fair measure of his own failure to achieve any change. Pigs were firmly looked down upon as the food of the poor, and so, like poultry, they had to overcome a strong prejudice before farmers would look at them. Moreover, the breeds were inferior, and slow to fatten. It was different in France, where pork was said by some to be the Frenchman's main meat.[118]

In 1918 Long was still complaining of the farmer's apathy, and dismayed that bacon valued at £23 million was imported; the home industry in his view was 'a disgrace to a great agricultural nation'. It was not that country cottagers had no pork on their tables. They were acknowledged to be breeding tens of thousands of animals, but the pork was eaten at home. Flora Thompson's *Lark Rise to Candleford* made that memorably clear when she described how 'the family pig was everybody's pride and everybody's business' in her cottage home. Mother boiled the potatoes for it, and the children on their way home from school gathered sow thistles, dandelions, and choice long grass, or on wet evenings collected snails in a bucket to feed it tasty titbits. Still, in some places better strains of animals were being fed now, and some even elegant housing found for them. It was no longer so usual to feed pigs on grass, acorns, and beechmast. Instead, they were fed in sties on barley and maize and fattened more quickly. Nevertheless, the fact remained that official figures for pigs in 1918 showed a decline since 1908.[119]

After 1918 English dairy farms played a further diminishing role in keeping pigs since milk was their sale product rather than the butter, which would have left plenty of skimmed milk to feed them. Pork prices fell to the lowest levels in the early 1930s, and English pork and bacon could not compete for quality with the Danish. Since much pig feed was imported from abroad, Astor and Rowntree finally concluded in 1938 that the business could be most efficiently rationalized by keeping pigs at ports, in buildings situated next to grain mills on the quaysides! Pig production, in their view, was 'not an integral part of British agriculture'.[120] The role of pigs in making a contribution to a multiple income from several sources had thus vanished from the sight of observers and advisers on policy, and this in a phase of agricultural fortune when multiple activities were always one of the most successful prescriptions for survival.

The merit of multiple activities, including pigs, in farming is most convincingly and memorably portrayed in George Henderson's account of his own farming success, *The Farming Ladder* (1944) in the inter-war years. He and his brother took over a run-down farm of 85 acres at Enstone, Oxfordshire, in 1924, on the oolitic limestone of the Cotswolds. Their deliberate plan was to follow several different activities at once, and keep careful accounts separating each, so that each paid its way. While 'British agriculture slipped down the precipice of post-war depression', they resolutely avoided 'mainstream farming', and instead built up a highly productive small farm on the basis of alternatives. They dubbed poultry 'the most important branch of our farming both from the point of view of profit and of the maintenance of fertility'. So they kept hens, selling eggs, then rearing and selling day-old chicks, then fat poultry; they also kept ducks and geese. They established a pedigree herd of Jersey cattle, from which they reared and sold two-year old calved heifers. From a sheep flock they sold fat lambs. With pigs, they first bought in stores and fattened them, but then set up a pedigree herd of Large Whites, from which they sold gilts and boars to other breeders. Finally, they grew the best-quality grain to sell as seed, and bought in cheaper grain to feed their stock. The fertility of their land was improved by their tireless husbanding of natural manure. Their small farm paid them handsomely through two decades of generally lean years for farmers in the 1920s and 1930s.[121]

As a concept, 'alternative agriculture' was not discussed in the farming literature between 1879 and 1939, yet its frame of reference was understood, and underlay much that was written at the time. Alternatives might be called 'supplements' or even 'fancy farming', but the fact remained that their various branches received prodigious attention in magazines and books, and, in order to reach everyone, publications were sold in both expensive and in the cheapest pamphlet formats. One of the most perceptive writers on the phenomenon as a whole was Edwin Pratt, viewing it around 1900 when it was still seen as a new situation, and not yet accepted as the normal state of affairs. He called his book in 1906 not *Alternative Agriculture* but *The Transition in Agriculture*. He saw the large amount of work which it created, and the large amount of food which it produced even though some, or much, was ignored by the statisticians because they laid down their own rules, to exclude enterprises under one acre. So, he explained ironically, if 100 acres were divided into one-acre lots (and some landowners were, indeed, dividing some of their land at this time into small parcels for the benefit of labourers and smallholders), the official statistics, far from showing more food being produced, showed 100 acres of land having gone out of cultivation! He saw also, more clearly than others, some of the concomitant facilities and developments which were needed to sustain and bolster alternative agriculture.[122] They promised to create a more congenial environment in which it could flourish. They are the themes of the next chapter.

8 ❧ CONTEXT AND CONCLUSION

THE alternative strategies developed by farmers and landowners in the later nineteenth century deserve consideration in a broader economic and cultural context. Just as widely separated periods of alternative agriculture have shown common trends, so similarities can be seen in the way events unfolded in the wider world of cultural attitudes and social relations. These are the themes to be followed in this chapter, and they stem from the view that an understanding of repeated events, when framed against a wider background, will help us to judge in a yet more informed way the changes occurring today, which are the subject of Chapter 9.

Vegetarianism

One of the repetitious themes that emerges from phases of alternative agriculture, and which was certainly prominent in the late nineteenth century, concerns changes in diet. Since the search for alternative strategies in farming involves the production of different and novel foodstuffs, it expands the available range of vegetables, fruits, and herbs, and at the same time improves their quality. It is not perhaps surprising, then, that their virtues in diet come to be more closely examined, and then more systematically commended. One of the results is a trend towards vegetarianism.

In the 1880s and 1890s vegetarianism took a conspicuous leap forward. That being so, our curiosity, inevitably, turns to the period 1650–1750, and there too we find vegetarianism emerging in a tentative way. The further question then arises whether the first wave of alternative agriculture after the Black Death introduced a similar trend.

Surveying the subject chronologically, and moving from darkness into light, we see no conspicuous advocates of vegetarianism in the late Middle Ages. If there were any, it is unlikely that they would have been found outside a highly restricted social class of religious men and women. The most recent study of monkish diets offers no encouragement for that proposition, suggesting rather that the monastic houses had lapsed into meat-eating by the fourteenth century, and persisted in this practice until the monasteries were dissolved. But it is not impossible that religious women were more ascetic in this respect, and certainly one informal community at Ipswich is on record as abstaining from meat-eating.[1] It is possible to envisage a single nunnery or monastery, or single individuals, upholding a return to a more austere meatless diet in the wake of the trauma induced by the scourge of virulent plague. Even a gentle surge of vegetarianism among a few thinkers and philosophers, outside the enclosed religious orders, is not unthinkable. The question can be raised, though it must go unanswered.

In the seventeenth century, in contrast, vegetarian attitudes were, indeed, manifest. John Robins, the Ranter under the Commonwealth, was strictly vegetarian, 'until many a poor soul was almost starved under his diet', writes Christopher Hill. But more enthusiasts for garden foodstuffs were moderates, recommending fruit and vegetables as a healthy diet, without clearly pledging themselves to forgo all meat. The Reverend John Beale, who did much to foster improvements in orchards and cider-making, is found discussing the principles of a good diet at an intellectual level, and enthusing over the taste of mushrooms; these were a novel experience for him, at the table of Sir Henry Wotton, a much-travelled diplomat. John Milton and Isaac Newton have been cited as vegetarians, as well as John Ray, the botanist, and Alexander Pope.[2] But while these contemporaries favoured vegetables in diet, it is unlikely that they refrained altogether from eating meat. A certain ambivalence would have been reasonable, such as is found in William Coles, a dedicated botanist writing in the mid-1650s, who had every reason to recognize the value of food plants. He was convinced that they did not give as good nourishment as flesh, but at the same time recognized that the Pythagorean philosophers, vegetarians in their day, had lived longer than any of his contemporaries. Perhaps his view represented the reflections of many more.[3]

Outright vegetarianism as a firm principle of diet emerged publicly in the 1690s, when it was proclaimed in print by Thomas Tryon, a quixotic London merchant, who may have been influenced by a year spent in Barbados. In the West Indies, he became conversant with the life and work of negroes on the sugar plantations, and those observations may have prompted some speculation on the merits of a vegetarian regime. Throughout his life Tryon was a restless seeker after new occupations and fresh ideas, fearlessly advocating singular viewpoints. He urged, for example, the preservation of labour-intensive industries that would employ the poor, rather than labour-saving inventions that would not. He wanted free schools for poor children set up in London. He voiced strong prejudices against foreigners in England who robbed native craftsmen of work. As for his dietary principles, these were seemingly more extreme than those of his predecessors: he forbade the eating of fish, flesh, or anything that had been killed, and when once he was converted to this principle he lived on a diet of herbs, fruit, grain, eggs, dairy products, and water. Aphra Behn was a fervent disciple, commending his beliefs in verse: 'I've tried thy methods and adore thy theme,' she wrote.[4]

Just how many other followers Tryon recruited, it is impossible to say. After his death in 1703 lone voices were raised intermittently in the eighteenth century in support of a wholly vegetarian diet, but the momentum of the seventeenth century had plainly been lost, and, when its advantages were pressed at all, they were argued from a significantly different viewpoint. In 1767 one book of dietary advice was specifically addressed to the poor, advocating pulses (especially peas) and nuts (in this case, pickled walnuts), but this was on the grounds that they were cheap.[5]

Thus vegetarian enthusiasm on the Tryon model lay virtually dormant for almost a century and a half; seen from the viewpoint of this investigation into alternative agriculture, it could be said that mainstream agriculture killed it. It did not begin to revive until the mid-nineteenth century, with the foundation in 1847 of the Vegetarian Society. Its supporters at that date, however, were far from recruiting a strong following. The marked change in its fortunes came about in the 1880s and 1890s, at the moment when the new phase of alternative agriculture gathered momentum. This created a more favourable environment and the movement won converts as never before.[6]

One of the leading propagandists of vegetarianism in the 1880s was a woman doctor, Anna Kingsford, who became a Vice-President of the Vegetarian Society. Her contribution deserves to be recalled for its prophetic quality. In 1880 she completed a thesis on vegetable diets in the Faculty of Medicine in Paris, and in 1881 published *The Perfect Way in Diet*. Her arguments in favour of vegetarianism were broadly conceived, and not based on grounds of health alone. Indeed, she showed a vision which, for its clarity and far-sightedness, can be much better appreciated now than then. She saw vegetarian diets as a way of feeding large numbers of people on less land, of providing work, and reducing imports.[7] As the times were favourable, the movement caught on, vegetarian lectures were delivered in Manchester in 1887 and 1888, and many books appeared in that and the next decade.[8] In contrast with the situation ten years before, when vegetarianism was dubbed 'a mere fad', a survey in 1889 proclaimed the existence of twenty-nine vegetarian restaurants in London, seven in Manchester, and one or more in Liverpool, Leeds, Birmingham, Bristol, Nottingham, Newcastle, Portsmouth, and other large towns. An 'active crusade' was under way through public meetings, lectures, discussions, vegetarian dinners, and the publication of several regular journals.[9] These favourable circumstances will need to be recalled when we come to survey the present-day phase of alternative agriculture, for a similar wave of vegetarian sentiment is again conspicuous.

Short of adopting outright vegetarianism, another group of people at this time was noticeably influenced in favour of new food habits by a closer acquaintance with the food habits of immigrants from abroad. In this respect, a strong similarity is seen with circumstances in the late sixteenth and seventeenth centuries, when Flemish, Dutch, and French immigrants also settled in England. At both periods, the influences were strongest in and around towns, and in southern and eastern England, and on both occasions familiarity with foreign food habits was further strengthened by the fact that some foreigners became market gardeners, operating on a new scale and at new levels of proficiency.[10]

In London, where the best supply of fruit and vegetables was available in quantity, substantial French and Italian communities were increasing in Soho from the early nineteenth century, bringing their taste for vegetables, salads, and fruits from their homelands. Whereas a cookery book of 1784 had denounced French cooks for their doubtful moral character as well as their cooking, a more sympathetic attitude supervened a century later, which Angeliki Torode has attributed to the fact that Englishmen were travelling more widely in Europe. That is certainly part of the story. But foreigners changed attitudes also by living and working in England. The famous French cook Alexis Soyer, who invented the field kitchen in the Crimean War, showed in cookery books such as his *Shilling Cookery for the People* (1855) what cheap and good meals could be made from stews and soups in the Continental style, incorporating more vegetables than meat.[11] A still more influential writer was Georgiana Hill, who later wrote a *History of Women* (1896, in 2 vols.), but started her long career by publishing cheap cookery books which sold at 6d. each. Her first book, *The Cook's Own Book: A Manual of Cookery for the Kitchen and the Cottage* (1860), began a series which flowed thick and fast thereafter, with recipes from France, Spain, Portugal, and India. They sold in thousands of copies. Cooks of all classes were introduced to menus with a foreign flavour. Then Frenchmen like André Simon and Marcel Boulestin settled in England, demonstrated French cooking styles, and won a reputation among the gastronomes for their writing and cooking.[12]

From a different direction entirely came the initiative of the Baroness Angela Burdett-Coutts, that generous giver to the poor, launching a grandiose scheme to help people in East London to buy fresh vegetables and fruit. Between 1864 and 1869 she spent nearly a quarter of a million pounds, building Columbia Market in Stratford. It was a veritable palace, even a cathedral, of iron and stone,

19. A new vegetable and fruit market for East London. Columbia Market, a monumental Gothic-style market in Bethnal Green, constructed around a quadrangle, was built by Baroness Burdett-Coutts with the generous intention of making vegetables and fruit more readily available to the poor of East London. It was in advance of its time, and failed for lack of attention to the social context in which it was being built. This illustration appeared in the *Illustrated London News*.

with aisles, columns 35 feet high, and flanking arcades in decorated Gothic. Twenty years later, in 1885, C. W. Stubbs thought its existence had encouraged garden-farming locally, but as a marketing aid the project was a disaster. Plainly in the 1860s it ran ahead of its time; might it have succeeded twenty years later when a horticultural revolution was well launched? The usual explanation for its failure rests on the deep hostility it encountered from the street costermongers and wholesalers, and the prohibition by the Baroness of trade on Sundays, a deep-rooted local custom. If fruit- and vegetable-selling expanded in East London in subsequent decades, it had nothing to do with Columbia Market.[13]

Nevertheless, other changing food habits from the 1880s onwards suited the needs of the agricultural moment; although they certainly did not amount to a revolution affecting the whole nation, they mattered in central London, where lay the main market for alternative produce. A congenial cultural context was being built up, hedged in by the limitations of the age. One of these can be glimpsed in the remarks of a writer on watercress in 1897. W. W. Glenny prefaced his survey of its history and cultivation with the remark that much more salad was eaten in eastern and Continental countries than in England; and overseas a salad should be dressed with oil and vinegar. However, in England this was only practised by those who favoured French cookery, and it as yet found slight favour among the lower and middle classes 'who prefer to eat their salad in a simple and primitive way'. So watercress found favour in England among all classes because it was the one salad plant which was best eaten alone, unadorned, and not mixed with other greenstuff. According to Glenny, the idea for a commercial trade in watercress came from Erfurt in Germany, and was started in England by William Bradbery in 1808 at Springhead, near Northfleet, Kent. A salad revolution from abroad was under way, but it would proceed only so far, and no further, waiting until the later twentieth century to resume its course.[14]

Large versus Small Farms

Another cluster of interests, and of discussions leading to action at this period, centred on the size of farms which offered the best hopes of a profitable agriculture. Not surprisingly, the tide of opinion was turning against large farms, and, although it did not move overwhelmingly in favour of small farms, it stirred up an animated debate, and gathered some eloquent spokesmen in their favour. Indeed, Rider Haggard claimed that nothing concerning the future of the land excited so much controversy as this.[15] It mirrored a situation which can be seen, somewhat less clearly, during the second phase of alternative agriculture, notably in the second half of the seventeenth century. Yet again, after the Black

Death in the mid-fourteenth century, the subject must certainly have given food for thought even though no overt, recorded debate has survived. In that case, it was actions which spoke louder than words.

In the late twentieth century, the debate for and against large or small farms seems to be shifting its centre of gravity, after a long period when 'mainstream' influences dominated, and it seemed that small farms were destined to disappear. Resistance surged in 1975 when a Small Farmers' Association was set up to curb the zeal of government for amalgamating small farms into larger units, and a new campaign was launched in 1985 to enlarge the membership.[16] Since the last phase of alternative agriculture came to an end, other circumstances have, of course, changed radically. Planning regulations now restrict the freedom of owners to dispose of their land to meet different needs. What is required first, therefore, is a change of attitude, which will ease acceptance of a new strategy. But we can already discern something of that sort in the emerging scene which could bring the question of large and small farms to the forefront with similar urgency to that seen on earlier occasions.

Some, indeed many, of the successful smallholdings in the late nineteenth century were carried on alongside other occupations which yielded a secondary source of income. That was also the situation in the period 1650–1750; indeed, the success of what historians have called the dual economy has prompted much investigation by them in the last thirty or forty years. So we are observing a not entirely alien development nowadays with the growth of teleworking from home and home-based handicraft industries, affording a living which relies on two or more sources of income.[17]

As for a movement in favour of smaller holdings of land after the Black Death, no such proposals are known to have been discussed in any theoretical literature, and indeed it could hardly be expected, since peasant holdings were already small, and many had grown smaller in the boisterous years of mainstream agriculture in the twelfth and thirteenth centuries. But in practice the subdivision of large farms was conspicuous when manorial lords all over England gradually gave up farming their home farms. The great mortality of men had made labour too expensive, and when lords turned against direct farming for themselves, they offered their manorial demesnes to tenants. Sometimes those tenants leased the land as a group, though they almost certainly cultivated it individually. This was, in practice, a move towards the breakup of large farming units into small, and one of its consequences was made very clear when the gentry resumed direct farming in the next phase of mainstream agriculture, a century and a half later. By then field boundaries had become blurred or lost, as peasant lessees had amalgamated pieces of demesne with other parts of their holdings.[18] The final outcome of this late medieval phase of alternative agriculture cannot be summed up in any general conclusion about the changing size of farms, since many peasants found the new economic conditions sufficiently favourable to them to build up their own somewhat larger units. A yeoman class with farms larger than those of the average husbandman was emerging. But the widespread leasing of demesnes certainly disturbed the existing pattern of land distribution in certain localities, and for a time checked the growth of the largest farms.

During the second experience of alternative agriculture, from the second half of the seventeenth century, a different mixture of events succeeded in hindering the emergence of large farms. This time the practical possibilities were improved by the Civil War and the setting up of a republic in 1649. Large quantities of Crown, Church, and Royalists' land were seized and sold by Parliament. In the event, most of this land passed to gentlemen, but here and there a large estate, even when first bought by a gentleman, was broken up into smaller units, arousing the suspicion that the new owner held sympathetic views towards the aspirations of smallholders.[19] With more certainty, judgement can be passed on the effect of the sales of forfeited Crown land, which were offered to soldiers in lieu of arrears of pay. In some cases, many small farms were set up on what had once been grand, royal estates. At Theobalds, Hertfordshire, the transformation caused Thomas Fuller to describe the new community as 'a little commonwealth; so many entire tenements, like splinters, flown out of the materials thereof'. In Berkshire, Windsor Great Park was subdivided, and about twenty families or more settled on it, while in Marylebone Park smallholdings were created for dairy farming. At Enfield a similar revolution was planned in 1659, this time inspired by the ideas of the Diggers, but it came too late in the life of the Republic and was stillborn.[20]

The 1650s were a decade in which idealism and a zest for innovative practices in farming strengthened arguments in favour of smallholdings. Profound interest was being aroused in the growing of vegetables, fruits, and industrial crops, and market gardeners everywhere were demonstrating the high productivity of land when cultivated intensively. Even the Royalist Sir Richard Weston was moved to deprecate those who coveted large quantities of land, and managed it badly. Having studied agriculture in the Netherlands, he was deeply impressed by the success of small farms: they gave work, and yielded bigger crops; spade husbandry and gardening methods saved seed; whole families could live off two to three acres.[21] The same observations, of course, lay behind the agitations of the Diggers, though they dashed their chances by claiming the right to take common lands for their holdings, and thus struck fear in the hearts of both landowners and ordinary farmers.[22]

After 1660 with the Restoration of the king, and the restoration of many considerable Royalist landlords, returning to their properties after an enforced absence, official sympathy in government and among the ruling class turned away from small farms. Nevertheless, the economic circumstances did not favour large farms, and those who remained wedded to arable farming found their fortunes deteriorating sharply, as grain prices slumped and persisted low. Historians have taken the general view that the number of small farmers declined markedly at this time, but they may be exaggerating the force of that trend; they have no more than single, scattered examples to support it, for no national survey is possible.[23] It is noticeable how those observers who knew most about labour-intensive crops and horticulture maintained their belief in smallholdings. Carew Reynel, who had spoken vehemently in favour of tobacco-growing because of the work it created was certain that 'the smaller estates the land is divided into, the better for the nation; the more people are maintained, and the land better husbanded.'[24] Another expert on horticulture, John Worlidge, writing a whole book on horticulture, was equally emphatic: 'it were much better for the public that the great farms were subdivided into lesser, that the people might have habitations and employments here at home, to keep them from straggling abroad, than to have so many great farms lie so neglected, to the great prejudice of the Commonweal.' Living in Hampshire, Worlidge may well have been looking out upon some large farms on the downlands lying neglected by 1677.[25]

The debate in favour of small farms gradually fell silent after 1660 as political power accumulated in the hands of larger landowners, and economic influence came into the hands of a new professional class of land agents who preferred to choose substantial men as lessees of their masters' land. Nevertheless, those who were engaged in horticulture, hop-growing, and dairying, or who cultivated industrial crops—frequently managed alongside a basic arable farm—demonstrated considerable success in practice. Sometimes, even, landowners are found urging dairying on their tenants. The areas of the country best suited to these specialities were localized, of course, and they only revealed themselves to the assiduous traveller, in out-of-the-way places.

When mainstream agriculture returned to dominate the scene after 1750, farms once more increased in size, and by the middle of the nineteenth century contemporaries acknowledged the dramatic results brought about by the many amalgamations of small into large units. A man ahead of his time heralded the next turning of the tide with a slim book in 1872 in favour of small farms. The Reverend William Lea, vicar of St Peter's, Droitwich, gave advice on how to make them pay, and argued with conviction that the nation had lost both socially and morally by the extinction of the small farmer, and the loss of the farming ladder. The positive role of the small farmer in depression was further underlined by Alfred Burrows, a land steward at Pluckley, Kent, asserting in 1882 from his own experience how few small farms stood vacant; rather, they were tending to be let at increased rents, while large farms went untenanted. In the course of the 1880s, smallholdings were put on the current agenda, and as a discerning Essex land agent saw things in 1896, 'history repeats itself'.[26] Ten years later Edwin Pratt reviewed the distinctly new directions being taken by farmers, as dairying, horticulture, and poultry-keeping expanded steadily.[27] Since all three activities were known to rest on the enterprise of small farmers (even though the success of these enterprises was now beginning to produce a new breed of larger entrepreneurs), the merits of small farms called again for recognition. It seemed to some with a liking for generalizations that they succeeded only on good soils and preferably near towns.[28] But that conviction could not be expressed too dogmatically when faced with the success of a far more numerous and widely distributed group of such cultivators in France. There the small farmer was strongly entrenched, and in no danger of being ousted from the land. Indeed, he was able to compete with spectacular success against English producers in the market for fruit, vegetables, and dairy goods. Opponents of smallholdings, therefore, had to resort to another argument, that the life was tantamount to slavery, and the long working hours and small rewards amounted to a living standard far inferior to that of the English agricultural labourer. To that judgement Arthur Arnold responded shrewdly that the French peasant might dress poorly, but he had money in the bank which the English labourer certainly did not have.[29]

When the argument was diverted thus, it raised questions about the quality of life and the different national cultures of England and France on which highly divergent opinions could be held. Even some of the government's official reporters on the depression in agriculture felt the need to moderate the severest English verdicts on peasant life in France. But perhaps no writer was better informed and gave more food for thought on this topic than Matilda Betham-Edwards, who had lived in France for long periods, travelled all over the country in the course of fifteen years following the journeys of Arthur Young, and spent many hours inside peasant houses, talking to their inhabitants. She was deeply impressed by the 'ease and well-being' of the French peasantry in 1892.[30] The debate for and against the life of the smallholder, as seen in France, is instructive because it so plainly raged between two opposing groups, starting out from thoroughly different cultural viewpoints. But the contrasted views can also be seen as being each entrenched in, and appropriate to, distinct historical ages. Those who favoured large farms measured efficiency in the economies of *labour* which were thereby achieved. Supporters of a French peasantry, arguing also for a revived English peasantry, measured food output per acre of *land*, and on that basis the smallholder could be seen to produce two or three times more food than the large farmer.[31] When the differences in viewpoints were further pursued, it was noticed that in France the peasants were usually owners of their land, and their independence was deemed an advantage in enhancing the quality of their lives. In England, in contrast, the opponents of smallholdings deplored this attachment to land as French folly, pointing out that an equally effective shield against the cold wind of depression lay in the partnership of landlords with their tenants, whereby in hard times landowners reduced their tenants' rents.[32]

Although in policy-making quarters in England, in Parliament and in government, the voices in favour of large farms finally dominated the debate, opinion was sufficiently divided for a body of opinion to be assembled in favour of small farms, and to procure some legislation in their favour, though its effects were disappointing. An unexpected partisan was Gladstone himself, making two speeches as early as 1879–80 praising *'petite culture'*. First, at a horticultural show in the grounds of Hawarden in August 1879, and then during the election campaign in Midlothian in 1880, he commended garden-like cultivation, and the production of more flowers, trees, shrubs, and fruits, following the example of the peasant proprietors of France. The first of these speeches drew an immediate response from Sir Henry Thompson in the *Nineteenth Century*, joining together arguments for small farms and for a better diet. Nature never intended fruits to be the privilege of the rich and great, he declared. The poor had as sound a right to them as to sunbeams; yet nineteen out of twenty inhabitants in London could not get green food on any terms, and those who did paid an exorbitant price.[33] Two speeches by Gladstone in the Commons in 1892, when another Small Holdings Bill was on the table, were reprinted by the Liberal Party in a penny pamphlet. 'It is the small holdings in France that have brought the agricultural wealth of that country to a point so marvellously and so almost incredibly large,' he roundly declared. The smallholdings that were hoped for in England were to be of thirty to fifty acres, built up in some cases by labourers acquiring land gradually. Knowledgeable advocates, including Gladstone, did not, of course, expect to set them up everywhere; they fully appreciated that regional differences would make them appropriate in some places and not in others, a fact that was fully borne out by experience.[34]

The English Commissioners appointed to investigate the agricultural depression in its more advanced stages, and reporting finally in 1896, came down firmly on the side of the large farmers. But their unsympathetic assessment of smallholdings was not an accurate reflection of all the assistant commissioners' reports in the 1880s. The latter had interviewed smallholders in a number of different regions, and, where they saw highly successful undertakings, they displayed a sympathetic and receptive frame of mind. It was the assistant commissioners in the West Country and the North who saw less success, and returned adverse verdicts. Andrew Doyle in the West Country was adamant that agricultural improvement was only possible on large farms, while Mr Coleman, returning from the North, concluded sardonically that 'however much the poetry may suffer', smallholdings were doomed as unproductive.[35]

The Senior Commissioners interviewed only large farmers and land agents, one of the latter saying emphatically that it was 'the greatest folly in the world to discuss such a thing' as peasant proprietorship favourably.[36] So the final report did not favour an extension of small farms, but it was criticized in many quarters for its unfair reporting, and it was not allowed to pass as though it were unanimous. Three commissioners dissented, and one of them, Francis Allston Channing, wrote a book of nearly 400 pages in support of a different viewpoint. In his view, the Commission's majority report favoured the existing land system and seemed to conclude that all the problems that were being faced by agriculturists could be left to take care of themselves. Critical of the present situation on many counts, he pointed out that smallholdings were not only economically successful, they were even beneficial to the large farmer in preserving a supply of efficient and skilled labour ready to hand. This was the opinion of Mr Wilkin of Tiptree Fruit Farm in Essex, who relied on the labour of small farmers to help him in busy seasons. Large and small farms, in short, were seen as interdependent, and the self-interest of the large farmer alone should have led him to help the survival of the small.[37]

The government could not entirely brush aside the eloquent pleas in favour of smallholdings and allotments, and so legislation was passed in 1892—Jesse Collings's Small Holding Act—allowing county councils to buy land for smallholders. But it did not oblige them to do so. Jesse Collings had introduced a smallholdings bill every year in his first four years as an MP in the House of Commons, but, despite his final success, the results in 1906 were described as 'melancholy'.[38] The demand for land was admitted, but so was the lethargy of councils and the opposition of landowners. As one observer perceptively remarked, councils represented 'the dominant influences in the country rather than the aspirations of the class wanting smallholdings', while the dislike shown by landowners was described more bluntly in 1910 as based on 'hearsay information or vague prejudice'.[39] An Act in 1907, the Small Holdings and Allotments Act, consolidated in 1908 with the earlier Act of 1892, was more forceful, but it still contended with continuing apathy or hostility. Cambridgeshire and Worcestershire County Councils won praise, the latter for its success in creating smallholdings at Catshill, near Birmingham, thereby bringing benefits to thirty-two nailers, whose industry had fallen away, and left them bereft of a living;

Shropshire County Council also took action in the north of the county after 1908, and had ninety-three smallholdings by 1914. In England as a whole between 1908 and 1914 some 14,000 holdings were created out of 200,000 acres.[40]

At the end of the war in 1918 the campaign for smallholdings again stirred into life because of the acknowledged need to provide land for returning army veterans. County councils resumed their duty of providing land, and eventually nearly 17,000 tenants were settled on a quarter of a million acres. A more ambitious venture still was tried at Patrington, Yorkshire, and Amesbury, Wiltshire, with the setting up of a group of small profit-sharing farms, organized around a central unit which provided machinery, and made co-operative purchases and sales. Meanwhile the theoretical debate on small farms was resumed, though less animatedly than before, and many small farms survived in reality all through the years to 1939. Remarkable among the fresh ventures of the 1930s was one activated by Lloyd George's bold proposal in 1930 (in the midst of acute depression and large-scale unemployment) to settle 100,000 families on 3 million acres of land. The Land Settlement Association was launched in 1934, with the support of government and distinguished public figures, and with the resources to create family farms that would give a living to unemployed industrial workers and miners. In 1936 it was expecting to acquire nineteen estates and settle 700 families. It contended with serious problems in finding land on suitable soils, and in training people to farm who came from a very different background; some of the sound principles for success, enunciated in the early 1900s, were either forgotten or brushed aside. So the choice of some sites, like that at Andover, Hampshire, proved a failure, whereas at Fen Drayton, in Cambridgeshire, it was a success. For the record, however, the story of these ventures has tended to be written off in pessimistic terms, without credit being given to the successes and the favourable verdicts of those families who made a new life on the land and found satisfaction in country living. An exception to the bleak verdicts was that of Lord Addison in 1939, claiming among smallholdings set up by County councils after 1918 a failure rate of no more than 15 per cent. The outcomes of all the varied experiments deserve more thorough investigation in historical perspective. They may yet receive it, if the subject of small farms captures public interest again, as it is likely to do in the more sympathetic state of opinion today. Crofts in the Scottish Highlands are already undergoing a 'renaissance' as a result of 'environmental, social and economic concerns'.[41]

While central and local government was forced into taking modest affirmative action to increase smallholdings, some of the most successful undertakings were those of sympathetic landowners and parsons who provided smallholdings on their own land. Cogent books and essays were written which inspired further ventures.[42] One of the most discerning of the writers was the Reverend Henry Dunster, vicar of Wood Bastwick, Norfolk, who wrote an article in 1884 on 'England as a market garden'. He noted how much fruit, vegetables, dairy produce, and eggs were being imported, and that their prices were rising. These were the foodstuffs which large farmers neglected but which suited small farmers admirably. He envisaged 'a coming revolution', and in the following year wrote a book containing far more detailed advice on the produce to be considered, giving chapters not only on the now familiar enterprises of small farms, but adding suggestions, such as flowers and plants for distillation as medicines and perfumes, and culinary herbs and plants. He was evidently well read, as well as being well informed, on East Anglia's plant habitats, for his proposals included caraway (once grown extensively, he said, in Essex and Suffolk), teasels (grown in Arthur Young's day in Essex), coriander, dill, angelica, liquorice, saffron, and tarragon, and, widening the range of choice far more than was usual, he commended sugar beet, buckwheat, canary seed, comfrey (as a forage plant), spurry, and more.[43]

Another energetic writer on the same lines was the layman K. B. Baghot de la Bere, of Burbage Hall, near Hinckley, Leicestershire, who owned and himself cultivated a small farm of twelve acres. He had experience in Wales also, wrote a great many small books under the name Kenard B. Edwards, and, in consequence, had a large circle of correspondents. He espoused the theories of von Thünen, without actually saying so: small holdings of 10–40 acres within a two-mile radius of a town would ensure the most advantageous use of land to both country and cultivator, and beyond that larger farms of 100 acres were desirable. On 10 acres, he argued, families could keep four cows, and sell milk; two or three breeding sows would produce pigs for fattening; mangolds, turnips, cabbages, and hay would feed the stock in winter with some purchased maize; while factory work in town would supplement this living. He himself added still more enterprises on his own small farm, keeping rabbits, poultry (for the eggs), bees, and selling vegetables.[44]

Yet another proponent of smallholdings was Arthur Arnold, MP for Salford, and writer of a book on the subject, called *Free Land*. His convictions rested on observations in the Channel Islands and parts of northern France and Belgium; he recognized the adverse marketing conditions faced by smallholders, and the fact that small farms were not 'the settled habit of a large number of people', but he expected they would be 'in time to come'.[45]

From this sample of the literature, it is clear that the discussion of smallholdings was a far from negligible theme in contemporary debate. Some of it, of course, ran on continuously from experiments which had started earlier, like the Chartist ventures at Minster Lovell, Oxfordshire, and elsewhere, begun in

1846–8. This longer experience of artificially created smallholdings suggested that townsmen did not generally succeed, and, at least at the outset, that small farmers needed alternative supplementary work.[46] The varying sizes of holdings called for a definition of what was a small farm, for plainly they spanned a wide range in different kinds of country. In northern England family farms were expected to be 50–100 acres, in East Sussex a smallholding was said to require 50 acres, whereas in the Lincolnshire fenlands 15 acres was sufficient to keep a family, and in the Isle of Axholme, 8–12 acres. In the New Forest less than 12½ acres served, while the Small Holdings Act of 1908 pronounced that a smallholding could range from 1 to 50 acres.[47]

Smallholdings, in short, came in innumerable different shapes and sizes, but that very fact was part of a body of experience that summed up the character of alternative agriculture. The whole system lacked tidy uniformity. Landlord Allcroft in Shropshire, for example, had wanted to ensure that his cottagers had milk for their children, so his allotments allowed 5 acres per cottager on which they kept two or three cows, raised pigs, and grew fruit (the fruit in some cases paying the rent); they could not have survived without other work in addition. Twofold sources of work for smallholders were frequently the secret of success elsewhere, as at Penstrase Moor, near Truro, Cornwall, a mining district where a barren strip of moorland had been reclaimed by removing a 6-inch layer of spar stones to reveal good loam underneath. Miners, with money saved in several cases from working overseas, prospered by mining and farming together. In Evesham, Worcestershire, where horticulture and a favourable custom of tenant right favoured smallholdings, larger farms were subdivided through the normal workings of the property market. The economic strategies of smallholders were bewilderingly diverse: they might well exasperate politicians seeking truths that could be expressed in a few crisp generalities.[48]

Some of the small farms cited in debate at this time were relatively recent experiments by landowners with a social conscience and strong convictions on the merits of small farms. They deserve notice since they seem to echo events under the Commonwealth in the seventeenth century. William James Harris, head of a firm of corn merchants in London and Liverpool, bought 2,000 acres in Devon in 1871, and cut up 400–500 acres into twenty-five smallholdings. In this case, his main concern was to arrest depopulation and the decline of arable farming, so his aspirations were out of tune with the time, but he hoped the end of the depression would brighten their prospects. His cultivators were expected to earn wages as well. Another experiment was that of Major Poore at Winterslow, near Salisbury, buying 200 acres in 1892, and selling 112 acres in small plots. Rider Haggard called him the Don Quixote of the Hampshire Downs, intending this as a compliment, for he had tilted at a windmill, and the windmill had fallen, leaving him triumphant. Fifty to sixty families lived on land which had previously accommodated three labourers, and extra employment was provided by tree-felling and hurdle-making in the vicinity. Mrs Poore had launched a women's venture in spinning and weaving the home-produced wool of the Hampshire Down sheep, though it proved unable to compete with homespun cloth from Ireland. Another benevolent helper of poor men was Sir Robert Edgecumbe, who created smallholdings out of Rew Farm in Winterbourne St Martin, Dorset. It was deemed a success at that time, for on 307 acres, bought in 1888, the population had been raised from 21 to 100 souls.[49]

One of the truths about smallholdings that became ever clearer as time went on was that they throve best in a countryside where the tradition of small peasant farms was of long standing. Their future was far less promising when they were introduced as a novelty into an alien landscape. This was recognized most readily in parts of Lincolnshire and East Anglia, and it explains the vigour and success of efforts to create more smallholdings there. In the more favourable environment prevailing after 1880 several associations for self-help sprang up in those counties. The Lincolnshire County Council took action to buy land as soon as the 1892 Act was passed. A Small Holdings Association at Spalding in the fens was formed, and Earl Carrington, a stalwart supporter, let 658 acres to it for distribution in 1–50-acre plots among 200 tenants. In 1900 another Voluntary Association was reported in Norfolk where farms in three parishes were acquired for smallholdings.[50]

Some of the most discerning and realistic discussions of the local requirements for successful smallholdings came from eastern England and especially from Louisa Jebb, who was associated with the Co-operative Small Holdings Society. She was their tireless advocate, and has left much the most informative description of smallholder farming drawn from personal visits to many different areas. One of her most effective accounts described the commoners in the New Forest. Their economy was called 'peculiar', for it still relied on common and pannage rights which had mostly been extinguished elsewhere, but it was enjoying 'exceptional prosperity'. Deep layers of ancient tradition lay beneath it, whereas this was lacking at Lambourne, Berkshire, where a scheme was launched by Lord Wantage with his Small Farms Company. Well-intended though it was, it did not show the success of G. E. B. Eyre in the far more favourable social climate of the New Forest, where he was determined to 'prevent the extermination of a thrifty, independent race of men who . . . might be trusted to work out their own salvation'.[51]

Against this background of an alternative agriculture that was found to be appropriate on small amounts of land, all the many idealist colonies that were set up during these same years fall into their correct place in the picture.

Whether inspired by anarchist, socialist, or religious ideals, all assumed that their livings would be won from the same pursuits. The arguments in favour were most forcibly put in the writings of Kropotkin, who settled in England in 1886, and urged the more intensive cultivation of land, including spade husbandry, in order to provide work and supply home-grown foodstuffs. Kropotkin saw Danish butter, Flemish and Jersey potatoes, French salads, and Canadian apples pouring into London—he claimed that two-thirds of Britain's food was imported—whereas all could be equally well produced in England.[52] His writings influenced many colonization schemes, most notably that set up at Clousden Hill on Tyneside by men who planned to follow up-to-date horticultural methods (using glasshouses), conducted through anarchist-communist social relations, so creating a new moral world. Like Kropotkin, the founders of the Clousden Hill colony favoured the integration of smallholdings with industrial work, though in the event this latter objective was not pursued. Maintaining social peace proved more difficult than economic profit, and it was mainly personal disputes which brought the colony to an end in 1898, at a moment when it was on the brink of adopting co-operative ideals.[53]

Clousden Hill was only one of many colonies in these years, some of which have not yet found their historians. They started out with varied convictions: a socialist colony was set up at Starnthwaite, near Kendal, in 1892; a group called Croydon's brotherhood church set up Whiteway colony, near Stroud, Gloucestershire; strict dietary principles, including vegetarianism, inspired the Norton colony, near Sheffield, established in 1896 by Hugh Mapleton, whose name lives on in the health-food firm. But they all built on the smallholders' strengths, relying on horticulture, dairying, and poultry.[54]

At the end of all this debate and many practical initiatives to meet the economic needs of the time, a balanced verdict would have been that both large and small farms had an equal claim to serve their countrymen efficiently with food. But in order to recognize this fact, and judge the two fairly, their observers had to measure their economic efficiency differently. Certain farming soils and specialities required large farms, which could use machinery to best advantage. Other pursuits were appropriate to family farms. In the North, for example, it was clear that family farms were entirely suitable for dairying and stockbreeding.[55] In yet other places, small farms flourished while requiring some additional wage work to support them, though this was not to be counted as an argument against them. They had strong social merits, for they were a ladder for those starting in the farming business, they brought variety into the routines of life, and they kept the countryside populated.[56]

One of the weaknesses in the situation of smallholders lay on the marketing side. The problem was being successfully solved in France through co-operation among smallholders, but the value of this principle was slow to be recognized in England. Some forms of partnership had been adopted in earlier phases of alternative agriculture. We have mentioned the occasional signs of land farmed 'to halves'. When new crops were being tried in the seventeenth century, the sharing of costs and profits between partners had been one method of sharing the risks. But such ventures were few and far between, none had a long life, and when profit-sharing was discussed again in the 1880s, it failed to win great support. The co-operative movement, on the other hand, opened out fresh possibilities of partnership at a convenient moment, and some experimental ventures among small farmers were beginning by 1900 to show encouraging results. The Smallholdings Association in south Lincolnshire had been in existence for some years when it developed a co-operative bank (by 1906), and planned co-operative buying and selling operations. The system of collection used by the poultry breeders around Heathfield, Sussex, which had sprung into existence spontaneously, was cited by Edwin Pratt as a successful working example of co-operation. Surveying a broader scene in 1906, he saw yet other efforts to co-operate—in buying fertilizers, in a co-operative dairy at Brandsby, near Easingwold, Yorkshire, in co-operative fruit-grading at Hereford, as well as combinations to lower freight rates on the railway.[57] By 1908 known societies supplying farm requisites numbered 128 in England and Wales. It was a beginning, but it lagged far behind achievements on the Continent, where the French, Dutch, Danes, and Germans, starting from a more deep-rooted cultural loyalty to peasant farming, had forged ahead much faster.[58]

Conclusion

A large number of different strategies were devised by farmers to meet the late nineteenth-century depression, and judgements of their merits depend on the angle in time and space from which they are viewed. Those who saw alternative agriculture as a temporary and regrettable diversion from mainstream agriculture ranked the various strategies differently from those who looked approvingly on their originality in meeting new problems, and who saw their long-term potential. An excellent example of a judge from the mainstream viewpoint was Lord Ernle, who wrote authoritatively in 1912 about the agricultural revolution, which was, after all, an achievement of mainstream farming. When smallholdings were contemplated in the Land Utilization Bill of 1931, he dubbed them an anachronism, 'economically . . . inferior to large farm units'. Others concurred in resisting the creation of 'a new peasantry'.[59] From a different angle, however, the same bias had provoked a much earlier outburst from Arthur Arnold, appearing before the Select Committee on Small Holdings in

1889: when comparing French and English agriculture, he deplored the fact that the committee always alighted on wheat. It was a criticism which could equally justly be levelled at agricultural historians today. A view of the scene from the standpoint of mainstream agriculture always meant sliding over the achievements of alternative agriculture. Yet the advances made in alternative phases were highly influential in the long term, and diversified its objectives.[60]

Since alternative agriculture thrives in a very different environment from that which prevails under mainstream farming, its appearance as an expedient strategy always runs against the grain of the previous phase, and it has to fight against entrenched, conservative attitudes. So it is fortunate that, in every age that is beleaguered with problems, a few far-sighted observers, critics, and innovators are found who do not stand around waiting for the mainstream trends to return. They see the need for a differently structured system, and they take up the challenge. Among those in the late nineteenth century who were less successful in persuading their contemporaries were the advocates of more small farms; but among the more successful were the gardeners and poultry-keepers among whom were many exploiting the small farms and holdings already in existence.

Standing back to see the scene in the broadest perspective were those who saw 'the great depression' in an optimistic, rather than pessimistic frame of mind. Highly original strategies were treated by them as hopeful and constructive signs of a successful future for agriculture. In the book by Edwin Pratt, *A Transition in Agriculture*, written in 1906 when he thought that farming was recovering from depression, he summed up the way ahead by saying, 'it may not be along the old lines but it is a recovery'. He was not looking at the manœuvres to save and restore mainstream agriculture; rather, he turned his gaze on the increasing demand for food other than wheat and meat. In those other activities lay hopes for the future, even though they were wont to be described as 'minor industries', a deprecatory term which aroused the deepest indignation in Charles Whitehead, one of the most vigorous spokesmen on behalf of fruit-growing.[61]

In order to find alternative activities, it is noticeable how Pratt had to wander, as we have done, all over the kingdom, looking at milk production in Essex, fruit in Gloucestershire, glasshouse crops in Hertfordshire, grapes in Sussex, rhubarb in Leeds, lettuces in Evesham, poultry in Heathfield, and pigs in the New Forest. Other features in the scene which raised Pratt's hopes were a miscellany of assorted, scattered experiments, presaging the acceptance of different food values, and inaugurating new economic relationships. They included a more scientific investigation into the nutritional merits of vegetables, fruit, and milk, co-operative ventures among farmers in buying materials, grading produce, and in marketing, and practical help given by friendly landlords to smallholders. These produced at least one example of métayage (the provision of stock and equipment by a supportive landowner, in this case Lady Carlisle at Castle Howard). Innovative activities under a regime of alternative agriculture were branching out in a multitude of different directions, but most were modest, local efforts, which only the assiduous seeker in out-of-the-way places was likely to uncover. The statisticians were the very last to become aware of them and give them regular attention.[62]

In the much longer perspective which we enjoy in the 1990s, the imaginative strategies of alternative agriculture from 1880 onwards can be seen in a different light from that of contemporaries. They expanded the frontiers of the farming business, continuing a half-finished story from the point at which efforts had faded around 1750. In a positive frame of mind, their undertakers met and accepted the challenges of a changed situation in a fresh and constructive way. They did not settle for manœuvres within the framework of a mainstream farming system that was then in retreat, and whose future was unpredictable. Not that the most promising strategies of alternative agriculture could be predicted. The innovations were tentative; they started in scattered corners of the kingdom, and they did not blow trumpets to attract attention. They could not possibly be measured until a very late stage when the statisticians finally woke up to their existence.[63] The activities which paved new ways ahead would have called for officials to take up their microscopes, whereas it was their wont to survey the scene with telescopes.

The diversification of an economy relies on the success of many concurrent changes, both in human ability to exploit natural and other resources, and in the attitudes of people to such possibilities. A change in food habits at this time was one sympathetic accompaniment, for new tastes and food preferences among the different social classes undoubtedly encouraged diversification. These went hand in hand with the growth of urban populations. Historians do not see any great increase in milk-drinking on health grounds until the First World War, when the low physical standard of recruits to the army was revealed. But before that happened, commercial dairying was invigorated when families who had lived in villages, ate much dairy produce, and may even have owned a cow, moved to towns. The success of fruit and vegetable producers was plainly assisted by the fact that these foods had hitherto been regarded as the luxuries of the well-to-do. For that reason they were a welcome novelty when made available to classes below.[64]

Some producers, it is true, did not see the fruit and vegetable market opening great prospects for them; they feared overproduction, and actually saw their fears confirmed by occasional gluts when fruit rotted unsold. But others were confident that the market could digest larger quantities indefinitely if the prices could be reduced. In fact, as events showed, a latent but frustrated demand lay in wait, which growers hastened to satisfy, and, in the light of another horticultural revolution which has occurred in the late twentieth century, we can appreciate the progress that was made. Yet plenty of room was left for another revolution to be ushered in in our own day, from the 1980s onwards. This is the subject of the next chapter.

PART IV

∾

THE FOURTH EXPERIENCE
1980S ONWARDS

9 ❧ ALTERNATIVE AGRICULTURE TODAY

A fourth phase of alternative agriculture began in the 1980s, and is evolving its many strategies under our eyes. No one can predict where they will lead, or which will triumph above the others, but their manifold variety is an encouraging sign that the essential requirement of this phase is being met, namely, extreme diversification, involving a readiness to consider a multiplicity of enterprises, and to give much attention to detail.

The onset of the new phase of alternative agriculture was perceptible around 1980, but matters were not brought to a head until spring 1984, when milk quotas were introduced in order to cut dairy production, and a near-record grain harvest in 1985 added to large stocks of wheat and barley that remained in store from the previous year. All this focused attention on the Food Mountain that had to be dismantled.[1] Maturing perceptions of the problem can be followed thereafter. A national debate was called for in 1989, when the options enumerated were: extensive farming, more forests, organic farming, diversified crops of all kinds (for food, industry, and medicine), and land for recreation. The principal cause for alarm at that time was seen in piecemeal decisions taken by default.[2] Three letter writers joined together to discuss the consequences for the uplands of the kingdom, perceiving that agricultural efforts to solve current problems were likely to be concentrated on the more favoured arable lowlands. They also saw technology playing a lesser role in shaping policy in the future, and more place being given to socio-economic considerations. Nevertheless, the practical solutions that they foresaw for the uplands centred on some of the same pursuits prescribed for the lowlands, commercial forestry, conservation, recreation, and access. These writers called for a strategy which avoided 'short-term responses to short-term and disparate policies'.[3]

The scene, in fact, was already in 1985 replete with diversified initiatives, and, in a certain sense, 'piecemeal decisions' were to be welcomed; the more individuals exploring new frontiers the better. Peas and beans were being recommended as livestock feed, to replace imported soybean and manioc. The EEC had decided to encourage lupins. Flax was under trial (for linen) in Northern Ireland and Scotland. A new company was set up by a seed merchant of Essex, John J. King and Sons, together with Bio-Research of Crewe to produce borage as a medicinal plant. Two years later, another seed company in Suffolk, Grainseed Ltd. of Eye, was in collaboration with a British chemical company to observe the results of growing different varieties of sunflowers in England.[4] Manifold enterprises were already under way, matching the lessons of history, that every conceivable initiative is worth a trial.

What is the situation after some fifteen years of stumbling into this new experience? A general view of the scene is taken at research centres in the universities. The University of Reading has a strong and long-standing commitment to both practical agriculture and the study of its history. At its Centre for Agricultural Strategy, the second director, Professor, now Sir, Colin Spedding, supported the notion of financial help to farmers in a period of transition, but urged public debate to advertise alternative strategies.[5] He did not, unfortunately, suggest that historians be consulted. If asked, they would have suggested, first, a search for the many individuals already laying paths into the future, for history shows that major changes are usually anticipated by a few idealists, patient, persistent individuals who have been following their personal convictions for many years before any crisis arose. New strategies have a long gestation period, as the seventeenth-century experience has shown most clearly, and that characteristic was again underlined in the study made by John Hargreaves in 1987 of some of the most innovative fruit and vegetable growers in England. They had long been dedicated growers with a certain philosophy of agriculture that did not run in the conventional grooves of current thinking, and they had converted their beliefs into practice at considerable personal risk and cost.[6] They now encounter a more encouraging environment. But their idealist dreams seemed outlandish in the 1950s and 1960s, and it has taken a long time for their lonely and unpopular opinions to be deemed far-sighted in the totally changed circumstances of today. Opposition to the excessive use of artificial fertilizers was one minority argument, staunchly upheld by Sir Albert Howard, canvassing in the 1930s for healthy soils that preserved and increased humus, and by Eve Balfour, who shared Howard's convictions, was the author of *The Living Soil* (1943), and founded the Soil Association. The change of viewpoint on this issue came too late to be relished by Sir Albert Howard, but before her death it lifted the spirits of Eve Balfour who had been collecting her evidence since the 1930s. Among farmers in the same decade, taking action to restore humus to a wasted farm, tribute must be paid to Arthur Hollins of Fordhall Farm in the West Country, reaching the same conclusions on the basis of observation and the wise advice of his agricultural labourer.[7]

Another hero of our time is surely Lawrence D. Hills, who founded the Henry Doubleday Research Association in 1954, naming it to commemorate a Quaker smallholder (1813–1902), a lone pioneer in the third phase of alternative agriculture, who commended the highly nutritive protein crop, Russian comfrey, in Britain. Lawrence Hills in 1954 was campaigning for home-grown, fresh foods, less dependence on the food of poor countries which needed the food for themselves, and promoting systems of organic farming which were self-sufficient in maintaining fertility. When mainstream agriculture brooked no resistance in the 1950s and the tide of uniformity was overwhelming diversity, Lawrence Hills's regular letters to the press evoked little response. In contrast, the Association's launching of a Seed Heritage Programme in 1992 with a 'seed library', to save the many varieties of vegetable seeds threatened with extinction by European and British legislation, crystallized an objective in the original inspiration, which in a different age meets with informed support.[8]

Because of their commitment to sustainable agriculture, organic food farms are wearing down some of the scepticism of commentators, so that they now hold a recognized place among systems of alternative agriculture. Not a few economists, working with statistics but without historical perspective, poured cold water on the future of organic farming.[9] But in 1990 the Royal Agricultural Show at Stoneleigh, Warwickshire, featured thirty-four exhibitors at its Organic Food and Farming Centre—three times larger than the previous year. The European Union gave support by its organic farming regulations, no. 2092 in 1991, and no. 2078 in 1992. The Danish and German governments set an example by giving their organic farmers a subsidy, while the British government allocated a small sum under a new Organic Aid Scheme in 1993.[10]

Before turning in more detail to the various initiatives under way at present, we should notice a not uninteresting parallel between the past and the present. Innovative, experimental farmers toil against obstacles, without certainty of success. They often have to choose fringe areas of land and disadvantageous sites simply because their resources are limited, even though their hopes are high. They cannot afford the best land with the best transport facilities, and some have hacked their holdings out of a wilderness. An assistant commissioner reporting to Parliament on alternative strategies in 1882 saw large quantities of strawberries and raspberries in west Kent growing on land 'which a few years ago was poor woodland'.[11] Similar locations can be perceived in the experiments of today, the pioneers often finding their best opportunities on rundown land in obscure places, where they secure it because competitors are few, and where they have scope for quiet experiments. They are found on the fringes of the farmers' best soils and outside the most favoured farming regions. Thus Edward and Penny Kain grow thirty-two unusual vegetables and twenty-three herbs, like rocket, exotic mustard greens, baby radiccio, several varieties of potato, chervil, and three varieties of basil, on what a reporter called a windswept Devon hilltop near Totnes. They cater for a restaurant in Dartmouth, and also grow soft fruit for their new business in fruit liqueurs. The Kains have been much supported by Frances Smith, an earlier pioneer of farm-to-restaurant supplies between Kent and London. She grows a large variety of unusual vegetables and herbs, using seed originally drawn from foreign countries, and when she started in 1987 one of her inspirations was Joy Larkcom's book of 1984, *The Salad Garden*. The innovative ventures of women feature prominently in more than a few case histories. Relevant in forging links with the past is the fact that Frances Smith's farm, comprising twenty-three acres and five polythene tunnels, is situated in Appledore, Kent. This place links her directly with a much earlier innovative endeavour to grow madder in the 1620s, when Appledore lay on the fringes of unattractive, undrained marshland.[11]

In other once less favoured countrysides, like the Weald of Kent, the Marches of Wales, or the fens of eastern England, more alternative ventures can be found but for another reason. These regions in the past were populated by small proprietors who have still not been totally wiped out of existence. Hence, the structure of landholding offers in such places the necessary small pieces for courageous adventurers to begin realistically on a modest scale. In fact, small-holdings and small farms offer the best beginning to many pioneers of new farming pursuits, whether to keep goats, grow mushrooms or organic vegetables, or return to farmhouse cheese-making. Regrettably, such circumstances have never conferred political influence.[12]

Initiatives being taken at the present follow several different directions, but few fail to recapture in some way memories of similar strategies used in the past: they urge better timber management, and the conversion of arable to pasture; they offer leisure activities, but this time to more people than did the deer parks and the game birds of the moorlands, which once gave pleasure only to the gentry; they foster the growing of varied plants, for industrial, for medicinal, and for aromatic use; and they produce more diversified foodstuffs, including vegetables, fruits, dairy produce, unusual meats, and fish. All are seen to have fresh potential, and those involved show an imaginative vision that expands their possibilities well beyond the scope envisaged for them in former phases of alternative agriculture.

One of the notable revivals for industrial purposes is the renovation of woodland, leading to a renewed interest in coppicing as an alternative occupation, and so returning to the practices of a former age. Coppicing regularly took on a new lease of life in earlier phases of alternative agriculture, and, this time round, its possibilities were already recognized in 1981 when one advocate deplored the

20. Coppicing. The coppicing, mainly of chestnut and ash, is centuries old on this farm in the Kentish Weald. This is Carroty Wood, on North Frith Farm, Hadlow, showing some of the best younger coppice on the estate. It was probably established about 1950, and has been cut about every 15 years for fencing stakes and palings. Local stories tell of high prices paid in the past for this particular cant of woodland by two proud but feuding woodcutting families. Coppicing does not submit readily to wood-processing machines, and so remains labour-intensive. The farmer here intends to continue to coppice, though perhaps on a reduced scale, and on a longer rotation. He does not see any likelihood at present of anyone locally planting larger areas of chestnut on this marginal Weald ground. But should we not, perhaps, expect demand to revive, and make it a profitable crop?

21. Charcoal-burning. The demand for charcoal for barbecues has revived this profitable use of wood-land. Here is Lol Graham, at work near Wendover, Buckinghamshire.

decades of neglect. Now, over a decade later, we see its revival in earnest. Coppicing is inspiring pride and interest, and nurturing a market in woodland crafts. It is encouraging more use of timber for industrial purposes, such as fencing, tool handles, and pulpwood for paper, and it is supplying a higher-quality charcoal than the 48,000 tonnes which are imported. Local authorities are giving active encouragement. In Kent, where 40 per cent of woodland is coppice, a Centenary Community Woodland Project was started in 1992 to encourage parish councils to create and manage their own woodlands and to value the produce, whether coppice stools, holly for Christmas, or blackberries. A Trees for Kent Advisory Panel was set up in that county to improve management, and similar initiatives have been taken in East Sussex in the Ashdown forest. At a more ambitious level, short-rotation coppice of willow and poplar is being considered as a source for conversion into fuel in power stations.[13]

Alarm at the heavy inroads being made into the large forests of other continents has stimulated initiatives at home to reduce dependence on foreign timber imports. Now it is being suggested that positive economies in the use of energy can result from building in timber rather than concrete and plastic. Plans are laid to make the United Kingdom in the longer term 24 per cent self-sufficient in timber, while oriented strand board, made from home-grown softwoods and forestry thinnings, and medium-density fibreboard, made from scrap timber with a veneer added, are being manufactured to reduce the need for imported hardwoods.[14]

Exploiting the uses of woodland further, plans have been laid to enlarge substantially the British forest acreage. In France woodland occupies 27 per cent, in West Germany 30 per cent whereas it covers only 10 per cent of Britain. A Midland Forest is planned by the Countryside Commission, covering 200 square miles of Derbyshire, Staffordshire, and Leicestershire, while plantings on the outskirts of cities are urged upon local authorities, both to increase forest products and to provide recreational facilities. Grants and tax concessions, already available to landowners, are now being recommended for farmers. Whereas the 'set-aside' policy introduced in 1988 takes land temporarily, or permanently out of cultivation, but does nothing with it, and is a negative and dispiriting measure, woodland-planting is one positive alternative, which has now been granted recognition in the European Union as a valid way of keeping land out of use. The current, energetic campaign of the Woodland Trust in enlisting public interest in woodland conservation and enjoyment reflects the new mood of appreciation for this alternative use of land.[15]

Turning the land 'permanently' to grass is another strategy for the present, thoroughly familiar since it was used in every earlier alternative phase. It is leading in some places, however, to more constructive moves by individuals to preserve, or recapture, unique landscapes that were in danger of being lost. Thus it becomes a more innovative undertaking, reflecting the fresh, late twentieth-century concern for preserving the variety of habitats in the world. In 1991 the government gave financial help (which it increased in 1993) to conserve and restore chalk grassland, lowland heath, coastal vegetation, river meadows and marshes, and heather moorland and hill landscapes. From late 1993 it became official EU policy to encourage farmers to set aside 18 per cent of their land for twenty years to create habitats such as woodlands and wetlands. Even before this measure, however, the sandy brecklands of East Anglia were being defended for their special qualities. This area has been reduced since 1900 to about a quarter of its former extent by forestry and arable farming. Its farmers are now receiving government and EU money to conserve what remains.[16] In another private venture, the attempt is being made by local people, setting up the Countryside Restoration Trust, to recover ancient watermeadows in Cambridgeshire. The meadows that were a seventeenth-century innovation have been thoroughly maltreated—ploughed and fertilized for cereals—and now lie desolate as set-aside land. Signs of appreciation of our ancient water-meadows will bring comfort to those, like Peter Martin at Britford, in Wiltshire, who long ago swam against the tide of mainstream agriculture, and continued valiantly to preserve, and to *use* his watermeadows for stock-raising.[17]

Other imaginative conversions of arable to grass are being undertaken in order to restore old meadows as they were before wholesale ploughing destroyed them. One example has been publicized in south Dorset, in a field called Scratchy Bottom, near Lulworth Cove, where Paul Simpson's father was once given incentives to plough, and now his son is given incentives to re-seed with meadow grasses and flowers, and allow the downland to regenerate.[18]

We have already seen how phases of alternative agriculture in the past gave a stimulus to the leisure pursuits of the rich, namely, hunting (hence the deer parks), wildfowling (hence the duck decoys), and game shooting (hence the breeding of pheasants, partridge, and other birds on heathland and moor-land). These past pleasures of the gentry class are not neglected now. Indeed, significant moves have been made to improve the habitats of game birds: Lord Peel is restoring the heather and wildlife to Swaledale, by coaxing and contriv-ing a reduction in sheep-grazing on the commons; and a management policy for game birds is now being explored on the Loddington estate, Leicestershire. This last involves research undertaken by a trust to commemorate Baron Aller-ton and his wife, who loved field sports and wildlife. But time has moved on, and in the late twentieth century a larger place is being made for the leisure pursuits of other classes. Farmers, in consequence, have turned land over to golf courses (perhaps too many, according to reports in 1995), mountain bike tracks, go-cart, stock car, and banger racing circuits, while riding schools flourish.[19]

Industrial plants have also returned to the scene for serious consideration, as they did most noticeably in the period 1650–1750. Some, moreover, are the same plants as were chosen in the past, though the merchant-traders who took the initiative with their farming partners in the sixteenth century are not the leaders now; they are replaced by research scientists seeking industrial manufacturers as partners. The scientists now hold the whip hand since they have the skill to modify plants genetically, and enhance their most promising attributes. In that process, the use of the plant may be turned in wholly new directions. This is happening to rapeseed, which appeared on the English scene as a serious crop in the 1560s, was established by the 1650s, and remained until the later nineteenth century. Its oil was then used for industrial purposes, in the cloth industry and for lighting. Its return in the 1970s brought an oil for human consumption, for although its high content of erucic acid threatened heart problems, a reduction was achieved in the mid-1970s. With the aid of subsidies from the EEC, rapeseed then spread comparatively rapidly for use as a vegetable oil, and in 1986 was described as the third most widely grown arable crop in England after wheat and barley.[20] Now its acreage must fall as subsidies are removed in accordance with the world trade agreement (GATT), and so its industrial potential returns to prominence. The oil is now modified to serve a different purpose, and is already being used experimentally to drive public transport vehicles, including a ferry in Italy, taxis in Berlin, two buses in Reading, two pleasure boats on the Norfolk Broads, and post office vans. Early in 1994 Rover car engines using rape oil were being tested. Through genetic engineering, scientists also see another use for rapeseed in cheap plastics.[21]

All oils from plants are under scrutiny now as renewable resources which may be substituted for mineral oils. The plants involved include trees as well as annuals, like sunflowers, which do not at present suit our climate, but could have a different future through biotechnology. Meanwhile as sources of energy yet other plants like sugar beet are considered for the making of bio-diesel, while fast-growing grasses for distillation into 'producer gas' are being investigated, and straw as a fuel stock for generating electricity is not ruled out.[22]

Industrial users of plants are also showing special interest in those plants which yield oils with unusual fatty acids, having unique chemical properties for specialized manufacturing purposes. The research scientists have many exploratory programmes under way, but their capital cost is high, and risk-conscious manufacturers do not respond readily to challenges with an uncertain future. Some surprising plants are under investigation. Caraway is one of those, of interest for its oil, which inhibits sprouting in potatoes. It was a field crop at Clanfield, Oxfordshire, in the seventeenth century, at a time when the making of comfits, that is to say, sugary sweets using caraway seeds had been introduced by immigrants and had firmly established itself in the kitchens of those who could afford sugar. Other plants under scrutiny are crambe (*Crambe abyssinica*), a member of the mustard family, and honesty (*Lunaria annua*), a common plant in our gardens, yielding a lubricant and hydraulic oil; marigold (*Calendula officinalis*) producing oil for coatings and cosmetics; and sprengel, of the spurge family (*Euphorbia lagascae*), containing a unique vernolic oil for industrial use.[23] In Somerset in 1983 trials were under way with the jojoba plant, the oil of which is used as a substitute for sperm whale oil in cosmetics and glove-making. In 1985 biotechnology was expected to adapt meadowfoam (*Limnanthes alba*) to the English climate for similar uses, and in 1993 scientists in the Netherlands reported hopefully on its future if the oil yield could be increased and made more reliable.[24]

Another industrial crop which has received attention recently is flax, which could revive the once well-established linen industry of Ireland. It is not so suggested for England, even though linen was made from English flax in the past, and a larger acreage was positively canvassed in the seventeenth century. The more productive oil-bearing varieties of flax, however, have returned in recent years, subsidized by the European Community in order to achieve self-sufficiency in linseed oil for paints, putty, and floor coverings. The blue flowers were at first a surprise and now a pleasure in the fields in June and July, and in 1993 covered 400,000 acres in Britain.[25]

Oils from plants are all bio-degradable, and so are commended on environmental grounds. So the future of this category of alternative crop, though unpredictable, is potentially large and lasting. But a multitude of other industrial possibilities are now being explored more deliberately, in order to use the proteins, starch, and fibres from plants, and the lignin from wood.[26] Advancing well beyond the research stage, hemp-growing for paper was started in England in 1980 by a courageous early pioneer, John Hanson of Lyme Regis, Dorset. Intent on positive action to conserve world resources, he passed one milestone when the index of the 1992 issue of the *Ecologist* was made of his hempen paper. In 1993 a consortium of twenty farmers, calling themselves Hemcore, was assembled, growing 1,500 acres of hemp in East Anglia. This crop will make more paper (of which a fine quality is at present being used for cigarettes and bibles), while the waste is being sold as horse bedding, for it is absorbent and makes good compost. This last idea came from France, where 10,000 acres of hemp are already grown. Yet another plan for using hemp as a fuel has now led to tests, with promising results, in Ireland, the Irish climate being eminently suitable for the new strain that has been developed. The plant grows in six months up to 14 feet; it is cheaper than wheat or barley to produce; and it burns as well as wood, and yields similar quantities of energy. In power stations it could replace Irish peat which is a diminishing resource.[27]

Other plans for hemp and flax have moved forward at the instigation of Harry Gilbertson and the Natural Fibres Organisation of Silsoe, Bedfordshire, and Robert Lukies, an Essex farmer. Gilbertson led the effort to invent a decorticating machine for extracting the tough stem fibres of these plants, and his engineering success holds out the possibility of exploiting the resilient qualities of these fibres in cloth-making and for specialist products such as 'revegetation blankets' in farming, and absorbent materials to soak up oil from polluted water. Lukies was planning in April 1995 to plant 1,000 acres of hemp at Great Dunmow, and underlined the merits of the crop in obliterating weeds and using only half the fertilizer used on cereals. If, as is hoped, this venture heralds 'a much-needed agricultural and industrial revolution'—in Germany too, where the industrial uses of hemp are being similarly explored—it will constitute the third part of a serial story begun in the sixteenth century. An act to increase the acreage of hemp and flax was passed in 1566, mainly to reduce imports, and cogent arguments for more forceful measures to the same end circulated in Westminster in the 1570s. Propaganda produced some positive results, and in the seventeenth century certain parts of England won a reputation for specializing in hemp and flax for canvas, sailcloth, sacking, ropes, and linen thread. The occupation lost momentum after 1750, and when hopes revived in the 1880s they were quickly dashed, for hemp was by then being carried more cheaply from Russia and Italy than from Norfolk to its buyers in North Yorkshire. A revival of flax was similarly discussed but dismissed since a large scutching mill in Suffolk had closed down in the 1860s, just too soon for flax to exploit its new chance. Even so, flax for paper was being grown by one intrepid Welsh farmer at Newport, Monmouth, in 1881.[28]

Willow has returned as another alternative crop not only for baskets, trays, and wickerwork furniture, but as a possible source of fuel, being harvested already for that purpose in Sweden. Basket-making sets up a parallel with the past, for in 1894 a surge in demand for willow for vegetable and fruit baskets gave it a good outlet. Willow was recommended for cricket bats in 1905, and again in 1927, when it was judged 'a profitable investment', if due care was taken in the choice and management of the trees. Against all odds willow managed to survive in the Somerset Levels, and now finds itself again in tune with the times; James Hector of Taunton won a prize as a grower and maker of hurdles and other garden products early in 1996, looking back, in his case, on a beginning with willow in the 1930s. At Brampton, in Suffolk, Robert Yates received publicity in 1992 for his products, having started willow-growing as an alternative

22. Willow-growing. This traditional crop in fenland country has survived in Somerset and East Anglia, and now benefits from a more favourable economic and social climate in which to sell its wares. Robert Yates is the farmer and basket maker in this photograph. He started growing 12 acres of willow beds in 1988 as an alternative crop on his 890-acre family farm at Brampton, Suffolk, and his first best-selling item proved to be a witch's house for children. He is shown here moving the roof of the house. He now makes arbours, hooded seats, and willow jumps for sports events, and executes special commissions.

crop in 1988. In Somerset a threat looms against the survival of willows through competing policies to raise water levels and attract wildlife into 'wetland' habitats. But other hopes are raised for it as a source of electricity, now that trials with new methods of harvesting are under way, urged on by the merits of willow as a 'green' fuel.[29]

A field crop, which has come and gone several times over, and came again in 1973 to Essex, was tobacco. Historians may still nurture a suspicion that this plant could have a medical use, for certainly such was the belief when it was introduced into Europe in the sixteenth century. Indeed, in 1995 the idea sprang again when a malaria vaccine was produced from tobacco leaves, and other researchers also suggested that, by wearing a skin patch of nicotine, sufferers from heart disease lowered the risk of blood clots.[30] But for the present it has passed away as a failed and undesirable venture. Natural dyes, on the other hand, seem at present to have a brighter future, since the fashion for fadeable colours persists: fadeable indigo jerseys have been advertised in positive terms for the virtue of their fading colours, and natural dyes command high regard. Used in Turkish carpets, for example, they earn high prices in the market. If natural dyes should find a commercial niche, then woad, madder, and weld could readily be grown again, just as they were in the second phase of alternative agriculture between 1650 and 1750. In 1995 hopes were high in several European countries, especially for woad, since a way has been found by English scientists to process it without inflicting its unpleasant smell on the neighbourhood when the leaves ferment.[31]

Herbal medicine, as we have seen, regularly prospers alongside vegetarianism in periods of alternative agriculture, and it certainly flourishes now. It was promoted in the years 1880–1914, and in the period 1650–1750, while it may have been modestly evident, though the documents are meagre, in the years 1350–1500.[32] In the past many plants were grown in gardens, rather than fields, under the conviction that their essential virtues—flavour, strength, and efficacy—were weakened when grown on a large scale. But this reservation did not apply after the seventeenth century; saffron, for example, was grown on large, though still modest, acreages; and liquorice was certainly a field crop in the seventeenth and eighteenth centuries,[33] as were woad and madder, used medically as well as for their dyes. In the course of the nineteenth century, English growers were ousted from the scene, as druggists came to rely on central Europe, notably Germany and Austria-Hungary for their main supplies. Whether English growers took renewed interest immediately after 1880 is not clear. But a remarkable leaflet was issued by the Ministry of Agriculture in 1914, revised in 1916, acknowledging that the outbreak of the Great War had 'completely changed the situation'. Prices for such herbs as foxglove, henbane, valerian, and dill had all risen sharply, for dandelion roots by 200–300 per cent and for belladonna by 600 per cent. 'The present time', it declared, 'is particularly favourable for the establishment of a home industry in the cultivation of medicinal plants.' *Materia medica* farms, apart from the one at Mitcham, existed at Carshalton, Hitchin, Long Melford, Market Deeping, and Wisbech. More were now encouraged, since current prices allowed them to absorb the high cost of labour, and might even permit exports. The leaflet gave practical advice on cultivation and marketing, and a list of desired plants. Local specialities, noted in passing, were dill from East Anglia, white poppy heads from Lincolnshire, and valerian from Derbyshire, where it was gathered wild from the woods and transplanted. As a result, Mrs M. Grieve, author of the later *Modern Herbal*, trained pupils to prepare herbs for the chemist, and one of the places where medical herbs flourished was Evesham, growing many dozens of acres of belladonna and blessed thistle.[34]

The scene, as it was presented in 1914, has a familiar look in the mid-1990s, though the economic logic is different. The role of medicinal plants has been enhanced in the last three decades of the twentieth century by a preference, when curing certain conditions, for herbal remedies, rather than chemical drugs, and by the recognition that plants could cheapen costs and could assist the poor populations of the world.[35] Will many more medical plants return again to the fields? Already evening primrose has become a familiar crop, used in the treatment of eczema, liver disease, multiple sclerosis, and other conditions. Sleeplessness submits to valerian, hops, and passion flower. Feverfew alleviates migraine. The evident benefits of hemp (*cannabis*) in relieving sufferers from multiple sclerosis is now stimulating a campaign to permit field cultivation (banned since 1971), and, if successful, will restore a traditionally known medicinal plant (favourably appraised in Nicholas Culpeper's *Complete Herbal* in the seventeenth century), to the fields and the pharmacopoeia. Bog myrtle (*Myrica gale*) is one of the most recent plants to be discovered and developed commercially, as an ointment that is found successful in dispelling midges. It promises to bring a crop for deliberate cultivation to the Scottish island of Skye. Yet another possible plant, whose potential is not yet fully realized, is purslane. In the early seventeenth century, Lord William Howard had it delivered to his door at Naworth castle, in Cumberland, and the botanists John Gerard and John Evelyn both welcomed it in salad. Its country name is pigweed, and that explains the insult thrown at it by William Cobbett in his gardening book in 1838, calling it 'a mischievous weed eaten by Frenchmen and pigs when they can get nothing else'. However, it was traditionally thought to be helpful in scorbutic ailments, and now it is promised a new lease of life with the discovery that its high quantity of alpha-linolenic acid protects against heart attacks. On the very day that this book was delivered to the publishers came news of an ambitious project to extract essential compounds and oils from plants such as lavender, rosemary, chamomile, thyme, sage, daffodils, and peppermint, for use in the pharmaceutical, perfumery, and food industries. It is being started with a substantial grant from the Ministry of Agriculture on the 250-acre James Barn Farm Estate at Naunton in Gloucestershire, and, in the words of the journalist's report, 'it is costing several millions of pounds and it has never been done on this scale before'. Finally, in the search for medicinal plants, special interest centres on finding a plant to combat the Aids virus, in which scientists in the laboratories in Kew Gardens are participants. Still wider vistas open out from research at Cambridge into the possibilities of injecting an active ingredient into plants to serve as a vaccine. A hybrid virus has been successfully injected into the cowpea plant, which multiplies in the leaves and so yields a cheap vaccine against foot-and-mouth disease. This procedure could hold out a fresh future for medicinal crops in the field.[36]

Aromatics constitute another revival from the past which brings a separate group of plants into the list of possibilities for alternative agriculture. Their first use lies in the perfume industry, but they are coming to be increasingly appreciated in the medical world. Aromatherapy is finding a place as an art of healing, and in 1989 was reported on trial in the surgical wards of the John Radcliffe Hospital, Oxford. Thus ancient learning is being recovered. It was considered newfangled in the 1970s, but, in fact, the use of essential oils was known in southern Europe in the fifteenth century, filtering through from the Arab world. It so captivated the rich of northern Europe by the sixteenth century that it led in Paris to the extravagant use of perfumed waters gushing from fountains during festivals. In England, one of the most conspicuous signs of the new fashion then was in the wearing of perfumed gloves.[37]

When we look for recurring rhythms in alternative agriculture, it is not surprising to find that a serious attempt to revive the cultivation of aromatic plants was made in the 1890s. In 1898–9 F. W. Burbidge wrote a cogent article on the virtues of their fragrant leaves (he thought them more effective than their flowers), claiming for their essential oils antiseptic powers, as well as commending their use in wines, liqueurs, and cordials. For supporting literature he harked back to the seventeenth century, citing William Temple's essay 'Of Health and Long Life'. This contained the writer's eloquent personal testimony to the 'reviving as well as pleasing' scents of herbs and flowers. Their effect struck Temple most forcibly when he visited the Indian warehouse in Amsterdam, filled with chests of mace, cloves, and nutmegs. But Burbidge also cited a two-volume work of J. Ch. Sawyer, *Odorographia*, published in 1892, as the most reliable text on perfumes, and a pamphlet from Schimmel of Leipzig of

1893. These and other writings of the 1880s and 1890s suggest that aromatics were enjoying a modest revival, as the agricultural circumstances would urge us to guess.[38]

The celebrated centres for the growing of aromatic plants in the last three centuries have moved about England in a seemingly random fashion, governed perhaps by the personal idiosyncrasies of individual growers, rather than by any specially favourable natural conditions. In the late nineteenth and early twentieth centuries Mitcham in Surrey held renown for growing peppermint, lavender, and thyme, whereas in the later eighteenth century lavender plantations had flourished in Berkshire, at Park Place, near Henley. Now in the later 1990s, the largest lavender farm in Britain is situated at Heacham, Norfolk, while a determined pioneer in the growing of roses for their oil is Peter Wilde, who has been at work in Yorkshire since 1987. Aromatic plants which grow freely in Britain are fennel, peppermint, geranium, lavender, hyssop, marigold, marjoram, rosemary, sage, and thyme. The list suggests some scope for new ventures, and it could be lengthened. On a visit to a perfumery in County Clare, Ireland, in 1993, yet other plants were suggested to this author: the perfumer there wished to see the cultivation of more angelica, clary sage, and lovage.[39]

A still larger category of plants suggesting themselves for consideration as alternative crops are those used for food. Mounting pressure accumulates in favour of the consumption of more vegetables and fruit, as, for example, when medical researchers stress anew their virtue in protecting against cancer. It is this claim which has been responsible for the great market success of broccoli in America. Plainly, there is much room for a change in diet in Britain, as the figures of vegetable consumption in the United Kingdom are the lowest among all European countries.[40] Progress has, nevertheless, been made in diversifying and expanding the consumption of vegetables and fruit in the United Kingdom in the last thirty years, thereby forging notable parallels with developments in the sixteenth–seventeenth centuries. Travel abroad for pleasure, deliberate searches overseas for new vegetables and fruits that will grow in England (Joy Larkcom's quest for salad plants overseas and her books come first to mind), and the dynamism of world trade have introduced many new foods to our tables, and refreshed the view taken of some familiar ones. The way has been paved for more alternative crops on the farm.[41]

Among familiar foods, potatoes are being examined with a more critical eye, in order to retrieve the many tastes of different varieties. Captain Donald MacLean at Dornock Farm in Crieff, Perthshire, grew a collection of 400 varieties; another experimenter is at work in Glamorgan; and the Henry Doubleday Research Association keeps a Potato Library, and constantly alerts us to the folly of allowing potato varieties to dwindle in number.[42]

23. Lavender-harvesting in the 1990s. Lavender-growing was associated in the late nineteenth and early twentieth centuries with Mitcham, Carshalton, and the Wandle valley, Surrey. Nowadays the main commercial centre is at Heacham, Norfolk, where 100 acres of lavender are grown, and the plant is harvested by machine.

Among possible new foods, the lupin continues under investigation. The sweet, narrow-leaved variety (*Lupinus angustifolius*) was being recommended in 1988 for bread, pasta, soup mixes, and cereal foods, and was awaiting approval as a safe foodstuff in 1993. More recently, the use of *Lupinus albus* has been publicized, as a livestock fodder, rich in protein (30–40 per cent) and containing also oil (8–12 per cent). The plant was often mentioned as a potentially valuable fodder crop in the seventeenth century, but it did not spread far, possibly because the varieties brought from the Continent did not grow readily in Britain.[43] From South America other food plants being evaluated include quinoa, a staple grain food in Peru, first made known to Europeans by the Spanish conquerors in the sixteenth century; ajipa, a succulent tuber-like horse chestnut; yacon, a sweet root with an apple flavour; and amaranth, a cereal with a high protein content.[44]

Other dimensions of the horticultural revolution that is under way at present involve new methods of growing vegetables, the choice of more and better varieties, or an extension of the growing season. The survey of enterprise all over Britain by John Hargreaves (1987), recorded the success of garlic in the Isle of Wight, where Colin Boswell of Mersley farms has become the master of the English crop, harvesting some 100 tonnes a year. Celery flourishes in the Isle of Ely, cucumbers are grown under glass on Humberside, organic tomatoes under glass on Pilling Moss, Lancashire, and asparagus (a crop whose future is likely to be improved by a nation-wide Growers' Association) in East Anglia and elsewhere. Diversification has lengthened the list of vegetables to include more varieties of onions, iceberg and red-leaved lettuces, oriental brassicas (Chinese leaves), endive, chicory, sorrel, courgettes, celeriac, calabrese, salsify (a reminder that this was named along with scorzonera and seakale in 1904 as a vegetable that deserved more attention), fennel, and squashes. Hopes are raised for the more deliberate cultivation of globe artichokes, dandelion leaves (regularly seen as a salad ingredient in French markets), rocket, and more varieties of mushroom.[45]

In reviewing present initiatives, John Hargreaves tapped local people for vivid stories of the heroic past of their grandfathers and great-grandfathers, when they first took land on Rixton Moss in Lancashire, and prepared it for horticultural use. It was offered to them in plots of twenty to twenty-five acres, at a nominal rent by the landowner. They were young, strong men of 20–25 years of age, taking their chance with nothing but a few handtools. They drained the moss, manured it with night soil from Manchester, and after twelve years of back-breaking toil brought it successfully into cultivation. They and their families lived in turf huts, old railway carriages, and sheds. Yet descendants of some of the original families, who still farm the mosses, hear the lands now described as 'highly productive agricultural areas', producing 'the best lettuce in the world'.[46]

Similar room for new initiatives is found in the fruit sector of the market. New, low-growing varieties of apples and pears are being planted, accompanied by an energetic campaign to enhance public appreciation of home-grown fruit. Openings are seen in the fact that pear consumption in Britain is the lowest in Europe, at 3lb. per person per annum. A new future for the almost-lost cherry trees, for damsons, greengages, and even medlars (for jelly) is reasonably predictable, while another phase of development is already under way with soft fruits, employing new varieties of strawberry, hybrid berries, like the tayberry, and introducing blueberries.[47]

A not unexpected renewal of our orchards has focused attention on nut trees, which have been greatly neglected since the 1880s and 1890s. Their neglect was visible for many years in parishes like Plaxtol and Ightham, in west Kent, where trees in many nut plats were left unpruned for years, and grew as high as 15 feet. Kentish cobnuts, a larger than usual hazel-nut, have continued on sale in small quantities in local shops throughout the period of mainstream farming, but were virtually unknown further afield. Nuts in general attracted attention in 1988 when the European Commission submitted proposals for modernizing orchards, and included nut trees with fruit trees. A Kentish Cobnuts Association was formed in 1990, in 1993 ten cobnut growers in Kent were offered stewardship grants, and an extension of marketing opportunities is the subject of research by Margaret Flemming (1995–6). The parish of Ightham, which has more than forty acres of cobnut plats, proceeded to retrieve a more correct memory of its past by bestowing a new sign on its Cobtree Inn in autumn 1993, removing the image of a cob horse, and restoring the tree. It is surely time to recall that walnut trees also grew successfully during earlier phases of alternative agriculture, in the later Middle Ages, and in the seventeenth to eighteenth centuries. Are they not due for revival now, since walnut oil is savoured as never before in the kitchen, and since medical research has suggested that walnuts, and other nuts, can halve the risks of heart attack?[48]

The search for an alternative agriculture has encouraged a reappraisal of the drinks available in the market, and so repeats seventeenth-century efforts to increase cider-drinking and improve cider quality. In the second phase of alternative agriculture the taste for cider was attributed to the Royalist soldiers encamped in the West Country during the Civil War. In the third phase of alternative agriculture, between 1879 and 1939, it was credited to the soldiers encamped in northern France in the 1914–18 war, and by 1927 the British were said to have become 'a nation of cider drinkers'. But the women too deserve credit for maintaining diversity, and the continuity of old traditions in our drinks, through the same period. Mrs C. F. Leyel, founder of the House of Culpeper and of the Society of Herbalists, kept alive the memory of tisanes, juleps, and cordials which are again in favour. But among them all, cider ranks as the first drink to benefit from the more adventurous tastes of the consumer; 100 million gallons were drunk in the year 1994–5. Pioneers in the 1950s, like J. L. Ward at Horam, Sussex, now have large established companies (in Mr Ward's case, the Merrydown Wine company), while small producers have their chance to win unique reputations for cider from their own apple orchards. In 1982 publicity was given to Richard Sheppy, farming near Taunton, Somerset, as the third generation of cider producers in his family. He branches out, as his forebears did not, brewing his own distinctive ciders for customers who buy from his farmgate as the Frenchman buys his wines. More recently still a journalist has described Ivor Dunkerton's success in Herefordshire in his 3,000-tree organic orchard, and has estimated that between 100 and 150 small and medium-sized producers make traditional ciders that now compete with wine.[50]

Following naturally from cider production has come cider brandy, a spirit which was being developed in a similarly hopeful frame of mind by Captain Wintour in the 1690s. Bertram Bulmer claimed in 1987 to be tasting at the King Offa distillery in Hereford the first cider brandy distilled for two centuries, while Julian Temperley of Pass Vale Farm, Burrow Hill, in Somerset, set up in 1989 the Somerset Cider Brandy Company and now sells far afield in London, and overseas.[51]

More varied drinks, alcoholic or not, are capable of commercial development, as Mrs Leyel's book of *Herbal Delights* bears witness. In Scotland the enterprise of Philippa Fraser at Moniack, near Inverness, has successfully established since 1979 the production of silver birch wine, elderflower, meadowsweet, and raspberry wines, and mead and sloe liqueurs. Plum liqueur and sloe gin are made by the Kain family on their farm at Dittisham, Devon. And since our roadsides are full of elderberry bushes, laden with flowers in June and July, it is not surprising that elderflower cordial is appreciated afresh, though, when it was made into a sparkling cordial and given the name of elderflower champagne, it dragged Guy Woodall of Thorncroft vineyard, Surrey, into a lawsuit with the French.[52]

For the connoisseur of whisky, barley germinated on a floor, and dried over a fire of local peat is being used to revive the making of a distinctive 'briny', single-malt whisky at Springbank, Campbeltown, at the foot of the Mull of Kintyre in Scotland. Through the determination of the owner, Hedley Wright, member of a long-standing maltster family, this labour-intensive method of malting barley has brought life back to the maltings in Campbeltown, where reputedly a hundred distilleries were at work in the eighteenth century. More innovative drinks, or ancient ones revived, may yet appear, like that being explored in 1987 after a potsherd from about 2000 BC was found on the Hebridean island of Rum, seemingly broken from a brewing vessel. Pollen grains showed heather, royal fern, meadowsweet, grain, and herbs, and promised to unlock the secret ingredients of the long-lost heather ale.[53]

In the fields, the most striking change, accompanying the more varied drinks that are now brought into the market-place, has been the spread of vineyards since the 1970s, some located on, or suspected to lie on, the same sites as vineyards of the Middle Ages. A pioneer at work in 1938 was George Ordish, planting a few vines at Yalding, Kent. After 1945 Edward Hyams and Ray Barrington Brock followed his example, the latter setting up at his own expense the Viticultural Research Station at Oxted, Surrey, in 1946. Having achieved encouraging results, and helped many more beginners to get started, this station had to close in 1970; it was still a private venture, which an unimaginative government refused to finance. Nevertheless, the momentum was maintained. A professional vineyard owner, Major-General Sir Guy Salisbury-Jones of Hambledon, Hampshire, is nowadays named as the first commercial leader in the field, but 'if he is the father' (of English vineyards nowadays), then we are told that Margaret Gore-Browne of Beaulieu, Hampshire, was surely 'the mother'. A milestone counted along the way was the founding of the English Vineyards Association in 1967, and one of the most celebrated of the new generation of vineyards is that at Lamberhurst, Kent, started in 1972, and having now sixty acres of vines. Vineyards spread swiftly in the 1980s, and in 1993 the commercial ones numbered 436, while private vineyards, if counted, would push the total higher. In 1993 wine production amounted to 1. 75 million litres, and English wines did well at wine-tastings and in competitions. But vine growers contend with two handicaps, the high excise duty, far higher than anything paid in other European countries, and EU regulations imposing limits on the quantities of 'table' and 'quality' wines which may be produced.[54]

Past phases of alternative agriculture have always stimulated innovations and expansion in dairying, and, as a branch of agriculture, it has established itself so firmly on the scene that it can hardly be regarded in the twentieth century as an alternative pursuit. Nevertheless, its origins and its notable expansion in phases of alternative agriculture still colour its fortunes, and are most readily reflected in its ability to adapt and diversify under stress. At the present time the milk quotas introduced in 1984 have curbed enterprise by setting harsh limits on milk output. Among those dairy farmers who persist, therefore, ice creams, made of whole milk, and with many varied flavours, have proved to be one strategy for survival.[55] In the light of its past history, it is a pity that many other possibilities of development have clearly been frustrated by the policymakers,

24. Vines. The vineyard at Lamberhurst in Kent is now one of the best established of recent creations, having been set up in 1972, and winning awards for its wines at home and in Europe. Here the workers are resting in the midst of a bumper crop in 1995.

for the market has shown a readiness to accept many novel milk products, like *crème fraîche, fromage frais*, and many unfamiliar cheeses, which are imported from the Continent, which might have been made in Britain. Even in such discouraging circumstances, however, a revival of farmhouse cheese-making is under way, restoring something of the great variety of local cheeses which was a notable feature of the seventeenth century. It is remarkable also for restoring women once more to a responsible place, and crediting them with notable achievements, in the dairy.[56]

Yet other innovations cluster in the dairying sector, using the milk of goats and sheep, and so reviving another two alternative pursuits from the past. Great hopes for ewe flocks were expressed in 1981 when ewes' milk cheeses and yoghurts found a receptive market in Britain, and now ice cream is added to the list. One hundred milking flocks were recorded in 1981, which were thought to have increased to between 120 and 150 by 1992. Sheep-milking is encouraged by the British Sheep Dairying Association, whose secretary, Olivia Mills, is herself owner of a ewe flock and was once a student of medieval agriculture.[57] A promising future for goats' milk cheeses was predicted by Jane Grigson in 1987, and Carolyn Fairbairn's prospering cheese dairy in the grounds of Crofton Hall, at Thursby in Cumbria, was celebrated in a newspaper article in January 1996. The goat's future has been enhanced by improvements in the breeds reared, and their numbers are rising. They were estimated at 100,000 in Britain in 1981, and both hill and lowland farmers were being urged in 1982 to keep goats, not only for their milk, but also for their hides, and for their meat; the meat is much appreciated by Muslims if ritually killed.[58] The introduction of angora goats from Australasia added a further incentive to goat-keeping, for angora wool (mohair) is a speciality fibre, much sought after nowadays for its light, soft qualities and elasticity. It is worth remarking of this venture too how prominent are the women in goat-keeping, as they were noticeable in the 1930s also. They are the most frequently cited pedigree goat-breeders and the winners of prizes, underlining again their part in leading the way to alternative agricultures. In adhering to small herds, however, women are in danger of being squeezed out by the hygiene regulations of the European Union, since new rules for the dairies impose heavy expenditure on buildings which the smaller herd keeper cannot afford.[59]

Among meats, various alternatives are being supplied by specialists, who find a worthwhile market among enthusiasts. They are breeding deer for venison once more, as in the parks of the seventeenth and eighteenth centuries, and this is seen not only in Scotland but in Essex also; they are breeding wild boar and a British Wild Boar Association was set up in 1989; pigs are being crossed with wild boar to give their meat a distinctive flavour; bison are being bred for meat,

25. Goats. Goat-keeping is an alternative farming pursuit, satisfying a demand for milk, cheese and other dairy products, meat, mohair, cashmere, and skins. Here is Mrs Ruth Goodwin, who has kept a herd of goats for thirty-three years, first at Horley, and then at Albury, Surrey, but who, because of the new European hygiene regulations which penalize the small farmers, is not able to sell her milk for human consumption. However, she supplies her own household with milk and cheese, and produces cashmere for spinners.

of which the largest herd is found at West Knoyle, Wiltshire; snails find a market mostly overseas; and ostriches are reared for their meat, feathers, and leather, supported by a newly formed British Domestic Ostrich Association, which counted fifty breeders in the UK in 1993, and was vigorously publicized recently by the Ostrich Farming Corporation, aiming to establish production in the UK and on the Continent.[60] Yet another source of meat lies with goose-keeping. Significantly, it was discussed in 1899, though the times were then unfavourable, because changing tastes had driven goose-meat out of fashion, replacing it with turkey. But an eloquent advocate of goose-meat at that time, living in Theale in Berkshire, pointed to French success, especially around Toulouse, and recommended that the meat be sold in joints, a practice that is common in Hungary. The present-day success of the goose was forecast in 1982, and is amply demonstrated today by Judy Goodman of Great Witley, Worcestershire, who started goose-rearing when her husband's dairy was hit by the milk quotas in 1984, and who, at Christmas in 1995, slaughtered 3,000 geese (and 1,000 bronze turkeys). She knows from experience how the taste for goose-meat has returned to favour.[61]

Finally, yet another alternative venture for farmers is fish-farming. Rainbow trout-farming is one such venture, and in one case in Oxfordshire, at Milton Common, a medieval fish pond was cleaned out in 1972 to make way for it. In 1982 fears for the overproduction of trout were expressed, but other specialities have emerged, like the breeding of ornamental fish, to diversify the story. Spare pieces of farmland in North Devon were reported in 1985 being put to this use, and attractive profits had diverted one breeder from his original plan to breed edible carp. Now competition in the fishing-grounds of Europe underlines the need for yet more attention to fish-farming inland.[62]

*

Present-day alternative agriculture is following a pattern which this book has made familiar through its investigation of three earlier occasions. But the repetitions are not only conspicuous in the practical activities by which farmers choose to earn a living. They reveal themselves also in the broader circumstances that are changing around them; or, if changes are not actually noticeable as yet, they are presaged by a changing climate of opinion. This is evident in the discussion of farm sizes. Large farms, the larger the better, are no longer seen to be the most desirable farming units. Voices are being raised to appreciate the social and agricultural value of family farms and smallholdings. The very fact that the *Spectator* chose to remind readers in 1995 of the landowner in the last century, Sir Robert Edgecumbe, dividing a farm of 343 acres into twenty-five holdings betokened fresh sympathies. Why retrieve his memory at this time? In

26. Geese. Goose has returned as a favoured meat for the Christmas dinner, and also to celebrate Michaelmas on 29 September. This has given a boost to the rearing and fattening of geese on a traditional, free-range system; they do not lend themselves to intensive rearing. Mrs Judy Goodman, seen here, produced 3,000 geese for Christmas in 1995 and hopes to produce 3,500 in 1996, as well as 1,500 free-range bronze turkeys. She comes from a Leicestershire farming family, and now farms with her husband and sons at Great Witley in Worcestershire. Her husband's dairy farm was hard hit by milk quotas, and so, having started with a few geese in 1982 as a hobby, which she kept in a paddock next to the garden, she increased their numbers to 100 in 1984. She was a regional finalist in 1986 for a National Farmers' Union Mutual Marketing Award, and benefited from the great publicity which she received in 1989 as a winner of the poultry section of the BOCM–WFU–*Farmers' Weekly* Awards for Women in Agriculture. She has been commended by distinguished food writers for her high-quality product. The farm also produces asparagus, and pick-your-own strawberries and raspberries.

fact, Edgecumbe was only one of a number of landowners with the same philosophical beliefs who took such action in the later nineteenth century; several others have already been named in Chapter 8 above. More significantly still, this recollection from the past drew comment from Paul Heiney in *The Times*, remarking of Edgecumbe's venture that 'if the experiment were repeated today, the response [from applicants to take the holdings] would be equally huge'. 'In forcing the smallholders out of business,' he declared, 'we have destroyed a national treasure.'[63]

The creation of satisfying and productive work on the land is one of the smallholders' contributions to a society seeking solutions to the large problem of unemployment. Their achievement stands in contrast to that of star performers in business: the more jobs they slash, the more they are acclaimed. In other directions, the smallholders are also being seen in a fresh light. A recent, thoughtful study by Robert Netting of *Smallholders, Householders* has examined the lifestyle of this very durable class of farmers, not only in following a sustainable agriculture (which is better appreciated now than for many a decade past), and securing a stable rural population, but in quietly conserving and enlarging plant resources which large farmers have squandered. Mauro Ambrosoli in a much longer historical survey of four centuries in western Europe, 1500–1900, also illuminates this last achievement. Underpinning his agricultural and botanical observations lies a foundation of weighty documentary evidence, showing the role of small farmers, *alongside* large farmers, landowners, and botanists, in assisting the revolution by which the legumes—clover, lucerne, and sainfoin—were absorbed into mainstream farming regimes. The positive merits of small farms are a theme which will be certain to feature increasingly in the literature henceforward, adding to the perceptions of some distinguished writers who underlined this truth between 1900 and 1939. The need for co-operation among small farmers was another theme repeatedly urged in the period 1880–1939, and though it did not make a deep impression on farming practice in Britain then, we may expect it also, differently structured perhaps, to undergo a fresh lease of life.[64]

One of the circumstances which has threaded its way patiently but silently through this text, but which may come to exert some influence for change in the future, is regional specialization. Alternative agriculture relies for its success on regional differences, and the more there are the better. But the regions have been forced by a dictatorial mainstream regime to serve the market through a national framework. This constraint has robbed it of some of its strengths, suppressed its greatest virtues, and sometimes deprived it of the power and the will to survive. As alternative agriculture gathers momentum, however, it could strengthen the conscious appreciation of regional individuality, and manœuvre rigid marketing policies into more flexible arrangements that would help specialist farmers and food producers. Some signs of this happening were publicized in August 1995 under the marketing slogan of 'Food from Britain'; what this meant, in fact, was 'Local Food from Regional Britain', but connoisseurs of regionalism and alternative farming were clearly not among those who chose the phraseology.[65]

Farmers working in the fields rarely have the chance to realize when they are repeating old strategies, though some reflections must be prompted when they clean out old fish ponds for trout-farming, prune again the cobnut trees in their much neglected nut plats, or return to the more professional coppicing of woodland. But even without historical reminders, diversification is clearly seen as the way forward, and so a major lesson from the past serves its turn again. Events have moved under their own momentum, but they have led to action which the historian must generally endorse. One of the most striking experiences, however, has been to observe the way the economic urgency of finding alternative strategies has transformed the whole intellectual and philosophical framework underpinning agriculture. One set of assumptions seemed destined to stand for ever; yet they are being dismantled and replaced by another. Activities, once despised, have become virtuous and once virtuous activity is now despised. As a result, for example, government money was provided in the nick of time to preserve and value an old Kent orchard of Bramley apple trees, planted in 1906, which a few years before was destined to be uprooted and destroyed as worthless.[63] The philosophical framework of agricultural life is, indeed, in turmoil in the 1990s, and so it is surely unnecessary to waste too many words defending the study of history. It both broadens perspectives, and yields a longer view of our past. Far from being a useless exercise, it could promote more soundly based plans for the future.

❧ CONCLUSION

A study of alternative agriculture in the past and the present calls for two separate themes to be discussed in conclusion. One concerns the overarching structure under which historians have to place the concept of alternating phases of mainstream and alternative agriculture. They have hitherto divided agricultural history along different lines, tending to stress a continuum of effort towards increasing mainstream foodstuffs. While acknowledging intermittent interruptions and setbacks, they have not seen any common characteristic in those intervening so-called 'depressions'. The other theme for a conclusion must centre on the lessons which farmers and policymakers may draw from repetitious experiences, four times over. Of these two discussions, the second has to be deemed the more significant because it could have practical consequences. It is best underlined if it stands as a final conclusion. First, we take up the more comfortable task for the historian of exploring the changes to be made in our interpretation of past events.

This account of alternative agriculture has resulted in a division of English agricultural development over six and a half centuries into different periods from those conventionally recognized. But historical conventions are not timeless; they reflect the viewpoint of one age, and in changed circumstances the scene from another vantage point may well look different. Indeed, it cannot be otherwise, for, as time moves on, it changes the priorities of farmers who actually work the land. That experience must inevitably alter the perspective of historians looking for the main trends and the significant watersheds.

Accepting the notion of a changing historical viewpoint, however, is not easy, when minds have long been accustomed to view the scene from a different standpoint. Yet such revisions have occurred before. A brief survey of the way writing on agriculture has shifted its ground in the past will not be out of place here, in order to underline that point. Before the nineteenth century, writers on farming were not historians in search of a long process of development, but were principally concerned with the practicalities. The first books of husbandry, printed in the sixteenth century, were straightforward texts of advice on mainstream farming, describing ways of preparing the land for planting and harvesting the main food crops—cereals—and on keeping livestock. Only one or two unusual authors alerted their readers to newer ventures; the work of Reynolde Scot on hops in 1574 was one of the remarkable early examples.

Then in the mid-seventeenth century, the literature faithfully reflected the transition to a new phase. The change was gradual, for one phase always overlaps the next, but the year 1650 makes a serviceable signpost, roughly marking the significant moment of transition, as defined by the books. Through the 1650s the attention of writers was diverted from an all but single-minded concern for mainstream agriculture to alternative strategies. This called for more detailed information and some encouraging words to be given to landowners and farmers, pondering new ventures. It was a task readily undertaken by writers in that decade, living under a new Commonwealth government, and feeling themselves facing wholly new opportunities when a monarchy was replaced by a republic. Thus, whereas Walter Blith wrote in 1649 a fairly ordinary account of farming procedures, having little that was new to say about standard practices, by 1652 his readers had alerted him to some interesting new projects, and so appeared *The English Improver Improved*. The old book was rewritten to include improvements, involving clover, sainfoin, lucerne, woad, weld, madder, hops, saffron, liquorice, rape and coleseed, hemp, flax, and orchard and garden fruits. An alternative agriculture was plainly in sight.[1]

Thereafter, between 1650 and 1750, appeared some highly professional books on horticulture and special crops, which diversified the subject-matter of farming books in gentlemen's libraries, as well as crops in the farmers' fields. This diversification made it necessary for writers and reporters to pass qualitative, rather than quantitative, judgements on the farming scene. If they had counted the acreages involved in growing alternative crops, they would not have produced any impressively large figures: neither a hop garden nor a saffron garden, for example, was likely to occupy more than three acres of land. But when judged from the point of view of the individual cultivator, counting his cash in hand, and reckoning his returns from small acreages, these items, despite high labour costs, could make all the difference in hard times between solvency and bankruptcy.[2]

In the middle eighteenth century the wheel turned again. The year 1750 is acceptable as the moment signalling the transition from an alternative to a mainstream regime; the precise dating of the watershed that is used here follows the lead of the economic historians who set the beginnings of an industrial revolution at this date, and who also postulate an agricultural revolution beginning alongside. But, in fact, some twenty years earlier, in 1731, change was on the horizon when Jethro Tull published his *New Horse-Houghing Husbandry*, introducing the seed drill and the horse hoe into the arable fields. Among his motives for these innovations were his extreme irritation at his labourers' resistance to novel methods, and his resentment at having to pay them higher wages than before. His experiments and the impulse behind them were the first sign that another age was dawning. Indeed, the transitional character of the moment was signalled in the very title of Tull's book. Its subtitle was *An Essay on the Principles of Tillage and Vegetation, introducing a Sort of Vineyard Culture into the Cornfield . . . by the Use of Implements lately Invented*. In short, the alternative agriculture of the vineyards had given the arable farmer some fresh ideas.[3]

After Tull followed a group of celebrated writers, dominating the literature at the turn of the eighteenth-to-nineteenth century (among them, William Marshall, Arthur Young, and the many writers for the Board of Agriculture), all intent on improving the yield of mainstream foodstuffs. In Arthur Young's case especially, they were distinctly unsympathetic towards peasant farming.[4]

For more than a century, the drive to increase cereal production accelerated, assisted by fertilizers from external sources, including seeds from abroad for making oilcake (English rapeseed was on the way out), bones, and guano, and followed by the manufacture of phosphates and nitrates, resulting from the work of the chemists Justus Liebig in Germany and Lawes and Gilbert in England. Agricultural progress was now firmly measured quantitatively, in cereal yields, and a sounder statistical basis was assembled when, first, some crop returns were collected during the Napoleonic wars, and then more searching and regular statistics were gathered after 1866.[5]

With the next dramatic turn of events in 1879, when the profits of cereal farmers collapsed, alternatives again became the order of the day. In this new age, which demanded different agricultural strategies from those that had served for well over one hundred years, interest in the history of agriculture was first effectively awakened. While agricultural commentators wrote informatively on all new practices, scholars began for the first time to write major works on the fortunes of farming in the past. The timing is partly explained by the fact that many documents were now being made more accessible for study. A concerted attempt to preserve and calendar historical records had been under way since 1838, and although political, constitutional, and ecclesiastical history commanded the first attention, scholars were drawn by the severity of the depression after 1879 to examine agricultural history as well.

It took some time for the historians to focus their thoughts and then assemble their evidence, but the result was a spate of books in the years 1907–15, followed by another far less closely clustered series after 1918. As for the major preoccupations in that phase of alternative agriculture, they were concerned with the characteristic themes of the age, the decline of the peasantry, the effects of enclosure on that outcome, the distribution of land between large and small owners, the role of small farmers, and the diversification of produce. Apart from the effects of enclosure, which has remained on the agenda, but has come to be studied for a different reason, notably as a contribution to agricultural productivity, these issues were entirely different from those which came to dominate the agenda subsequently, following the war of 1939–45.[6]

When mainstream agriculture returned after 1939, and historians resumed the study of farming history, after a hiatus between 1939 and about 1950, they showed a rising interest in topics associated with mainstream agriculture, and in tune with its chief objectives. They have been especially concerned with measuring agricultural productivity, and the timing of 'the agricultural revolution'. That revolution has generally been narrowly construed as the relationship between cereal yields and the input of labour and capital. Such matters as poultry, dairying, and fruit-growing have been treated as lesser side-issues, while rabbit warrens, dovecotes, and tobacco have been ignored as eccentricities.[7]

In fact, the first attempt at studying the productivity of cereals went back to 1927 when W. H. Beveridge endeavoured to measure the yield and price of corn in the Middle Ages.[8] His interest was at odds with the mood of his time, though it is an illustration of the way in which single individuals regularly anticipate events, and come to be recognized as precursors of another phase. But, in the event, Beveridge moved away from this subject in the 1930s into a more ambitious study, not of yields, but of prices and wages.[9] It was only in the 1970s, at the climax of the farmers' drive for higher cereal production, that historians turned assiduously to the task of gauging cereal productivity in the past. A major, early contribution to the discussion was J. Z. Titow's calculations of cereal yields in the Middle Ages on the estates of Winchester abbey. The most recent is that by Bruce Campbell and Mark Overton, surveying six centuries and heroically bringing together in a continuous series six hundred years of cereal yields in Norfolk between 1250 and 1850. This long time-span is usually separated into three periods, because the documentary sources in each phase are not directly comparable.[10]

Lying behind these studies were assumptions derived from the work of Professor M. M. Postan, linking cereal yields with changing population levels. He had argued, on the basis of medieval experience, that when rapid population growth inflated the demand for cereals in the thirteenth century, the land was cultivated to exhaustion, and in consequence yields fell. Insufficient food supplies induced weakness, sickness followed, and so plague spread, causing high mortality. The Black Death in the mid-fourteenth century was a Malthusian crisis that had long been waiting to happen.[11]

This proposition became something of an orthodoxy in the 1960s and 1970s. But it is noticeable in the latest work of Campbell and Overton that their graph of rising and falling yields does not uphold that theory. Rather, it suggests the reverse, that cereal yields rose in periods of rising population, when the demand was insistent, and fell when population levels were stable or in decline, and demand subsided.[12] That conclusion comes close to matching the trends and the period divisions suggested here, in which phases of mainstream and alternative agriculture are separated. Cereal yields are seen to reflect a more complex relationship between land and people, and so require to be set in a broader circumstantial context. The very reverse of the results postulated by Postan then emerge. A wholly feasible and reasonable strategy was adopted in periods of mainstream agriculture when the demand for cereals was high. On such occasions, when labour was plentiful, more attention was paid to fastidious and labour-intensive cultivation. In periods of labour shortage, the demand was met with the aid of machines. When yields fell, it was not because the land had been overworked in order to satisfy extreme demand, but because the labour given to cereal-growing was withdrawn, and energy was turned to other, more profitable pursuits, a situation which always prevails in phases of alternative agriculture. To identify and substantiate such trends, however, it is essential to study the whole farming scene, including all the alternative activities in farming, and not simply confine the investigation to the management of the arable rotation and the complementary role of livestock.

The key descriptive words which differentiate the major phases of agricultural development can be expressed in terms of 'specialization in periods of mainstream agriculture' and 'diversification in phases of alternative agriculture'. The distinction is actually present in Campbell and Overton's long survey of cereal production, for, in the later Middle Ages, when alternative agriculture dominated the scene they note the increasing cultivation in the arable rotation of legumes, including not only peas and beans but vetches, seemingly introduced in the later fourteenth century, while in the later seventeenth century they underline the use of clover, lucerne, sainfoin, and turnips. But Campbell and Overton give short shrift to other special crops which accompanied that diversification between 1650 and 1750, when in fact they are another symptom of the same trend.

This brief survey of themes in agricultural history suggests that historians must now expect a change to occur in the topics commanding their attention. Some will assuredly resemble those which came to the fore in the earlier period of alternative agriculture, between 1880 and 1939. These include the decline of the peasantry, the distribution of land between large and small farms, and the diversification of produce. In fact, some signs of this have been evident since about 1984: several historians in recent years have focused attention on the survival of the peasantry in certain regions of the kingdom in the nineteenth and twentieth centuries, a fact of life which had long passed unnoticed. The distribution of land in farms of different sizes, and between different social classes, is coming under scrutiny in a local context. Some of the merits of diversification on peasant farms have recently been conceded in a sympathetic study of nineteenth-century agriculture in Italy, published in the context of a volume of essays, which aroused other expectations, being entitled *Agricultural Productivity in Europe.*[13]

Other themes which cluster around an expanding alternative agriculture, and which may be expected to reappear, concern agricultural co-operation, farming partnerships, including the holding of land 'to halves', and studies of labour-intensive crops that stress their economic and social consequences. Women's initiatives in paving the way for new strategies are also likely to receive more attention; as we have seen, 'minor farming pursuits' were persistently nurtured by women in the background of mainstream farming, but in changing times they were taken up with fresh energy, though this led to their falling under the control of men.[14] In sum, we may expect historians henceforward to tackle seemingly new themes in agricultural history, though those with long memories will recognize them as old themes, long neglected.

*

What of the lessons which farmers and policymakers may take to heart from the past? Judging by the experience of the three previous phases of alternative agriculture, the strong assumption of our age that omniscient governments will lead the way out of economic problems will not, in practice, serve. The solutions are more likely to come from below, from the initiatives of individuals, singly or in groups, groping their way, after many trials and errors, towards fresh undertakings. They will follow their own hunches, ideals, inspirations, and obsessions, and along the way some will even be dismissed as harmless lunatics.[15] The state may help indirectly, but it is unlikely to initiate, or select for support, the best strategies; and, out of ignorance or lack of imagination, it may positively hinder. We have seen how, in the sixteenth century, government ministers were concerned to reduce the import of industrial products and promote home-grown commodities, and named such crops as rapeseed, woad, and madder. This was no more than an aspiration of policymakers, accompanied by propaganda. It stimulated some individual enterprises, whose long-term implications should not be summarily dismissed. We do not have sufficient evidence to judge the gains in experience which counted in the long run. In the short term, however, government prodding failed. But decades later fresh experiments by individuals succeeded because of the markedly different economic and social circumstances.

Another example of official intervention shows in the history of tobacco-growing when government in the seventeenth century closed the door on a new opportunity by banning its cultivation, but found itself, in practice, unable to prevent it being grown when it became an ideal crop for poor men. Only after some sixty years, and a campaign of more brutal government repression for the last thirty, was it driven from the fields, and then a fall in the price of American tobacco may be considered to have been the more effective instrument in eliminating it from the scene. In the nineteenth century, the government inadvertently helped the fruit growers by lifting duties on imported sugar in 1874, thereby finding for the fruit farmers a voracious market for their plums in the jam factories. But the government's measure was an entirely accidental consequence, and certainly not planned to assist alternative agriculture.

The possibility that the policies, now imposed by the EU and the UK government, may ruin a promising future for vineyards in this country is a contemporary example of official measures that could have damaging consequences for the aspirations and pioneering endeavours of individuals. Another example threatened when the Ministry of Agriculture resolved in 1989 to ban the sale of cheese made with unpasteurized milk, just at the moment when farmhouse cheese-making was beginning to recover from decades of decline. Fortunately, in this case, the threat of extinction goaded the cheesemakers into forming their own Specialist Cheesemakers' Association, and the government was persuaded to reconsider its policy. The confrontation between opposing views, in this case, might well have ended less satisfactorily; official policies too often spring from assumptions inculcated in the period of mainstream agriculture, which are inappropriate in the new phase. Among the most glaring examples still is the deference shown towards the interests of large farmers, to the neglect of the medium and small farmers, yet these last will assuredly be some of the most original initiators of new projects. In short, the successes of alternative agriculture remain uncertain for many reasons.[16]

This survey of the present-day scene has the advantage of being set against a more than usually detailed historical background, and is thereby coloured by the experiences of more than one generation of our forebears, going over the same ground. Repetitions abound, as we have seen, and they underline the relevance of the past to the present. Indeed, on occasion, the historian is tempted to anticipate certain directions which the future will take: for example, the recent rehabilitation of cobnut plats in the Weald of Kent, planted in the 1880s and neglected for many decades, is one current development which this author, living in the area, confidently predicted. Despite the profound changes that differentiate the economic, social, and political circumstances of the 1990s from the fourteenth, seventeenth, and nineteenth centuries, the solutions found in

phases of alternative agriculture have more than a passing resemblance to each
other.

Unfortunately, the decision-makers hoping to solve present-day problems
generally have little or no knowledge of historical parallels with which to set the
present picture in perspective. Current assessments often prove to be rooted in
narrow assumptions which close the outlook on a much wider panorama of
possibilities. The National Research Council in the United States commissioned
a report in 1989, which resulted in a book entitled *Alternative Agriculture*. But
being centred on 'how the real world works', it accepted the continuance of
mainstream routines. From that viewpoint, it was concerned principally with
the way farmers might reduce costs, and reduce environmental pollution, while
remaining competitive in the market. It acknowledged the creativity of farmers
in developing entirely new solutions, but its eleven case studies, gathered in
1986, passed over the more adventurous enterprises with little comment, and
described instead fourteen farms whose systems claimed notice for reducing
soil erosion, and reducing the use of chemical fertilizers, pesticides, weedkillers,
and antibiotics, while continuing to grow the same crops. The generous use of
hand labour was noted in some cases, but that aspect prompted little further
reflection. The rational decision on one farm to treat a certain grass not as a
weed to be eliminated at great cost, but as an acceptable fodder crop, was noted,
but it was not recognized as an enlightened and adventurous innovation, similar to one strategy of alternative agriculture found in the seventeenth century
when legumes like clover, lucerne, and sainfoin were singled out from other
grasses, and nurtured as fodder crops. Significantly, the present-day American
farmer's inspiration to grow a weed as a crop came from a stint of farming in
South America.[17]

In a different vein, in England the Royal Agricultural Society published in
1985 a guide to nineteen possible alternative crops. They were all selected
because they could be gathered by the combine harvester. The proposals
included neglected cereals, like oats and rye; crops recently made familiar as
alternatives to wheat and barley: rapeseed; durum wheat (for pasta); linseed,
and lupines; plants that were, and are as yet, climatically unsuitable, but which
might be genetically altered, like sunflowers, and soybeans; and herbs for medicinal use like evening primrose, borage, and fenugreek. In a final miscellany of
potential crops, the list offered lentils as a plant of the Mediterranean region and
Turkey, but confessed to having 'very limited information' about its cultivation.
The investigators were totally ignorant of the fact that lentils as a fodder crop
would have been seen anywhere in England between Lancashire and Kent in the
seventeenth and eighteenth centuries.[18]

Both the above reports on alternative agriculture in the 1980s bravely looked into the future, but with blinkered eyes. Their vision lacked historical depth. Historians know that many ventures, hardly publicized as yet, are likely to outstrip the success of those that are best advertised now. All the initiatives being taken today, whether large or small, must be surveyed with an open mind, and we must be prepared for total surprises, made successful by accidental and unforeseeable factors.

Despite the historical parallels, however, some circumstances today are plainly unique to the present phase of alternative agriculture, and had no place in the past. One is the powerful role of Europe's Common Agricultural Policy, laid down at Brussels. It is not the choice of Britain alone, but is agreed by all partners in the European Union. So the choices that will triumph in the end have to fall within the areas in which farmers are allowed by all the partners in the EU to operate freely. As already noted, England's vine growers could be checked by regulations emanating from Brussels. Their directives so far have encouraged positive action in other directions in order to reduce grain and other surpluses. These have encouraged extensive, rather than intensive, farming, striving in particular to improve the environment for wildlife and human enjoyment. But they have also encouraged some alternative crops, such as nuts, linseed, and hemp for paper. The objectives shift yearly as fresh experience is brought to bear.

Other less predictable circumstances could, of course, play a part in determining the shape of the final story. If climatic changes exert a demonstrable effect on agricultural seasons, they will alter the zones in which certain farming enterprises can be carried on. Another nuclear accident could change overnight the demand for one food against another, or indeed for all mainstream foodstuffs. Another sudden oil crisis could totally distort the pattern of prices for foods and industrial materials. Looking further ahead, a precipitating factor in major change could result from action deliberately taken to deal with the long-term fuel crisis. Present-day agriculture relies heavily on the energy from non-renewable fuels, and some eloquent and far-sighted appraisers of the scene have repeatedly underlined the risks. In 1977 Philippa Pullar argued that mainstream agriculture had 'taken the wrong course', while in 1979 and 1980 G. W. Heath deplored the dangers inherent in that dependence, and the dishonesty of economists who measured efficiency without reckoning these hazards in their calculations. Those protests were made well within the memory of the oil crisis in 1974, and struck a chord of sympathy among a few, only to be forgotten as the sense of urgency faded. But extravagance in the use of energy could be called into the debate with greater insistence in the future. The same could happen to another weakness in the modern agricultural system, which aroused concern in the early 1990s, namely, the reliance of the developed world on feeding stuffs carried from hungry Third World countries, where they are more urgently needed to feed people.[20]

Another unpredictable factor lies in the changing policies and fortunes of single countries, which have always had the potential to exert a strong influence over the agriculture of trading partners. We have seen this in England's case in the seventeenth and nineteenth centuries. A curb on exports or imports immediately stirs action by the injured party. It happened in the early 1970s when the United States imposed an embargo on the export of soybeans to Europe, and the EC resolved to become self-sufficient in protein for livestock and vegetable oil. Hence the more than successful cultivation of oilseed rape in Germany, France, and England, which has transformed the landscape.[21] Britain's balance of payments deficit nowadays could be much reduced by other reductions in imported foods; from time to time that item is calculated, as in 1992 when it was reported that half a billion pounds was being spent by Britain on imported fruit from temperate climates, all of which could be produced at home.[22] The GATT agreement on world trade in 1994 imposes a free trade policy and so disallows any move towards protection among the participating countries. But the more aggressive initiatives of British farmers could still lead to the substitution of home-grown foods for imports.

In differentiating the possible commercial success of a variety of crops, predictions are rendered uncertain by yet another factor, namely, the volatility of fads and fashions. The RASE's booklet in 1985 on alternative crops, for example, did not offer great hopes for the sale of oats in the future, since farm horses were now few, and consumption by people, and by horses for racing and leisure, was expected to be static or to increase but slowly. The writer could not foresee the sudden publicity that would be given to the medical discovery that eating oats was highly beneficial in reducing the risks of heart attack.[23] At the same time some positive circumstances in our present-day lifestyles and new scientific skills could ease the path to alternative agricultures. The readiness to adopt new and different foodstuffs is spreading to a wider circle of the population, and flexibility and curiosity have grown (partly as a result of much increased foreign travel), along with an appreciation of the effects of diet on health. Publicity quickens the recognition and adoption of novel foodstuffs, and on this score radio, television, the newspapers, and the journals are more than efficient. Along with the willingness to accept novelty in food goes a more discriminating taste. Appreciating subtle differences of flavour is a faculty for which the French are more renowned than the British, but it is better understood and valued nowadays, as the taste for home-baked breads in great variety, including fermented rye bread, bears witness. The British population, moreover, clearly has the potential to eat more of the foodstuffs which figure on the list of favoured alternative food crops: Italians in 1989 ate 167 kilograms of vegetables per head of population, and Spaniards 182 kilograms, compared with only 65 kilograms eaten by the British.[24]

Further hopes for more diversified crops arise from the ability of the scientists to adapt novel plants genetically to suit the British climate and to enhance their most desirable attributes. Among foodstuffs, some publicized and under consideration in 1988 and 1990 were navy beans (for baked beans), sunflowers, and soybeans, for cultivation in southern England.[25] Other possibilities for genetic engineering could bring more industrial crops into the fields. In this search, initiatives in several countries are being co-ordinated within the European Union. Leadership in Europe belongs to the Dutch scientists, one of whom, Louis J. M. van Soest, characteristically pursued a personal interest in the 1980s well before any official recognition and assistance was forthcoming. For him the ideas for potential crops came from old journals, and especially from literature during the 1939–45 war, when the German war effort was hampered by the lack of raw materials formerly bought from abroad, and alternatives, for example, for rubber, were urgent.[26] The search among scientists for renewable industrial resources from plants has now spread world-wide, and was given a strong impetus by two symposia in the United States in 1988 and 1991. It is now being directed onto a broader path by the founding of a periodical in 1992, *Industrial Crops and Products: An International Journal.* Among many plants at present under investigation for their oil, waxes, and resins are fibre hemp, crambe (of the mustard family), elephant grass, dandelion, safflower, honesty, aster, and pyrethrum.[27]

Another category of potential crops emerges from the debate concerning the cost of medicines. Drugs supplied to the National Health Service increase in cost by about 11 per cent per annum. This trend runs in parallel with a certain current of opinion in favour of herbal remedies, which have long been discounted in favour of chemical drugs, because the latter have guaranteed purity and consistency. The disturbing side-effects of some chemical drugs, however, plus their cost, has tilted opinion somewhat, and restored more balance to the assessment of alternative, plant-based medicines. Moreover, they have special advantages for use in the poor countries of the world. Since the same shift of opinion towards herbal remedies was noted in the seventeenth century, and perhaps, though less clearly, in the late nineteenth century, it may be deemed a movement that is associated with phases of alternative agriculture.[28] Certainly, it offers opportunities to farmers, as is evident in their attention to the cultivation of such plants as evening primrose and borage.

While the special circumstances of the late twentieth century open up fresh dimensions to the problem of finding a satisfactory alternative agriculture, our historical survey teaches many lessons. It emphasizes the need for a multitude of solutions, rather than a few that must serve everyone. So, if farmers are driven by tidy administrators into narrow channels of conformity, their search for distinctive niches and diversity is stifled. Indeed, in no time at all, problems of overproduction loom in one sector, which provoke another mass movement, repeating the same problems in another sector. Diversity is the watchword; in fact, for the best insurance of individuals, diversity on single farms is also recommended. Thus we may rehearse the advice of the two French authors of *Maison Rustique*, in 1600: 'a good farmer will make profit from everything, and there is not (as we say) so much as the garlic and onion which he will not raise gain of, by selling them at fairs most fitting for their time and season, and so help himself thereof and fill his purse with money.'[29] The same sentiments were often repeated in the years 1880–1939. 'In these trying times', wrote the Reverend W. J. Pope in 1882, when recommending poultry-keeping, 'we cannot afford to despise small things.' Yet the best exponent for that recipe for survival must surely be the smallholder, described by Miss Whetham, who had a cottage and a little land in the 1930s, and lived by the River Severn. He picked sprouts, trapped rabbits, and made kennels in January, netted salmon, mended boats, and beat for shoots in February, did more of the same in March but also sold a pig, cut osiers and drove at fairs in April. So he continued for the rest of the year, adding yet more variety to life when he sold mushrooms, plums, blackberries, and wild ducks. In this case, as in the advice of writers at every encounter with alternative agriculture, gainful measures rely for their discovery on the careful observation of detail. We are already observing such opportunities being found today, by identifying the needs of minorities and so serving a specialized market, though that is not to say that the market will not eventually grow and be patronized by many.[30]

Since the most successful strategies are unpredictable, this should bring hope to the idealists and the pioneers of new ventures, battling against discouraging, dismissive criticism. Discouragement is seen at present, for example, in the government's lacklustre attitude to the prospects for bio-fuel (from rapeseed or other plants), in contrast with the positive endeavours that are officially favoured in France. But a more encouraging lesson from the past comes from the experience of Eve Balfour, Albert Howard, Arthur Hollins, and others who will for ever go unnamed, who put their faith in a sustainable agriculture in the 1920s and 1930s, whereas the tide of opinion did not turn in their favour until the mid-1980s. Idealists who take a new path plainly have to believe in their goals, whether they offer immediate profit or not.[31]

Another parallel with the past, justifying deep reflection in the present, concerns the rising tide of unemployment. Alternative agriculture regularly offers work that is highly labour-intensive, whereas the overriding objective in economic life at present is to reduce labour at all costs, and few voices are as yet raised to question that first principle of efficient business procedure. Yet it is, in fact, derived from the era of mainstream farming; the threat of bitter, and worsening, social unrest may well weaken the foundations on which that seemingly solid edifice was erected by economists to suit a different age. In the seventeenth and early eighteenth centuries, labour-intensive farm crops held out a lifeline to the unemployed, and were welcomed as such. Alongside the expansion of dual employment on land and in industry, they undoubtedly alleviated the problem of the poor between 1650 and 1750; as an urgent political issue, finding work for the poor temporarily faded. In the late nineteenth-century phase of alternative agriculture, Peter Kropotkin argued most eloquently in favour of labour-intensive work on the land. Demanding more horticulture, he stressed first and foremost the common sense of growing fruit and vegetables at home to replace rising imports, but he also pleaded the good sense of providing work for all. A policy of 'low labour and high technology' had met the situation until 1870, he argued, but after that it was no longer appropriate.[32] The same may be said today. A notable characteristic of many horticultural ventures is again their labour-intensity, and in a climate of opinion which also acknowledges labour as a therapy, it is striking how often the horticulturists themselves stress the satisfaction of their work, despite the hard manual labour.[33]

Since far-sighted individuals have forecast the impossibility of restoring full employment now that modern technology is daily reducing the work required, we plainly await another Peter Kropotkin to pronounce the same lesson all over again. The continuing obsessive drive to foster technology and shed labour at all costs belongs appropriately to the phase of mainstream agriculture, and not to the alternative phase. If this is recognized, may we perhaps see scope for the revival of saffron-growing in Saffron Walden and East Anglia? It is an expensive product which the English once grew to perfection.[34]

As another contribution to full employment, a further seventeenth-century solution deserves to be recalled. It offered to families in rural areas a mixture of agricultural and industrial work. Country workshops of nailmakers, scythe-smiths, potters, framework knitters, and many other crafts preserved families in the countryside in the seventeenth century, and these proved to be the precursors of an industrial revolution. This diversification of the rural economy, permitting agriculture and industry to coexist in the same communities, and even in the same households, avoided the painful social disruption which followed later when industrial growth demanded that workers live in towns. The more congenial partnership of agriculture and industry in the countryside is matched today by the coexistence of farming and teleworking in some rural areas, and sometimes in the same families.[35] Its merits can best be appreciated in the light of historical experience, for it could maintain or even increase village populations, and relieve the heavy pressure on towns. On social and economic grounds, it could offer benefits to many people.

A more wide-ranging discussion of all the necessary ingredients in a balanced urban and rural society is plainly needed while a strategy for alternative agriculture unfolds. The drive for high technology will doubtless continue; yet the human need for satisfying work and a sustainable routine has to be met as well. In the course of such an analysis of fundamentals, the meaning of efficiency has to be redefined for it cannot indefinitely acclaim technology without regard for its social consequences. In the words of a lone critic, crying in the wilderness in 1979, agriculture 'was once a labour-intensive, energy self-sufficient operation', but it 'has been transformed into one that is capital intensive and energy consumptive'. In other words, its so-called efficiency is expensive in ways that have been ignored, notably in its use of non-renewable energy resources. It may be that bio-fuel, wind, or sea power, can eventually come to the rescue. But in the mean time the more sustainable agriculture of peasant farming on the Continent and at home, which has the further advantage of populating the countryside and alleviating the physical and social problems of towns, deserves more informed sympathy and a stay of execution.[36]

A further parallel with the past concerns the initiatives of women in nurturing the first phases of new endeavours. Women have always had to use their ingenuity to infiltrate the interstices of an economy dominated by men. Sometimes their concerns have been described as trifles, though the apt rejoinder is that 'trifles make the sum of things'. But their activities, pioneered modestly in unnoticed places, have often proved to be a lifeline in adversity, and have then become commercial successes. This fact of life is earning some recognition in the more favourable environment obtaining now. A policy proposed by thoughtful US companies is seeking to draw on the ingenuity and ideas of groups in society who in periods of mainstream activity are ignored. The principle has been ponderously enunciated thus: that 'diverse teams of people may be better at solving knotty problems and making creative decisions than people who share the same attitudes, colour, gender, background, and lifestyle'. According to this philosophy 'diversity, properly handled, can be a source of strength in confronting complex issues'; following established grooves of thought to 'the exclusion of unconforming ideas' is not the way to unlock new doors, we are told. All this is really ancient wisdom couched in a new phraseology. As this study of alternative agriculture over centuries of experience has shown, two channels of creative influence have routinely been found at decisive moments of transition and they have rejuvenated agriculture: one has been opened up by contact with foreigners, and the other by women, whose farming initiatives have been absorbed, one by one, into the mainstream.[37]

Reflections on women's initiatives could prompt still further speculation on some of their current endeavours, noticed but hardly exploited as yet. They have made moves to break down the national market for home-produced foodstuffs into more intimate local units. Partnerships are being cemented here and there by local farms supplying all their mixed, and often innovative, range of fruit and vegetable produce to a circle of local purchasers, pledged to take everything sea-sonally available on a regular basis. The initiative was first launched by women in Japan, forming a purchasing network in association with one farm. It has been copied by a farming family in North Devon, which expected soon to dis-pose of all its highly varied vegetables and fruits to its regular customers.[38] It is a marketing device which addresses most directly the needs of farms in less acces-sible situations, but it illustrates the originality of strategies that can be devised at the grass roots to accompany alternative agriculture, and it may hold greater potential. It offers an example of a device which decentralizes the market and positively facilitates diversification, and it links noticeably with an initiative coming from the supermarket chains which also show an interest in promoting regional food specialities.[39] If a more self-sufficient regional organization of the food supply evolved for other reasons (say, to reduce the fuel wasted in long-distance transport), it would further help the enterprising, specialist producer.

At a certain level of commercial production, the diversification inherent in alternative agriculture can benefit greatly from co-operation among producers. The movement can be expected to expand again, and is, in fact, expanding in the circumstances prevailing now. In Lincolnshire already 65 per cent of vege-tables are sold through co-operatives, and perhaps some glimmerings of another style of co-operation are emerging from a different direction in the formation of associations of individuals, pioneering specialties like asparagus and ewes' milk cheese. These gather together members who are geographically scattered, but who share vital knowledge and experience.[40]

Many alternative strategies called into being by the present phase of alterna-tive agriculture are emerging from below, and, as history leads us to expect, they are nurtured by courageous and idealist individuals, many of whom survive on a shoestring. They are not always launched with great resources and expensive publicity. Among those who initiate their ventures modestly, many of the pioneers will be women, and many sites will lie off the main highways, lacking access to ready publicity; the byways in the Weald of Kent are one example of ideal terrain. Past parallels readily come to mind in the market gardeners of the nineteenth century who found a foothold on commons and wastelands around

London. And it may not be too far-fetched to bring the wisdom of the present day from a far-distant continent to bear on the English scene: policymakers in China have recognized that the best ideas come from the farmers themselves who 'act in advance of policy'; 'local change', they say, has often run 'ahead of policy'. Profiting from this lesson, Chinese statesmen have altered their agricultural programme, in order to encourage experimentation. In Europe, by contrast, where agriculture fell under the control of government in the nineteenth century, its freedom becomes daily more constrained.[41]

We shall not be surprised that some of the courageous adventurers and idealists who pursue new paths now made a start under mainstream agriculture, and have long since faced and lived through adversity and disappointment. Their success arrives at length, because the tide has turned in their favour. Others who have come late on the scene, and are still in the relatively early stages of their venture, should not be afraid to start small, exploiting the distinctive circumstances of their own locality. When viewing this scene, it is tempting to cite a passage from William James, written in an earlier phase of alternative agriculture in the 1890s, and cited as a favourite piece of wisdom by the economic historian George Unwin. He used it in a different context, but its message will be consoling to those who have to work the land in new ways and who start from a small base.

As for me, my bed is made; I am against bigness and greatness in all their forms, and with the invisible, molecular, moral forces that work from individual to individual, stealing in through the crannies of the world like so many soft rootlets, or like the capillary oozing of water, and yet rending the hardest monuments of man's pride, if you give them time. The bigger the unit you deal with, the hollower, the more brutal, the more mendacious is the life displayed. So I am against all big organizations as such, national ones first and foremost; against all big successes and big results; and in favour of the eternal forces of truth, which always work in the individual and immediately unsuccessful way, under-dogs always, till history comes, after they are long dead, and puts them on the top.[42]

Such remarks set the modest enterprises of pioneers in a longer perspective. It encourages them to pay attention to 'small things', for they may in the end produce large changes. That message encourages ingenuity and diversity, which, as experience shows, always lurks in modest, out-of-the-way places needing time and freedom to mature. The generalized regulations of a European agricultural policy, which fosters scale and uniformity, may serve in periods of mainstream agriculture, but it spells death when alternatives are needed. In this connection, it is instructive to note a strong movement of opinion in favour of rescuing bio-diversity from destructive regulations; agricultural diversity calls urgently for the same treatment.[43]

Finally, some food for thought lies in the use of the term 'depression' to describe phases, now and in the past, that have called for alternative strategies. The experience can equally well be regarded as a challenge, out of which long-term benefits may spring. We see how it is compelling us to view our natural world afresh, and it is certainly revealing a cycle of repeated events which teaches many lessons. Above all, it insists that we pay heed to the experience of history. James E. Thorold Rogers, who was the pioneer in the study of agricultural prices and ranks among the first of the English economic historians in the nineteenth century, pronounced the most explicit message on this score, in the form of a fable. His words, dramatically exposing man's folly in ignoring the lessons of history, make an apt conclusion to this survey.

The Sibyl offers her books, in which the future is forecast, to the Roman statesman, according to the legend. The price is refused twice, and, after each repulse, she destroys irrevocably one of the volumes, demanding the same price for the third. This is what Bacon called the wisdom of the ancients, and the moral is plain.[44]

NOTES

Notes to Introduction

1. Slee, 1989; Pesek, 1989.
2. Godrey Smith, 'Alarm clocks and milking as usual', *Sunday Times*, 18 May 1980.
3. The ten countries of the European Union in 1985-6 were meeting all their own needs *and more* in producing 20% more cereals than they could consume, 33% more butter, and between 7% and 8% more cheese, beef, veal, and poultry-meat.—Brassley, 1995: 7.
4. Santayana, 1954: 82, ch. 10.
5. Forty years are counted from the founding of the British Agricultural History Society, and the publication of the first *Agricultural History Review* in 1953.
6. The detailed studies are best exemplified in H. P. R. Finberg and Joan Thirsk, gen. eds., *The Agrarian History of England and Wales* (=AHEW), i–viii, Cambridge 1967– . For an example of a study stressing the onward and upward trend of grain and meat production, see Campbell and Overton, 1991.
7. Santayana, loc. cit.

Notes to Chapter 1

1. Bolton, 1980: 59–63; *AHEW*, ii. 726–7, 721; *AHEW*, iii. 2–6; R. M. Smith, 1991: 48–50.
2. *AHEW*, iii. 4–5; Bolton, 1980: 209–11.
3. Coulet, 1967: 240.
4. For one regional example of these strategies, see C. Dyer, 1980: 134, 146–52; also *AHEW*, iii. 83.
5. C. Dyer, 1980: 139; Bolton, 1980: 153, 156–9, 174–5, 177.
6. R. A. L. Smith, 1943, offers some of the most illuminating information on ewe flocks. The sheep-dairying enterprise of Canterbury Cathedral Priory was deliberately expanded under Prior Henry of Eastry (1285-1331) on Romney Marsh and in Thanet. Nevertheless, Smith does not always separate sheep-dairying from cow-dairying or the yield from flocks in wool as against milk. Dairying plainly declined after the Black Death, but Smith does not consider the possibility that it became a peasant enterprise instead. See Smith, 1943 (1969 edn.): 148 ff., esp. 159–60, 165. See also Cracknell, 1959: 11–16.
7. Richmond, 1981: 99; Brandon, 1971: 134. For considerable numbers of cattle alongside sheep, see the Catesby estates in Warws.—*AHEW*, iii. 91–2.
8. C. Dyer, 1983: 210, 214; id. 1989: 159.
9. *AHEW*, iii. 464–5. Evidence assembled by Ann Kettle for Shropshire suggests some growth of dairying, but it is far from conclusive. North Shropshire later became a noted dairying area.—VCH, *Salop.*, iv, 1989: 92–3, 150–4.
10. Denney, 1960: 27, 37–9.
11. The emergence of dairying in specialist areas, and not everywhere, has to be stressed. The woodpasture region eventually became the dairying area *par excellence* in Suffolk, whereas on the breckland dairying recovered after the Black

Death, slightly expanded in some places, but then retreated.—Bailey, 1989: 256–8, 294–5. For the tantalizing ambiguity of the evidence on ewe flocks, cow herds, and the relative importance of their products, see Biddick, 1989: 46–7, 94. For further reflections in the light of later events, see Ch. 7, p. 166.

12. Biddick, 1984: 165–77. See also B. M. S. Campbell, 1991: 156–9, in which it is said that mean livestock numbers on English demesnes were static, 1250–1350, but then rose, so that 16% more animals were carried in 1400 than in 1300. This figure includes pigs, though the author does not differentiate their changing numbers from those of sheep and cattle. See also Thornton, 1991: 186, noticing, but without comment, on the bishop of Winchester's estate at Rimpton, Som., 1208–1403, a herd of up to 100 pigs, compared with 26 dairy animals, and 250 sheep.

13. Bolton, 1980: 180–92.

14. Veale, 1957: 85–90.

15. Bailey, 1989: 128–35, 251–6; *AHEW*, iii. 236, 301, 394.

16. Bailey, 1988: 11–13; *AHEW*, ii. 946. Henry VII's night attire was adorned with black rabbit fur.—Veale, 1966: 15, 141, cited in Bailey, 1988: 12.

17. Cantor and Hatherly, 1979: 71; Birrell, 1992: 113.

18. Cantor and Hatherly, 1979: 71–80; Steane, 1985: 169; Cantor, 1970–1: 14; VCH, *Salop.*, iv. 10.

19. Richard Carew, cited in E. P. Shirley, 1867: 28; Royal Commission on Historical Monuments, *Northants*, vi, 1984: 92. The difficulty of estimating venison-eating is discussed in C. Dyer, 1989: 60–1. The most recent survey of deer-farming by Birrell does not differentiate qualitatively between centuries, but throughout stresses venison for household food and as gifts. But it does suggest in the later Middle Ages that parks were enlarged and ownership moved down the social scale. It also documents the more precise counting of deer, which may indicate slightly more commercial attitudes.—Birrell, 1992: 114–15, 121, 124.

20. *AHEW*, ii. 883–5, 945. A dovecote of the Knights Hospitallers in Herefs. has an inscription on the *tympanum* of the doorway, with the date 1326.—Croke, 1920: 46.

21. Richmond, 1981: 39; *AHEW*, iii. 392; VCH, *Salop.*, iv. 63 , 100.

22. C. K. Currie, 1991: 98.

23. Steane, 1970–1: 299–303; M. Aston, 1988*b*: *passim*. See also McDonnell, 1981.

24. C. K. Currie, 1991: 98.

25. Ibid. 99–100, 106–7; Roberts, 1966: 119–26. See also M. Aston, 1988*b*: *passim*.

26. C. K. Currie, 1991: 97, 101–2; Roberts, 1968*b*: 161.

27. Guérin, 1960: 132, 157 ff., 131. See also Edeine, 1974: i. 80–85.

28. Roberts, 1964: 219; id. 1968: 111; C. Dyer, 1989: 106–7.

29. Emery, 1962: 383–5. For a discussion of moats and their uses on the Continent, see Aberg and Brown, 1981: *passim*.

30. Epstein, 1992: 181, 186–7, 200–19; Smith and Christian, 1984: 5, 35; Googe, 1577: 31; *AHEW*, iv. 44, 172–3, 450; Lobo Cabrera, 1987: 193–8. For woad, see below, Ch. 4.

31. Holdsworth, 1991: 22.

32. B. M. S. Campbell, 1983: 41.

33. *AHEW*, iii. 301, 260; Googe, 1577: 3r.; C. Dyer, 1989: 62, 63; J. Harvey, 1984: 84–7, 90–2.

34. Bath, 1963: 87–8, 272–3; id. 1960: 132 ff.; Tits-Dieuaide, 1981: 373, 365–7; Irsigler, 1984: 719–47.

35. Bath, 1960: 132–40. An isolated reference has been found to buckwheat in Wales at an early date (1326) for feeding rabbits.—*AHEW*, ii. 843. For furze grown in England to feed rabbits, see Bailey, 1989: 254.
36. M. Aston, 1988*a*: p. 101.
37. J. Harvey, 1981: 76–143; id. 1984: 89–99; id. 1985: 83–101; id. 1972*a*: 14–21. See also McLean, 1989 edn.: 198.
38. *AHEW*, iii. 236.
39. C. Dyer, in *AHEW*, iii. 236–7, 126; Du Boulay, 1965: 443–6 and *passim*; Hare, 1981: 1–8, 13–15; Richmond, 1994: 165–9. I am much indebted to Prof. Richmond for this last reference.
40. C. Dyer in *AHEW*, iii. 83–4; Thirsk, in *AHEW*, iv. 229; Kerridge, 1967: ch. 3, *passim*, but esp. 181–2, 187, 189. For early signs of ley farming in coastal Sussex, see Brandon, 1971: 132–4.

Notes to Chapter 2

1. Bland, Brown, and Tawney, 1914: 271, 274–5.
2. Thirsk, 1978: 85–9.
3. Ibid. 29. The price index for all grains stood at 422 in 1582 but had dropped to 324 in 1584.—*AHEW*, iv. 819.
4. *AHEW*, iv. 819–20 (note that the year of each index number denotes the beginning of the cropping year; the harvest was taken the following year); Clark, 1985: 6–9.
5. Bland, Brown, and Tawney, 1914: 274.
6. But note the detailed examination of clover in Norfolk and Suffolk by Overton, 1985, showing its slow introduction until 1675, and the fact that its main advantage was seen as fodder.
7. *AHEW*, v. II. 301–3, and the documents there cited.
8. Ibid. 306–8.
9. Ibid. 306.
10. Ibid. 328–33. For more details on the financial concessions given to exporters of malt and barley in the first half of the 18th c., and the frauds which enhanced their value, see Ormrod, 1985: 28–33. On stronger beers and the increase of distillation, see P. Clark, 1983: 209, 211.
11. *AHEW*, v. II. 332–3; Johnson, 1963 edn., Introduction.
12. *AHEW*, v. II. 327, citing R. Harford, 1677, in *Harleian Miscellany*, iv, 1809: 489.
13. In writing of the crisis caused by the Black Death in 1348–9 Ian Kershaw, similarly, writes of an agrarian crisis in 1315–22, depicting it as part of a long preamble which culminated in 1348. In short, the Black Death accelerated existing trends.—Kershaw, 1973: 3–50.
14. Ash, 1941, i. 11–13, 17; Thirsk, 1992*a*: 18–21. Attention continued to be paid to the classical writers through the seventeenth and into the eighteenth century. See M. Stubbs, 1982: 471; Hunt, 1986: 160–1; Bradley, 1725.
15. M. Stubbs, 1982: 465–7, 479.
16. For these projects in detail, see Chs. 4 and 5 below.
17. Thirsk, 'Horses in early modern England', ead. 1984*c*: 381–6.
18. Thirsk, 1978: 24, 27.
19. See below, Ch. 4, p. 83. It is also likely that the earlier grant to Sir Henry Guildford

of the right to export hops and madder was connected with a willingness on his part to initiate the growing of hops and madder on his Kentish estates.—Furley, 1874, ii. 11. 449.

20. John Norden proclaimed this truth about neglected land in *The Surveyor's Dialogue*, 1607, repr. in Thirsk and Cooper, 1972: 110.

21. Partnerships are shown most clearly in tobacco-growing in Gloucestershire. See Thirsk, 'New crops and their diffusion', ead. 1984a: 259–85.

22. For an example of an innovative venture which was revived several times, and was finally, though briefly, successful in the early 18th c., see madder-growing, Ch. 5 below. For persistence with mulberry trees and silk production, though it culminated in failure, see also Ch. 5.

23. Thirsk, 1992a: 18–23. For Columella on horticulture, see Ash, 1941, iii. 3. The first edition of Columella in print was in 1510.—Conley, 1927: 18.

24. McLean, 1989, ch. 1. For indirect clues to the high standard of cultivation achieved in monastic gardens, see the seizure of six loads of fruit trees from Chertsey abbey when it was dissolved. They were removed to furnish Oatlands, a manor house newly acquired by Henry VIII in 1537, and undergoing extensive renovation.—Colvin, 1982: 213. The garden of the Old Deanery at Wells, Som., may also be an illustration of the fine gardens of churchmen. It was cultivated in 1551–4 and 1561–8 by William Turner, the father of English botany.—M. Aston, 1988a: 102.

25. Heresbach, 1577: 55. For Henry's imitation of Francis I, see his employment from 1532 onwards of John Le Leu, alias Wolf, of Normandy to bring courtly horticulture in the French mode to England. Wolf helped to beautify Nonsuch Palace, built to rival Francis I's Chambord.—Alsop, 1980: 252 ff.

26. Webber, 1968: 31–3.

27. Byrne, 1981: ii. 203.

28. Heresbach, 1577: 63. Googe's translation of Heresbach, cited here, followed the original Latin version, which had been written some years earlier still.

29. Rowse, 1962: 281; Thirsk, 1990a: 70. The present author saw an artichoke garden at Stanway House, in Glos., the home of Lord Niepath, in the late 1980s. Thomas Smith, Secretary of State under Elizabeth, is an excellent example of an Essex landowner paying close attention to his gardens and the farming of his estate.—Dewar, 1964: 68.

30. Fynes Moryson's *Itinerary*, 1908: iv. 165, 173. More general remarks were made by William Thomas, Clerk of the Privy Council in 1549, on Englishmen's increasing disposition to travel abroad (and hence their willingness to receive foreigners more civilly at home). Thomas also commented on differing food habits, noting that the common people of Italy ate more herbs and fruits, whereas the English ate more flesh, fowl, and fish.—W. Thomas, 1774: 9–11.

31. Rohde, 1922: 116. For the history of colewort, see Nieuwhof, 1969: 3–4. William Lawson (1617) described colewort as a good potherb, from which country housewives gave their pottage its name, and called cabbages *caell*. John Harvey, 1981: 73, writes of 'colewort or kale plants'. Some informative passages appear in Heresbach on varieties of cabbage, available in the mid-16th c.—Heresbach, 1577: 56r.–v.

32. Dietz, 1972; *passim*; Parkinson, 1629: 512; BL Lansdowne MS 81/48. I am assuming in this last document that the 'large onions' were Spanish, since the document was concerned with goods from Spain.

33. Byrne, 1949: 67. One of the most instructive lessons by a foreigner on serving and appreciating vegetables and fruit, as practised in Italy, was the account by Giacomo Castelvetro, writing in 1614 for Lucy Countess of Bedford. See the handsome edition of this work by Riley, 1989.

34. *CSPVen.* 1617–19: 319.

35. Heresbach, 1577: 48r.–v.; Thomas Harriot, cited in J. W. Shirley, 1983: 154.

36. Heresbach, 1577: 67v. More eloquent still on home-grown medicinal herbs was Timothy Bright, 1580 and 1615; *passim.*

37. Thirsk, 1985: 265–6; Rohde, 1971: 55, 57–8. In BM MSS, Royal MS 7C XVI, said to be one of Thomas Cromwell's papers, the names of 54 distilled waters, prepared between 1 May and 16 July, 1539 are recorded, together with another 24 waters (generally different) left over from the previous year. For the importance which Sir Thomas Smith, clerk of the Privy Council, attached to his medicinal distillations, see Dewar, 1964: 142–3. For more on the early history of distillation, see C. Anne Wilson, 1975, and 1984, *passim,* and 'Stillhouses and stillrooms', forthcoming. Forbes, 1948: 57, 68–9, 83–4, deals with 'the growing popularity of distillation' in Italy in the 15th c., its spread to northern Europe, especially the Netherlands, the gradual perfecting of procedures, and a new design of alembic in the later 15th c. But he does not consider the possibility of cheaper or simpler equipment. The theories of Paracelsus in the 16th c. may have been a crucial factor in explaining increasing interest.—Underwood, 1953: 406–11.

38. Henrey, 1975, i. 88–9; Coles, 1657, Epistle to the Reader; Sackville MSS, HMC 80: 71; Ornsby, 1877: 30, 32, 87, 88, 162, 179, 182, 296, 315, 319, 356, 359; Griffiths, 1987: 440, 453. For herbal ales, see P. Clark, 1983: 98–9. Thomas Hill's remark in the Epistle of *The Profitable Art of Gardening,* 1574, that gardening was the handmaid of physic and surgery goes to the heart of the matter. In some cases it was the medicinal uses of vegetables and fruit which first attracted attention to them. Cherries, according to Fitzherbert (1598 edn.), only had a medicinal use, and this is implied by William Temple in his *Essays,* 1680, 1692, where 'common cherries' for him unfailingly cured indigestion.—Temple, ed. Nicklin, 1903: 144. It is worth noticing a special interest in herbs in the Percy family, going back to the early 15th c. and still evident in the early 17th c. For a rare, early 15th-c. treatise on the medicinal qualities of herbs, found in the Percy library, see Rohde, 1971: 203. For the experiments of Henry Percy, ninth earl of Northumberland and Sir Walter Ralegh, when Percy joined Ralegh in the Tower of London after the Gunpowder Plot, see Thirsk, 1987: 45.

39. Coles, 1657: 121; Thick, in *AHEW,* v. II. 505–6; Parkinson, 1629: 469, 470, 494, 496, 500, 503. Note especially the statement that the English learned from the Dutch about spinach and how to stew it in its own moisture, and add butter.—Ibid. 496.

40. Borthwick Institute, York, Tithe Cause Papers of the Dean and Chapter of York, D & C court, 1595/9; 1614/2; 1628/2; 1676/1. I wish to thank Dr John Addy for these references. The tithed produce at Great Driffield (and, indeed, elsewhere) provokes curiosity about the gentry living there at the time. Driffield in the 13th c. was the site of a royal residence of some importance. It later passed to the house of Aumale.—Brown, Colvin, and Taylor, 1963: 923–4. Kirby Malzeard's precocious interest in root vegetables may be connected with its proximity to Jervaulx abbey.

41. *CSPD* 1656: 328.

42. Thick, in *AHEW*, v. II. 503–6.
43. Wrigley and Schofield, 1981: 528; Bland, Brown, and Tawney, 1914: 373.
44. Thirsk, 1978: 4–5; T. Hill, 1982 edn.: 13–21, 26–38, 46 ff., 132. For cogent arguments in 1576 concerning the labour needed if hemp, flax, and rapeseed were grown in large quantity, see PRO SP12/107/51.
45. *AHEW*, v. II. 515, 581.
46. Thick, 1990*a*: 291–3.
47. BL Lansdowne MS, 74, fos. 75v.–6; Hirst, 1986: 123.
48. *AHEW*, v. II. 544–59; Webster, 1975: *passim*; Speed, 1659; 'To the Reader'. The 'wide community of endeavour' to improve husbandry after 1649 joined some Royalists with the Parliamentarians. A strong stimulus came from the experience of having seen the agriculture of many different parts of Britain during the wars.
49. Blith, 1653: *passim*; Parkinson, 1629: 512; Coles, 1657: 138, 33, 173.
50. Speed, 1659: *passim*, and what appears to be the original MS, BL Add. MS 33509. See also Worlidge, 1675: 162–3. On sow thistles, see Syme, 1863–86: v. 153. The similarity of Speed's remarks with those of Weston can be seen in Weston's *Discours*, 1652: 11–14. He recommended a rotation of flax, turnips, and clover, seen between Ghent and Antwerp. 'French furze', always so called, was routinely recommended by others. See John Aubrey, *c*.1670–80 (Bodleian Library MS, Aubrey 2, fo. 90v); John Evelyn and John Beale in correspondence, 1664 (transcripts in Wellcome Institute, Oxford); John Mortimer, 1707; Richard Bradley, 1727; and a letter of 1685, in which it was claimed that French furze grew more thickly (Univ. College of North Wales Library, Bangor, Penrhos Coll., Penrhos V, 96). Was it *Ulex Gallii* or *Ulex strictus*, which has softer and more succulent shoots (see Grieve, 1931, 1985 edn.: 366–8)? English writers emphasized the value of French furze as fuel, but it was fed to cattle in France and deemed very wholesome. As it was green in winter, it was cut and ground (in apple grinders for quickness) and so fed to livestock. Whole fields were sown with it in Normandy, Brittany, and Poitou. See Duhamel du Monceau, 1767: 82. During the third experience of alternative agriculture, French furze was tried in England on the Woburn experimental farm in 1897 as fodder for bullocks and sheep, but it was thought to require too much labour to bruise it for feeding, and the trial was abandoned.—Voelcker, 1923: 141–2. On bees, see Raylor, 1992: 92–105, and a review by D. Hey in *AHR* 41/2, (1993), 190.
51. The variety of available choices is matched in Hartlib's diary, naming those who were growing liquorice, saffron, rhubarb, flowers, 'roots, plants, and seeds from the Indies', and clover.—Sheffield Univ. Library, Ephemerides, 1649, J-2, 1654, TT-TT6, SSSS6–8.
52. Fussell, 1947: 47–9; Sheffield Univ. Library, Hartlib MS 66/27/1 (letter from John Moore to Hartlib, n.d.); Coles, 1657: 83 and Epistle to the Reader.
53. Hartlib, 1652: 8–9; Parkinson, 1629: 461; Coles, 1657: 38–9; T. Hill, 1594: 59. The discussion about field and garden crops was confused. Richard Banckes in 1552 claimed that herbs grown in fields were better than those grown in gardens, and those grown on hills were best. Hill acknowledged that field-grown plants were stronger, but deemed them in substance inferior, though he agreed with Banckes about herbs grown on hills.
54. Bodleian Library MS Aubrey 2; Plot, 1705: 158; Hunts. RO, Inventory of Edward Lavender of Bury cum Hepmangrave, 1737. I wish to thank Dr Stephen Porter for this reference.

55. Hartlib, 1652: 6, 8; 1651 edn.: 106.
56. Gentles, 1971: 36–9; Thirsk, 1991: 48.
57. Darby, 1956: 87, 275, 279.
58. Sir Thos. Culpeper, 1668: A2r.–v. 'To see 500 or 1,000 acres of land in one farm', added Culpeper, 'is methinks better becoming New than Old England'. See also Carew Reynel in the same vein in 1674: 20.

Notes to Chapter 3

1. According to Henrey, 1975: i. 169, 'Compared with the years 1600–50 the second half of the seventeenth century in England witnessed a great increase in the number of gardening books published.' This was not a peculiarly English phenomenon. A study of the books found in libraries in the Lyons area shows that over half (56%) of all books published on agronomy between 1646 and 1720 were concerned with horticulture, and between 1720 and 1743 62%.—Durand, 1979: 191, cited in *AHEW*, v. II. 589.
2. *AHEW*, v. II. 562–4.
3. Henrey, 1975: i. 183–4.
4. Ibid. 187–91. It is totally appropriate that, during the fresh horticultural renaissance under way in the late 20th c., the proposal should be announced to put the surviving third of Evelyn's manuscript (originally a work of 900 pages) into print for the first time.—Bowle, 1981: 250 n. 12(1).
5. Henrey, 1975: i. 185, 189–90. On the nurserymen and seedsmen, see Harvey, 1975: 42–9, and Thick, 1990*b*, *passim*.
6. Worlidge, 1677; 172–8. Fruit as food for the poor in times of corn scarcity had also been commended in Mascall, 1654: 52,
7. *AHEW*, v. I, ch. 6, *passim*; *AHEW*, v. II. 549–50, 309–11, 560, 344–6; Langley, 1753, *passim*; Minchinton, 1975: 66.
8. See below, pp. 56–7.
9. *AHEW*, v. II. 374–8. Evelyn's words were echoed by Worlidge: 'What can be more profitable than woods or trees'. Cited in R. Williams, 1987: 79.
10. Thirsk, 1978: *passim*; Gee, 1767: 2. For a letter in 1665 encouraging hemp and flax, and addressed to Samuel Pepys, whose office as 'clerk of the king's ships' gave him influence in this regard, see *CSPD* 1665–6: 121. For flax in Kent, see Ormrod, 1995: 98–100.
11. *AHEW*, v. II. 555–7, 568.
12. *AHEW*, v. I. 302, 78, 104; v. II. 555–6, 569; Henrey, 1975: 193; Banister, 1799: 162–71; Mavor, 1801: 290. Nathaniel Fiennes's authorship was suggested by Frank Emery in an unpublished essay.
13. For an early discussion of lucerne in Hartlib, see Sheffield Univ. Library, 'Ephemerides', 1650, F-G4: Banister, 1799: 190–3, 196–7; *AHEW*, v. I. 224, 254, 302, 366; v. II. 572; Mavor, 1801: 290. Mavor, in fact, believed that lucerne was 'the most productive of all the artificial grasses'.
14. Thick, 1990*a*: 279–96; Thick, 1993: 132–51; Clark, 1983: 112; Kerridge, 1967: 270–7; Overton, 1985: 207–16.
15. *AHEW*, v. II. 556; v. I. 224; Mavor, 1801; 291–2 (it was well known from the mid-17th c. that spurry was an excellent fodder for cows, and was so used in France, Brabant, Holland, and Germany); Beddows, 1969: 317–21. On spurry, see Hartlib,

Ephemerides, 1652, CC–CC2, DD–DD5, and Houghton, 1727–8: ii. 373. On parsley, Houghton, 1681: 138, and Worlidge, 1704, *sub nomine*; on lupines, Hartlib, 1651: 49, and Worlidge, also mentioning lentils, 1675: 138. (Lentils are found growing in many scattered places at this period, including common fields.—*AHEW*, v. I. 106, 112, 213, 220; Brassley, 1988: 40, 200). Russell Garnier, 1896: 95–6, concluded that spurry and burnet were abandoned, when other meadow grasses were perfected.

16. *AHEW*, v. I. pp. xxiii, xxviii–xxix, 40, 142–3, 146, 152–4, 164, 183, 186, 189–90, 231–4, 281, 285, 290–1, 324, 338–9, 378–80; *AHEW*, v. II. 12–13, 61, 361–3, 387, 446–7, 486–7; Edwards, 1978: 175–90; Valenze, 1991: 146, 148–9. Expanding cheese production is well illustrated in the Vale of Berkeley, Glos., in the size of herds and quantities of cheese, by Horn, 1994: 70–1, 93–5.

17. Mascall, 1620: 257–8, 279; *AHEW*, iv. 50–1, 416; *AHEW*, v. I. 287, 342, 344, 380; *AHEW*, v. II. 2, 336–7, 387–8, 445–6; Kerridge, 1967: 86, 125; Thirsk, 1978: 91, 95; Worlidge, 1675: 161. For pigs in High Suffolk, fed in dairies *and* woods in the early 17th c., and sold to London and for victualling ships, see Reyce, 1902: 37. For pigs fed on cinquefoil and clover in summer, and mast and acorns in the autumn, see John Beale, writing to Hartlib in 1657.—Sheffield Univ. Library, Hartlib MSS, 62/23/2.

18. *AHEW*, iv. 44, 172, 194; Choyselat, 1580: *passim*; Thirsk, 1991: 48; Worlidge, 1675: 163–6; Boston RO, Whaplode Acre Book; Defoe, 1928: 59–60.

19. Broad, 1980: 77–89.

20. Griffiths, 1987: 457; Williams, 1987: 78, citing Latham and Matthews, 1974: 201.

21. Ibid. 95; *AHEW*, v. II. 377–8.

22. Bowle, 1981: 192. Dudley Lord North recommended ponds as an aid to housekeeping in 1669 in his *Observations and Advices Oeconomical*, 30. Carp was regarded as a luxury fish around 1600, as Hollyband's Dialogue of French instruction suggests. Offered stewed carp by his host, the guest replied: 'You will put yourself to great cost.' 'Care you not for the charges,' replied the gallant host.—Byrne, 1949: 30.

23. *AHEW*, v. I. 274; v. II. 576; Moore, 1703: 161–5; North, 1713: 26, 71–2. For a carp pond carefully cleaned and stocked with 127 brace of carp at Harpswell, Lincs., in 1723, see Lloyd, 1973: 14. Note also Sir John Lowther's construction of ponds, stocked with carp and tench, between 1731 and 1733 at Flatt Hall, near Whitehaven, Cumberland.—Beckett, 1981: 34.

24. *AHEW*, v. II. 366–71. For a new deer park at Belton, Lincs., for Sir John Brownlow, see *CSPD* 1690–1: 172. The view of the deer park as a private larder, and of venison as a 'gift currency' at this time is shared by R. Williams, 1987: 86–8, 94. The gentry's sales of venison and game to the town are a contemporary observation by Alexander Pope, introduced into his *Second Epistle of the Second Book of Horace*, lines 234–5. I wish to thank Prof. Aubrey Williams for this reference.

25. Sheail, 1978: 347–8, 353–4; *AHEW*, v. I. 237–8, 271, 274; Tittensor, 1986, *passim*. See also below, Ch. 4.

26. *AHEW*, v. II. 544; Northants RO, Isham Correspondence, IC 537; Speed, 1659: 3; BL Add. MS, 33509.

27. KAO, Clayton MSS U214/E7/30–63; Sheail, 1978: 345, 348–50; PRO E134, 28 Chas. II, Mich. 11; *AHEW*, v. I. 308–9; Manchester Univ., John Rylands Library, Ry. Ch. 2541. On warrens in Ashdown forest, I wish to thank Dr Brian Short. On the enclosure and warrens there, see also Merricks, 1994: 115–28, esp. 120, 124.

28. Anon., 1710, 'The case of the distressed warreners'; *AHEW*, v. I. 308–9; Sheail, 1978:

352. For an earlier agreement (1663) between a manorial lord and a warrener, requiring the latter to supply 25 couples to the lord weekly, or otherwise when asked for, see Clinton, 1911: 158.

29. *AHEW*, v. I. 96, 299; Worlidge, 1675: 68; BL Sloane MS 3569, fo. 103; Colville, 1904: 32-3; Elstob, 1933: 159; Bradley, 1725: 49.

30. *AHEW*, v. II. 647-8, 808-9: Severn, 1986: *passim*, though the author misdates the bulk of the recorded dovecotes to the later, rather than the early, 18th c.

31. Worlidge, 1675: 166, 213; Severn, 1986: 7.

32. *AHEW*, v. I. 191. This pigeon-keeper was noted for his strongly Parliamentarian sympathies during the Interregnum. Was it then that he first flouted the lord's monopoly? See also Brassley, 1988: 122, 169, 207, for a Cambridgeshire parson regularly gathering 9*s*. p.a. from the owner of a dovecote, 1703-7; and Bradley, 1727: 16-17, noting that in February pigeons fetched three or four times the price received in March.

33. W. Coles in *Adam in Eden*, 1657: 347, claimed that in Kent and Essex 'there be men of good worth whose estates consist in hop grounds', but this does not unambiguously say that all their wealth came from hop grounds.

34. *AHEW*, v. I. xxx, 166-7, 176, 275-6; Houghton, 1727-8, ii. 457. For more on hops, see Ch. 4 below.

35. Sheffield Univ. Library, Hartlib MSS., 41/1/144-5. For a new orchard at Fulbeck, Lincs., in 1676, see Manchester Univ., John Rylands Library, Ry.Ch. 2585. For the 'infallible claim that fruits were a sovereign remedy for infirmities', see La Quintinye, 1693: 94.

36. Hartlib, 1652 edn.: 16-17; Millett and Graham, 1986: 149; McLean, 1989: 234, 243; Harvey, 1981: 84, 122, 123; *AHEW*, v. II. 567. For walnut oil imported into England from Germany, see Irsigler, 1984: 735. For its medicinal and craft uses, see Parkinson, 1629: 595; Sowerby, 1652: 5.

37. Norden, 1607: 240; Thirsk, 1992c. 304, 309-10, 316 ff.

38. BL Add. MS 38599, no. 17, fos. 54v.-55; Lockyer, 1981: 215; Everitt, 1966: 33; Bowle, 1981: 113.

39. Fuller, 1987: 362-3; Cox, 1720-30, v. 440; T. M. James, 1969: 132-3. For a sound, general verdict on the walnut tree, see Worlidge, 1675: 80, 101-2.

40. A prosecution at Surrey Quarter Sessions for the theft of walnuts at Reigate in 1662 concerned an orchard belonging to Elizabeth, Countess Dowager of Peterborough.—Jenkinson and Powell, 1935: 255. Interest in nut trees even extended to the growing of pistachio nuts, when *c*.1719 Henry Marsh grew them in his celebrated garden at Hammersmith, where they survived 'several years' and produced nuts.—McGarvie and Harvey, 1983: 22.

41. Marshall, 1818: ii. 445; Herefordshire RO, Ledbury tithe book, A61.

42. PRO C78/592/13.

43. Thirsk and Cooper, 1972: 80; Chester RO, Chester Diocese, Consistory Court files, EDC 5 (1671). I wish to thank Dr Addy for this reference.

44. See e.g. Worlidge, 1677: 172-8; Evelyn, 1699: *passim*. For John Locke's complete conversion to the value of vegetables, fruit, and herbs, in diet and as medicine, see Locke, 1978: *passim*, but esp. the correspondence in the 1680s and 1690s, pp. 53-4, 239-41, 508-9, 513. For more spacious arguments, applicable to all classes, and noting that in Europe a quarter of the diet in winter came from herbs and roots, see Bradley, 1729: 16-17, 36-8.

45. Worlidge, 1675: 132–3.
46. Bradley, 1729: 37.
47. Evelyn–Beale correspondence, 3 Oct. 1664, and 3 May 1667. (I wish to thank the Wellcome Centre, Oxford, and Dr Mayling Stubbs, the transcriber of these letters, for permission to use these transcripts.) The interest in mushrooms may have been stimulated in fashonable circles by the fact that François de La Varenne in *Le Cuisinier français* (1651) had particularly recommended mushrooms in cooking (along with asparagus and a bouquet garni).—Bowle, 1981: 231.
48. BL Sloane MS, 629, fos. 252 ff.
49. Colville, 1904: 72.
50. GLRO, M1, 1718/10.
51. Kalm, 1892: 91.
52. GLRO, M1, 1682/18; 1684/93.
53. *AHEW*, v. II. 562–3; Lancs. RO, DDBa/D10/B8; Speed, 1659: ch. 6. The uncertain use of turnips is evident in Topham's *Letters from Edinburgh*, 1776, where fruit was limited in variety, and small turnips were presented for dessert.—Topham, 1776: 229.
54. CJ XVII, 1711–1717, 4 May 1713, p. 311; Bradley, 1729: 16.
55. PRO E134, 3 Geo. I, Mich. 4.
56. Bodleian MS, Aubrey 2.
57. Som. RO, DD/SP 1691; 1730/31; Beavington, 1965: 95–7.
58. Bodleian MS, Aubrey 2; Cottis, 1985: 261 and *passim*. It may be significant that Anthony Ashley, grandfather of the Earl of Shaftesbury, is credited with the introduction of the cabbage to England from the Netherlands where he had lived temporarily in order to transcribe works by the cartographer, Lucas Waghenaer.—C. Wilson, 1968: 87, cited in Ferrier, 1989: 446. I am much indebted to Professor A. van der Woude of Wageningen for this reference.
59. Rohde, 1971: 214–16.
60. Ibid. 216–18.
61. McGarvie and Harvey, 1983: 25.
62. Lambeth Public Library, UH 96/1062.
63. *AHEW*, iv. 175 (note also the mustard of Durham, 'proverbial for its excellence' by the 1740s.—*AHEW*, v. I. 56); Hunts. RO, Probate inventory of Edward Lavender, 1737.
64. Plot, 1705 edn.: 155; *AHEW*, v. I. 214–15. Caraway and coriander were noted as significant crops in Essex in 1920 by Grieve; in fact, coriander could yield 15,000 lb. an acre.—Grieve, 1920: 34, 44.
65. J., S., Gent, 1697: 125, 103.
66. *AHEW*, iv. 13, 40, 43, 177, 426, 592; *AHEW*, v. II. 339–41, 402, 567–8; Lewis, 1736: 20–1. I owe this reference to Dr D. A. Baker.
67. BL Cotton MS, Titus B V, fo. 292; Dietz, 1972: 1, no. 2; Syme, 1863–86: iv. 248; *AHEW*, v. I. 375, 215; PRO E134, 13 Wm III, Trin. 19. Just how market prices in the 19th c. swung from moderate rewards to riches is shown in the statement in 1865 that a pack of 9,000 teasel heads might fetch anything between £4 and £22.—Syme, loc. cit.
68. Thirsk, 'New crops and their diffusion', ead. 1984a: 259–85.
69. Fuller, 1987 edn.: 138; Edwards, 1976: 63; D. Barker, 1989: 20; Cottis, 1985: 223; PRO E 112, 455, no. 975; J. Harvey, 1987: 3. The invention of printing caused books on

medicinal herbs to be published and the information made more widely available. See e.g. *The Grete Herball*. 1529 edn., and Albertus Magnus, *Secrets of the Virtues of Herbs*, 1549.

70. Cornwall, 1977: 144; I wish to thank Miss Judith Oliver for the saffron figures from Cambs. inventories, and Mr Alan Bullwinkle for much varied information from wills, inventories, other documents, and printed sources, on saffron in Cambs. and Essex; Bradley, 1736: 158; VCH, *Cambs.*, vi. 108, 131, 225, 238–9, 254; viii. 60, 75, 147, 187, 213, 223, 232, 242; Saffron Walden Museum, Leaflet 13, p. 4.

71. Anon. 1732*a*, *An Account of Saffron*, Dublin Society, 1732: *passim*; VCH, *Cambs.*, vi. 92; Norfolk RO, Townshend loan (I owe the details of this Bacon archive to the kindness of Sheila Cooper, Nesta Evans, and Prof. Hassell Smith); Houghton, 1727–8: iv. 287, citing *Trans. Philosophical Soc.* 12 (1678). *An Account of Saffron* described Cambridgeshire growers cropping for two years and fallowing in the third.

72. E. Evans, 1976: 19, 46–7; William Salt Library, Stafford, S Ms 429, iii I; information kindly supplied by letter by Prof. Eric Evans.

73. Thirsk, 1978: 177.

74. D. A. Baker, 1985: 237; Som. RO, Consistory Court Papers, D/D/C, 1739.

75. Markham, 1613: 2nd book, p. 31; Parkinson, 1629: 11; J. Harvey, 1972*b*: *passim*, esp. 13; Coles, 1657: 272; Hollybande, 1573: 112; Powell and Jenkinson, 1938; 71; PRO E134, 3 Jas. II, Easter 2.

76. Thirsk, 1978: 142–4, 146.

77. At Evesham Arthur Young reckoned in 1768 that 300–400 acres were given over to gardening (its asparagus was celebrated), and produce went to Bath and Bristol.—Webber, 1968: 25. While the area was known for its many smallholders, note also John Evelyn's dedication of *Acetaria*, 1699: 191, to John Lord Somers of Evesham. On asses' milk in Canterbury, see D. A. Baker, 1985: 434–6, and Putney, in *AHEW*, v. I. 290. Lord Chancellor John Methuen in Ireland was greatly helped in illness by asses' milk in 1697.—*CSPD* 1697: 178. Pehr Kalm encountered this specialty in 1748 on a journey from Gaddesden (Herts.) to Woodford (Essex).—Kalm, 1892: 160.

78. Colville, 1904: 76, 20, 27–8, 30; Rowse, 1962: 283; Beale, 1675–6: 363; Beale and Lawrence, 1677: 2. A qualitative change in the status of vegetables and fruit after the mid-17th c. is not a peculiarly English phenomenon, but is evident in Holland too. Dutch artists took pride in depicting vegetables and fruit in their paintings, and Gabriel Metsu's picture of *The Vegetable Market at Amsterdam*, c.1661–2 (Paris, Louvre), is one of the highlights. See Ferrier, 1989: 428–46.

Notes to Chapter 4

1. Irsigler, 1984: 725–6. Selective breeding in the late 20th c. has eliminated the erucic acid which formerly made rapeseed unpalatable for human consumption. See below, Ch. 9.

2. Godrey Smith, 'Alarm clocks and milking as usual', *Sunday Times*, 18 May 1980; Thirsk and Cooper, 1972: 499–500.

3. B. M. S. Campbell, 1983: 41.

4. Moorhouse, 1981, in Crossley, 1981: 115; Thirsk, 1978: 68.

5. Thirsk, 1978: 68. I owe to Dr Todd Gray a further reference to rapeseed in this decade, found in Consistory Court Records, Norwich RO, 1550s, fo. 77, c.1558,

showing tithe taken on rapeseed at 'Lington', an unidentified place.

6. Thirsk, 1978: 68–9.
7. Ibid. 69.
8. Smith and Baker, 1983: 90, 106, 109–10.
9. Thirsk, 1978: 70; Moir, 1957: 256–7.
10. Moir, 1957: 257–8, 260–2; PRO E134, 2 Car. I, Easter 19.
11. Moir, 1957: 262, 258; *AHEW*, iv. 653.
12. PRO E134, 2 Car. I, Easter 19.
13. PRO E112/179/2; E134, 2 Car. I, Easter 19.
14. Ibid.; Thirsk and Cooper, 1972: 496–500.
15. PRO E112/179/2: E134, 2 Car. I, Easter 19; Thirsk, 1978: 70; Northants RO, Finch Hatton MS, vol. 119; PRO E178/5438.
16. Anon. 1646, *The Anti-Projector*, 8; CJ VIII, p. 183.
17. Joint RO, Lichfield, 1698 R, inventory of Thomas Renshawe; *AHEW*, v. 1. 56.
18. Lincs. AO, Inventory 205/62; Hart, 1832: 9. Net profits per acre for wheat, barley, beans, and peas are those given by Samuel Trowell in 1739 in *A New Treatise of Husbandry*, pp. 156–7, cited in D. A. Baker, 1985: 569–70. For the feeding of rapeseed to cattle and sheep, see Mortimer, 1707: 120–1; Houghton, 1727–8: iv. 21.
19. See e.g. Dugdale's descriptions of the area around the Wash and in Axholme, in Darby, 1956: 275, 283; Worlidge, 1687: 45–6.
20. David Griffiths in a letter to *The Times*, 30 July 1983: 'At harvest time it [i.e. rapeseed] is extremely vulnerable to seed loss, especially in a dry, hot spell. Being a few days late with swathing can easily cost £50 per acre.'
21. Lincs. AO, Inventory 212/25. For Benedict Webb's reference to the value of rapeseed in employing the poor in the 4–6 weeks before harvest, see PRO E134, 2 Car. I, Easter 19. According to another observer, the crop was sown at Lammas (19 August).—Hart, 1832: 9.
22. I owe this information on the West Midlands trade to the kindness of Dr Graeme J. Milne of the Portbooks Programme, University of Wolverhampton, who supplied me with all references to the coastal trade in rapeseed and rape oil, found in the portbooks between 1693 and 1720. The original documents are held in the PRO.
23. Thirsk, 1978: 138; Falkus, 1976, in Coleman and John, 1976: 260.
24. Devon RO, Bedford MSS, W1258, LP, 5/2.
25. I thank Vivien Billington warmly for news of the wild woad plants still found nowadays; Clark and Wailes, 1935–6: 69; Nigel Hawkes, 'Set-aside farmers are moved to grow woad', *The Times*, 17 June 1995, p. 4. The growth of interest in woad (and indigo) since the late 1980s is noteworthy, and is best seen in two international conferences, of which the first was held in Erfurt in 1992, and the second in Toulouse in June 1995, the latter bringing together some eighty people, mostly from Europe and Asia. In Dec. 1995 was announced a grant from the Leverhulme Trust to an agricultural botanist at Reading University to study 'the scientific basis of indigo production from woad'.—*The Times*, 27 Dec. 1995, p. 18.
26. Hants RO, Jervoise of Herriard Collection, Sherfield MSS 44M69/L30/76. I wish to thank Mr Jervoise for permission to cite this document and others below.
27. Orders of 1621 in Norwich City Archives, Assembly Books, AB 6/125d–126, cited in Allison, 1955: 660; Wills, 1979: 3.
28. BL Lansdowne MS 49, no. 58, fo. 139.

29. Ponting, 1976: 77.
30. Ruddock, 1951: 81–2, 88. (See also PRO C1, 273, 52 for a Chancery dispute concerning woad brought from Genoa); Caster, 1962: 87–8.
31. This describes the competitive scene in the simplest terms. It deserves more careful analysis. Woad had been grown in the Garonne valley much earlier, and some supplies reached England as well as going eastward to Spain, but the scale of French production increased when Toulouse commanded the marketing of woad.— Caster, 1962: 87–91. See also Huxley, 1992: 214–26. The vicissitudes of Italian woad production and marketing are well illustrated in Lee, 1982: 141–56, and the phases of fortune seem to dovetail with the French experience. See also Ruddock, 1951: 212.
32. O. Coleman, 1961: 321.
33. Ponting, 1976: 75–6.
34. Lee, 1982: 141–2.
35. This paragraph is based on the very full account in Mägdefrau, 1973: 131–48. A revival of interest in the woad-growing history of the Erfurt area is recorded in a number of publications since 1988 by H. E. Müllerott, and published by the Thüringer Chronik Verlag.
36. BL Lansdowne MS 49, no. 47.
37. Mägdefrau, 1973: 137, 141–2.
38. Luther, 1967, liv. 132, no. 1281 (I wish to thank Dr Mary Prior for this reference); Mägdefrau, 1973: 142. The last woad mill in Germany, at Pferdingsleben near Gotha, did not close until 1910.—Wills, 1979: 4.
39. O. Coleman, 1961: 321–4.
40. Thirsk, 1978: 27–8. It is probably significant that woad from the Azores began to be traded by the Bernuy family, of Burgos, Spain, in the 1540s (or possibly a little earlier than this), after fifty years in which they had been engaged in selling the woad of Toulouse. Some of their woad regularly went from Burgos to England and Flanders.—Huxley, 1992. 214–26.
41. Thirsk, 1978: 28.
42. We do not know for certain the owner of this piece of Lymington land, but it may be significant that the manor, having been confiscated for the attainder of Henry, marquess of Exeter, in 1539, passed to various grantees thereafter, and was at this date, 1548, in Crown hands.—VCH, *Hants*, iv. 646. For the virtue of saline soils, see Young, 1813; 174.
43. Bettey, 1978: 114–15. For Robert Cecil at Cranborne, see *DNB, sub nomine*.
44. BL Lansdowne MS 49, nos. 54, 57.
45. Thirsk, 1978: 29; Surrey RO, Guildford Muniment Room, Loseley MSS 1966/1 and 1965. I wish to thank Mr J. R. More-Molyneux of Loseley Park for allowing me to consult and cite these MSS.
46. PRO SP 63, 126, 16.
47. West Sussex RO, Ep II, 5, 3, fos. 68–76. I am much indebted to Dr Christopher Wickham for this reference. One man in Sussex disturbs this geographical and chronological generalization. John Woodward of Fishbourne claimed in 1585 to have grown woad for seven years on 2 acres of arable, for six years on another 3 acres, and for shorter periods of one, two, or three years on another collection of seven pieces of land, amounting to 32 acres in all. This takes Woodward's original effort back to 1578, the year when the first alarms sounded about the sharply rising

price of woad. It was caused by a heavy duty imposed by the French in 1577.—PRO E163, 15, 1; Thirsk, 1978: 27; Kellenbenz, 1976: 29.

48. For the Cope family growing woad in Oxfordshire, see BL Lansdowne MS 49, no. 59; PRO C2, Jas. I, C22, 82. See also Thirsk, 1978: 21–2.

49. C. R. J. Currie, 1976: map 5 and p. 364.

50. Burnby and Robinson, 1976: 8.

51. Wills, 1979: 6.

52. R. S. Smith, 1961: 41.

53. See above and below, p. 83 and p. 90.

54. BL Lansdowne MS 49, no. 57.

55. PRO E163, 15, 1; VCH, *Sussex*, ii. 24; ix. 137–8, 207, 233; vii. 31. The same William Devenish of West Hampnett supplied some 200 quarters of woad seed to launch a woad-growing project in Ireland *c.* 1591.—PRO LR9/86.

56. Hants RO, Jervoise of Herriard Coll., 44 M69/L57/4 and 11; also loc. cit. 2, 57, and 8.

57. Bettey, 1978: 14–15; PRO E163, 14, 9. For woad in Bucks., see that at Brill in Bernwood forest in 1611 (PRO SP 14, 54, 15); at Buston in Aston Abbots in the 1730s (Oxon. RO, DIL XV e, 3d); and in the early 18th c. at Tyringham, near the R. Ouse (VCH, *Bucks.*, iv. 482).

58. Guildford Muniment Room, Loseley MS 1966, 2.

59. PRO E163, 15, 1.

60. Ibid.

61. Youngs, 1976: p. 151.

62. *CSPD* 1581–90: 326, 339.

63. Youngs, 1976: 152; *CSPD* 1580–1625, Addenda, p. 207. This last makes it clear that while the acreage was restricted, it was recognized that much work would be given to the poor.

64. Youngs, 1976: 152; *CSPD* 1591–4: 525. For individual licensees, by parish, see BL Lansdowne MS 49, no. 59.

65. BL Lansdowne MS 49, no. 59.

66. PRO St. Ch 5, A 35, 21. I owe this reference to Dr Adrienne Rosen. See also Hughes and Larkin, 1969: 213 (no. 802).

67. Notestein, Relf, and Simpson, 1935: vi. 300; ii. 297.

68. BL Lansdowne MS 49, nos. 57, 43, 54, 59. For Northants, see below. For Glos., where woad remained till the 19th c., see R. Perry, 1945: 109.

69. Stone, 1949: 46.

70. Ponting, 1976: 75. Chemists at the woad and indigo conference in Toulouse in June 1995 gave the scientific explanation.

71. Guildford Muniment Room, LC 1966, 3.

72. Hardy, 1905: 37; Brownlow, 1652: 46.

73. Northants RO, Isham MSS, IL3630, 3592, 3606, 5279.

74. VCH, *Hunts.*, iii. 144–5.

75. Thirsk, 1978: 4–5. See also Guildford Muniment Room, Loseley MS, 1966, 3.

76. Guildford Muniment Room, Loseley MS 1966, 3; *CSPD* 1580–1625: Addenda, p. 207.

77. Bettey, 1978: 114. See also PRO SP 14, 54, 15 for a dispute at Brill, Bucks., between commoners and lord concerning woad and work for the poor.

78. Slack, 1975: 8–12.

79. Thirsk, 1984*b*: 287–307.

80. Mildon, 1934: chs. 15–18.

81. Oxon. RO, DIL XV, e, 3d.

82. R. S. Smith, 1961: 27 ff.

83. Centre for Kentish Studies, Maidstone, U55, E100, 76.

84. Bodleian Library, MS Aubrey 2.

85. PRO E134, 9 Chas. I, Easter 10.

86. Oxon. RO, DIL XV, e, 3d.

87. Leics. RO, Misterton Parish Registers. I wish to thank Dr John Goodacre for these references.

88. Young, 1813: 174, 179. T. Stone described Cartwright as lord of the manor of Brothertoft in 1800. See H. O. Clark and Wailes, 1935–6: 80.

89. Wills, 1979: 4.

90. Guildford Muniment Room, Loseley MS 1966, 3.

91. BL Lansdowne MS 49, no. 52. For the yields of 2 and 3 tons per acre, see H. O. Clark and Wailes, 1935–6: 91.

92. BL Lansdowne MS 121, no. 21; Lansdowne MS 49, no. 52.

93. *AHEW*. iv. 653.

94. Blith, 1652: 225.

95. Worlidge, 1675: 41–2.

96. PRO C5, 8, 101. I wish to thank Mrs Lucy Roe for drawing my attention to this case, and for allowing me to use her transcript of the accounts of William Baldwyn.

97. These destinations are taken from the woad accounts of Robert Payne for Wollaton, Notts., of Geo. Bedford and Henry Sherfield for Blagdon Park, Dorset, and of Lionel Cranfield for Milcote, Warws.

98. Leics. RO, DG 7, 1, 19a; DG 7, 1, 74; Hunts. RO, Connington Coll., acc. 40, add. ix i.

99. Reading Univ. Library, Farm Records Coll., Glo 6, 1, 1.

100. VCH, *Bucks.*, iv. 482; Billingsley, 1798: 115.

101. Skipp, 1978: 106 and *passim*.

102. Blith, 1652: 227–34; Thirsk, 1983: 306–7. See also Worlidge, 1675: 41.

103. Morton, 1712: 17.

104. Centre for Kentish Studies, Maidstone, DRb, At 3; D. A. Baker, 1985: 245.

105. VCH, *Hunts.*, iii. 144. I wish to thank Dr Stephen Porter for this reference; Young, 1813: 174–82.

106. Darwin and Meldola, 1896–7: 36–7. The exact locations of the other three enterprises are identified by Wills, 1979: 4. See also H. O. Clark and Wailes, 1935–6: 69–95. Paul Brassley, a Lincolnshire native and reader of my manuscript, tells me that Skirbeck still has a pub called The Woadman.

107. Wills, 1979: 10, 16, 18–20.

108. Ibid. 4, 14, 20.

109. This evolution is significantly different from that in East Germany around Erfurt, where peasants continued in charge of woad when the great merchants lost interest in the later 17th c.—Raschke, 1988: 6–7.

110. The government's attitude towards tobacco-growing is an example of unsympathetic and destructive intervention in the 17th c.—Thirsk, 1984*a*: 259–85.

111. Thirsk, 1978: 4–5.

112. This account leans heavily on the very thorough work of Dennis A. Baker, 1985: 471 ff.

113. Bath, 1963: 178–80.
114. See below, Ch. 5, on madder.
115. Awty, 1981: 59; D. A. Baker, 1985: 476–7.
116. Scot, 1574: p. iv, cited in D. A. Baker, 1985: 478.
117. For Essex hops, see Emmison, 1978: 103, 235, 287, 307.
118. Burn, 1781: iv. 242; Thirsk and Cooper, 1972: 109.
119. Markham, 1613: 90–1.
120. Ibid. 89; Thirsk, 1978: 182–3, 67; Markham, 1613: 93–101, 91.
121. BL Lansdowne MS 12/5, fo. 7, cited in D. A. Baker, 1985: 482; *AHEW*, v. ii. 299.
122. D. A. Baker, 1985: 479 ff.
123. Banister, 1799: 206, 226, 231. On farmer-gardeners, see Thick, in *AHEW*, v. ii. 504.
124. Thirsk and Cooper, 1972: 86; *AHEW*, iv. 106. This last work, continuing up to 1640, does not mention a hop trade in the West Midlands, whereas *AHEW*, v. ii. 299, and Thirsk and Cooper, 1972: 337–9, referring to the 1650s and later, contain significant contemporary comments on Herefordshire hops, and show them as serious competitors with the hops of south-east England.
125. Worlidge, 1675: 133–46.
126. Ibid.; KAO DR b/Pi7/6A; U23 E6. For a considerable increase in hop-growing at Coleshill, Berks., in 1719–22, showing hops worth £21 in 1719 and over £274 in 1722, see Cottis, 1985: 252.
127. D. A. Baker, 1985: 617, 622, 639.
128. Banister, 1799: 205, 236–9.
129. Charles Whitehead in 1899 expressed indignation at what he called the somewhat derisive terms used to describe Kent's farming activities. Without them, he said, farmers would have been in an almost hopeless state of depression. This theme will recur below.—Whitehead, 1899: 485.
130. In 1794 the hops within 2½ miles of Canterbury were still computed at 1,500 acres, and were said not to have varied materially for some years.—Canterbury Cathedral Library, Irby Deposit, U 11, 430, no. 86; Whitehead, 1890a: 321–5. For hop acreages in the years, 1807–51, see *AHEW*, vi. 1058–9. For the later history of West Midland hops, compared with Kent, see Pocock, 1958: 75–80.
131. For the chequered years after 1914, and until 1957, see *AHEW*, viii. 189–90; Pocock, 1957: 128. For present hopes for hops, see Roger Protz, 'Hops spring eternal', *Observer Colour Supplement*, 12 Nov. 1995, p. 61; David Brown, 'Mini-hop lowers growing costs', *Telegraph*, 19 Sept. 1995, p. 10. I wish to thank Mr Nigel Chew for this reference.
132. For two recent accounts of later hop history, see Filmer, 1982, a richly illustrated book, and Lawrence, 1990, which vividly recounts the success of one farmer, Edward Albert White, at Beltring, Paddock Wood, Kent, prospering in another age of alternative agriculture, from the 1870s till his death in 1922, by engaging in a variety of different activities at the same time. The wisdom of this procedure is another theme in alternative agriculture, developed below. Alongside dairying, fruit- and vegetable-growing, forestry, charcoal-burning, and horse and cattle breeding, he manufactured insecticidal hop- and fruit-washes.—Lawrence, 1990: 35–40.

Notes to Chapter 5

1. Bath, 1963: 272.

2. B. M. S. Campbell, 1983: 41.

3. Brewer, 1870: iv. I. 125.

4. Tawney and Power, 1924: i. 329; Hulme, 1900: 45.

5. Rymer, 1704–32, xvii. 410–15, repr. in Thirsk and Cooper, 1972: 19.

6. Allen, 1982: 178. I wish to thank David Allen for drawing my attention to this. William Turner was doubtless thoroughly familiar with the madder plant for he had spent some considerable time visiting the Rhine country, Holland, and East Friesland, and making expeditions to the islands off the Dutch coast. He cannot have failed to visit Zealand, the principal centre of madder-growing.—*DNB, sub nomine.*

7. Hants RO, Jervoise of Herriard Collection, Sherfield MSS, 44M69/L33/24. I wish to thank Mr Jervoise for permission to consult and cite these documents. Government interest in the madder project is made clear in PRO SP 16, 44, no. 1.

8. Sherfield MSS, 44M69/L33, nos. 24, 9, 10.

9. Ibid., nos., 9, 10, 24.

10. Ibid., no. 10.

11. Ibid.

12. Ibid., nos. 10, 24, 17.

13. Ibid., no. 15.

14. Ibid., nos. 15, 16.

15. Ibid., nos. 11, 12, 13, 14, 24, 18.

16. Ibid., nos. 24, 14, 45, 17, 19. For the evidence that Culpeper was the landlord, see the note of rent paid to him: ibid. 44M69/L55/78.

17. Ibid. 44M69/L33, nos. 19, 20; Moir, 1957: 259.

18. Sherfield MSS, 44M69/L33, nos. 10, 23.

19. Ibid., nos. 21, 22, 24; Woodcroft, 1969: 515.

20. Ibid., nos. 25, 26, 32.

21. *CSPD* 1625–49: Addenda, p. 442.

22. Sherfield MSS, 44M69/L33, nos. 29, 35, 33, 36–9, 46; *CSPD* 1631–3: 77, 402, 478.

23. Sherfield MSS, 44M69/L33, no. 36; *CSPD* 1635–6: 429, 551; *CSPD* 1636–7: 211.

24. *CSPD* 1637: 47.

25. Fuller, 1952: 252; Blith, 1652: 234; id. 1653: 235.

26. Sheffield Univ. Library, Hartlib MSS, 70/7, 62/45/2–3, 66 /27/1; *CSPD* 1656–7: 88; Fuller, 1952: 252; PRO SP 29/7, no. 136.

27. Woodcroft, 1969: 526. A much later reference to past success with madder mentioned that Dutch merchants grew it, and 'amassed great estates by it.' It may relate to this episode.—Anon., 1732*b*: *The Great Improvement of Commons that are Enclosed*, London Univ. Library, Goldsmith's Collection.

28. PRO E134, 31 and 32 Chas. II, Hil. 6. Another lawsuit in Chancery featuring the same James Smith shows him in 1658 buying from dealers indigo which had been imported by the East India Company.—PRO C78, 732, 8.

29. PRO E134, 31 and 32 Chas. II, Hil. 6.

30. Ibid.

31. VCH, *Glos.*, viii. 204; Miller, 1758: 21; Houghton, 1727–8: ii. 372.

32. Chapman and Chassagne, 1981: 1–11, 158, 217–18; Ponting, 1977: 18, 19; Schaefer, 1941*a*: *passim*, but esp. 1400–3; id. 1941*b*: *passim*, but esp. 1412–13.

33. Anon. 1765: *Impartial Considerations on the Cultivation of Madder in England.* This

tract is bound in a volume of Acts of Parliament of 1765 in BL, shelfmark 213. i. 4(100). I am much indebted to Dr Dennis Baker for this reference.

34. Hudson and Luckhurst, 1954: 90.
35. P. Miller, 1758: pp. v–viii, 37.
36. Ibid., *passim*, but esp. pp. v, vii.
37. Ibid., p. ix; *DNB, sub nomine*, and Le Rougetel, 1990.
38. Ponting, 1977: 17; P. Miller, 1758: 3.
39. P. Miller, 1758: 21; Anon. 1765: 1; Fuller, 1952: 252; *DNB, sub* Philip Miller.
40. P. Miller, 1758: 19.
41. Hudson and Luckhurst, 1954: 59, 89–90; *Trans. Roy. Soc. of Arts*, 2 (1789), 6 (I wish to thank Dr Juanita Burnby for this reference); PRO E134, 31 and 32 Chas. II, Hil. 6.
42. Jacob, 1774: 97–100.
43. Chassagne, 1980: 119–20.
44. Resentment at the advantages enjoyed by the French 'growing madder free of taxes' surfaces in Anon., 1765. See also Duhamel du Monceau, *Éléments d'Agriculture*, Paris, 1762. This was translated into English by Philip Miller in 1764, and the 1767 edition of Miller's translation shows the 54 pages on madder.—1767: ii. 151–205.; Hudson and Luckhurst, 1954: 90.
45. Hants RO, Sherfield MSS, 44M69/L33, no. 45.
46. P. Miller, 1758: 34.
47. Anon., 1765.
48. Sheffield Univ. Library, Hartlib MSS, 66/27/1 and 70/7; Arbuthnot, 1800: *passim*; Ponting, 1977:20; Schaefer, 1941*a*: 1403; Wiskerke, 1952: 127.
49. The mulberry leaves in Dorset are grown under plastic. For the silk farm at Compton House in Dorset, see the publicity leaflet, *Worldwide Butterflies and Lullingstone Silk Farm*. For the silk farm originally in Kent, see Dyke, 1949: *passim*.
50. Thirsk, 1978: 40–2, 47–8, 68, 103–4, 144–6; N. Evans, 1985: *passim* but esp. 50–2.
51. BL Cotton MS Titus B V, 185; L & P. Hen. VIII, vol. 13, part 1, p. 206.
52. Dietz, 1972: nos. 46, 146, 11; HMC 80, Cranfield MSS, 17, 26.
53. J. Clarke, 1839: 69–73.
54. Cust, 1891: 97–8; Ashton, 1969: 115; W. A. Shaw, 1911: 25.
55. See further below, p. 129.
56. *CSPD* 1603–10: 344, 398; [Stallenge], 1609, *Harleian Miscellany*, ii, 1809: 218–22.
57. [Stallenge], loc cit.
58. Ibid. 208.
59. Paterson, 1978: 455.
60. Hatch, 1957: 45.
61. BL Harleian MS 4807, no. 29, fos. 57–8.
62. PRO SP 14/47, no. 109.
63. *CSPD* 1603–10: 540. The procedure locally is clearly seen in Devon, to which a letter was sent entreating the Earl of Bath and named knights and gentlemen to accept 5,400 mulberry trees at three farthings each.—Hamilton, 1877: 234–5.
64. I wish to thank Dr Christopher Currie for this suggestion.
65. *Observer*, 5 June 1977, p. 11. See also Colvin, 1982: 245, 248.
66. Colvin 1982: 214.
67. Paterson, 1978: 455. In 1650, when Theobalds was surveyed for sale by Parliament,

it had a Mulberry Walk, and a Green Walk with 72 mulberry trees.—PRO E317, Herts. 26.

68. Hatch, 1957: 3.
69. Colvin, 1982: 110, 115.
70. Bonoeil, 1622: 11. This was contained in *His Maiesties Gracious Letter to the Earl of Southampton, Treasurer, and to the Councell and Company of Virginia . . .*, London, 1622.
71. PRO SP 14/47, no. 109.
72. Shaw, 1911: 23.
73. Bonoeil, 1622: *passim*, but esp. 65–9, 71–2. Bonoeil referred to his friends in Languedoc, and may have come from there himself, but in the handling of the worms he described a method used in Messina. The means by which knowledge was transmitted from Messina to Languedoc and then to England calls for investigation. Some helpful suggestions on the connections between Sicily and France appear in Sabin, 1931: 6. Bonoeil's treatise was printed for the benefit not only of Virginia, but also of the Somers islands, where silk production was also initiated.
74. Hatch, 1957: 5–7.
75. Powell, 1977: 83.
76. Hatch, 1957: 8–11, 17.
77. Ibid. 3–61. Note esp. the official requirement (1623–4) that every plantation build a two-storeyed house for silkworms, and that every garden be planted with at least four mulberry trees. George Sandys, the governor of Virginia, had both. Similar orders were renewed in 1642. By the 1660s the mulberry tree was the most frequently cited tree marking land boundaries.
78. Hamer, 1935: 126–7; Clarke, 1839: 110, 123–31, 180–90.
79. I wish to thank Dr Barbara Todd for the information on Abingdon.
80. Hartlib, 1655: *passim*; Sheffield Univ. Library, Hartlib MSS, Ephemerides 1652, CC–CC3. See also Coles, 1657: 83 ff.
81. Hartlib MSS, Ephemerides, 1652 DD–DD2.
82. Stubbs, 1989:339; *AHEW*, v, ii. 538; Sheffield Univ. Library, Hartlib MSS, Ephemerides, 1654, VV–VV2; Darby, 1956: 274.
83. Worlidge, 1687: 190, 102–3.
84. Sheffield Univ. Library, Hartlib MSS, 66/27/1. The use of dandelions and lettuce was reported by John Moore, writing from Dublin about the experience of a kinswoman.
85. Worlidge, 1687: 103.
86. I owe this reference to the kindness of Dr John Broad, citing Verney MS EC, 23 June 1724.
87. Chaloner, 1953: 781–3.
88. Worlidge, 1704: under Mulberry.
89. Clarke, 1839: 75.
90. Ibid. 77–8.
91. Hamilton in 1877 thought that the many mulberry trees then growing in South Devon dated from this time.—Hamilton, 1877: 235. The present author, visiting the site of the Walsinghams' home at Scadbury, Kent, in 1993, was told of a mulberry tree near by, only recently uprooted in a storm. As Sir Thomas Walsingham was a

gentleman of standing in Kent, he may be expected to have planted a good number. However, some mulberry trees in England are even older than this.— Amherst, 1896: 160.

92. Peterson, 1965: 1, 20; US Dept. of Agriculture, 1966: 4. See also Rabak, 1935: 1–14; Knowles and Miller, n.d.: 1–23.

93. US Dept. of Agriculture, 1966: *passim*; Peterson, 1965: 18.

94. Sheffield Univ. Library, Hartlib MSS, Ephemerides, 1639: B–C2. See also above, pp. 82–3, 105. Good illustrations and a bibliography appear in Hanelt, 1961: 114–45. I wish to thank Dr Hans-Heinrich Müller for this reference.

95. *CSPD* 1663–4: 217, 378; HMC IX, *House of Lords MSS, 1672–3*, 27–8.

96. HMC IX: 27–8.

97. Reynel, 1674: 87.

98. Plot, 1705 edn.: 157–8; Bodleian MS, Hearne's Diaries, 158, p. 8. I owe this reference to the late Frank Emery.

99. I owe this information on Colonel Vernon to Dr Janet Cooper.

100. Mortimer, 1707: 131.

101. PRO SP 29, 443, no. 43.

102. Ibid.

103. Foster, 1891, 1892: 214. This Eustace Burnaby of Northamptonshire was thought to be a son of Sir Richard Burnaby, and to have died young. If his early death is an error, he could have been the grower of safflower. At his death he held land at Grandborough, on the R. Leam in Warws., south of Rugby, on the borders of Northamptonshire.

104. PRO PROB 11/376.

105. Plot, 1686: 205; J. M. Wilson, 1847: i, under *Barley*; *CSPD* 1661–2: 480; 1663–4: 217, 378. John Beale in 1657 had wanted to advance the growing of French barley, which 'by the notorious oppression of apothecaries' sold at a fancy price of 4s. the light pound.—Sheffield Univ. Library, Hartlib MSS 52/18–19.

106. Houghton, 1727: iv. 354–5.

107. Ibid. 354; Hudson and Luckhurst, 1954: 167; *CSPD* 1694–5: 32.

108. Urry, 1930: 193; Houghton, 1727: ii. 459; Kalm, 1892: 61.

109. Perry, 1945: 109–10; photograph of weld, *The Times*, 26 June 1996, p.26; also in *Harrogate and North Yorkshire News*, 21 June 1996, p.7.

110. Worlidge, 1675: 148–9; *Fuller's Worthies*, 1987 edn.: 192.

111. Blith, 1653: 224–7; Speed, 1659: 106.

112. D. A. Baker, 1985: 243–5; *Fuller's Worthies*, 1987 edn.: 192; Banister, 1799: 197.

113. Blith, 1653: 226–7.

114. Banister, 1799: 197–202.

115. Ordish, 1977: 20; Bondois, 1929: 286, 297.

116. *AHEW*, i. ii. 103–4, 117–18; Ordish, 1977: 22; *AHEW*, ii. 121.

117. Ordish, 1977: 23.

118. Bolton, 1980: 152; Steane, 1985: 276–7; Ch. 1 above; Bath, 1963: 144. The mounting imports of wine from France are usually attributed to the marriage of Eleanor of Aquitaine to Henry II in 1152, bringing the wine region around Bordeaux into English hands until 1453, or, as in Hyams, 1949: 40, to peace and a marriage alliance with France, 1303 and 1308. Hartlib followed the substance of this argument in *Hartlib's Legacie*, 1652: 23. But authors sometimes also link French imports with the

need to suppress vineyards at home in order to produce more grain.—Ordish, 1977: 31.

119. Heresbach, 1577, Epistle to the Reader. William Camden in 1586 also attributed the disappearance of vines to slothfulness.—Ordish, 1977: 33.

120. Heresbach, 1577, Epistle to the Reader.

121. Ordish, 1977: 13.

122. *CSPD* 1547–80: 316; Markham, 1613: 70, 87, 130–2; Colvin, 1982: iv, II. 213.

123. Hartlib, 1652: 22–4, 27–8; Hartlib, 1655a: 24; Sheffield Univ. Library, Hartlib MSS, Ephemerides, GG–GG2.

124. Stubbs, 1982: 479.

125. Amherst, 1896: 327–30.

126. Elstob, 1933: pp. ix–xiv, xxviii–xxix, 153, 157–65.

127. Henrey, 1975: i. 175–8; ii. 479–81. A work by S.J., *The Vineyard*, 1727, reiterated hopes of financial gain for ordinary farmers growing vines if once a person of quality set the example.—Loc cit., A3v.–A4. For more historical illustrations, without a sense of the chronology suggested here, see Hyams, 1949: ch. 1.

128. Ordish, 1977: 35–6, 39, 43–5; Pratt, 1906: 89, 93, 96–7.

129. Bodleian Library, MS Aubrey 2.

130. Plot, 1686: 380.

131. Rowse, 1962: 283.

132. Ordish, 1977; 41–3.

133. C. Martin, 1971: 153–60.

134. Pococke, 1888: 166.

135. Thirsk, 1984a: 284.

136. Ibid. 265–70, 283. Partnerships have a history in western Europe which, for their beginnings, structure, membership, and conventions of association, merit further study. For partnerships in Holland in windmills and oil refineries, and interests as small as a 1/64th part in trading voyages, see De Vries, 1976: 118.

137. The role of the Salters' Company was addressed in my paper on 'Seventeenth-century village life in Old England', given at the Plimouth Plantation in Sept. 1988, but unpublished.

138. Thirsk, 1992a: 15–34.

139. Payne, 1589: 8; Hants RO, Jervoise of Herriard Collection, Sherfield MSS, 44M69/L57, nos. 2, 4–9; Bettey, 1978: 117; *Acts of the Privy Council, July 1628–April 1629*, 82–3, no.265; Thirsk, 1983: 308.

140. *AHEW*, vi. 303–5.

141. *AHEW*, v. II. 581–6; Warws. RO, L6/1363. I owe this reference to the kindness of Dr Todd Gray. It should be emphasized that the relative advantages of drilling rows or broadcasting seed, and of hoeing by machine or by hand, were still being debated at the end of the 18th c. See Billingsley, 1798: 274–9.

Notes to Chapter 6

1. Historical experience was prominent in the evidence of witnesses before the Royal Commission of 1894, when most of them discussed 19th-c. currency changes. A much longer view was taken by R. L. Everett, MP, describing the price inflation in Europe in the sixteenth century, following upon the opening of the silver mines at Potosi in South America. This increased the monetary stock of Europe fivefold, he

claimed, and caused a fourfold increase in prices. 'The history of agriculture is really one great illustration of the close connexion between the supply of money and prices in my judgment. That is the result of my historical research, and of quotations from authorities of all kinds.'—BPP 1894, XVI, pt. II, C7400–II, pp. 138–200, 331–54. Tobacco-growing in the 1880s was recognized by some as being a revival from the past (see below, pp. 155–6). So was the return to favour of small farms, after a period when the future seemed to lie only with large farms. On this, see the Essex land agent, Alfred Darby.—BPP 1896, XVII, C8021, p. 356.

2. *AHEW*, vi. 91.

3. Chambers and Mingay, 1966: 157–9.

4. Prince, 1989: 50 ff. For a strong push in this direction during the French and Napoleonic wars, see F. M. L. Thompson, 1963: 220–22.

5. E. Evans, 1976: 19, 46–7. For continuing horticulture in the Vale of Evesham, see J. M. Martin, 1985: 41–50.

6. Sheail, 1971: 98, 101. If the warrens continued, Sheail remarks that they were poorly managed.

7. BPP 1881, XVI, p. 388. It is noticeable in William Mavor's *General View of the Agriculture of Berkshire*, in 1801, how many special crops are listed as 'not usually cultivated', though suitable for Berkshire soils. They included cabbages and carrots for livestock feed, hops, woad, dill for hay for ewes with sucking lambs, flax, and lavender. Mavor was urging a programme that was inappropriate for the time.—Mavor, 1801: 227–34.

8. D. R. Chapman, 1888: 173; Whitehead, 1884: 12; BPP 1896, XVII, C8021, p. 2; BPP 1839, VIII, C398, pp. 377 ff.; Sharp, 1982: 59, 100 ff.

9. Sharp, 1982: 55, 86, 99, 187, 188. For the declining interest in rhubarb between the 1760s and 1820s, to be expected in the general circumstances postulated here, see Foust, though different reasons are given by the author.—Foust, 1992: 126–9.

10. BPP 1881, XVII, p. 829.

11. Prince in *AHEW*, vi. 41.

12. Haggard, 1902: ii. 316–19.

13. Bear, 1888: 97–112.

14. *AHEW*, vi. 92–3; Ernle, 1961: 349, 374–5.

15. BPP 1881, XVI, p. 372; 1882, XIV, pp. 12–13; Whitehead, 1882: 71.

16. An effective summary account of part of this period up to 1900 is contained in Stearns, 1932: 84–101, 130–54.

17. Whetham, 1978: 70–1, 80–96, 102–8, 113, 120–2.

18. Street, 1933: 4–5; Whetham, 1978: 226, 229–35. For similar judgements on the period 1875–1939 as all of a piece, chronic depression in agriculture being briefly interrupted by the First World War, see Perry, 1974: 13; Newby, 1987: 104; F. M. L. Thompson, 1991: 211 ff.; and, most recently, Perren, 1995.

19. Caird, 1888: 124–5, 139; BPP 1881, XVII, pp. 145, 964; 1894. XVI, pt. II, C7400–II, p. 71; 1894, XVI, pt. I, C7400–I, p. 25; 1896, XVII, C8021, p. 118.

20. BPP 1894, XVI, pt. I, C7400–I, p. 188; 1894, XVI, pt. II, C7400–II, p. 121; 1881, XVII, p. 587.

21. BPP 1894, XVI, pt. I, C7400–I, pp. 42, 57; 1881, XVII, p. 750.

22. BPP 1881, XVII, p. 140; BPP 1896, XVII, C8021, p. 66.

23. BPP 1894, XVI, pt. II, C7400–II, p. 475.

24. BPP 1894, XVI, pt. I, C7400–I, p. 188; 1894, XVI, pt. III, C7400–III, pp. 256–8.

25. BPP 1881, XVII, p. 140; Haggard, 1902: ii. 329.

26. See e.g. James Howard, 1880: 435–41; Faunce de Laune, 1882: 229–64, 604–09; Anon. 1882: 366–8; Randell, 1882: 368–70; Fream, 1888: 415 ff.; Wrightson, 1890: 282; Stapledon, 1914. I thank Paul Brassley for this last reference.

27. See BPP 1881, XVI, pp. 300, 361, 372, 376, 378, 410, 413, 420, 443, 447; 1882, XV, C3375–I, pp. 2, 15, 31, 75, 90; 1895, XVII, p. 266; Caird, 1888: 125.

28. BPP 1895, XVII, C7764, p. 18; Orwin and Whetham 1971: 267, 350.

29. BPP 1895, XVII, C7915, pp. 20, 48–9, 96; BPP 1896, XVII, C8021, pp. 596, 430–1, 282; BPP 1894, XVI, pt. I, C7365, p. 11.

30. The use of leys in the late Middle Ages is difficult to uncover, for lack of detailed evidence. The practice may have been known in northern England before it became familiar in the Midlands, though it is found at Wymeswold, Leics., in the early 15th c.—Thirsk, 1967: 178; Kerridge, 1967: 193–5, and Ch. 3 above.

31. Peel, 1923: 29; Jones, 1933: 21–41; Wheldon *et al.*, 1931: 62–125; Stapledon, 1944: 130–43 (note that this essay was written in 1918 and paid tribute to the earlier demonstration of ley farming by Robert H. Elliot at Clifton Park); Stapledon and Davies, 1942: *passim*; Griffith, 1936: 33–53; Whetham, 1978: 31–2, 174–5; Russell, 1966: 244–6.

32. BPP 1881, XVI, pp. 450, 453.

33. BPP 1896, XVII, C8021, pp. 60, 61, 110; 1894, XVI, pt. III, C7400–III, p. 87; 1895, XVII, C7915, pp. 96, 74.

34. Lucerne was the subject of an experiment in this period on a heavy clay soil, not the most suitable for this legume. It was designed by James Mason at Eynsham Hall, near Oxford, in order to accumulate nitrogen on a poor soil. Significantly Mason went to Thanet to collect practical advice. He did not test the result fully, for he did not follow the lucerne with arable crops, but laid down what proved to be a fine pasture instead.—A. D. Hall, 1904: 106–24. For more on Mason, see also below, n. 37.

35. BPP 1881, XVII, pp. 850, 852, 937; 1882, XIV, p. 107; Voelcker, 1880: 130–49, and in subsequent vols. of the *JRASE*, *passim*.

36. BPP 1882, XIV, pp. 94–101, 109; Haggard, 1902: i. 527–31. In 1931, among 'Notable Farming Enterprises', the achievements of A. H. Brown were celebrated. In growing grain continuously, he had been inspired by reading about Mr Prout's system.—Robinson, 1931: 151–62.

37. BPP 1881, XVII, pp. 324–5. A system using some of the same ideas was followed by James Mason at Eynsham Hall, on Oxford clay. It was described after his death by A. D. Hall in 1904. Mason used his knowledge of chemistry to devise a system of deep ploughing and aeration in order to release minerals from the subsoil. He satisfied himself that this method did successfully release potash compounds.—A. D. Hall, 1904: 106–24.

38. BPP 1894, XVI, pt. I, C7400–I, pp. 185, 139; Haggard, 1902: i. 420.

39. BPP 1895, XVII, C7915, p. 70; Ormrod, 1985: 16–17, 81–93; *AHEW*, v. II. 330–49.

40. Robinson, 1931: 151–62. This farmer followed Prout, but he also had many sidelines, borrowed from the regimes of alternative agriculture.

41. Andrews, 1881: 408; BPP 1881, XVII, p. 911.

42. BPP 1881, XVII, p. 977.

43. Jenkins, 1886: 729–56; E. J. Beale, 1887: 59–63.

44. The books were named by De Laune, 1887: 232, as E. Beale, *English Tobacco Culture* (1887), an informative work on the various experiments of Carter and large landowners, A. A. Erskine, *Tobacco Growing in Great Britain and Ireland* (no date found), P. Meadows Taylor, *Tobacco, a Farmer's Crop* (1886), and F. W. Fairholt, *Tobacco: Its History and Associations* (1859).

45. C. J. Beale, 1887: 3–4, 83–8.

46. De Laune, 1887: 213–51. Tobacco trials were also conducted by Lord Walsingham in Norfolk (see Jenkins, 1886: 732) and in Essex (see Arnold, 1888, p. 571).

47. Thirsk, 1984*a*: 259–85.

48. Jenkins, 1886: 733, 739; De Laune, 1887: 216 ff.; Arnold, 1888: 572. Tobacco had been grown in Ireland in the 1830s and been welcomed as a peasant crop. It had also been grown in 1782 in the Vale of York, and at some time in Scotland at Kelso, and at Newstead in Roxburghshire.—Arnold, 1888: 570–1.

49. De Laune, 1887: 216; Arnold, 1888: 570; BPP 1894, XVI, pt. I, C7365, p. 38.

50. Harte, 1973: 91–110. For hemp and flax in East Anglia, see N. Evans, 1985: 16–20, 41–6, 50–4, 103–4, 125–7, 163; and in Kent, see Ormrod, 1995.

51. Andrews, 1881: 408–10; Jenkins, 1881: 430–3; Stratton, 1882: 455–74.

52. BPP 1896, XVII, C8021, pp. 106, 114.

53. BPP 1894, XVII, pp. 253, 266.

54. BPP 1896, XVII, C8021, pp. 431–2; 1895, XVII, C7915, p. 73; N. Evans, 1985: 166–7.

55. Haggard, 1902: ii. 316–19. Similarly discrepant rates were cited by outraged fruit and vegetable growers, comparing transport costs to English markets from France and from southern England. See BPP, 1881, XVII, p. 905, showing that 1 ton of hops from Staplehurst, Kent, to London (41 miles) cost 37*s*. 4*d*., whereas the same quantity from Boulogne to London (99 miles) cost 19*s*. 7*d*. Other examples showed the French paying about half the cost for twice the distance.

56. Anon. 1890*b*: 441–9; Whetham, 1978: 165–9; Bridges and Dixey, 1925: 59–88; Pretyman, 1928: 1–9; Bridges and Dixey, 1934: 7, 12–13, 22–3, 34; Agricultural Statistics, 1937–8; *JRASE* 99 (1938), 440; Douet, forthcoming, ch. 5.

57. Pocock, 1965; 17.

58. Ibid. 17, 21–2; Mingay, in *AHEW*, vi. 41, 1042, 1056–9. Measured on a scale which put the quality of East Kent hops at the top with a mark of 100, Farnham (Surrey) hops were rated at 95, Worcester hops at 90, Weald of Kent hops at 70, and Sussex hops at 60.—BPP 1882, XV, C3375–I, p. 40.

59. BPP 1881, XVII, p. 818. Kent was by now the main hop county: 86% of all English hops were grown in the south-east: 64% of the total were grown in Kent, 14% in Sussex, 5% in Hampshire, and 4% in Surrey.—BPP 1882, XV, C3375–I, p. 39. The astonishing ups and downs of hop-growing were given by an east Kent farmer in 1881 relating his experience since 1864; yields had varied from 1¼ cwt. to 16 cwt. an acre, and prices from 10*s*. to 294*s*. a cwt.—BPP 1882, XV, C3375–I, p. 39.

60. BPP 1881, XVII, p. 911; BPP 1882, XV, C3375–I, pp. 39–40; Whitehead, 1890*a*: 324, 348.

61. BPP 1881, XVI, p. 409. Farnham was then growing 1500a. of hops, more than half the Surrey acreage of 2,370a.—Ibid.

62. Whitehead, 1893: 260; BPP 1896, XVII, C8021, p. 300.

63. BPP 1894, XVI, pt. I, C7365, pp. 28, 35.

64. BPP 1894, XVI, pt. II, C7400–II, pp. 76, 262.

65. BPP 1895, XVII, C7915, p. 58.
66. BPP 1896, XVII, C8021, p. 118; BPP 1894, XVI, pt. I, C7400–I, p. 219. For a similar situation in Hants, see Sheail, 1971: 140–1.
67. N. D. G. James, 1981: 190–1; BPP 1894, XVI, pt. II, C7400–II, p. 76; 1895, XVII, C7915, pp. 58, 87; Sheail, 1971: 113–14.
68. Sheail, 1971: 110–13, 115–18, 126–7, 138–41; BPP 1881, XV, p. 144; BPP 1896, XVII, C8021, p. 12; BPP 1895, XVII, C7915, p. 87; Haggard, 1902: i. 57; VCH, *Wilts.*, xi. 177.
69. Sheail, 1971: 112–13, 126.
70. Price, 1884: pp. vii–viii, 5–6.
71. Sheail, 1971: 125, 144–6, 195–201; BPP 1895, XVI, C7728, p. 25; BPP 1894, XVI, pt. I, C7334, p. 92; BPP 1895, XVII, C7915–I, p. 41.
72. Curtis, 1903: 16–49.
73. BPP 1894, XVI, pt. I, C7400–I, pp. 178, 186; Haggard, 1902: ii, 179. Nelthorpe may have been following the advice of Professor Curtis, the author of the 1903 survey, for Curtis had also advised capital expenditure on woodland planting in 1888.— Curtis, 1888: 337–65.
74. BPP 1882, XV, C3375–I, p. 42.
75. BPP 1882, XV, C3375–I, pp. 42–3; Tallant, 1880: 114–21.
76. BPP 1882, XV, C3375–I, p. 43.
77. See e.g. the fifth Marquess of Ailesbury at Savernake, Wilts., whose finances were much straitened in the 1890s, and who rehabilitated a decayed estate by, *inter alia*, making the game and deer in the forest self-supporting by expanding the sales of birds and venison, and by the vigorous letting of the shooting rights.—F. M. L. Thompson, 1963: 314.
78. Curtis, 1903: 16–49.
79. Whetham, 1978: 123, 169–71; Beevor, 1927: 46–9; Ch. 9 below, p. 229.

Notes to Chapter 7

1. The article by David Taylor, 1974: 153–9, noticeably employs the conventional term 'depression' while presenting contrary evidence of prosperity among dairy farmers. On the 'rise of modern dairying', see Wrightson, 1890: 279.
2. Fussell, 1966; D. Taylor, 1974, 1976, and 1987.
3. Farmer, 1991: 401–3, 464. For a fine study of women's commanding role in the dairy, see Valenze, 1991: 142–69, though the author does not see the alternating phases of mainstream and alternative agriculture occurring within the period of her article, *c.*1740–1840.
4. Denney, 1960: 37–9.
5. *AHEW*, v. II. 328 (the earlier statute of 1550–1 was a short matter of fourteen lines only); *AHEW*, v. I. 361–3, 486–9.
6. *AHEW*, v. I. 131, 152–4; Edwards, 1978: 175–90.
7. Bear, 1888: ch. 5; Long, 1887: 124.
8. D. Taylor, 1974: 156.
9. Bear, 1888: 97–104; D. Taylor, 1987: 48.
10. Fletcher, 1961: 21.
11. Long, 1887: 124, 149. James Long had considerable knowledge of European farming. He was professor of dairy farming at the Royal Agricultural College at Cirencester, occupied two farms of his own in Hants and Herts., and wrote many

books on various aspects of alternative agriculture and smallholder farming.—
BPP 1894, XVI, pt. II, C7400–II, pp. 395–403; Long, 1885.

12. Jenkins, 1882: 521–34; id. 1883: 155–84.

13. BPP 1894, XVI, pt. I, C7400–I, p. 145; 1896, XVII, C8021, p. 599; D. Taylor, 1987: 50–1.

14. D. Taylor, 1987: 51–2; BPP 1894, XVI, pt. I, C7400–I, pp. 31, 145, 109; 1882, XV, C3375–V, pp. 54–5; 1894, XVI, pt. II, C7400–II, p. 135. I have argued elsewhere that women's initiatives tend to promote diversity, while men's promote uniformity. Dairying is one illustration of these contrasting viewpoints, though it is missed by Valenze, 1991, see n. 3 above.

15. BPP 1894, XVI, pt. II, C7400–II, p. 252.

16. D. Taylor, 1987: 50, citing *JRASE*, 2nd ser. 2 (1865), 344. The financial advantages of milk sales persisted despite technical progress in butter- and cheese-making with the introduction of the centrifugal separator and other aids.—Whetham, 1964: 376–7.

17. D. Taylor, 1987: 56. Foreign cheese imports doubled between the late 1860s and 1914.—Ibid. 49.

18. Ibid. 56–7, 60.

19. Fletcher, 1961: 27; D. Taylor, 1987: 49, 56.

20. D. Taylor, 1974: 153.

21. Bear, 1888: 98; Whetham, 1964: 377. For success in Shropshire, culminating in a factory in 1932 using milk for tinned cream and condensed milk, and for Cadbury's decision in 1911 to buy milk for chocolate-making, see Perren, 1989: 242.

22. Bear, 1888: 98; D. Taylor, 1987: 62.

23. D. Taylor, 1976: 586; id. 1987: 64; id. 1974: 153; Astor and Rowntree, 1938: 251.

24. Milk for making cheese in England fell from 70% of the total in 1860 to less than 25% by the 1920s.—D. Taylor, 1976: 589.

25. The association of fruit with gardens and not farms is discussed in Sharp, 1982: 8, 25. In some counties, as a result, the *General Views of Agriculture* (e.g. for Surrey) at the end of the 18th c. say very little about fruit- and vegetable-growing.

26. BPP 1882, XV, pt. II, C3375–II, p. 28.

27. Anon. 1888: 407–38; Whitehead, 1882: 71–104. Whitehead's article was reissued by the Royal Agricultural Society as a pamphlet, price 1s.

28. Whitehead, 1884: 28; id. 1890a: 197–9; Anon. 1890a: 454–6. Compensation for improvements was a serious issue (Whitehead, 1882: 103–4). Evesham gardeners had it by ancient custom, while others had none. Tenant right, as it was called, was adopted nationally by the Act of 1895, but it was not backdated, and only affected leases made after Jan. 1896.—Haggard, 1902: i. 357. In the Vale of Evesham the custom played into the hands of the best growers because they could bid most for tenant right, which sometimes exceeded the freehold value of the land.—Sidwell, 1969: 48. On Evesham tenant right and its origins, see also J. M. Martin, 1985: 46.

29. BPP 1882, XIV, p. 376.

30. BPP 1882, XV, C3375–I, p. 42; Hargreaves, 1987: 82–4, 108. Albert Pell, member of the Council of the Royal Agricultural Society, and a farmer in the Isle of Ely and in Northants, noting the increasing use of artificial fertilizers in farming generally, concluded that land 'is just as much a manufactured article as the cloth in the coat I am wearing.'—BPP 1894, XVI, pt. II, C7400–II, p. 130.

31. Wright, 1886: *passim*; id. 1893; 119; Anon. 1888: 417–18.

32. BPP 1881, XVII, p. 829; 1882, XV, C3375–V, p. 34.
33. Morgan, 1888: 886; Whitehead, 1882: 75; id. 1889: 172–3, 179; id. 1883: 371; BPP 1881, XVII, pp. 829, 831, also 907.
34. Bear, 1899: 30–4; Whitehead, 1883: 368–87 esp. 371; id. 1889: 156–80.
35. Thick, in *AHEW*, v. II. 512; Sidwell, 1969: 45, 47; BPP 1895, XVII, C7871, p. 6; Pratt, 1906: 132.
36. Haggard, 1902: i. 337–9, 460; Sharp, 1982: 136.
37. BPP 1881, XVII, pp. 829–30; 1881, XVI, p. 403: 1882, XV, C3375–I, p. 42; Sharp, 1982: 112, 116; Bear, 1899: 31.
38. BPP 1895, XVII, C7842, p. 7.
39. Bunyard, 1899: Preface.
40. Haggard, 1902: i. 356, 288; G. M. Robinson, 1976: pp. 11–13; BPP 1906, LV, p. 218. The comment on celery-growing came from a land agent of Wainfleet, speaking generally of Lincolnshire smallholdings.
41. Whitehead, 1889: 116; Bear, 1897: 213.
42. Whitehead, 1889: 163; Haggard, 1902: i. 344, 347, 355.
43. For a study of Harmondsworth, see Sherwood, 1973.
44. Bear, 1897: 215–16; BPP 1896, XVII, C8021, p. 64; 1895, XVII, C7842, p. 42.
45. Haggard, 1902: ii. 55–7, 186–7; BPP 1906, LV, Cd 3278, p. 21. In the Friskney district near Boston celery and potatoes had also become a routine by 1906.—Ibid.
46. Bear, 1897: 215.
47. Platt, 1602: *passim*; Bradley, 1736 edn.: *passim*.
48. Chapman, 1888: 171–4. The edition by H. G. Bull of *Pomona* in 2 vols., 1876–85, was richly illustrated by two women artists. A coloured plate, no. XIX, was recently reproduced as a postcard by the Library of the Royal Botanic Gardens at Kew.
49. Haggard, 1902: i. 290; BPP 1896, XVII, C8021, pp. 2–4, 99–103; Chapman, 1888: 175; BPP 1895, XVII, C7871, p. 6.
50. Haggard, 1902: i. 351, 347.
51. D. Harvey, 1964: 97; Whitehead, 1889: 173–4; BPP 1896, XVII, C8021, p. 408.
52. D. Harvey, 1964: 98; Whitehead, 1889: 165. On the discovery of the Evesham plum, see Sidwell, 1969: 47, 49, and J. M. Martin, 1985: 50.
53. Pidgeon, 1888: 486–92.
54. Voelcker, 1896: 500–20.
55. Ibid. 502.
56. Haggard, 1902: i. 352–3; Whitehead, 1889: 174; Voelcker, 1896: 518.
57. See Ch. 3 above.
58. Bunyard, 1899: 77.
59. BPP 1882, XV, C3375–I, p. 41; Whitehead, 1882: 72, 92; Bear, 1899:35; Whitehead, 1889: 165–6 (Barcelona nuts are also mentioned as having been planted in the same area of Kent at this time); Whitehead, 1904: 49–50.
60. Whitehead, 1904: 49, 26; Dunster, 1885: 96.
61. Bear, 1898: 289, 513, 520.
62. Thick, 1990: *passim*; J. Harvey, 1972*b* *passim*.
63. Bear, 1898: 289; Assbee, 1897: 394.
64. Bear, 1898: 520–1.
65. Ibid. 549.

66. Ibid. 520, 522, 534. For the Edmonton–Enfield area, see Burnby and Robinson, 1983: *passim*, and Pam, 1992: 146–52.

67. Bear, 1898: 292, 311, 535–40; Haggard, 1902: ii. 213.

68. Bear, 1898: 290, 525, 518, 520, 526, 524, 291. At Spalding narcissi took over when snowdrops succumbed to disease, and the Dutch stiffened competition by sending larger crocus bulbs than the smaller English kind.

69. Bear, 1898: 288–9.

70. Thick, in *AHEW*, v. ii. 513–14.

71. Bunyard, 1897: 349, 350.

72. Assbee, 1897: 404, 398; Bear, 1899: 270–6. Bear claimed that no other industry had shown such expansion between 1879 and 1899 as fruit under glass.—1899: 267.

73. Assbee, 1897: 398, 405; Burnby and Robinson, 1983: 13. For more on the glasshouses for fruit, including some experimental movable glasshouses, see Bear, 1899: 267–306. For the Lea valley, see Pam, 1992: 151; for Edmonton High Street, Palmer, 1936. I wish to thank Mr David Pam for help in identifying Palmer.

74. Assbee, 1897: 400; Sutton, 1897: 392.

75. Sutton, 1897: 388–9, 380, 378.

76. Ibid. 374, 388, 381, 385, 397, 386, 362.

77. Bear, 1898: 304, 549, 526.

78. BPP 1881, XVII, pp. 824, 829, 830; BPP 1897, XV, pp. 83–5.

79. Wright, 1920: appendix.

80. BPP 1882, XV, C3375-I, pp. 9–10, 42; BPP 1881, XVII, pp. 905, 907, 919–20; Haggard, 1902: i. 350.

81. Whitehead, 1889: 176; id. 1892: 589; Pratt, 1906: 133, 146, 189–94; Sharp, 1982: 218 ff. The Frenchman's care in sending his fruits to markets 'beautifully arranged' in small packages and attractive baskets drew comment in 1905 in contrast with the roughly packed containers of 15, 28, or 48 lb. used by the English.—BPP 1881, XVII, p. 905. The English had evidently lost an art for which the London gardeners were admired in the early 18th c.

82. BPP 1895, XVII, C7915, pp. 28, 53. Also C. L. Campbell, 1895: 181; Bear, 1897: 222; Whitehead, 1889: 175. For more on co-operation, see Ch. 8 below.

83. McKay, 1908 (Daily Mail edn. 1909): *passim*; Weathers, 1913: 203–26, esp. 204–5. (I am much indebted to Malcolm Thick for introducing me to these two works); Fraser, 1910: 235–9; Pratt, 1906: 146; Jenkins, 1880: 86, 90. Another vivid account of the practical details involved in French gardening is given in Nussey and Cockerell, 1909.

84. Whitehead, 1889: 170–2; Bear, 1898: 517, 520; Bear, 1899: 282–3; Brown, 1985: 24, 39.

85. Whitehead, 1889: 170–2; Roach, 1985: 44–6.

86. Fraser, 1910: 235; McKay, 1909: preface, p. iv.

87. One commercial innovation which counts as an exception is watercress. It is alleged to have entered the list of salad plants in England in 1808 and found a niche in suitable places having a supply of flowing water.—Glenny, 1897: 611–22. But a woman street crier is depicted selling watercress 'for scorbutic ills' much earlier than this in London, in 1796. Watercress was evidently sold for medicinal use before the German idea was born of eating it as a salad plant. This was a not uncommon transformation in plant use. (I wish to thank Sean Shesgreen for the early evidence of watercress, in London, found in *Newbery's Cries of London as they*

are daily exhibited in the streets, 1796. Copy in the Houghton Library, Harvard University.) On chicory, see BPP 1904, XVI, pp. 377–81; on tomatoes in Evesham, see Haggard, 1902: i. 350; on turnip tops, see BPP 1882, XV, C3375–I, p. 42.

88. Bunyard, 1899: 95–100; Goodale, 1892: 600–13.

89. Hatton, 1921: 49; Rew, 1927: 24–32; H. V. Taylor, 1929: 127–40.

90. Rew, 1927: 16–32; Darke, 1937: 90–105; Gleed, 1931: 201–13; Anderson, 1928: 50–77; Carslaw and Graves, 1937: 35–52; H. G. Robinson, 1931: 151–62; H. V. Taylor, 1929: 127–40. For a fuller survey of the solutions of different regions, see Whetham, 1978: ch. 11.

91. Jenkins, 1880: 81–95; Vilmorin, 1890: 874–6.

92. The antiseptic and other medicinal uses of aromatic plants were discussed in Burbidge, 1898–9: *passim*. It is significant that the books which he cites on aromatic plants date from the mid- to end of the 17th c. and begin again in 1865–93. The Board of Agriculture and Fisheries listed the most desired medicinal plants in 1914, revised in 1916, in a leaflet, no. 288, entitled *The Cultivation and Collection of Medicinal Plants in England*. Mrs M. Grieve was both practical and learned, publishing a number of slim pamphlets on culinary, fragrant, and other herbs. Mrs Hilda Leyel edited Mrs Grieve's papers as *A Modern Herbal*, 1931 (of which another edition appeared, 1985). See also Dorothy Gertrude Hewer, 1944, who ran the Herb Farm and school at Seal, Kent, from about 1925 and was described in 1941 as 'one of our foremost authorities on the subject', and her successor, Margaret Brownlow, 1957.

93. Thirsk, 1991: 48; Defoe, 1928 edn.: i. 59–60.

94. Whitehead, 1899: 474; Cobbett, cited by Jesse Collings in BPP 1889, XII, p. 6 (much earlier Defoe had noted Dorking in Surrey as the market for the fattest geese.— Defoe, 1928 edn.: i. 153); E. Brown, 1899: 320, 350; Cathcart, 1899: 165–9. Exactly the same buoyant growth of poultry-keeping took place after 1880 in Russia, when mainstream agriculture was failing. It is described by Thompstone, 1992: 52–63.

95. Pope, 1882: 104–14; BPP 1896, XVII, C8021, p. 440.

96. BPP 1882, XIV, p. 418.

97. BPP 1882, XV, C3375–IV, p. 18. This management was later urged by Haggard, 1902: i. 116.

98. BPP 1882, XIV, p. 435; 1882, XV, C3375–II, pp. 43–4. Also described by Druce, 1882: 503–7; Short, 1982: 17.

99. Although future local research may revise this verdict.

100. Brian Short's description of the Heathfield district is especially enlightening on this aspect.—Short, 1982: 17–19.

101. Ibid. 19–23; Mascall, 1581; Lewis Wright in *Encyclopaedia Britannica*, 11th edn., 1911, xxii. 218.

102. BPP 1895, XVI, C7623, *passim*; Short, 1982: 23; BPP 1896, XVII, C8021, p. 436; Whitehead, 1899: pp. 474–5. Lean birds were bought from Ireland at three months and were fattened in 3–4 weeks, being crammed three times a day.—BPP 1895, XVI, C7623, p. 11. The adoption of cramming at Birdsall, E. Yorks., on Lord Middleton's home farm was described in 1899. It was overseen by someone who claimed considerable experience, partly gathered in the service of a poultry firm in Leadenhall Market.—Cathcart, 1899: 161–3.

103. BPP 1895, XVI, C7623, p. 4 and *passim*.; Short, 1982: 24, 21. The First World War put

an end to cramming, and when changes afterwards shifted the emphasis to egg production, the geographical area in Sussex moved eastwards.—Short, 1982: 25-8.

104. BPP 1896, XVII, C8021, p. 15. On Aylesbury ducks, see Fream, 1894: 290-333, and *Encyclopaedia Britannica*, 1911, xxii. 219. Living memories are contained in Sanders, 1990: 147. 'Years ago Eaton Bray was awash with ducks . . . Ducks were even driven loose to Standbridgeford station, and despatched live, by rail.' In another household, plucking started daily at 5 a.m., wicker baskets were loaded on carts for the station by 8 a.m., and the ducks were in Leadenhall market by midday. I wish to thank Mrs Joan Curran for this reference.

105. Defoe, 1928 edn.: ii. 14-16; BPP 1896, XVII, C8021, pp. 15-16.

106. BPP 1896, XVII, C8021, p. 64.

107. Haggard, 1902: ii. 390.

108. BPP 1896, XVII, C8021, pp. 437, 440.

109. Pratt, 1906: 151-64; BPP 1896, XVII, C8021, pp. 436, 441; Cathcart, 1899: 157; *Encyclopaedia Britannica*, 1911, xxii. 220; Rew, 1903: 120-1.

110. BPP 1896, XVII, C8021, p. 437; *Encyclopaedia Britannica*, 1911, xxii. 219; E. Brown, 1899: 320, 338, 340, 350-1.

111. BPP 1895, XVII, C7871, pp. 8-9, 82-3. For another influential woman in the poultry business, see Mrs Kezia Collins of Cade Street, Heathfield, who may have launched Heathfield into its leading place as a poultry centre, by devising the plan in 1788 of sending poultry by carrier to London.—Short, 1982: 19.

112. BPP 1896, XVII, C8021, p. 439. Many more details of French management were given in Jenkins, 1883*b*: 184-206, in which he reprinted an article by C. L. Sutherland on west central France.

113. *Encyclopaedia Britannica*, 1911, xxii. 215, 219, 217.

114. Rew, 1927: 300; House, 1923: 93-109; Whetham, 1978: 179-80; Holderness, 1929: 55-69; Astor and Rowntree, 1938: 230.

115. Elkingon, 1929: 140-62; Denham, 1933: 83-100.

116. Astor and Rowntree, 1938: 246-7.

117. Whetham, 1978: 70-1, 80-2.

118. Long, 1886: Preface, 8, 299.

119. Long, 1918: Preface, 1-4, 7-8, 108 ff., and photos of Sir Gilbert Greenall's piggery. See also Long, 1886: 48 ff., 347 for Lord Morton's piggery at Tortworth Court.

120. Whetham, 1978: 82-96, 102-8, 113, 120-2.

121. Henderson, 1944: *passim* but esp. 21, 40. I wish to thank Paul Brassley for introducing me to this most pertinent lesson in alternative agriculture on small farms. For general remarks on the same period, see also Perren, 1995: 45-50.

122. Pratt, 1906, *passim*, but esp. ch. 1 and p. 98. For a similar survey for the *Morning Post* in 1900, with precise examples, see Graham, 1900, *passim*, and esp. 116.

Notes to Chapter 8

1. White, 1993: 15-18, 23-7, 38; Gilchrist and Oliva, 1993: 73-4; see also 60-5. It may be worth noting that the Cathars on the Continent of Europe were vegetarians.

2. C. Hill, 1990: p. 164. I owe the information concerning John Beale to Dr Mayling Stubbs, who examined John Beale's letters to John Evelyn in Christ Church, Oxford. On the vegetarians, see Evelyn, 1699: 124, 129, 137, 142, 154; Williams, 1883: vi, 106, 107, 111, 318; J. C. Dyer, 1982: viii, ix. Ray is cited, ibid. 107, saying that

'man was never meant to be a carnivorous animal, and a table of plant food was much more sweet and healthful than one of reeking flesh of butchered and slaughtered animals.'

3. Coles, 1656: 50.

4. Gordon, 1871: *passim*; Tryon, 1699: *passim*. Tryon's life is vividly described by himself in *Some Memoirs*, 1705.

5. Anon. 1767: 1–2, 73. One seemingly lone voice was that of Thomas Ash of Myddle, Salop., who abstained 'from blood and things strangled', as well as 'being too nice in observing the Canons . . . of the first Counsel of the Apostles at Jerusalem'.— Hey, 1981: 227.

6. J. C. Dyer, 1982, *passim*. Whether this period also saw an invigorated interest in herbal medicines, in preference to chemical drugs, is worth further enquiry. For some suggestive examples of books on herbal remedies, see O. P. Brown, 1871 and 1890; Brook, 1887; and Fernie, 1897.

7. Kingsford, 1881: 97 ff. and *passim*.

8. J. C. Dyer, 1982, *sub nomine*; Marsh, 1982: 196. Jane Grigson also stressed the many vegetarian cookery books appearing in the 1880s and 1890s, when reviewing the Bibliography by Elizabeth Driver, 1989, in the *Times Literary Supplement*, 22–8 Dec. 1989.

9. 'What is Vegetarianism? by a Vice President of the Vegetarian Society', *Cassell's Family Magazine*, July 1889, 347–9. This anonymous article was almost certainly written by Anna Kingsford, since the description of the author and the arguments used fit her exactly.

10. See above, Ch. 2, p. 36.

11. Torode, 1966: 117; Hutchins, 1967: 395–8.

12. Georgiana Hill, 1860, 1862 (it is unfortunate that many of her books in the British Library were destroyed during the last war); David, 1964: 60.

13. Stern, 1966: *passim*; Healey, 1978: 166–8; Stubbs, 1885: appendix I.

14. Glenny, 1897: 205–28. See also above, p. 295, n. 87.

15. Haggard, 1902: ii. 38–9.

16. See e.g. Mary Heron's letter in the *Independent*, 10 Nov. 1989; John Young, 'Small farm holders spread net', *The Times*, 21 Jan. 1985.

17. Compare e.g. the observations of a New Forest landowner, George Edward Briscoe Eyre, that a really active smallholder would have three livings—from land, common rights, and industry (i.e. dealing, higgling (i.e. trading in poultry, etc.), or hauling). More evidence from Lincolnshire and counties to the north of higgling with small-scale farming is found in BPP 1881, XV, p. 231. For keen observation over a wider scene, see Jebb, 1907*c*: 12, 30, 34, 37, 43.

18. Thirsk, 1992*a*: 16–17, 24, and the authorities there cited. See also above, Ch. 1.

19. Thirsk, 1992*b*: 188.

20. Gentles, 1971: 36, 38–9; Sharp, 1992: 268; Pam, 1977: 13.

21. Hartlib, 1651: 8, 11.

22. Thirsk, 1992*b*: 182–4 and the sources there cited.

23. Following the lead given by A. H. Johnson in *The Disappearance of the Small Landowner*, 1909, repr. 1963. See 1963 edn., Introduction, pp. xii and 135–6. For more uncertainty on the chronology and the general verdict, see Ginter, 1991: *passim*.

24. Thirsk, 1978: 142.
25. Worlidge, 1677: 176.
26. Lea, 1872, *passim*; Burrows, 1882: 11–12. A minority report by three members of the Royal Commission on Agricultural Depression in 1896 stressed the unfortunate consequences of earlier amalgamations into large farms between 1850 and 1880, for now owners had not the capital to break them up again.—BPP 1896, XVI, C7981, p. 22. For a careful account of the scholars' verdicts on the movement from small to large farms at this time, not forgetting the snares in the official statistics, see Grigg, 1987: 179–89.
27. Pratt, 1906: 2–3.
28. BPP 1881, XV, p. 237; 1881, XVI, pp. 388–9; BPP 1882, XIV, pp. 165–6.
29. BPP 1882, XIV, pp. 316–7; BPP 1889, XII, p. 32.
30. Betham-Edwards, 1892, Introduction, *passim*, esp. pp. xix, xxi. See also below, Conclusion, n. 4.
31. BPP 1881, XVI, p. 261; 1882, XIV, pp. 159–66, 214; 1889, XII, pp. 30–1.
32. BPP 1882, XIV, pp. 316–17; 1882, XV, p. 57; 1894, XVI, pt. II, C7400–II, pp. 70–1; BPP 1889, XII, pp. 19–43. To the French example of small farms should be added the equally successful Danish ones, producing cheese, butter, and bacon. Their system was publicized by Rider Haggard (1913), though he despaired because English farmers would not learn lessons from it. But its principles were upheld in practice by George Henderson in Oxfordshire in the 1920s and 1930s, whether he read Rider Haggard or not, though he could not benefit, as did the Danes, from any co-operatives (see above, Ch. 7, p. 197).
33. Grindon, 1879: *passim*.
34. Gladstone, 1892: *passim*. See also BPP 1894, XVI, pt. III, p. 42; 1895, XVII, C7871, p. 46.
35. BPP 1881, XVII, pp. 92–3, 118; 1882, XV, C3375–III, pp. 74–5, C3375–V, pp. 42–3.
36. BPP 1881, XV, p. 158.
37. Channing, 1897: pp. xi, xiv, chs. 2, 7, 10, and 15; BPP 1889, XII, pp. 31–2; Haggard, 1902: i. 460. On the contribution of smallholders to local economies, see D. J. Hall, 1992.
38. For the steps leading finally to an Act, see Bone, 1976: 653–61.
39. Fay, 1910: 503; BPP 1906, LV, Cd 3278, p. 79; 1907, LXVII, p. 8.
40. Haggard, 1902: i. 340–3; Fay, 1910: 502–5. For more detail on the legislation, see Bone, 1976: 653–61; VCH, *Salop.*, iv. 263. The Salop holdings were reported in 1957 to favour intensive dairying.
41. Whetham, 1978: 137–9, 301–2; E. Thomas, 1927: *passim*; Addison, 1939: 241–60; Orwin, 1930: 109–14; Land Settlement Association, 1936, Jan. issue; McReady, 1974: *passim*; James Cusick, 'Young see crofting as "agriculture of the future"', *Independent*, 17 July 1992, 2. A writer who favoured co-operative or cottage farms in 1884, using an argument that strikes a chord today, was the Revd. Henry Solly. He welcomed the notion of a mixture of work on the land and in industry, which would constitute a more healthy life and would escape the social problems of the towns, which, in his day, meant, above all, poor housing.—Solly, 1884: 3, 9. For the present surge of interest among historians in small farms, see Winstanley, 1996, and the bibliography therein.
42. Winfrey, 1906: 222–4, 227; Orwin and Whetham, 1964: 331–5. Rider Haggard noted

the practical examples set by parsons in their active support for smallholdings.—
Haggard, 1902: ii. 325.

43. Dunster, 1884: 603–9, 598, and *passim*. An unusual venture was that of a small cultivator who grew violets, and sent them to Paris as sugared violets, a valuable
article, it was said.—BPP 1889, XII, p. 108. Most medicinal plants by 1914 came to
Britain from central Europe; when war began, they were recommended for
cultivation at home, because foreign supplies dried up.—Board of Agriculture
Leaflet 288.

44. BPP 1882, XIV, pp. 156–65. Baghot claimed 20,000 correspondents in the course of
his seventeen years of publishing.

45. BPP 1882, XIV, pp. 200–18, 225–6. Arthur Arnold was a vigorous witness before the
Select Committee on Allotments and Small Holdings.—BPP 1889, XII, 313,
pp. 19–34. For another robust writer, see Impey, 1886: *passim*.

46. Hadfield, 1970: 223 and *passim*; BPP 1882, XV, C3375–III, pp. 73–4. A separate literature, not discussed here, advocated the setting up of allotments. See Barnett, 1967:
162–83.

47. BPP 1881, XVII, p. 128; 1896, XVI, pt. I, p. 104; 1889, XII, pt. I, pp. 117, 197–201, 369;
1896, XVII, C8021, p. 76; 1894, XVI, pt. I, C7374, p. 6; Fay, 1910: 502–14.

48. BPP 1881, XV, p. 83; 1882, XIV, pp. 157–8; 1882, XV, pp. 5–7; G. M. Robinson,
1976: 18. For higgling as a second source of income for smallholders, see BPP 1881,
XV, p. 231.

49. BPP 1894, XVI, pt. I, C7400–I, pp. 95, 139, 173; Haggard, 1902: i. 9, 274–9.

50. BPP 1906, LV, Cd 3278, pp. 79, 15–16, 99; Winfrey, 1906: 224. (This author, Richard
Winfrey, was chairman of the Holland County Council Small Holdings Committee, and of the Lincolnshire and Norfolk Small Holdings Association, later becoming an MP. He was also a member of Peterborough Town Council.—BPP 1906, LV,
p. 79); Haresign, 1983: 31. Lord Carrington, who became President of the Board of
Agriculture in 1905, increased smallholdings on his land from 61 in 1868 to 190 in
1906, and from 100 allotments in the same period to 2,205. He even built dairies
onto all existing cottages.—BPP 1906, LV, p. 258, 80. His forebear had assisted in
creating allotments a century earlier.—Barnett, 1967: 178. For more on the Norfolk
case and in general, see Haggard, 1902: ii. 39, 506–8. For Lincolnshire, see Haresign,
1983: *passim*, though this author's general verdict on the failure of smallholdings is
greatly overstated. It partly results from an unrealistic expectation that smallholdings would 'solve' the problem of depopulation, and partly from a foreshortened
view of the history of smallholdings in the fens of Lincolnshire.

51. Jebb, 1907: 171–9; BPP 1906, LV, Cd 3278, pp. 15 ff. Louisa Jebb was invited by the
Cooperative Small Holdings Society to collect evidence on the circumstances in
which smallholdings succeeded, in order to help in the framing of legislation. She
visited them, classified them, and gave a balanced appraisal in a book, 1907*b*. See
also ead. 1907*c* and 1909. The unusual procedure of a small landowner in West
Norfolk, who recognized the value of common rights, deserves notice. He had cut
up a farm into four or five smallholdings of about 20 acres each, and actually created a common of 20–25 acres, to give them a cow run. It struck the reporter as
'rather a new departure'.—BPP 1896, XVII, C8021, p. 433; BPP 1894, XVI, pt. I,
C7400–I, p. 123. For a broad survey of experience with smallholdings in six counties, including large numbers on the estates of Lord Tollemache in Cheshire and

Lord Savile in Yorkshire, see Bear, 1893: *passim*, as well as Jebb, 1907*b*, noted above.

52. Kropotkin, 1974: ch. 2, esp. 53–4, 58, 60.

53. The history of Clousden Hill is well researched and sympathetically appraised in Todd, 1986: *passim*.

54. The markedly honest and balanced account of the Whiteway colony, written by a member of 35 years' standing, deserves to be singled out.—N. Shaw, 1935. For this and other colonies, see Todd, 1986: 11–12; Marsh, 1982: 99 ff.; Hardy, 1979: *passim*.

55. BPP 1894, XVI, pt. I, C7400–I, pp. 185–6; 1881, XVII, pp. 128–9. For a later verdict along the same lines, see E. Thomas, 1927: 5.

56. BPP 1894, XVI, pt. II, C7400–II, p. 84; 1896, XVII, C8021, p. 79; 1889, XII, p. 196; 1906, LV, Cd 3278, pp. 20–1. A report was called for into the decline in agricultural population, 1881–1906. See BPP 1906, XCVI, Cd. 3273, pp. 583 ff.

57. S. Taylor, 1884. This was dedicated to the Rt. Hon. Henry Fawcett, MP, Professor of Political Economy at Cambridge, described as one of the earliest and staunchest supporters of profit-sharing. It is significant, but not surprising, that profit-sharing is evoking fresh interest in the 1990s. The literature of the 1880s and 1890s deserves to be reread. See e.g. *The Encyclopaedia Britannica*, 11th edn., xxii, under Profit-Sharing. On co-operation, see BPP 1906, LV, Cd 3278, pp. 80, 101; Pratt, 1906: 170–1, 178–83, 189; Haggard, 1902: ii. 142–3; Horace Plunkett Foundation, 1930: *passim*.

58. Fay, 1910: 505–13; Impey, 1909: 16. Louisa Jebb was emphatic in 1909 that smallholders must co-operate or go under. Earl Carrington, President of the Board of Agriculture in 1909, shared her fervent belief in co-operation.—Jebb, 1909: 22, 3–4. For comparison, see the growth of a French syndicate of peasant farmers, buying fertilizers, pesticides, seeds, tools, and machines.—A. R. H. Baker, 1986: 45–59.

59. Cooper, 1989: 46, 202, citing Hansard, 5th ser. 1931, lxxx. 88.

60. BPP 1889, XII, p. 38. In overlooking alternative agriculture, commentators also overlooked women's work. See the example of the farm on which the farmer's wife 'looked after the minor products of the farm'. Yet the farm in question started small, and became a farm of 1,000 acres, based on trees, a dairy, poultry, and garden produce; in other words, all but trees were originally the women's 'minor products'!—Wright, 1889: 5–6. See also Cathcart, 1899: 156–7: whenever he asked people if poultry paid, he received no definite answer, but was always told that the women liked them and regarded the takings as their perk. That, seemingly, closed the conversation.

61. E. A. Pratt, 1906: *passim*; Whitehead, 1899: 485.

62. E. A. Pratt, 1906: *passim*. On Lady Carlisle, see Grey, 1891: 780.

63. For two of many criticisms of the statistics, see BPP 1882, XV, p. 42, and Bear, 1899: 30–1.

64. D. Taylor, 1987: 62; Whetham, 1970: 9–10; Astor and Rowntree, 1938: 46, 251–2, 301, 428–9.

Notes to Chapter 9

1. 'Price deal hopes', *Observer*, 21 July 1985; 'Concern over grain mountain', *The Times*, 14 June 1985; 'Grain glut blights farms', *Observer*, 12 Jan. 1986.

2. Tim Radford, 'To the green and pleasant?', *Guardian*, 22 Dec. 1989, Environment, 2.

3. Derek Barber and others, 'Long-term strategy' (letter), *The Times*, 10 Jan. 1985, 11.

4. 'Grain glut starts', *The Times*, 18 Feb. 1985; 'Making sunflowers grow', *The Times*, 25 Aug. 1987.

5. John Young *et al.*, 'Can wheat fields be turned into woods?', *The Times*, 28 Nov. 1986, 14; 'Bad news for British farmers' (letter), *Independent*, 24 Aug. 1990.

6. Hargreaves, 1987: 59-61 and *passim*. On the idealists and eccentrics who anticipate the future, see also Slee, 1989: 30.

7. A. Howard, 1943; id. 1945; Balfour, 1943; Francis Blake, 'Cultivating the organic garden' [obituary of Lady Eve Balfour], *Guardian*, 23 Jan. 1990; Whetham, 1978: 322-5; Seddon, 1989: 217-23; Holland, 1984: 30, 70, 89, 104, 130-41. For a later venture into organic farming in 1970, see Wookey, 1987: *passim*.

8. The Henry Doubleday Research Association issues literature from its centre at the Ryton Organic Gardens, Ryton-on-Dunsmore, Coventry. For the seed bank, see Michael Hornsby, 'Vegetable library sows the seeds of rebellion', *The Times*, 4 July 1992.

9. Rosemary Collins, 'Market ready for more organic food', *Guardian*, 29 May 1986; 'Gummer backs switch', *The Times*, 4 Oct. 1994, 10; 'Benefits of organic farming dismissed', *Independent*, 25 Aug. 1992.

10. 'Government cash urged', *Independent*, 3 July 1990; *Farmers' Weekly*, 119/2 (8 July 1993), 16. Government aid was still deemed a meagre sum in 1994.—'Green grow the crops', *The Times*, Home, 31 May 1994, 5.

11. BPP 1882, XV, p. 42 (in fact, strawberries were still growing in former woodland *c.*1954 at North Frith Farm, Hadlow); Emily Green, 'Call a spud a spud', *Independent*, Food and Drink, 22 May 1993, 32; Joy Larkcom, 'Random harvest', *Observer*, 20 May 1979, 40; Emily Green, 'They call her the lettuce lady', *Independent*, Food and Drink, 9 May 1992, 35. For madder at Appledore in the 1620s, see above, pp. 110-11.

12. In 1986 it was said that organic growers were either large-scale owner-occupiers or smallholders.—Rosemary Collins, 'Market ready', *Guardian*, 29 May 1986. For farmhouse cheesemakers, see Michael Durham, 'Britain churns out the cream of cheeses', *Observer*, 10 Apr. 1994, 5; Alan Road, 'Organic growth', *The Times*, 18 Apr. 1995, 35.

13. Caroline Brannigan, 'The woodcraft folk', *Argus Country Extra*, June 1995, 9; George Peterken of the Nature Conservancy Council, *The Times*, 9 Jan. 1981, 11. In 1993 UK sales of charcoal amounted to 60,000 tonnes p.a., of which 3% came from English sources.—'Charcoal saving the rainforest', *Courier*, 8 Jan. 1993. For a venture in Hangman's Wood, South Ockendon, Essex, see Nicholas Schoon, 'Charcoal burners capitalise on nature', *Independent*, 4 Apr. 1992; Oliver Tickell and Nick Nuttall, 'Burning desire to buy British', *The Times*, Weekend, 3 June 1995, 11; Fred Pearce, 'Seeing the wood for the trees', *New Scientist*, 14 Jan. 1995, 12-13. In summer 1993, it was hoped that the EU would recognize coppice for the non-rotational set-aside scheme.—*Farmers' Weekly*, 9 July 1993, 26; Sarah Sturt, 'Bid to create woodlands', *Courier*, 21 Feb. 1992, 5; 'New life for an ancient source', *Elements: Environment Newspaper of Kent County Council*, summer 1992, 4; 'Traditional skills being kept alive', *Courier*, 27 Aug. 1993, 2; Bea Cowan, 'New stories from old chestnuts', *The Times*, 18 Dec. 1993; Nick Nuttall, 'Minister backs renewable energy', *The Times*, 21 Dec. 1994; Oliver Tickell, 'Burning issue of coppicing', *The Times*, Weekend, May 13, 1995, 17.

14. *Timber, Times Supplement*, 16 Mar. 1995, *passim*.

15. Nicholas Schoon, 'Woodland vision', *Independent*, Home section, 28 Nov. 1992, 5; John Young, 'Fallow fields', *The Times*, Home News, 9 Dec. 1987, 7. The Royal Institution of Chartered Surveyors recommended the increase in the forested area of Britain in 1982; see 'Forestry and Land Use', RICS 1982, reported by John Young, 'Call for increase in forests', *The Times*, 9 Feb. 1982; also John Young, 'Farming surpluses: 1', *The Times*, Home News, 22 Dec. 1986, 5; Roger Milne, 'Putting the land out to grass', *New Scientist*, 17 Dec. 1987, 10; Michael Hornsby, 'Farmers win right to convert unused acres to woodland', *The Times*, Home News, 27 Jan. 1995, 10; Invitation to New Members, issued Mar. 1995 by the Woodland Trust, Grantham, Lincs.; Andy Smith, 'Farmers sow the seeds', *Observer*, 16 Apr. 1995.

16. Michael Hornsby, 'Throwing money at the custodians', *The Times*, 2 July 1991; Nicholas Schoon, 'Extra funds for "green" farmers', *Independent*, 11 Aug. 1993. But for cautionary words on the need for skilled management over a long period to recreate habitats such as marshes, heaths, and chalk grassland, see Roger Milne, 'Putting the land out to grass', *New Scientist*, 17 Dec. 1987, 10–11. Already in 1987 the Queen's speech to Parliament promised to encourage the planting of farm woodland.—*The Times*, 26 June 1987, 4; N. Schoon, 'Unique wilderness', *Independent*, 13 Mar. 1993.

17. Maer Kennedy, 'Dung and destiny', *Guardian*, 23 July 1993; Andrew Morgan, 'A farmer not waving but drowning', *Independent*, 14 Mar. 1992, 42.

18. Oliver Gillie, 'Scratchy Bottom returns', *Independent*, 14 Apr. 1993, 7.

19. Christopher Warman, 'How sheep spoil the shoot', *The Times*, 6 Aug. 1986; Duff Hart-Davies, 'Leave it to the birds', *Independent*, 20 Oct. 1993; Geoffrey Lean, 'Lord Peel's heather moor policy', *Observer*, 10 Aug. 1986; Adrian Holloway, 'Golden Bear finds new cave', *Independent*, 15 May 1993; Steve Boggan, 'Farmers use EC cash', *Independent*, Home News, 5 Dec. 1991, 5. Alan Hamilton, 'Golf course owners bunkered by debt', *The Times*, Home News, 17 July 1995, 6. Approved riding schools have trebled in the last fifteen years.—Geoffrey Lean, 'Ponies are chewing up the countryside', *Observer*, 2 May 1993.

20. 'Rapeseed oil revisited', *Lancet*, 7 Dec. 1974; Schering Agriculture, *Growing Double Low Oilseed Rape Varieties*, 1989, 3–4; *Oilseed Rape*, Leaflet P2278, MAFF Publications, Alnwick, Northd., 1986.

21. John Emsley, 'It fuels buses', *Independent*, 23 Nov. 1992. French research was reported in a letter from Julian Smith in the *Observer*, 27 Jan. 1991. For boats on the Norfolk Broads, see Andy Coghlan, 'Biofuel cruises', *New Scientist*, 9 Oct. 1993, 22. For the competitive price, see Charles Abel, 'British biodiesel is competitive', *Farmers' Weekly*, 11 Dec. 1992, 29. For a survey in general, see John Emsley, 'Energy and fuels', *New Scientist*, Inside Science, 68, 15 Jan. 1994, 1–4; 'Postman Pat goes green', *Observer*, Business, 20 Aug. 1995, 3. But see also Kurt Kleiner, 'Altered crop threatens poor nations', *New Scientist*, 17 June 1995, 10. On Rover trials, Kevin Eason and M. Hornsby, 'Rover gears up for flower power', *The Times*, Home News, 13 Jan. 1994, 9. On plastics, Nick Nuttall, 'Scientists develop cheap plastics', *The Times*, Home News, 31 May 1994, 1. See also Ch. 4 above, pp. 72 ff.

22. 'Sunflower power tests', *The Times*, 9 Feb. 1981; Advt. by Plant Breeding Institute, Cambridge, in *Farmers' Weekly Supplement*, Dec. 1992, 11; John Timson, 'Science Report', *The Times*, 18 June 1987; Sarah Lonsdale, 'Farmland lying fallow',

Observer, 9 Feb. 1992, 8; John Newell, 'Grasses which could yield fuel', *The Times*, 27 Aug. 1986; Kate de Selincourt, 'Europe's home-grown fuel', *New Scientist*, 16 Oct. 1993, 22–4.

23. Van Soest and Mulder, 1993. I wish to thank Dr Louis van Soest for discussing these initiatives in Holland and elsewhere with me.

24. Martin Wainwright, 'Somerset firm could help save whales', *Guardian*, 3 Jan. 1983; 'Crop could replace whale oil', *The Times*, 14 Sept. 1985; Van Soest and Mulder, 1993: 63.

25. Richard Ford, 'Ulster flax fields back in bloom', *The Times*, 9 Apr. 1985; 'Design for linen', *The Times*, Special Report, 13 June 1985, 21; Geoffrey Lean, 'Euro rules set aside old conflicts', *Observer*, 11 July 1993, 24; *Farmers' Weekly*, 25 Oct. 1991, 56.

26. For a far-sighted survey in 1950–1, see *Crops in Peace and War: The Year Book of Agriculture, 1950–51*, US Dept. of Agriculture, Washington, 1951: *passim*. It can be set beside a Dutch publication of 1987: Van Soest *et al.* 1987.

27. 'High hopes for the first legal cannabis crop', *Independent*, 12 July 1993, 3; James Ehrlichman, 'Legality on paper for cannabis', *Guardian*, 19 Feb. 1993; David Sharrock, 'Cannabis on a new high', *Guardian*, Environment, 13 Aug. 1993, 18–19; Audrey Magee, 'Irish have high hopes for cannabis, fuel of the future', *The Times*, Home News, 17 August, 1996, p. 7.

28. Oliver Tickell, 'Hemp and flax lead the fibre revolution', *The Times*, Weekend, 28 Jan. 1995, 19; *CSPD* 1547–80: 517, 519; Nick Nuttall, 'Hemp returns', *The Times*, Home News, 11 Apr. 1995, 5; Denis Staunton, 'Germans roll up for joint venture', *Observer*, World News, 20 Aug. 1995, 15; Oliver Tickell, 'Old fibre gets set for renaissance', *New Scientist*, 19 Aug. 1995, 19. See also above, pp. 28–9, 46–7, 158–9.

29. Baillie, 1894: 234–50; Pratt, 1905: 21–3, 32–4; 1927: 80–5; 'Enterprising wicker man weaves a wicked witch', *Observer*, 16 Feb. 1992; 'Hurdler leaps into hot spot', *The Times*, 27 Feb. 1996, 25; Michael Prestage, 'Wildlife plan threatens survival', *Independent*, Home News, 18 Mar. 1992, 10; TV programme, 'Tomorrow's World', 9 Dec. 1994.

30. William Temple, 1903: 134, 143; Underwood, 1953: 414; Nigel Hawkes, 'Vegetable vaccines', *The Times*, Overseas News, 12 Apr. 1995, 13; 'Nicotine finding', *The Times*, Home News, 30 Sept. 1995, 2.

31. Penny Plain Catalogue, spring/summer 1993. The Research and Development Project for Natural Dyes was created in 1981, under the direction of Dr Harald Böhmer, and sponsored by Marmara University to promote the use of natural dyes in Turkey. The potential of woad-growing, botanically and economically, is being investigated at the Long Ashton Research Station, and was reported in David J. Hill, 1992. It received fresh notice in June–Dec. 1995, following an international conference on natural dyes at Toulouse in June 1995. See Balfour-Paul, 1995: 77–81. See also Nigel Hawkes, 'Set-aside farmers are wooed to grow woad', *The Times*, 17 June 1995, 4; Roger Dobson, 'Woad returns in "green" jeans', *Independent*, 3 Sept. 1995.

32. Jeremy Laurance, 'Great cures or mumbo jumbo?' *The Times*, Focus, 5 July 1995, 20; J. Harvey, 1981: 86 ff.

33. For liquorice grounds extending over more than 100 acres in Pontefract in 1818, see Marshall, 1818: i. 401.

34. A herb farm at Holbeach, Lincs., still in existence in 1931, was said to have started the cultivation and distilling of peppermint seventy years before, which means about 1860. The beginnings of herb-growing in other places are not easily dated. In Mitcham it goes back to 1800 or earlier.—Grieve, ed. Leyel, 1984, pp. xiv, 537; Hargreaves, 1987: 138; Board of Agriculture and Fisheries, Leaflet 288, 1914, revised 1916. A Herb Farm was set up at Seal, Kent, c.1925, by Dorothy G. Hewer, and continued until 1968. See Hewer, 1944. I wish to thank Monty Parkin for all his research into the Seal Herb Farm among local people.

35. 'Vast store of plant drugs', *The Times*, 6 Sept. 1978. *Information World Review* in Jan. 1996, p. 110, announced a new journal abstracting information on the medicinal properties of plants, entitled *Review of Aromatic and Medicinal Plants*.

36. Jos Kleijnen, 'Evening primrose oil', *British Medical J.* 309/6958 (1 Oct. 1994), 824–5; John Young, 'Healing plant may bring joy', *The Times*, 8 July 1985; Jeremy Saise's letter, *Sunday Times*, 18 Oct. 1987; Sarah Lonsdale, 'Final battle', *Observer*, 29 Aug. 1993; T. Stuttaford, 'The primrose path', *The Times*, 4 Oct. 1994; 'With the help of herbs', *Focus*, 15–16 Dec. 1992, 14; Julian Chomet, 'Herbal migraine remedy', *Sunday Times*, 13 Feb. 1983, though in this case drug companies were seeking to isolate the active substances and procure a patent on them; Mark Handscomb, 'Cannabis: Why doctors want it to be legal', *Independent*, 23 Feb. 1993, 14; Culpeper, n.d.: 183; James McGhee, 'Myrtle oil keeps bloodsucking midge at bay', *New Scientist*, 1 July 1995, 20; Stephen Goodwin, 'Folklore remedy...', *Independent*, 11 Aug. 1995, 7; Ch. 2 above, pp. 33–5; Grieve, ed. Leyel, 1984: 660; Cobbett, 1838: 127; 'How walnuts and purslane can save your heart', *New Scientist*, 18 June 1994, 8; 'Cotswold crop may lead fight against killer disease', *Cotswold Journal*, 14 Mar. 1996; Liz Hunt, 'Scientists look to plants for Aids treatment', *Independent*, 31 Dec. 1992; Andy Coghlan, 'When beans means vaccines', *New Scientist*, 11 July 1992.

37. Rosalyn Lewis, 'Where fragrant oils replace the familiar hospital smell', *Independent*, 4 July 1989; F. Wilson, 1991: p. iii and *passim*; Rimmel, 1865: 200–1; Lough, 1953: 163, 196.

38. Burbidge, 1898–9: 134–76; Temple, 1903: 130–1.

39. Burbidge, 1898–9: 150; Mavor, 1801: 232; 'Lavender harvesting then and now', *The Times*, 26 July 1984 (For a well-researched history of lavender, see Festing, 1989. I thank Ken Gravett for this reference.); Beryl Downing, 'Bewitched by a million English roses', *Independent*, 5 Jan. 1991, 41; Rimmel, 1865: 200. For Irish experience, I wish to thank Prof. Nicholas Canny and Brian Mooney of Vincent Perfumes, Ireland's only working perfumery, at the Burren Perfumery, Carron, Co. Clare. See also Grieve, 1926.

40. Chris Mihill, 'Fruit and vegetable diet helps avert cancer', *Guardian*, 25 Nov. 1993; Celia Hall, 'Fresh evidence backs cancer link to diet', *Independent*, Home, 15 Sept. 1993, 3; 'Broccoli and the C-word', *Amer. Philosophical Soc. News*, 7/2 (June 1992), 7; David Nicholson-Ward, 'Britons show stress', *Independent*, Home, 23 Sept. 1992, 5.

41. Joy Larkcom, *The Salad Garden*, 1984. This was the work which greatly influenced Frances Smith at Appledore. See also Larkcom, *Oriental Vegetables*, 1991. For a vivid account of Joy Larkcom's first plant-seeking journey into Europe, see 'Random harvest', *Observer*, 20 May 1979, and for her visit to China in 1985, see Anna Pavord, 'New arrivals in the cabbage patch', *Independent*, 31 Aug. 1991, 41.

42. Emily Green, 'Call a spud a spud?', *Independent,* Food and Drink, 22 May 1993, 32; Jane Grigson, 'Getting back to our roots', *Observer Colour Supplement,* 12 July 1987, 44–6; Fiona Beckett, 'Spuds you'd like to taste', *Independent,* Food and Drink, 19 Feb. 1994, 4.

43. Pearce Wright, 'Horticulture. Flower garden favourite', *The Times,* 23 Aug. 1988; Susan Watts, 'Plan to make a meal of lupin seeds', *Independent,* 12 July 1993; Robin McKie, 'Technology. Coming soon', *Observer,* 8 Jan. 1995; Folkingham, 1610: 30; Hartlib, 1651: 49; Worlidge, 1687: 38; Bradley, 1725: 60, 66.

44. J. Tremaine, 'The lost crops of the Incas', *The Market Place* (Magazine of the Eastern Costa del Sol), Oct. 1991 (no p. nos.) This article urged new, young English settlers in southern Spain to buy land where tropical plants were *in situ,* and to experiment with the new suggestions! For the first account of quinoa, see Avalle-Arce, 1970: 169–70. For salsify and other suggestions in 1904, see Udale, 1904: 94. For recent possibilities from Wye College, see Nix, 1995: 3 ff., 'Cash crops'.

45. For an appeal in 1974 against the trend to reduce variety, see Roy Hay, 'Gardening: successes and failures', *The Times,* 29 Dec. 1974; Alex Renton, 'Scientists shape the strawberry's future', *Independent,* 3 July 1990; Hargreaves, 1987: *passim*; Graham Rice, 'Garlic bred', *Observer, Life Supplement,* 24 Oct. 1993, 49. For another garlic grower in Bramber, W. Sussex, see Malcolm Smart, 'Garlic—the sweet smell of success', *Guardian,* Home News, 7 Nov. 1979, 16. On sorrel, see Sophie Grigson, 'First taste of spring', *Independent,* Food and Drink, 1 May 1993, 34. On rocket, see Jane Grigson, 'Rocket takes off again', *Observer Magazine,* 4 Oct. 1987, 76. The pioneer grower of cardoons is Clarissa Dixon-Wright, growing them in Lincolnshire for adventurous London restaurateurs.

46. Hargreaves, 1987; 82–4.

47. Ibid. 129, 149–50; Roach,1985: 74–5, 175; Joanna Blythman, 'Bing's big hit days are over', *Independent,* 26 June 1993. A brief reference in the press to the fact that 'there's no such thing as a good greengage now' was timely.—*The Times Magazine,* 26 Aug. 1995, 4. For the medlar, see Ruth Weiss, 'A curious fruit', *Garden,* 117/11 (Nov. 1992), 538–9. The pioneer cultivator of blueberries was David Trehane in Dorset, setting up a commercial plantation in 1957.—Joanna Blythman, 'Picking up the English country blues', *Independent,* Food and Drink, 15 Aug. 1992, 28.

48. Bill Cater, 'Growing low for high profits', *The Times,* Focus: Kent, 8 Feb. 1991, 29; 'Green matters', *Here and Now* (Tonbridge and Malling Borough Council, Official Newspaper), June 1993, 5, and Oct. 1993, 5; Christopher Jackson, *Business News of Europe from Christopher Jackson, MEP for Kent East,* Jan. 1989, 6; Clive Fewins, 'It's crunch time for the cobnut growers', *The Times,* c.18 Aug. 1993; Kentish Cobnuts Association, *Newsletters*; Roach, 1985: 236–43; Judy Sadgrove, 'Nuts each day', *Observer,* 19 July 1992, 3; 'How walnuts and purslane can save your heart', *New Scientist,* 18 Jan. 1994, 8. Dr Flemming's report on the marketing of cobnuts, supported by the Canterbury Farmers' Bicentenary Fund, is forthcoming.

49. Leyel, 1937.

50. *AHEW,* v. ii. 303, 310; Barker, 1927: 65–6. For the increasing demand for cider in public houses in the early 1980s, see Derek Harris, 'Cider makers roll out the barrels', *The Times,* 28 June 1982; 'Bulmer raises glass . . .', *The Times,* 13 July 1995, 1; John Young, 'Cider apple growers told of risks', *The Times,* 5 Jan. 1985. Traditional cider joined the Campaign for Real Ale in 1990.—Nicholas Roe, 'The Somerset

cider clearances', *Independent*, 12 May 1990, 40; Craig Seton, 'Wine of the apple', *The Times*, 15 Feb. 1982; Joanna Pitman, 'Cider casts off its bumpkin image', *The Times*, 5 July 1994.

51. *CSPD* 1696: 390; photograph with caption of Bertram Bulmer, *The Times*, 4 Aug. 1987; Nicholas Roe, 'The Somerset cider clearances', *Independent*, 12 May 1990, 40; photograph, *Independent*, Home News, 28 Aug. 1991; John Burns, 'Scrumpy-tious apple brandy', *Farmers' Weekly*, 11 Dec. 1992, Farmlife, 1–2.

52. David Black, 'First of the season's wine—in Scotland', *The Times*, 11 May 1984, 23; Andrew Eames, 'Fermenting in the laundry', *Independent*, 16 Dec. 1989; Emily Green, 'Call a spud a spud?', *Independent*, Food and Drink, 22 May 1993, 32; Kathy Marks, 'French say claims for "noble" English drink are all froth', *Independent*, 19 Jan. 1993; ead., 'Elderflower drink bursts the champagne bubble', *Independent*, 9 Feb. 1993.

53. Michael Jackson, 'Barley and peat on the Mull of Kintyre', *Independent*, Food and Drink, 18 Apr. 1992, 30; Mary Beith, 'A drop of the ancient stuff', *The Times*, 28 July 1987.

54. Ordish, 1977: 47–53; 'Harvest time (at Pilton manor, Somerset)', *Guardian*, 31 Oct. 1979; 'Try some English wine', *Focus*, 27–8 Dec. 1994. The figures for 1992–3 were somewhat higher: see Mary Fagan, 'English wines to drink to', *Independent*, 12 July 1993; Steve Boggan and Rhys Williams, 'English wines enjoy a taste of success', *Independent*, Home News, 28 Aug. 1993, 5. In 1984 Pulham vineyards, Norfolk, beat 38 wines from 25 countries to win the gold medal at an international tasting in London.—'Winning wine', *The Times*, 11 Sept. 1984. In 1993 Thames Valley vineyards, near Twyford, Berks., were noted prize-winners.—Boggan and Williams, op. cit. For the work of Margaret Gore-Browne in making vineyards in the 1960s, see her obituary, *The Times*, 26 Aug. 1976, 14, and her book, *How to Plant a Vineyard*. For a general survey of vineyards in 1981, see *English Wine Then and Now*, English Wine Centre, Alfriston, E. Sussex, and for the constraints of EC regulations, Anthony Rose, 'Flying the flag for English wine', *Independent*, Food and Drink, 29 June 1991, 35, and Rhys Williams, 'EC rules handicap English vineyards', *Independent*, 31 Mar. 1993, 2.

55. Martyn Halsall, 'A Case of diversify or die', *Guardian*, New Business, 23 Mar. 1992, 10; Peter Elson, 'Pastures of dairy ice', *The Times*, 1 Jan. 1994, 4.

56. *Farm Cheeses from the British Isles*, Neal's Yard Dairy, London, 1993; Harbutt, 1995; *passim*; Jack Crossley, 'For the love of a good cheese', *Times Weekend*, 22 July 1995, 11.

57. David Brown, 'Boom in ewe milk cheese', *Sunday Telegraph*, 21 June 1981; 'Sheep's milk is ice cream winner', *Courier*, 10 Dec. 1993, 13. I wish to thank Mrs Olivia Mills for her letter and literature on the British Sheep Dairying Association.

58. Jane Grigson, 'The year of the goat', *Observer Magazine*, 18 Oct. 1987, 86; 'Goat-keeping on the increase', *Oxford Mail*, 7 Dec. 1981; Nicholas Lander, 'First, get your goat', *Financial Times*, 13–14 Jan. 1996, 11.

59. Ena Kendall, 'Farmers urged: Go in for goats', *Observer*, 1 Aug. 1982, 4; John Young, 'Goat goes for record £14,700', *The Times*, 25 May 1987; Sue Arnold, 'Indisputably a big cheese', *Observer*, 2 Oct. 1994; Raey Campbell, 'Farming for fibre', Fibre Corporation, n.d. (literature supplied by Dewar Angora Stud, Newlands Farm, Barmby Moor, York. The demand for other special wool fibres has led to the breeding of

llamas and alpacas on some farms.—'Bird brainwave', *Observer*, 14 Feb. 1988); Michael Gaisford, 'Scrapie test knocks goat trade', *Farmers' Weekly*, 8 July 1993, 22, 33; Anon., 'Mohair and cashmere', *Farmers' Weekly*, 11 Dec. 1992, 37. (This news item emphasized the handicaps of goatkeepers who receive no government subsidy, in contrast with sheep-keepers.) For European regulations on dairies to which the small breeders cannot conform, see *Observer*, 5 Dec. 1993, 5.

60. Veronica Heath, 'Game for the masses', *The Times*, 25 July 1995, 18; TV programme, 2 July 1995, on Sheila and Nick Charrington's deer and venison at Layer Marney, Essex. For three snail enterprises, see letters from Roy E. Groves, of the Snail Centre, Wisborough Green, Sussex, in *Times Magazine*, 14 Jan. 1995, 5; from John Newell in Sandwich, Kent, in *Independent*, 8 Dec. 1987; and from Jacques Aubree and Rick Ozzard, near Frome, Som., in *Observer*, 31 May 1987 (a British Snail Farmers' Association was formed in 1986 and had 40 members in 1987). For ostriches, see 'Bird brainwave', *Observer*, 14 Feb. 1988; Anon., 'Top prices for big birds', *Farmers Weekly*, 9 July 1993, 15; Karen Zagor, 'Problems could hatch from ostriches', *The Times*, 23 Dec. 1995, 26.

61. Bill Frost, 'Sharpshooters take aim', *The Times*, 17 Mar. 1994, 3; Robin Young, 'Healthy buffalo', *The Times*, Home News, 15 Feb. 1995, 7; E. Brown, 1899: 313-51; 'British palate recalls the ... goose', *The Times*, 6 Nov. 1982, 20; Michael Hornsby, 'Geese carve a slice of the market', *The Times*, 12 Dec. 1994; Mrs Goodman's personal communication.

62. Peter Trickett, 'Medieval fishpond has good catches in store', *Oxford Mail*, 27 Apr. 1972, 3; Michael Pollitt, 'Trouble spot for fish', *Oxford Mail*, 27 Feb., 1982; John Young, 'Farmers break into goldfish market', *The Times*, 9 Apr. 1985. The renovation of ponds for whatever purpose is now a skilled occupation in considerable demand.—Kath Rowland, 'Restoring ponds to their full glory', *Courier*, 5 Nov. 1993; Letter from Prof. S. J. Pirt, 'Fish farming', *The Times*, 20 Apr. 1995, 19.

63. Paul Heiney, 'Smallholders barely holding on', *The Times*, Weekend, 22 July 1995, 8. Sir Robert Edgecumbe's division of Rew farm was appreciatively described in Haggard, 1902: i. 273-9.

64. Tim McGuire, 'High salaries should be linked to executives who can create real jobs', *The Times*, Business Letters, 13 July 1995; Netting, 1994: *passim*; Ambrosoli, 1996: *passim*. Because of its historical perspective and documentary evidence, Ambrosoli's book goes some way to answer the criticism of Netting's book by Paul Richards, concerning the proof needed to show how genetic variety in plants is conserved by small farmers.—Richards, 1994: 8.

65. Brian Collett, 'Regional food groups will help to promote small producers', *The Times*, 29 Aug. 1995. See also Nigel Hawkes, 'Supermarkets damage British fruit growers', and the spirited response from J. Sainsbury plc.—*The Times*, 5 Jan. 1996, 5, and 11 Jan. 1996, 19.

66. On the fundamental need of a healthy economy for diversification in all sectors of activity, see Goldsmith, 1994: 38. The old orchard saved was Marie Cooper's in Lughorse Lane, Yalding, Kent.—Oliver Gillie, 'Tall trees of Kent', *Independent*, 14 Aug. 1993, 5.

Notes to Conclusion

1. *AHEW*, v. II: chs. 16, 18, and 19. Also available in Thirsk, 1990 (2).

2. Ibid.
3. *AHEW*, v. II. 585-9. While 1750 makes an approximate dividing line, 1740 emerges as the more significant date in recent analyses of grain production and prices.— Jackson, 1985: 333-51 and the earlier authorities therein cited.
4. It is entertaining and instructive to read of French peasant agriculture in the eyes of Matilda Betham-Edwards, going over the same ground as Arthur Young, but a hundred years later, *c.*1892. Where Young in 1787-9 saw peasant farming in the blackest terms, 'pitiable management', 'a miserable system' (this was land 'to halves'), 'an unimproved poor and ugly country', and 'a countryside of privilege and poverty', Miss Betham-Edwards saw fat peasant farmers, ease and independence, and warmly praised the system of land 'to halves', which she described as another name for co-operative agriculture; in her view, 'nothing has done more to improve the condition of the peasant and of husbandry within the last fifty years.' The transformation was partly the result of the Revolution giving land to the peasants, but also partly due to the successes of alternative agriculture after 1870, which rewarded peasants rather than large farmers.—Betham-Edwards, 1892; Introduction and *passim*.
5. F. M. L. Thompson, 1968: 67-70.
6. Thirsk, 1984*d*: 1-3.
7. Tribe, 1978: 64; P. J. Perry, 1970: 139-40.
8. Beveridge, 1927: *passim*.
9. Beveridge, 1939.
10. Titow, 1972; Campbell and Overton, 1993. This last article summarizes all the literature on the subject between 1972 and 1993.
11. Postan, 1966: 549-632.
12. Campbell and Overton, 1993: 38-105, esp. 41-2.
13. Reed, 1984 and 1986: *passim*; Mills, 1980 and 1984: *passim*; Howkins, 1994: *passim*; O'Brien and Toniolo, 1991: 385-409, esp. 408, and Thirsk, 1995: 272-3.
14. This is evident in Valenze, 1991: esp. 143-5, 161.
15. Hargreaves, 1987: 59-61. For strong criticism of government policy, see C. W. Scott, 'What the politicians sowed', reviewing Clifford Selley, *Ill Fares the Land, Daily Telegraph*, 6 Mar. 1972.
16. 'English wines to drink to', *Independent*, 12 July 1993; Harbutt, 1995: 7; letter from Peter White, 'Subsidies exclude small farms', *Observer*, 13 Feb. 1994, 24; Michael Hornsby, 'Multinationals creaming off the fat of the land', *The Times*, Home News, 22 Aug. 1994, 6. These dispirited comments on government policy are noticeably different from one speech of John MacGregor when newly appointed as Minister of Agriculture in 1987, pledging warm support for family farms.—John Young, 'MacGregor pledges support for family farms', *The Times*, 18 July 1987. See also Carruthers, 1993: 525-7.
17. Pesek, 1989: *passim*, but esp. 279-81.
18. Royal Agricultural Society of England, 1985. For lentils in the 17th and 18th c., see *AHEW*, iv. 172; v. I. 106, 112, 213, 220; Kerridge, 1967: 31, 47, 49, 59, 77, 82, 213.
19. Brassley, 1995: 3-16; 'Linseed support here to stay', *Farmers' Weekly*, 25 Oct. 1991, 56.
20. Colin Spedding, reported in John Young *et al.*, 'Can wheat fields be turned into woods?', *Independent*, 28 Nov. 1986, and in a letter to the *Independent*, 24 Aug. 1990.

For the setting up at Oxford of a new centre studying climatic change, see *The Times*, Home News, 30 Sept. 1991, 6; Philippa Pullar, 'Farming: Are we feeding ourselves to death?', *The Times*, 19 Jan. 1977; G. W. Heath's letters in *The Times*, 19 Nov. 1979 and 6 May 1980.

21. Askew, 1989: 4.
22. Anna Pavord, 'The best of British comes from overseas', *Independent*, Weekend, 20 June 1992, 34. See also 'The grocer's bill we can't afford', *Guardian*, 4 May 1993.
23. Royal Agricultural Society of England, 1985: 8. Also, for nuts halving the risks of cancer, see Judy Sadgrove, 'Nuts each day', *Observer*, 19 July 1992, 3; and for fruit and vegetables protecting against heart disease, Nigel Hawkes, 'Will a fruit and vegetable diet make you live longer?', *The Times*, 16 May 1995, 15.
24. 'Small baker prospers with upper-crust loaf', *The Times*, 15 Apr. 1978; David Nicholson-Lord, 'Britons show stress', *Independent*, Home News, 23 Sept. 1992, 5. See also Hargreaves, 1987: 129 for pear consumption in Britain, the lowest in Europe.
25. Pearce Wright, 'Genetic beans could help to close trade gap', *The Times*, 11 Apr. 1988; 'New crops for new weather', *Guardian*, 5 Mar. 1990; Robin Young, 'The British baked bean', *The Times*, 4 July 1994.
26. Personal interview in June 1993, with L. J. M. van Soest at Wageningen.
27. Janick and Simon, 1989; Van Soest and Freek, 1993. The new journal is published by Elsevier Science Publishers, Amsterdam and New York. I wish to thank Dr van Soest for his considerable help with this subject.
28. 'Stores cash in on increasing appetite for natural remedies', *Independent*, Home News, 2 June 1993, 8.
29. Estienne and Liebault, cited in Thirsk, 1980: 633.
30. Pope, 1882: 114; Whetham, 1978: 321-2. For others on the same theme between 1880 and 1900, see Dunster, 1885: 171; John Coleman, Assistant Commissioner, in BPP 1881, XV, pt. I, pp. 206, 124; Burton, 1883: 3 and *passim*; and for the French following multiple activities, see Anon. 1896: 387-92. For diversity on fruit and vegetable farms today, see Hargreaves, 1987: 70-4, 106-7, 138-42, 146-7, 196-7.
31. Edward Long, 'EC Funds fuel France's bio-diesel alternative', *Farmers' Weekly*, 11 Dec. 1992, 44, and id., Weekly Opinion, p. 5; As a measure of success to date, see Centre for Alternative Technology (founded, be it noted, in 1974), *Visitors' Guide*, 15, and Trisha Fermor, on the organic farm of Donald Cooper at Yalding, Kent, transferred since his death to the Henry Doubleday Research Association, *Courier*, 5 Feb. 1993, 2.
32. Kropotkin, 1974: ch. 2, pp. 52 ff. For other contributions to this debate, see also Edward de Bono, 'Jobs for all on the pyramid principle', *Observer*, 21 Feb. 1993, and letter, *Independent*, 20 Feb. 1993; Goldsmith, 1994: 105-7.
33. Hargreaves, 1987: 38, 60, 67, 79, 86, 92, 108, 118; Keith Wheatley, 'Life on the Ail of Wight', *Observer Magazine*, 22 Nov. 1987, 90. For a searching appraisal of unemployment and 'the social consequences of high technology', see the letters of S. Gourlay, *The Times*, 6 Mar. 1978, 19; and 'The total madness of EC agricultural policy', *Independent*, 1 Dec. 1992.
34. B. A. Hopkinson, letter, *Independent*, 4 Aug. 1993, 19; Edward de Bono, 'Jobs for all', *Observer*, 21 Feb. 1993; id., letter, *Independent*, 20 Feb. 1993; Andrew Glyn, letter, *Independent*, 29 Mar. 1993.

35. Nick Evans, 'Community salutes a hi-tech saviour', *Guardian, Information Technology*, 2 Nov. 1993; 'Homework for the grown-ups', *Courier, Homebuyer*, 1 Jan. 1993, 5. For teleworking, launched in the Scottish highlands, see Nicholas Bannister, 'IT puts Highlands on line', *Guardian*, 15 Nov. 1993, 11. For the new construction of a televillage near Crickhowell, Wales, though not combined with any agricultural pursuit, see Paul Penrose, 'A community of kindred spirits', *The Times*, 23 June 1995, 31.

36. G. W. Heath, letter, *The Times*, 19 Nov. 1979. Another on the same lines from John Seymour of Pembrokeshire, *The Times*, 17 Mar. 1978, contested the argument of Kenneth Mellanby that 'only large mechanized farms can solve our future food problems'. For varied, appreciative evaluations of family farms, see T. B. Mills, letter 'To be a farmer', *The Times*, 7 Aug. 1978; Mary Heron, letter on 'A policy for world sales and family farms', *Independent*, 10 Nov. 1989; Michael Brown, letter 'Grass roots', *The Times*, 7 June 1980; Gasson and Errington, 1993; Carruthers, 1993; Hamlin and Shepard, 1993: 39–52; Berkeley Hill, 1993: 359–70. I thank Paul Brassley warmly for the last four references.

37. Simon Caulkin, 'Minorities get the vote', *Observer*, Business, 14 Nov. 1993, 8. This reported the views of Bob Lattimer, a human resources consultant of Towers Perrin in the USA, reporting the growing belief among some US companies that they needed ideas 'outside the established groove'. A fresh exploration of those phases which favoured the adoption of women's initiatives (phases of alternative agriculture are the ones suggested here) could refine the debate on women's fluctuating fortunes in the economy. See the survey by Bridget Hill, 1993.

38. The initiative of Jan and Tim Dean of North Devon was publicized in a television programme, 18 May 1993, describing farmers who were not sufficiently near a town to supply town shops and who could not comply with the demand for produce of the exact shape and size required by the supermarkets. Among vegetables supplied to their customers were kohlrabi, celeriac, and salsify. See also Frances Bissell, 'The Times cook', *Times Magazine*, 3 June 1995, 51; 'Safeway lets local producers supply a flavour of the area', *The Times*, 15 Feb. 1994, 31.

39. Oliver Gillie, 'Buying British could close food gap', *Independent*, 16 Mar. 1993.

40. Hargreaves, 1987: 139, 37–9; Brundreth, 1951: 9. For an instructive account of village co-operatives in Lincolnshire, set up in the 19th-c. phase of alternative agriculture, and fading in a mainstream phase, see Kaye, 1994: 80–7.

41. A. M. Everitt, personal communication; Bernstein, 1992: 231, in a review of Kelliher, 1992; Koning, 1994; John Young, 'Landowners appeal for ministry of rural affairs', *The Times*, 15 Feb. 1995.

42. Unwin, 1927: 462–3, citing *The Letters of William James*, 1920: ii. 90. See also Daniels, 1926, p. v.

43. The detailed attention of small farmers was commended by a Berkshire farmer, discussing woad in 1801: 'it is seldom, indeed, that great farmers will attend to minute crops.'—Mavor, 1801: 230. On the struggle to preserve bio-diversity, see Pearce, 1994: 5.

44. On Thorold Rogers, see Harte, 1971, pp. xix–xx. The citation is given in Gibbins, 1913, page facing the preface. For an emerging perception of the value of knowing some history, if only relatively recent history, see Caroline Palmer, 'Lest we forget', *Observer*, Business, 8 Jan. 1995, 8.

BIBLIOGRAPHY

ABERG, F. A., and BROWN, A. E., eds., 1981, *Medieval Moated Sites in North-West Europe*, BAR, International Ser. 121, Oxford.

ADDISON, LORD, of STALLINGBOROUGH, 1939, *A Policy for British Agriculture*, London.

ALLEN, D. E., 1982, 'A probable sixteenth-century record of *Rubia tinctorum*', *Watsonia*, 14: 178.

ALLISON, K. J., 1955, 'The Wool Supply and the Worsted Cloth Industry in the Sixteenth and Seventeenth Centuries', Leeds Ph.D. thesis.

ALSOP, JAMES, 1980, 'John Le Leu, alias Wolf: French arboriculturist at the Tudor court, precursor of later Huguenot gardeners', *Proc. Huguenot Soc. of London*, 23/4: 252–4.

AMBROSOLI, MAURO, 1997, *The Sown and the Wild: Botany and Agriculture in Western Europe, 1350–1850*, Cambridge.

AMHERST, HON. ALICE, 1896, *A History of Gardening in England*, 2nd edn., London.

ANDERSON, A. W., 1928, 'Farming in Yorkshire', *JRASE* 89: 50–77.

ANDREWS, MICHAEL, 1881, 'On the modes of culture and preparation of flax as practised in Ireland and on the Continent', *JRASE* 2nd ser. 17: 408–10.

Anon. 1646(?), *The Anti-Projector, or the History of the Fen Project*, London.

Anon. 1710, 'The case of the distressed warreners of England, humbly presented to the honourable Parliament' (no. 151 in London University, Goldsmith's Library, 1930, *Catalogue of the Collection of Broadsides*, London).

Anon. 1732*a*, *An Account of Saffron*, Dublin Society, Dublin.

Anon. 1732*b*, *The Great Improvement of Commons that are Enclosed* (London Univ. Goldsmith's Collection).

Anon. 1765, *Impartial Considerations on the Cultivation of Madder in England*. (A tract bound in a volume of Acts of Parliament of 1765 in BL, shelfmark 213.i.4 (100).)

Anon. 1767, *Primitive Cookery: or the Kitchen Garden Display'd* . . ., 2nd edn., London (BL 1037e41 (2)).

Anon. 1888, 'Article V. [Review of books, and 1887 agricultural returns], *Quarterly Rev.* 166, April: 407–38.

Anon. 1882, 'Report of the consulting biologist on laying down land to permanent pasture', *JRASE* 2nd ser. 18: 366–8.

Anon. 1890*a*, 'Vegetable and fruit farming', *JRASE*, 3rd ser. 1: 454–6.

Anon. 1890*b*, 'The cultivation of sugar beet', *JRASE* 3rd ser. 1: 441–9.

Anon. 1896, 'Agriculture in France' [from the Report of the British Consul of La Rochelle, Western France, 1896, C. 7919], *JRASE* 3rd ser. 7: 387–92.

ARBUTHNOT, MR, 1800, *On the Culture and Curing of Madder*, Dublin Society, Dublin.

ARNOLD, EDWIN LESTER, 1888, 'The future of English tobacco', *Nineteenth Century*, 24, July–Dec.: 569–73.

ASH, H. B., ed. and trans., 1941, *Lucius Junius Moderatus Columella on Agriculture*, London and Cambridge, Mass.

ASHTON, ROBERT, 1969, *James I by his Contemporaries*, London.

ASKEW, MELVYN F., 1989, *Growing Double Low Oilseed Rape Varieties*, Schering Agriculture, Nottingham.

ASSBEE, J., 1897, 'The progress of market garden cultivation during Queen Victoria's reign', *J. Roy. Hortic. Soc.* 21/1: 393–410.

ASTON, MICHAEL, ed., 1988*a*, *Aspects of the Medieval Landscape of Somerset: Contributions to the Landscape History of the County*, Somerset County Council, Bridgwater, Som.

—— ed., 1988*b*, *Medieval Fish, Fisheries, and Fishponds in England*, BAR, British Ser. 182 (1), Oxford.

ASTON, T. H., COSS, P. R., DYER, CHRISTOPHER, and THIRSK, JOAN, eds., 1983, *Social Relations and Ideas: Essays in Honour of R. H. Hilton*, Cambridge.

ASTOR, VISCOUNT, and ROWNTREE, B. SEEBOHM, 1938, *British Agriculture: The Principles of Future Policy*, London.

AVALLE-ARCE, JUAN BAUTISTA, 1970, *El Inca Garcilaso en sus 'Comentarios'*, Madrid.

AWTY, BRIAN G., 1981, 'French immigrants and the iron industry in Sheffield', *Yorkshire Archaeological J.* 53: 57–62.

BAILEY, MARK, 1988, 'The rabbit and the medieval East Anglian economy', AHR 36/1: 1–20.

—— 1989, *A Marginal Economy? East Anglian Breckland in the Later Middle Ages*, Cambridge.

BAILLIE, EDMUND J., 1894, 'Willows and their cultivation', *JRASE* 3rd ser. 5: 234–50.

BAKER, A. R. H., 1986, 'The infancy of France's first agricultural syndicate: the syndicat des agriculteurs de Loir-et-Cher, 1881–1914', *AHR* 34/1: 45–59.

BAKER, D. A., 1985, *Agricultural Prices, Production, and Marketing with Special Reference to the Hop Industry: North-East Kent, 1680–1760*, New York and London.

BAKER, G. M., *see* Smith and Baker.

BALFOUR, EVE B., 1943, *The Living Soil and the Haughley Experiment*, London.

BALFOUR-PAUL, JENNY, 1995, 'The woad trade of Toulouse, and the second international conference on woad, indigo, and other natural dyes', *Dyes in History and Archaeology*, 13, Textile Research Associates, York, 77–81.

[BANCKES, RICHARD], 1552, *A Boke of the Propreties of Herbes called an Herball . . .*, London.

BANISTER, JOHN, gent., of HORTON KIRBY, KENT, 1799, *A Synopsis of Husbandry . . . from a long and practical Experience in a Farm of considerable Extent*, London.

BARKER, B. T. P., 1927, 'The cider industry and the farmer', *JRASE* 88: 65–79.

BARKER, DIANA, 1989, 'Tithe disputes in Tudor Berkshire', *Berkshire Old and New*, 6: 16–23.

BARNETT, D. C., 1967, 'Allotments and the problem of rural poverty, 1780–1840', in E. L. Jones and G. E. Mingay, eds., *Land, Labour, and Population in the Industrial Revolution: Essays Presented to J. D. Chambers*, London, 162–83.

BATH, SLICHER B. H. VAN, 1960, 'The rise of intensive husbandry in the Low Countries', in J. S. Bromley, and E. H. Kossmann, 1960, 130–53.

—— 1963, *The Agrarian History of Western Europe, AD 500–1850*, London.

BAUGH, G. C., ed., 1989, *The Victoria History of Shropshire*, iv. *Agriculture*, London.

BEALE, E. J. ed., 1887, *English Tobacco Culture, being a Description of the First English and Irish Tobacco Crops of 1886*, London.

BEALE, JOHN, 1675–6, 'Advertisements occasioned by the remarks printed in Numb. 114 ... with some hints for the horticulture of Scotland', *Philosophical Transactions of the Royal Society*, 10/116: 357–67.

—— and LAWRENCE, ANTHONY, 1677, *Nurseries, Orchards, Profitable Gardens and Vineyards encouraged, the present Obstructions removed and probable Expedients for the better Progress proposed ... in several Letters ... directed to Henry Oldenburg, esq.*, London.

BEAR, W. E., 1888, *The British Farmer and his Competitors*, London.

—— 1893, *A Study of Small Holdings, written for the Cobden Club*, London.

—— 1897, 'The food supply of Manchester', *JRASE* 3rd ser. 8: 205–28.

—— 1898, 'Flower and fruit farming in England', *JRASE* 3rd ser. 9: 286–316, 512–50.

—— 1899, 'Flower and fruit farming in England, III and IV', *JRASE* 3rd ser. 10: 30–86, 267–313.

BEAVINGTON, F., 1965, 'Early market gardening in Bedfordshire', *Trans. Inst. British Geographers*, 37: 91–100.

BECKETT, J. V., 1981, *Coal and Tobacco: The Lowthers and the Economic Development of West Cumberland, 1660–1760*, Cambridge.

BEDDOWS, A. R., 1969, 'A history of the introduction of timothy and cocksfoot into alternate husbandry in Britain, part 1', *British Grassland Soc. J.*, 14/1: 317–21.

BEEVOR, SIR HUGH R., 1927, 'The immediate advancement of sylviculture', *JRASE* 88: 46–9.

BERNSTEIN, THOMAS P., 1992, 'Peasants, power, and reform in China under Deng Xiaoping', *J. Peasant Studies*, 19/3 and 4: 229–33.

BETHAM-EDWARDS, MATILDA, ed., 1892, *Arthur Young's Travels in France during the Years 1787, 1788, 1789*, 4th edn., London.

BETTEY, J. H., 1978, 'The cultivation of woad in the Salisbury area during the late sixteenth and seventeenth centuries', *Textile History*, 9: 112–17.

BEVERIDGE, W. H., 1927, 'The yield and price of corn in the Middle Ages', *Economic J., Econ. Hist. Supplement*, 1: 155–67, repr. in Carus-Wilson, 1954–62, i. 13–25.

—— 1939, *Prices and Wages in England from the Twelfth to the Nineteenth Century*, i. *Prices Tables: The Mercantile Era*, London.

BIDDICK, KATHLEEN, 1984, 'Pig husbandry on the Peterborough Abbey estate from the twelfth to the fourteenth century AD', in Caroline Grigson and Juliet Clutton-Brock, *Animals and Archaeology, iv. Husbandry in Europe*, BAR, International Ser. 227, Oxford, 161–77.

—— 1989, *The Other Economy: Pastoral Husbandry on a Medieval Estate*, Berkeley and London.

BILLINGSLEY, JOHN, 1798, *General View of the Agriculture of the County of Somerset*, Bath.

BIRRELL, JEAN, 1992, 'Deer and deer farming in medieval England', *AHR* 40/2: 112–26.

BLAND, A. E., BROWN, P. A., and TAWNEY, R. H., 1914, *English Economic History: Select Documents*, London.

BLITH, WALTER, 1652, *The English Improver Improved*, 3rd impression, London.

—— 1653, *The English Improver Improved*, 3rd edn., London.

BOLTON, J. L., 1980, *The Medieval English Economy, 1150–1500*, London.

Board of Agriculture and Fisheries, 1914, Leaflet 288, *The Collection and Cultivation of Medicinal Plants in England*, revised 1916.

BONDOIS, PAUL M., 1929, 'Colbert et la fabrication du bas (1655–83)', *Revue d'Histoire Économique et Sociale,* 17: 275–329.

BONE, QUENTIN, 1976, 'Legislation to revive small farming in England, 1887–1914', *Agricultural History,* 49: 653–61.

BONOEIL, JOHN, 1622, *A Treatise of the Art of making Silke . . .,* in *His Maiesties Gracious Letter to the Earle of Southampton,* London.

BOWLE, JOHN, 1981, *John Evelyn and his World: A Biography,* London.

BRACE, HAROLD W., 1960, *History of Seed Crushing in Great Britain,* London.

BRADLEY, RICHARD, 1725, *A Survey of the Ancient Husbandry and Gardening collected from Cato, Varro, Columella, Virgil, and others . . .,* London.

—— 1727, *The Country Gentleman and Farmer's Monthly Director,* 2nd edn., London.

—— ed., 1727–8, see Houghton 1727–8.

—— 1729, *A Philosophical Enquiry into the late severe Winter,* London (London University, Goldsmith's Library collection).

—— 1736, *The Country Housewife and Lady's Director,* repr. 1980, London.

BRANDON, P. F., 1971, 'Demesne arable farming in coastal Sussex during the later Middle Ages', *AHR* 19/2: 113–34.

BRASSLEY, P. W., 1995, 'The common agricultural policy of the European Union', in R. J. Saffe, ed., *The Agricultural Notebook,* 19th edn., Oxford, 3–16.

—— LAMBERT, A., and SAUNDERS, P., 1988, *Accounts of the Reverend John Crakanthorp of Fowlmere, 1682–1710,* Cambs. Rec. Soc., 8, Cambridge.

BREWER, J. S., ed., 1862–1910, *Letters and Papers, Foreign and Domestic, of the Reign of Henry VIII,* London, iv. I, xiii, I.

BRIDGES, A., and DIXEY, R. N., 1925, 'A study of the sugar-beet position', *JRASE* 86: 59–88.

———— 1934, *British Sugar Beet: Ten Years' Progress under the Subsidy,* Oxford.

BRIGHT, TIMOTHY, 1580, *A Treatise wherein is declared the Sufficiencie of English Medicines for Cure of all Diseases cured with Medicine,* London.

—— 1615, *A Treatise . . . whereunto is added a Collection of Medicines growing for the most part within our English Climate,* London.

BROAD, JOHN, 1980, 'Alternate husbandry and permanent pasture in the Midlands, 1650–1800', *AHR* 28/2: 77–89.

BROMLEY, J. S., and KOSSMANN, E. H., 1960, *Britain and the Netherlands: Papers Delivered to the Oxford–Netherlands Conference, Utrecht.*

BROOK, RICHARD, 1887, *Brook's Family Herbal,* London.

BROWN, A. E., *see* ABERG and BROWN.

BROWN, EDWARD, 1899, 'Geese and geese breeding', *JRASE* 3rd ser. 10: 313–51.

BROWN, MAISIE, 1985, *The Market Gardens of Barnes and Mortlake,* Barnes and Mortlake History Society.

BROWN, O. PHELPS, 1871–1890, *The Complete Herbalist or the People their own Physicians by the Use of Nature's Remedies,* London.

BROWN, P. A., *see* BLAND, BROWN, and TAWNEY.

BROWN, R. ALLEN, COLVIN, H. M., and TAYLOR, A. J., 1963, *The History of the King's Works,* ii, London.

BROWNLOW, MARGARET, 1957, *Herbs and the Fragrant Garden*, London.

BROWNLOW, RICHARD, 1652, *Reports: A Second Part of Diverse Famous Cases in Law*, London.

BRUNDRETH, SIR FREDERICK, 1951, 'Agricultural cooperation today', *The Times Survey of British Agriculture*, July.

BUCHANAN, H. B. M., 1909–10, 'How to work a smallholding at a living profit, XIV, Pigs that pay', *Country Home*, 4, Oct.–Mar. 41.

BULL, H. G., 1876–85, *Herefordshire Pomona, containing original Figures and Descriptions of the most esteemed Kinds of Apples and Pears*, 2 vols., Hereford.

BUNYARD, GEORGE, 1897, 'Progress in fruit culture during Queen Victoria's reign, 1837–97', *J. Roy. Hortic. Soc.* 21/1: 343–63.

—— 1899, *Fruit Farming for Profit*, Maidstone.

BURBIDGE, F. W., 1898–9, 'Fragrant leaves v. sweet scented flowers', *J. Roy. Hortic. Soc.* 22: 134–76.

BURN, RICHARD, 1781, *Ecclesiastical Law*, 4 vols., London.

BURNBY, JUANITA, and ROBINSON, A. E., 1976, *And They Blew Exceeding Fine: Robert Uvedale, 1642–1722*, Edmonton Hundred Historical Society, Occasional Paper, NS 32.

———— 1983, *'Now turned into Fair Garden Plots' (Stow)*, Edmonton Hundred Historical Society, Occasional Paper, NS 45.

BURROWS, ALFRED. J., 1882, *The Agricultural Depression and how to Meet it; Hints to Landowners and Tenant Farmers*, London.

BURTON, MRS J. H., 1883, *My Home Farm*, London.

BYRNE, MURIEL ST CLARE, 1949, *The Elizabethan Home: Discovered in Two Dialogues by Claudius Hollyband and Peter Erondell*, London.

—— ed., 1981, *The Lisle Letters*, 6 vols., Chicago and London.

CABRERA, M. LOBO, *see under* LOBO.

CAMDEN, W., 1727, *Magna Britannia*, London.

CAIRD, JAMES A., 1888, 'Recent experiences in laying down to grass', *JRASE* 2nd ser. 24: 124–56.

CAMPBELL, BRUCE M. S., 1983, 'Agricultural progress in medieval England: Some evidence from eastern Norfolk', *EcHR* 2nd ser. 31/1: 26–46.

—— 1991, 'Land, labour, livestock and productivity trends in English seignorial agriculture, 1208–1450', in Campbell and Overton, 1991, 144–82.

—— and OVERTON, MARK, eds., 1991, *Land, Labour and Livestock: Historical Studies in European Agricultural Productivity*, Manchester.

———— 1993, 'A new perspective on medieval and early modern agriculture: six centuries of Norfolk farming, c.1250–c.1850', *Past & Present*, 141: 38–105.

CAMPBELL, C. LEE, 1895, 'Hardy fruit growing in the future', *JRASE* 3rd ser. 6: 177–82.

CANTOR, L. M., 1970–1, 'The medieval parks of Leicestershire', *Trans. Leics. Archaeolog. and Nat. Hist. Soc.*, 46: 9–24.

—— and HATHERLY, J., 1979, 'The medieval parks of England', *Geography*, 64/2: 71–85.

CARRUTHERS, PETER, 1993, 'Policies for people and production' [Report on Proceedings of a Symposium on 'Crisis on the Family Farm. Ethics or Economics?'], *Food Policy*, 18/6: 525–7.

CARSLAW, R. McG., and GRAVES, P. E., 1937, 'Farm organization on the Black Fens of the Isle of Ely', *JRASE* 98: 35–52.

CARUS-WILSON, ELEANORA M., ed., 1954–62, *Essays in Economic History*, i.

CASTELVETRO, GIACOMO, 1989, *The Fruit, Herbs, and Vegetables of Italy: An Offering to Lucy, Countess of Bedford*, trans. and introd. Gillian Riley, London.

CASTER, G., 1962, *Le Commerce du Pastel et de l'Épicerie à Toulouse de 1450 environ à 1561*, Bibliothèque méridionale, Faculté des Lettres de Toulouse, 2nd ser. 37.

CATHCART, HON. A. H., 1899, 'Fattening and marketing of poultry', *JRASE* 3rd ser. 10: 156–71.

CHALONER, W. H., 1953, 'Sir Thomas Lombe (1685–1739) and the British silk industry', *History Today*, 3/11, Nov.: 778–85.

CHAMBERS, J. D., and MINGAY, G. E., 1966, *The Agricultural Revolution, 1750–1880*, London.

CHANNING, F. A., 1897, *The Truth about Agricultural Depression: An Economic Study of the Evidence of the Royal Commission*, London.

CHAPMAN, D. R., 1888, 'Recent improvements in cider and perry making', *JRASE* 2nd ser. 24: 171–95.

CHAPMAN, S. D., and CHASSAGNE, S., 1981, *European Textile Printers in the Eighteenth Century: A Study of Peel and Oberkampf*, London.

CHARTRES, J., and HEY, D., eds., 1990, *English Rural Society, 1500–1800: Essays in Honour of Joan Thirsk*, Cambridge.

CHASSAGNE, SERGEI, 1980, *Oberkampf, un Entrepreneur capitaliste au Siècle des Lumières*, Paris.

—— *see also* CHAPMAN and CHASSAGNE.

CHOYSELAT, PRUDENT, 1580, *The Discours Oeconomique of Prudent Choyselat: The First Book in English on Poultry Husbandry*, ed. H. A. D. Neville, repr. 1951, Reading.

CHRISTIAN, DAVID, *see* SMITH and CHRISTIAN.

CLARK, H. O., and WAILES, REX, 1935–6, 'The preparation of woad in England', *Trans. Newcomen Soc.* 16.

CLARK, PETER, 1983, *The English Alehouse: A Social History, 1200–1830*, London.

—— ed., 1985, *The European Crisis of the 1590s: Essays in Comparative History*, London.

CLARKE, JOHN, 1839, *A Treatise of the Mulberry Tree and Silkworm and on the Production and Manufacture of Silk*, Philadelphia.

CLEERE, HENRY, and CROSSLEY, DAVID, 1985, *The Iron Industry of the Weald*, Leicester.

CLINTON, W. O., ed., 1911, *A Record of the Parish of Padworth and its Inhabitants, compiled chiefly from Original Documents by Mary Sharp*, Reading.

COBBETT, WILLIAM, 1838, *The English Gardener . . . concluding with a Kalender . . .*, London.

COCKERELL, O. J., *see* NUSSEY and COCKERELL.

COLEMAN, D. C., and JOHN, A. H., eds., 1976, *Trade, Government, and Economy in Pre-industrial England*, London.

COLEMAN, OLIVE, ed., 1961, *The Brokage Book of Southampton, 1443–44*, ii, Southampton Records Ser., 6.

COLES, W., 1656, *The Art of Simpling*, London.

—— 1657, *Adam in Eden*, London.

COLVILLE, JAMES, ed., 1904, *Letters of John Cockburn of Ormistoun to his Gardener, 1727–1744*, Scottish History Soc., 45, Edinburgh.

COLVIN, H. M., 1982, *The History of the King's Works*, iv. *1485–1660*, pt. II, London.

—— *see also* BROWN, R., ALLEN, COLVIN, and TAYLOR.

CONLEY, C. H., 1927, *The First English Translators of the Classics*, New Haven.

COOPER, ANDREW FENTON, 1989, *British Agricultural Policy, 1912–36: A Study in Conservative Politics*, Manchester and New York.

COOPER, J. P., *see* THIRSK and COOPER.

CORNWALL, JULIAN, 1977, *Revolt of the Peasantry, 1549*, London.

COSS, P. R., *see* ASTON, COSS, DYER, and THIRSK.

COTTIS, JANIE, 1985, 'Agrarian change in the Vale of White Horse, 1660–1760', Reading Univ. Ph.D. thesis.

COULET, NOEL, 1967, 'Pour une histoire du jardin. Vergers et potagers à Aix-en-Provence: 1350–1450', *Le Moyen Âge*, 73: 239–270.

COX, T., 1720–30, *Magna Britannia et Hibernia Antiqua et Nova*, or *a New Survey of Great Britain*, 6 vols., London.

CRACKNELL, BASIL E., 1959, *Canvey Island: The History of a Marshland Community*, Occasional Paper 12, Dept. of English Local History, Leicester University.

CROKE, A. O., 1920, *A Book of Dovecotes*, London.

CROSSLEY, D. W., ed., 1975, *Sidney Ironwork Accounts, 1541–73*, Camden Soc. 4th ser. 15.

—— ed., 1981, *Medieval Industry*, CBA Research Report 40, London.

—— *see also* CLEERE and CROSSLEY.

CULPEPER, N., n.d., *Culpeper's Complete Herbal*, Foulsham Reprint, Slough, Berks.

CULPEPER, THOS., 1668, *A Tract against the High Rate of Usury, presented to the High Court of Parliament, A.D. 1623 . . . by Sir Thomas Culpeper, Sen., Knight*, London.

CURRIE, C. K., 1991, 'The early history of the carp and its economic significance in England', *AHR* 39/2: 97–107.

CURRIE, C. R. J., 1976, 'Smaller domestic architecture and society in North Berkshire, c.1300–c.1650, with special reference to Steventon', Oxford D.Phil.

CURTIS, CHARLES E., 1888, 'The principles of forestry', *JRASE* 49: 337–65.

—— 1903, 'The management and planting of British woodlands', *JRASE* 64: 16–49.

CUST, LADY ELIZABETH, 1891, *Some Account of the Stuarts of Aubigny in France (1422 –1672)*, London.

DANIELS, G. W., 1926, *George Unwin: A Memorial Lecture*, Manchester and London.

DARBY, H. C., 1956, *The Draining of the Fens*, 2nd edn., Cambridge.

DARKE, W. F., 1937, 'Vegetable production on the mixed farm', *JRASE* 98: 90–105.

DARWIN, FRANCIS, and MELDOLA, R., 1896–7, 'A visit to an English woadmill', *Nature*, 55/2 Nov: 36–7.

D'AUBANT, ABRAHAM, *see* THOMAS, WILLIAM, 1774.

DAVID, ELIZABETH, 1964, *French Provincial Cooking*, Harmondsworth, 1964.

DAVIES, W., *see* STAPLEDON and DAVIES.

DEFOE, DANIEL, 1928, *A Tour through England and Wales*, 2 vols., Everyman edn., London.

DENHAM, H. J., 1933, 'Notable farming enterprises, iv. A commercial experiment in poultry farming', *JRASE* 94: 83–100.

DENNEY, A. H., 1960, *The Sibton Abbey Estates: Select Documents, 1325–1509*, Suffolk Records Soc. 2.

DE VRIES, JAN, 1976, *The Economy of Europe in an Age of Crisis, 1600–1750*, Cambridge.

DEWAR, MARY, 1964, *Sir Thomas Smith: A Tudor Intellectual in Office*, London.

DIETZ, BRIAN, ed., 1972, *The Port and Trade of Early Elizabethan London: Documents*, London Record Soc. 8.

DIXEY, R. N., *see* BRIDGES and DIXEY.

DOORGEEST, M., *see* VAN SOEST, DOORGEEST, and ENSINK.

DOUET, ALEC, forthcoming, *Norfolk Agriculture, 1914–1972*.

DRIVER, ELIZABETH, 1989, *A Bibliography of Cookery Books published in Britain, 1875–1914*, London.

DRUCE, S. B. L., 1882, 'A Poultry farm in Huntingdonshire', *JRASE* 2nd ser. 18: 503–7.

DU BOULAY, F. R. H., 1965, 'Who were farming the English demesnes at the end of the Middle Ages?', *EcHR* 2nd ser. 17/3: 443–55.

DUHAMEL DU MONCEAU, 1767, *The Elements of Agriculture by M. Duhamel du Monceau*, trans. and revised by Philip Miller, 2 vols., Dublin.

DUNSTER, REV. HENRY P., 1884, 'England as a Market Garden', *Nineteenth Century*, 16, July–Dec.: 598–610.

—— 1885, *How to Make the Land Pay, or Profitable Industries Connected with the Land and Suitable to all Occupations, Large or Small*, London.

DURAND, GEORGES, 1979, *Vin, vigne, et vignerons en Lyonnais et Beaujolais (XVIe–XVIIIe siècles)*, Paris.

DYER, C., 1980, *Lords and Peasants in a Changing Society: The Estates of the Bishopric of Worcester, 680–1540*, Cambridge.

—— 1983, 'English diet in the late Middle Ages', in T. H. Aston, *et al.*, eds., *Social Relations and Ideas: Essays in Honour of R. H. Hilton*, Cambridge.

—— 1989, *Standards of Living in the Later Middle Ages: Social Change in England, c.1200–1520*, Cambridge.

—— *see also* ASTON, COSS, DYER, and THIRSK.

DYER, JUDITH C., 1982, *Vegetarianism: An Annotated Bibliography*, Metuchen, NJ, and London.

DYKE, ZOE, LADY HART, 1949, *So Spins the Silkworm*, London.

EDEINE, BERNARD, 1974, *La Sologne. Contribution aux études d'ethnologie métropolitaine*, 2 vols., Paris.

EDWARDS, P. R., 1976, 'The farming economy of N.E. Shropshire in the seventeenth century', Oxford Univ. D.Phil. thesis.

—— 1978, 'The development of dairy farming on the north Shropshire plain in the seventeenth century', *Midland History*, 4/3 and 4: 175–90.

ELKINGTON, W. M., 1929, 'Poultry in agriculture', *JRASE* 90: 140–62.

ELSTOB, IVY, ed., 1933, *The Garden Book of Sir Thomas Hanmer, Bart.*, London.

ENSINK, ELS., *see* VAN SOEST, DOORGEEST, and ENSINK.

EMERY, F. V., 1962, 'Moated settlements in England', *Geography*, 47: 378–88.

EMMISON, F. G., 1978, *Elizabethan Life: Wills of Essex Gentry and Merchants proved in PCC*, Chelmsford.

EPSTEIN, S. R., 1992, *An Island for itself: Economic Development and Social Change in Late Medieval Sicily*, Cambridge.

ERNLE, LORD, 1961, *English Farming, Past and Present*, 6th edn., London.

ERRINGTON, ANDREW, *see* GASSON and ERRINGTON.

EVANS, ERIC, 1976, *The Contentious Tithe*, London.

EVANS, NESTA, 1985, *The East Anglian Linen Industry: Rural Industry and Local Economy, 1500–1850*, Pasold Studies in Textile History, 5, Aldershot, Hants.

EVELYN, JOHN, 1664, *Sylva . . . to which is annexed Pomona . . . also Kalendarium Hortense or Gard'ners Almanac*, London.

—— 1699, *Acetaria. A Discourse of Sallets*, London.

EVERITT, A. M., 1966, *The Community of Kent and the Great Rebellion, 1640–60*, Leicester.

FALKUS, M., 1976, 'Lighting in the dark ages of English economic history: town streets before the industrial revolution', in D. C. Coleman and A. H. John, eds., *Trade, Government, and Economy in Pre-industrial England*, London.

FARMER, DAVID, 1991, 'Marketing the produce of the countryside, 1200–1500', in Edward Miller, ed., *AHEW*, iii, Cambridge, 324–430.

FAY, C. R., 1910, 'Small holdings and agricultural cooperation in England', *Quarterly J. of Economics*, 24: 499–514.

FERNIE, W. T., 1897, *Herbal Simples, Approved for Modern Uses of Cure*, 2nd edn., Bristol and London.

FERRIER, LINDA STONE, 1989, 'Gabriel Metsu's vegetable market at Amsterdam: seventeenth-century Dutch market paintings and horticulture', *The Art Bulletin: A Quarterly Published by the College Art Association of America*, (New York), 71/3.

FESTING, SALLY, 1989, *The Story of Lavender*, Sutton, Surrey.

FILMER, RICHARD, 1982, *Hops and Hop Picking*, repr. 1986, Princes Risborough, Bucks.

FINBERG, H. P. R., ed., 1972, *The Agrarian History of England and Wales*, i, pt. II. AD 43–1042, Cambridge.

FISHER, F. J., ed., 1966, *Calendar of the Manuscripts of the Rt. Hon. Lord Sackville of Knole, Sevenoaks, Kent*, ii. *Letters Relating to Lionel Cranfield's Business Overseas, 1597–1612*, HMC 80, London.

FLETCHER, T. W., 1961, 'Lancashire livestock farming during the Great Depression', *AHR* 9/1: 17–42.

FOLKINGHAM, W., 1610, *Feudigraphia*, London.

FORBES, R. J., 1948, *Short History of the Art of Distillation . . .*, London.

FOSTER, JOSEPH, 1891, 1892 , *Alumni Oxonienses; the Members of the University of Oxford, 1500–1714, Early Series, A–D*, 4 vols., Oxford.

FOUST, CLIFFORD M., 1992, *Rhubarb: The Wondrous Drug*, Princeton.

FRASER, A. B. S., 1910, 'My French garden at Withdean, Patcham, Sussex', *Country Home*, Feb., 235–9.

FREAM, W., 1888, 'The Herbage of old grass lands', *JRASE* 2nd ser. 24: 415–47.

—— 1894, 'Some minor rural industries', *JRASE* 3rd ser. 5: 290–303.

FULLER, THOMAS, 1952 edn., *The Worthies of England*, ed. John Freeman, London.

—— 1987 edn., *Fuller's Worthies*, ed. Richard Barber, London.

FURLEY, ROBERT, 1874, *A History of the Weald of Kent, with an Outline of the History of the County to the Present Time*, 2 vols., Ashford.

FUSSELL, G. E., 1947, *The Old English Farming Books from Fitzherbert to Tull, 1523–1730*, London.

—— 1966, *The English Dairy Farmer, 1500–1900*, London.

GARNIER, RUSSELL, 1896, 'The introduction of forage crops into Great Britain', *JRASE* 3rd ser. 7: 77–97.

GASSON, RUTH, and ERRINGTON, ANDREW, 1993, *The Farm Family Business*, Wallingford.

GEE, JOSEPH, 1767, *Observations on the Growth of Hemp and Flax in Great Britain*, London.

GENTLES, IAN, 1971, 'The management of the Crown lands', *AHR* 19/1: 25–41.

GIBBINS, H. DE B., 1897; 8th edn., 1913, *Industry in England. Historical Outlines*, London.

GILCHRIST, ROBERTA, and OLIVA, MARILYN, 1993, *Religious Women in Medieval East Anglia*, Studies in East Anglian History, 1, Centre of East Anglian Studies, Norwich.

GINTER, DONALD E., 1991, 'Measuring the decline of the small landowner', in B. A. Holderness and M. Turner, eds., *Land, Labour, and Agriculture*, London, 27–47.

GLADSTONE, W. E., 1892, *The Tory Small Holdings Bill: Two Speeches delivered by the Rt. Hon. W. E. Gladstone, M. P., in the House of Commons, on March 24 & April 8*, London.

GLEED, C. J., 1931, 'The strawberry industry of South Hampshire', *JRASE* 92: 201–13.

GLENNY, W. W., 1897, 'Watercress: Its history and cultivation', *JRASE* 3rd ser. 8: 607–22.

GOLDSMITH, JAMES, 1994, *The Trap*, London.

GOODALE, G. L., 1892, 'Cultivated plants of the future', *JRASE* 3rd ser. 3: 600–13.

GOOGE, BARNABY, 1577, *Foure Bookes of Husbandry*, London. (*See also under* HERESBACH.)

GORDON, ALEXANDER, 1871, 'A Pythagorean of the seventeenth century', Paper read before Liverpool Literary and Philosophical Soc., 3 April, Liverpool.

GRAHAM, DAVID, *see* MILLETT and GRAHAM.

GRAHAM, P. ANDERSON, 1900, *The Revival of English Agriculture*, London.

GRAVES, R. McG., *see* CARSLAW and GRAVES.

GRAY, TODD, 1995, *Devon Household Accounts, 1627–59: Part One*, Devon and Cornwall Record Soc., NS 38.

GREY, ALBERT, 1891, 'Profit-sharing in agriculture', *JRASE* 3rd ser. 2: 771–93.

GRIEVE, MRS M., 1920, *Culinary Herbs: How to Grow and Where to Sell, with an Account of their Uses and History*, Chalfont St Peter.

—— 1926, *Plants of Sweet Scent and their Employment in Perfumery*, Chalfont St Peter, 1926.

—— ed. C. F. Leyel, 1931, new edn., 1985, *A Modern Herbal*, London.

GRIFFITH, MOSES, 1936, 'The improvement of hill grazings. The Cahn Hill experiments', *JRASE* 97: 33–53.

GRIFFITHS, ELIZABETH, 1987, 'The management of two East Norfolk estates in the seventeenth century: Blickling and Felbrigg, 1596–1717', Univ. of East Anglia Ph.D. thesis.

GRIGG, DAVID, 1987, 'Farm size in England and Wales, from early Victorian times to the present', *AHR* 35/2: 179–89.

GRINDON, LEO HARTLEY, 1879, *Food for Everybody: Mr Gladstone on Gardening. Suggestions for the Utilization of Unprofitable Farm Lands and of the Columbia Market, Bethnal Green*, London and Manchester.

GUARDUCCI, ANNALISA, ed., 1984, *Agricoltura e trasformazione dell' ambiente, secoli XIII–XVIII*, Prato.

GUÉRIN, ISABELLE, 1960, *La Vie rurale en Sologne aux XIV et XV siècles*, Paris.

HADFIELD, ALICE MARY, 1970, *The Chartist Land Company*, Newton Abbot.

HAGGARD, H. RIDER, 1902, *Rural England: Being an Account of Agricultural and Social Researches Carried out in the Years 1901 and 1902*, 2 vols., London.

—— 1913, *Rural Denmark and its Lessons*, London.

HALL, ADRIAN, 1992, *Fenland Worker-Peasants: The Economy of Smallholders at Rippingale, Lincolnshire, 1791–1871, AHR* Supplement Ser. 1.

HALL, A. D., 1904, 'The agricultural experiments of the late Mr James Mason', *JRASE* 65: 106–24.

HALL, DAVID J., 1992, 'Production of natural indigo in the United Kingdom', in N. and H. E. Müllerott, eds., *Beiträge zur Waidtagung. Woad Cultivation, Indigo Dyeing, Awa Indigo, North Africa, North France, United Kingdom, Japan, Past and Present (Arnstadt)*, 4/5, pt. 1: 23–6.

HALLAM, H. E., ed., 1988, *The Agrarian History of England and Wales*, ii. *1042–1350*, Cambridge.

HAMER, MARGUERITE B., 1935, 'The foundation and failure of the silk industry in provincial Georgia', *North Carolina Hist. Rev.* 12: 125–48.

HAMILTON, A. H. A., 1877, 'The attempted introduction of the culture of silk into Devonshire in the reign of James I', *Trans. Devon Association*, 8: 234–5.

HAMLIN, CHRISTOPHER, and SHEPARD, PHILIP T., 1993, *Deep Disagreement in U.S. Agriculture: Making Sense of Policy Conflict*, Boulder, Colo., San Francisco, and Oxford.

HANELT, P., 1961, 'Zur Kenntnis von *Carthamus tinctorius L*', in L. R. Mansfeld and H. Stubbe, eds., *Die Kulturpflanze . . .*, Berlin, ix. 114–45.

HARBUTT, JULIET, 1995, *Guide to the Finest Cheeses of Britain and Ireland*, Specialist Cheesemakers' Association, Newcastle under Lyme.

HARDY, DENNIS, 1979, *Alternative Communities in Nineteenth-Century England*, London.

HARDY, W. J., ed., 1905, *Notes and Extracts from Sessions Rolls*, i, Hertford.

HARE, J. N., 1981, 'The demesne lessees of fifteenth-century Wiltshire', *AHR* 29/1: 1–15.

HARESIGN, S. R., 1983, 'Small farms and allotments as a cure for rural depopulation on the Lincolnshire fenland, 1870–1914', *Lincs. History and Archaeology*, 18: 27–36.

HARFORD, R., 1677, 'Proposals for building in every county a working-almshouse or hospital, as the best expedient to perfect the trade and manufactory of linen cloth . . .', *Harleian Miscellany*, ed. W. Oldys, iv, London, 1809, 489–94.

HARGREAVES, JOHN, 1987, *Harvests and Harvesters: Fruit and Vegetable Growing in England*, London.

HART, JAMES, 1832, *The Journal of Mr James Hart . . . one of the Commissioners deputed by the Church of Scotland to congratulate George I on his Accession . . .*, Edinburgh.

HARTE, N. B., 1971, *The Study of Economic History: Collected Inaugural Lectures, 1893–1970*, London.

—— 1973, 'The rise of protection and the English linen trade, 1690–1790', in N. B. Harte and K. G. Ponting, eds., *Textile History and Economic History: Essays in Honour of Miss Julia de Lacy Mann*, Manchester, 74–112.

HARTLIB, SAMUEL, 1651, *His Legacie*, London.

—— 1652, *His Legacie*, 2nd edn., augmented, London.

—— 1655*a*, *His Legacie*, 3rd edn., London.

—— 1655*b*, *The Reformed Virginian Silkworm*, London.

—— 'Ephemerides' [Hartlib's Diary], MS in Sheffield University Library, publication forthcoming.

HARVEY, DAVID, 1964, 'Fruit growing in Kent in the nineteenth century', *Archaeologia Cantiana*, 79: 95–108.

HARVEY, JOHN, 1972*a*, 'Medieval plantsmanship in England: the culture of rosemary', *Garden History: The Journal of the Garden History Society* 1/1: 14–21.

—— 1972*b*, *Early Gardening Catalogues*, London and Chichester.

—— 1975, 'Leonard Gurle's nurseries and some others', *Garden History*, 3/3: 42–9.

—— 1981, *Mediaeval Gardens*, London.

—— 1984, 'Vegetables in the Middle Ages', *Garden History*, 12/2: 89–99.

—— 1985, 'The first English garden book: Mayster Jon Gardener's treatise and its background', *Garden History*, 13/2: 83–101.

—— 1987, 'The square garden of Henry the poet', *Garden History*, 15/1: 1–11.

—— *see also* McGARVIE and HARVEY.

HATCH, CHARLES E., JUN., 1957, 'Mulberry trees and silkworms: Sericulture in early Virginia', *Virginia Mag. of History and Biography*, 65/1: 3–61.

HATHERLY, J., *see* CANTOR and HATHERLY.

HATTON, R. G., 1921, 'Progress in methods of practical fruit growing', *JRASE* 82: 49–116.

HEALEY, EDNA, 1978, *Lady Unknown: The Life of Angela Burdett-Coutts*, London.

HENDERSON, GEORGE, 1944, *The Farming Ladder*, London.

HENREY, BLANCHE, 1975, *British Botanical and Horticultural Literature before 1800*, 3 vols., Oxford.

HERESBACH, KONRAD, 1577, *Foure Bookes of Husbandry*, trans. Barnaby Googe, London.

HEWER, D. G., 1944, *Practical Herb Growing*, London.

HEY, DAVID, ed., 1981, *The History of Myddle*, London.

HILL, BERKELEY, 1993, 'The "myth" of the family farm: Defining the family farm and assessing its importance in the European community', *J. of Rural Studies*, 9/4: 359–70.

HILL, BRIDGET, 1993, 'Women's history: A study in change, continuity, or standing still?', *Women's History Review*, 2/1: 5–22.

HILL, CHRISTOPHER, 1972, *The World turned upside down: Radical Ideas during the English Revolution*, London.

—— 1990, *A Nation of Change and Novelty: Radical Politics, Religion, and Literature in Seventeenth-Century England*, London.

HILL, GEORGIANA, 1860, *The Cook's Own Book: A Manual of Cookery for the Kitchen and the Cottage*, London.

HILL, GEORGIANA, 1862, *Foreign Desserts for English Tables*, London.

HILL, PAUL, *see* NIX with HILL.

HILL, THOMAS [=Mountain, Dydymus], 1594, *Gardener's Labyrinth*, repr. 1982, London.

HIRST, D., 1986, *Authority and Conflict: England, 1603–1658*, Cambridge, Mass.

Historical Manuscripts Commission, 80, ii, see under Fisher, 1966.

HOLDERNESS, H., 1929, 'The livestock of Lancashire', *JRASE* 90: 55–69.

HOLDSWORTH, CHRISTOPHER, 1991, *The Piper and the Tune: Medieval Patrons and Monks*, Stenton Lecture, 1990, Reading University.

HOLLINS, ARTHUR, 1984, *The Farmer, the Plough, and the Devil: The Story of Fordhall Farm, Pioneer of Organic Farming*, Bath.

HOLLYBANDE, CLAUDIUS, 1573, *The French Schoolmaister*, London.

Horace Plunkett Foundation, 1930, *Agricultural Cooperation in England: A Survey*, London.

HORN, JAMES, 1994, *Adapting to a New World: English Society in the Seventeenth-Century Chesapeake*, Chapel Hill, NC, and London.

HOUGHTON, JOHN, 1681, *A Collection of Letters for the Improvement of Husbandry and Trade*, London.

—— 1727–8, *A Collection for the Improvement of Husbandry and Trade*, ed. Richard Bradley, 4 vols., London.

HOUSE, C. A., 1923, 'Poultry keeping on the farm', *JRASE* 84; 93–109.

HOWARD, SIR ALBERT, 1943, *An Agricultural Testament*, New York and London.

—— 1945, *Farming and Gardening for Health and Disease*, London.

HOWARD, JAMES, 1880, 'Laying down land to grass', *JRASE* 2nd ser. 16: 435–41.

HOWKINS, A., 1994, 'Peasants, servants and labourers: The marginal workforce in British agriculture, *c*.1870–1914', *AHR* 92/1: 49–62.

HOYLE, R. W., ed., 1992, *The Estates of the English Crown, 1558–1640*, Cambridge.

HUDSON, DEREK, and LUCKHURST, K. W., 1954, *The Royal Society of Arts, 1754–1954*, London.

HUGHES, P. L., and LARKIN, J. F., eds., 1969, *Tudor Royal Proclamations*, iii. *The Later Tudors, 1558–1603*, New Haven and London. *See also* LARKIN and HUGHES.

HULME, E. WYNDHAM, 1896–1900, 'The history of the patent system under the prerogative and at common law', *Law Quarterly Rev.* 46: 141–54, and 61: 44–56.

HUNT, JOHN DIXON, 1986, *Garden and Grove: The Italian Renaissance Garden in the English Imagination, 1600–1750*, Princeton.

HUTCHINS, SHEILA, 1967, *English Recipes and Others*, London.

HUXLEY, SELMA, 'Diego de Bernuy. Ejemplo de un mercader no lanero', *Historia de Burgos*, iii. *Edad Moderna(2)*, Caja de Ahorros Municipal de Burgos, 195–229.

HYAMS, EDWARD, 1949, *The Grape Vine in England*, London.

IMPEY, FREDERIC, 1886, *'Housed Beggars': Or the Right of the Labourer to Allotments and Small Holdings*, London.

—— 1909, *Small Holdings in England*, London.

IRSIGLER, FRANZ, 1984, 'Intensivwirtschaft, Sonderkulturen, und Gartenbau als Elemente der Kulturlandschaftsgestaltung in den Rheinlanden (13–16 Jahrhundert)', in Guarducci, 1984, 719–47.

J., S., 1727, *The Vineyard, being a Treatise showing the Nature and Method of Planting . . . being the Observations made by a Gentleman in his Travels*, London.

JACKSON, R. V., 1985, 'Growth and deceleration in English agriculture, 1660–1790', *EcHR* 2nd ser., 38/3: 333–51.

JACOB, EDWARD, 1774, *The History of the Town and Port of Faversham in . . . Kent*, London.

JAMES, N. D. G., 1981, *A History of English Forestry*, Oxford.

JAMES, T. M., 1969, 'The walnut trade in Croydon', *Surrey Archaeolog. Coll.* 46: 132–3.

JANICK, J., and SIMON, J. E., eds., 1989, *Advances in New Crops: Proceedings of the First National Symposium on New Crops, 23–26 Oct. 1988, at Indianopolis, U.S.A.*, Portland.

JEBB, LOUISA, 1907a, 'The English aspect of the smallholding question', *Economic Journal*, 17: 171–9.

—— 1907b, *The Small Holdings of England: A Survey of Various Existing Systems*, London.

—— 1907c, *How Landlords can Create Smallholdings: Some Examples*, London.

—— 1909, *The Smallholdings Controversy: Tenancy v. Ownership*, London.

JEEVAR, PETER, 1977, *Dovecots of Cambridgeshire*, Cambridge.

JENKINS, H. M., 1880, 'Note on market gardening and vine culture in the north-west of France', *JRASE* 2nd ser. 16: 80–103.

—— 1881, 'Flax-farming in the Netherlands', *JRASE* 2nd ser. 17: 430–33.

—— 1882, 'Dairy farming in the Netherlands', *JRASE* 2nd ser. 18: 521–34.

—— 1883a, 'Dairying in Denmark', *JRASE* 2nd ser. 19: 155–84.

—— 1883b, 'Notes on Continental poultry keeping', *JRASE* 2nd ser. 19: 184–206.

—— 1886, 'Notes on the cultivation of tobacco in the north-west of Europe', *JRASE* 2nd ser. 22: 729–56.

JENKINSON, HILARY and POWELL, DOROTHY L., eds., 1935, *Surrey Quarter Sessions Records. The Order Book for 1661–3 and the Sessions Rolls from Michaelmas 1661 to Epiphany 1663*, Surrey Record Soc., 36.

———— see also POWELL and JENKINSON.

JOHN, A. H., see COLEMAN and JOHN.

JOHNSON, A. H., 1909, *The Disappearance of the Small Landowner: Ford Lectures*, repr. 1963, London.

JONES, MARTIN G., 1933, 'Grassland management and its influence on the sward', *JRASE* 94: 21–41.

KALM, PEHR, 1892, *Pehr Kalm's Account of his Visit to England on his Way to America*, trans. Joseph Lucas, London.

KAYE, DAVID, 1994, 'No paper boots at the village co-ops', *The Countryman*, 99/6: 80–7.

KELLENBENZ, H., 1976, *The Rise of the European Economy: An Economic History of Continental Europe from the Fifteenth to the Eighteenth Century*, London.

KELLIHER, DANIEL, 1992, *Peasant Power in China: The Era of Rural Reform, 1979–1989*, New Haven and London.

KERRIDGE, ERIC, 1967, *The Agricultural Revolution*, London.

KERSHAW, IAN, 1973, 'The great famine and agrarian crisis in England, 1315–22', *Past & Present*, 59: 3–50.

KEYNES, G. L., 1937, *John Evelyn: A Study in Bibliophily and a Bibliography of his Writings*, Cambridge.

KINGSFORD, ANNA, 1881, *The Perfect Way in Diet: A Treatise Advocating a Return to the Natural and Ancient Food of our Race*, London.

[——], 1889, 'What is vegetarianism? by a vice-president of the Vegetarian Society', *Cassell's Family Magazine*, July, 347–9.

KNOWLES, P. F., and MILLER, MILTON D., n.d., *Safflower in California*, Manual 27, California Agricultural Experimental Station, Extension Service, Univ. of California, 1–23.

KONING, NIEK, 1994, *The Failure of Agrarian Capitalism: Agrarian Politics in the U.K., Germany, the Netherlands and the U.S.A., 1846–1919*, London.

KOSSMANN, E. H., *see* BROMLEY and KOSSMANN.

KROPOTKIN, PETER, 1974, ed. Colin Ward, *Fields, Factories and Workshops Tomorrow*, London.

LAMBERT, A., *see* BRASSLEY, LAMBERT, and SAUNDERS.

Land Settlement: The Official Journal of the Land Settlement Association, 1935–6, nos. 2–5.

LANGLEY, BATTY, 1753, *Treatise on Cider*, London.

LA QUINTINYE, JEAN DE, 1693, *The Compleat Gard'ner, or Directions for cultivating and right ordering of Fruit-Gardens and Kitchen-Gardens . . .*, London.

LARKCOM, JOY, 1984, *The Salad Garden*, repr. 1993, London.

—— 1991, *Oriental Vegetables*, London.

LARKIN, J. F., and HUGHES, P. L., eds., 1973–83, *Stuart Royal Proclamations*, i., *Royal Proclamations of King James I, 1603–25*; ii. *Proclamations of King Charles I, 1625–46*, Oxford. (*See also* HUGHES and LARKIN.)

LATHAM, ROBERT, and MATTHEWS, WILLIAM, eds., 1974, *The Diary of Samuel Pepys*, viii. 1667, London.

LAUNE, C. FAUNCE DE, 1882, 'On laying down land to permanent grass', *JRASE* 2nd ser. 18: 229–64, 604–9.

—— 1887, 'Tobacco as a farm crop for England', *JRASE* 2nd ser. 23: 213–52.

LAWRENCE, ANTHONY, *see* BEALE and LAWRENCE.

LAWRENCE, MARGARET, 1990, *The Encircling Hop: A History of Hops and Brewing*, Bicknor, Kent.

LAWSON, WILLIAM, 1617, *The Countrie Housewife's Garden . . . together with the Husbandry of Bees*, London.

LEA, REVD. WILLIAM, 1872, *Small Farms: How They Can be Made to Answer by Means of Fruit Growing*, London.

LEE, EGMONT, 1982, 'Woad from Citta di Castello, 1476–1484', *J. European Econ. Hist.* 11/1: 141–56.

LE ROUGETEL, HAZEL, 1990, *The Chelsea Gardener: Philip Miller, 1691–1771*, London.

LEWIS, JOHN, 1736, 2nd edn. [first edn. 1723], *The History and Antiquities, Ecclesiastical and Civil, of the Isle of Tenet, in Kent*, London.

LEYEL, MRS C. F., 1937, *Herbal Delights, Tisanes, Syrups, Confections, Electuaries, Robs, Juleps, Vinegars, and Conserves*, London. (*See also* GRIEVE, 1931.)

LLOYD, C. M., ed., 1973, *Letters from John Wallace to Madam Whichcot*, Lincs. Record Soc., 66.

LOBO CABRERA, MANUEL, 1987, 'El comercio de pájaros canarios bajo Felipe II', *Studia Historica, Historia Moderna* (Salamanca) 5: 193–8.

LOCKE, JOHN, 1978, *The Correspondence of John Locke*, ed. E. S. de Beer, iii, Oxford.

LOCKYER, ROGER, 1981, *Buckingham: The Life and Political Career of George Villiers, First Duke of Buckingham, 1592–1628*, London.

LONG, JAMES, 1885, *British Dairy Farming, to which is added a Description of the Chief Continental Systems*, London.

——— 1886, *The Book of the Pig: Its Selection, Breeding, Feeding and Management*, London.

——— 1887, 'British dairy farming: Two means of promoting its greater prosperity', *JRASE* 2nd ser. 23: 123–68.

——— 1918, *British Pigs: The Art of Making Them Pay*, London.

LOUGH, JOHN, ed., 1953, *Locke's Travels in France, 1675–9*, Cambridge.

LUCKHURST, K. W., *see* HUDSON and LUCKHURST.

LUTHER, M., 1967, *Table Talk*, in *Luther's Works*, ed. Theodore G. Tappert, Philadelphia, liv.

McDONNELL, J., 1981, *Inland Fisheries in Medieval Yorkshire, 1066–1300*, Borthwick Paper 60, Borthwick Institute of Historical Research, University of York.

McGARVIE, MICHAEL, and HARVEY, JOHN, 1983, 'The Reverend George Harbin and his memoirs of gardening, 1716–23', *Garden History: The Journal of the Garden History Society*, 11/1: 6–36.

McKAY, C. D., 1908; Daily Mail edn, 1909, *The French Garden: A Diary and Manual of Intensive Cultivation*, London.

McLEAN, TERESA, 1989 edn., *Medieval English Gardens*, London.

McREADY, K. J., 1974, *The Land Settlement Association: Its History and Present Form*, Plunkett Foundation for Cooperative Studies, Occasional Paper 37.

MÄGDEFRAU, WERNER, 1973, 'Zum Waid- und Tuchhandel Thüringischer Städte im späten Mittelalter', *Jahrbuch für Wirtschaftsgeschichte*, 2: 131–48.

MALDEN, W. J., 1890, 'Crops for pickling and preserving', *JRASE* 3rd ser. 1: 710–32.

MARKHAM, GERVASE, 1613, *The English Husbandman*, London.

MARSH, JAN, 1982, *Back to the Land: The Pastoral Impulse in England, from 1880 to 1914*, London.

MARSHALL, WILLIAM, 1818, *The Review and Abstract of the County Reports to the Board of Agriculture from the Several Agricultural Departments of England*, i. *Northern Department*; ii. *Western Department*, York.

MARTIN, CLAUDE, 1971, 'David Geneste: A Huguenot vine grower at Cobham', *Surrey Archaeolog. Coll.*, 68: 153–60.

MARTIN, J. M., 1985, 'The social and economic origins of the Vale of Evesham market gardening industry', *AHR* 33/1: 41–50.

MASCALL, LEONARD, 1581, *The Husbandly Ordring and Governmente of Poultrie . . .*, London.

——— 1620, *The Government of Cattell*, London.

——— 1654, *The Country-man's Recreation: Or the Art of Planting, Graffing, and Gardening in three Books*, London.

MATTHEWS, W., *see* LATHAM and MATTHEWS.

MAVOR, WILLIAM, 1801, *General View of the Agriculture of Berkshire*, London.

MELDOLA, R., *see* DARWIN and MELDOLA.

MERRICKS, LINDA, 1994, 'Without violence and by controlling the poorer sort. The enclosure of Ashdown forest, 1640–93', *Sussex Archaeological Collections*, 132: 115–28.

MILDON, W. H., 1934, 'Puritanism in Hampshire and the Isle of Wight from the reign of Elizabeth to the Restoration', London University Ph.D. thesis.

MILLER, EDWARD, ed., 1991, *The Agrarian History of England and Wales*, iii. *1348–1500*, Cambridge.

MILLER, MILTON D., *see* KNOWLES and MILLER.

MILLER, PHILIP, 1758, *The Method of Cultivating Madder as it is now practised by the Dutch in Zealand*, London.

MILLETT, MARTIN, and GRAHAM, DAVID, 1986, *Excavations on the Romano-British Small Town at Neatham, Hampshire, 1969–79*, Hampshire Field Club Monograph 3, Farnham and District Museum Society.

MILLS, D. R., 1980, *Lord and Peasant in Nineteenth-Century Britain*, London.

—— 1984, 'The nineteenth-century peasantry of Melbourn, Cambridgeshire', in R. M. Smith, ed., *Land, Kinship, and Lifecycle*, Cambridge.

MINCHINTON, WALTER, 1975, 'Cider and folklore', *Folklife*, 13: 66–79.

MINGAY, G. E., *see* CHAMBERS and MINGAY.

MOIR, ESTHER, 1957, 'Benedict Webb, clothier', *EcHR*, 2nd ser. 10/2: 256–64.

MOORE, SIR JONAS, 1703, *England's Interest or the Gentleman and Farmer's Friend*, London.

MOORHOUSE, S. A., 1981, 'The medieval pottery industry and its markets', in CROSSLEY, 1981, 96–125.

MORGAN, FRANK A., 1888, 'The fruit growing revival', *Nineteenth Century*, 24, July–Dec.: 879–90.

MORTIMER, JOHN, 1707, *The Whole Art of Husbandry*, London.

MORTON, JOHN, 1712, *The Natural History of Northamptonshire*, London.

MORYSON, FYNES, 1908, *An Itinerary containing his Ten Yeeres Travell through the Twelve Dominions . . .*, 4 vols., Glasgow, iv.

MULDER, FREEK, *see* VAN SOEST and MULDER.

NETTING, ROBERT McC., 1994, *Smallholders, Householders: Farm Families and the Ecology of Intensive, Sustainable Agriculture*, Stanford, Calif.

NEWBY, H., 1987, *Country Life: A Social History of Rural England*, Totowa, NJ.

NICKLIN, J. A., ed., n.d., *Essays of Sir William Temple*, London.

NIEUWHOF, M., 1969, *Cole Crops, Botany, Cultivation and Utilization*, London.

NIX, JOHN, with HILL, PAUL, 1995 (26th edn.), *Farm Management Pocketbook*, Wye, Kent.

NORDEN, JOHN, 1607, *The Surveyors Dialogue*, London.

NORTH, DUDLEY LORD, 1669, *Observations and Advices Oeconomical*, London.

NORTH, ROGER, 1713, *A Discourse of Fish and Fishponds, done by a Person of Honour*, London.

NOTESTEIN, W., RELF, F. H., and SIMPSON, H., eds., 1935, *Commons Debates, 1621*, New Haven.

NUSSEY, HELEN and COCKERELL, O. J., 1909, *A French Garden in England: A Record of the Successes and Failures of a First Year of Intensive Culture*, London.

O'BRIEN, P. K., and TONIOLO, GIANNI, 1991, 'The poverty of Italy and the backwardness of its agriculture before 1914', in B. M. S. Campbell and M. Overton, eds., 1991, *Land, Labour, and Livestock: Historical Studies in European Agricultural Productivity*, Manchester, 385–409.

OLDERSHAW, A. W., 1923, 'Crops for ensilage', *JRASE* 84: 39–49.

OLIVA, MARILYN, *see* GILCHRIST and OLIVA.

ORDISH, GEORGE, 1977, *Vineyards in England and Wales*, London.

ORMROD, DAVID, 1985, *English Grain Exports and the Structure of Agrarian Capitalism, 1700–1760*, Occasional Papers in Economic and Social History, 12, Hull University.

—— 1995, 'The industries of Kent, I. 1640–1800', ch. 3 in A. Armstrong, ed., *The Economy of Kent, 1640–1914*, Woodbridge, 85–109.

ORNSBY, REVD. GEORGE, ed., 1877, *Selections from the Household Books of the Lord William Howard of Naworth Castle*, Surtees Soc. 68.

ORWIN, CHRISTABEL S., 1930, *The Future of Farming*, Oxford.

—— and WHETHAM, EDITH H., 1971 edn., *History of British Agriculture, 1846–1914*, Newton Abbot.

OVERTON, MARK, 1985, 'The diffusion of agricultural innovations in early modern England: Turnips and clover in Norfolk and Suffolk, 1580–1740' *Trans. Inst. British Geographers*, NS 10: 205–21.

—— 1993, *see* CAMPBELL and OVERTON.

PALMER, ALFRED J., 1936, *Old Edmonton*, Edmonton (repr. in Newsletter of the Edmonton Hundred Historical Society, Nov. 1995).

PAM, DAVID, 1977, *The Rude Multitude (Enfield and the Civil War)*, Edmonton Hundred Historical Society, Occasional Paper, NS 33, Edmonton.

—— 1992, *A History of Enfield*, ii. *1837 to 1914: A Victorian Suburb*, Enfield Preservation Society, 1992.

PARKINSON, JOHN, 1629, *Paradisi in Sole . . .*, London.

PATERSON, ALLEN, 1978, 'Loved by king and peacock: The mulberry tree in Britain', *Country Life*, 163/420, 23 Feb.: 455.

PAYNE, ROBERT, 1589, *A Briefe Description of Ireland made in this Yeare, 1589 . . .*, London.

PEEL, W. R., 1923, 'Stock farming on arable land', *JRASE* 84: 29–38.

PERKINS, J. A., 1983, 'Allotments in nineteenth-century Lincolnshire', *Lincs. History and Archaeology*, 18: 21–5.

PERREN, R., 1989, 'Agriculture, 1875–1985', VCH Salop, iv, ed. G. C. Baugh, London.

—— 1995, *Agriculture in Depression, 1870–1940*, Cambridge.

PERRY, P. J., 1970, 'An agricultural journalist on the "Great Depression": Richard Jefferies', *J. of British Studies*, 9/2: 126–40.

—— 1974, *British Farming in the Great Depression, 1870–1914*, Newton Abbot.

PERRY, R., 1945, 'The Gloucestershire woollen industry, 1100–1690', *Trans. Bristol & Glos. Arch. Soc.*, 66: 49–137.

PESEK, JOHN, Chairman of the Board on Agriculture, National Research Council, 1989, *Alternative Agriculture*. Committee on the Role of Alternative Farming Methods in Modern Production Agriculture, Washington, DC.

PETERSON, W. F., 1965, *Safflower Culture in the West-Central Plains*, Agricultural Information Bulletin 300, USA, Dept. of Agriculture, Washington.

PIDGEON, DAN, 1888, 'Fruit evaporation in America', *JRASE* 2nd ser. 24: 486–92.

PLATT, SIR HUGH, 1602, *Delightes for Ladies*, London.

PLOT, ROBERT, 1686, *The Natural History of Staffordshire*, Oxford.

—— 1705, repr. 1972, *The Natural History of Oxfordshire*, Oxford.

POCOCK, D. C. D., 1957, 'Fluctuations in hop cultivation and classification of hop regions in south-eastern England', app. II of Dept. of Hop Research, *Annual Report*, Wye College, Kent, 124–33.

—— 1958, 'Hop cultivation and hop regions in the West Midlands', app. II of Dept. of Hop Research, *Annual Report*, Wye College, Kent, 75–80.

—— 1965, 'Some former hop-growing centres', *AHR* 13/1: 17–22.

POCOCKE, RICHARD, 1888, *The Travels through England of Dr Richard Pococke . . . during 1750, 1751, and later Years*, ed. J. J. Cartwright, Camden Soc. 1.

PONTING, K. G., 1976, 'Indigo and woad', *Folklife*, 14: 75–88.

—— 1977, 'Madder', *International Dyer and Textile Printer*, 24, June: 17–21.

POPE, REVD. W. J., 1882, 'The Poultry of the farm', *JRASE* 2nd ser. 18: 104–14.

POSTAN, M. M., ed., 1966, *The Cambridge Economic History of Europe*, i. *The Agrarian Life of the Middle Ages*, 2nd edn., Cambridge.

POWELL, DOROTHY L., and JENKINSON, HILARY, eds., 1938, *The Order Books and the Sessions Rolls, Easter 1663–Epiphany 1666*, Surrey Rec. Soc. 39.

POWELL, WILLIAM S., 1977, *John Pory, 1572–1636: The Life and Letters of a Man of many Parts*, Chapel Hill, NC.

POWER, EILEEN, *see* TAWNEY and POWER.

PRATT, EDWIN A., 1906, *The Transition in Agriculture*, London.

PRATT, E. R., 1905, 1927, 'The East Anglian timber willow', *JRASE* 66: 19–34, and 88: 80–6.

PRETYMAN, ERNEST G., 1928, 'Sugarbeet: Position and outlook', *JRASE* 89: 1–9.

PRICE, R. J. LLOYD, 1884, *Rabbits for Profit and Rabbits for Powder: A Treatise upon the New Industry of Hutch Rabbit Farming in the Open upon Warrens specially Intended for Sporting Purposes*, London.

PRINCE, H. C., 1989, 'The changing rural landscape, 1750–1850', in *AHEW*, vi, ed. G. E. Mingay, 7–83.

RABAK, F., 1935, 'Safflower, a possible new oil-seed crop for the Northern Great Plains and the Far Western States', Circular 366, Aug., US Dept. of Agriculture, Washington, 1–14.

RANDELL, C., 1882, 'Laying down clayland intended for permanent pasture', *JRASE*, 2nd ser. 18: 368–70.

RASCHKE, HELGA, 1988, 'Der Waidhandel in Gotha seit dem Indigoimport', *Beiträge von der Waidtagung am 19 September, 1987, in Pferdingsleben*, Gesellschaft für Heimatgeschichte, Kulturbund der DDR, Gotha, 2–7.

RAYLOR, TIMOTHY, 1992, 'Samuel Hartlib and the "Commonwealth of Bees"', in Michael Leslie and Timothy Raylor, eds., *Culture and Cultivation in Early Modern England: Writing and the Land*, Leicester and London, 91–129.

REED, M., 1984, 'The peasantry of nineteenth-century England: A neglected class?', *History Workshop J.* 18: 53–71.

—— 1986, 'Nineteenth-century rural England: A case for "peasant studies" ', *J. of Peasant Studies*, 14/1: 78–99.

RELF, F. H., *see* NOTESTEIN, RELF, and SIMPSON.

REW, R. H., 1903, 'The food production of British farms', *JRASE* 64: 110–22.

—— 1927, 'The output of English farming', *JRASE* 88: 16–32.

REYCE, ROBERT, 1902, *Suffolk in the XVIIth Century: The Breviary of Suffolk by Robert Reyce, 1618*, ed. Lord Francis Hervey, London.

REYNEL, CAREW, 1674, *The True English Interest*, London.

RICHARDS, PAUL, 1994, 'With love and sweat' [Review of Netting, *Smallholders, Householders*], *Times Literary Supplement*, 9 Sept., 8.

RICHARDSON. R. C., ed., 1992, *Town and Countryside in the English Revolution*, Manchester.

RICHMOND, COLIN, 1981, *John Hopton: A Fifteenth-Century Gentleman*, Cambridge.

—— 1994, 'The transition from feudalism to capitalism in the archives of Magdalen College, Oxford: A note', *History Workshop J.* 37: 165–9.

RILEY, GILLIAN, *see* CASTELVETRO.

RIMMEL, EUGENE, 1865, *The Book of Perfumes*, London.

ROACH, F. A., 1985, *Cultivated Fruits of Britain: Their Origin and History*, Oxford.

ROBERTS, B. K., 1964, 'Moats and Mottes', *Medieval Archaeology*, 8: 219–22.

—— 1966, 'Medieval fishponds', *Amateur Historian*, 7/4: 119–26.

—— 1968a, 'A study of medieval colonization in the forest of Arden, Warwickshire', *AHR* 16/2: 101–13.

—— 1968b, 'Fish culture in sixteenth-century Poland. Review article', *AHR* 16/2: 161–3.

ROBINSON, A. E., *see* BARNBY and ROBINSON.

ROBINSON, G. M., 1976, *Late Victorian Agriculture in the Vale of Evesham*, Research Paper 16, School of Geography, Oxford University.

ROBINSON, H. G., 1931, 'Notable farming enterprises, II. Mr A. H. Brown's Farms of Northwood Farm, North Hayling, Hants', *JRASE* 92: 151–62.

ROHDE, ELEANOUR S., 1922, *The Old English Herbals*, London; repr. 1971, New York.

ROWNTREE, B. SEEBOHM, *see* ASTOR and ROWNTREE.

ROWSE, A. L., 1962, *Ralegh and the Throckmortons*, London.

Royal Agricultural Society of England, 1985, *A Guide to Alternative Combinable Crops*, Stoneleigh, War.

Royal Commission on Historical Monuments England, 1984, *County of Northampton*, vi, London.

RUDDOCK, ALWYN, 1951, *Italian Merchants and Shipping in Southampton, 1270–1600*, Southampton Rec. Series, i.

RUSSELL, SIR JOHN, 1966, *A History of Agricultural Science in Great Britain*, London.

RYMER, THOMAS, ed. G. Holmes, 1704–32, *Foedera...*, 20 vols., London.

S., J., GENT., 1697, *The Experienc'd Fowler; or, The Gentleman, Citizen, and Countryman's Pleasant and Profitable Recreation*, London.

SABIN, A. K., 1931, *The Silkweavers of Spitalfields and Bethnal Green*, Victoria & Albert Museum, London.

Saffron Walden Museum, n.d., *The Saffron Crocus*, Leaflet 13, Saffron Walden.

SANDERS, MAURICE H., 1990, *Characters of Wood, Wurlitzer, and Wesley: Maurice Sanders Looks Back*, Courtney Publications, Ashwell, Baldock, Herts.

SANTAYANA, GEORGE, 1954, *The Life of Reason*, i. *Reason in Common Sense*, 1-vol. edn., London.

SAUNDERS, P., *see* BRASSLEY, LAMBERT, and SAUNDERS.

SCHAEFER, G., 1941*a*, 'The cultivation of madder', *Ciba Review*, 39, May: 1398–1406.

—— 1941*b*, The history of Turkey red dyeing', *Ciba Review*, 39, May: 1407–16.

SCHOFIELD, R. S., *see* WRIGLEY and SCHOFIELD.

SCOT, REYNOLDE, 1574, *A Perfite Platforme of a Hoppe Garden*, London.

SEDDON, QUENTIN, 1989, *The Silent Revolution: Farming and the Countryside in the 21st Century*, London.

SEVERN, JOHN, 1986, *Dovecotes of Nottinghamshire*, Newark, Notts.

SHARP, BUCHANAN, 1992, 'Rural discontents and the English Revolution', in Richardson, 1992, 251–72.

SHARP, T. J., 1982, 'The development of the fruit industry in Kent, 1680–1914, with particular reference to the mid-Kent area', University of Kent, Ph.D. thesis.

SHAW, NELLIE, 1935, *Whiteway: A Colony on the Cotswolds*, London.

SHAW, W. A., ed., 1911, *Letters of Denization and Acts of Naturalization for Aliens in England and Ireland, 1603–1700*, Huguenot Soc. 18.

SHEAIL, JOHN, 1971, *Rabbits and their History*, Newton Abbot.

—— 1978, 'Rabbits and agriculture in post-medieval England', *J. Historical Geography*, 4/4: 343–55.

SHEPARD, PHILIP T., *see* HAMLIN and SHEPARD.

SHERWOOD, P. T., 1973, *Agriculture in Harmondsworth Parish: Its Growth and Decline, 1800–1970*, West Drayton District Local History Society, West Drayton.

SHESGREEN, SEAN, 1990, *The Criers and Hawkers of London: Engravings and Drawings by Marcellus Laroon*, Stanford, Calif.

SHIRLEY, E. P., 1867, *Some Account of English Deerparks*, London.

SHIRLEY, JOHN W., 1983, *Thomas Harriot: A Biography*, Oxford.

SHORT, BRIAN, 1982, ' "The Art and craft of chicken cramming": Poultry in the Weald of Sussex, 1850–1950', *AHR* 30/1: 17–30.

SIDWELL, R. W., 1969, *A Short History of Commercial Horticulture in the Vale of Evesham*, Vale of Evesham Historical Soc., Research Papers, 2: 43–51.

SIMON, J. E., *see* JANICK and SIMON.

SIMPSON, H., *see* NOTESTEIN, RELF, and SIMPSON.

SKIPP, VICTOR, 1978, *Crisis and Development: An Ecological Case Study of the Forest of Arden, 1570–1674*, Cambridge.

SLACK, PAUL, ed., 1975, *Poverty in Early Stuart Salisbury*, Wiltshire Rec. Soc. 31.

SLEE, BILL, 1989, 2nd edn. [1st edn. 1987], *Alternative Farm Enterprises: A Guide to Alternative Sources of Income for the Farmer*, Ipswich.

SMITH, A. HASSELL, and BAKER, GILLIAN M., eds., 1983, *The Papers of Nathaniel Bacon of Stiffkey*, ii. *1578–85*, Centre of East Anglian Studies, Univ. of East Anglia, Norwich.

SMITH, R. A. L., 1943, and 1969 edn., *Canterbury Cathedral Priory: A Study in Monastic Administration*, Cambridge.

SMITH, R. E. F., and CHRISTIAN, DAVID, 1984, *Bread and Salt: A Social and Economic History of Food and Drink in Russia*, Cambridge.

SMITH, R. M., 1991, 'Demographic developments in rural England, 1300–48: A survey', in Bruce M. S. Campbell, ed., *Before the Black Death: Studies in the Crisis of the Early Fourteenth Century*, Manchester, 25–77.

SMITH, R. S., 1961, 'A woad-growing project at Wollaton in the 1580's', *Trans. Thoroton Soc. Notts.*, 65: 27–46.

SOEST, LOUIS J. M. VAN, and MULDER, FREEK, 1993, 'Potential new oilseed crops for industrial use', *Lipid Technology*, May–June: 60–5.

—— DOORGEEST, MARTIJN, and ENSINK, ELS, 1987, *Introductie-Demonstratie tuin Potentiële nieuwe Gewassen (Informatie, Knelpunten en potentie)*, Centrum voor Genetische Bronnen Nederland Stichting voor Plantenveredeling (Foundation for Agricultural Plant Breeding), Wageningen.

SOLLY, REVD. HENRY, 1884, *Home Colonisation: Rehousing of the Industrial Classes; or Village Communities v. Town Rookeries*, London.

SOMERVILLE, WILLIAM, 1923, 'The laying down of land to grass', *JRASE* 84: 11–28.

SOWERBY, LEONARD, 1652, *The Ladies' Dispensatory*, London.

SPEED, ADOLPHUS, 1659, *Adam out of Eden, or an Abstract of Divers Excellent Experiments touching the Advancement of Husbandry*, London.

STALLENGE, W., 1609, 'Instructions for the Increasing and Planting of Mulberrie Trees, and the Breeding of Silke-Wormes for the making of Silke in this Kingdome', *Harleian Miscellany*, ed. W. Oldys, ii, London 1809, 218–22.

STAPLEDON, R. G., 1914, *Report on the Condition of the Seed Trade in the Aberystwyth College Area*, Aberystwyth.

—— 1943, *The Way of the Land*, London.

—— and DAVIES, W., 1942, *Ley Farming*, London.

STEANE, JOHN M., 1970–1, 'The medieval fishponds of Northamptonshire', *Northants Past & Present*, 4/5: 299–310.

—— 1975, 'The medieval parks of Northamptonshire', *Northants Past & Present*, 5/3: 211–33.

—— 1985, *The Archaeology of Medieval England and Wales*, London.

STEARNS, RAYMOND PHINEAS, 1932, 'Agricultural adaptation in England, 1875–1900', *Agricultural History*, 6/2 and 3: 84–101, 130–54.

STONE, L., 1949, 'Elizabethan overseas trade', *EcHR* 2nd ser. 2: 30–56.

STRATTON, RICHARD, 1882, 'Flax for paper-making', *JRASE* 2nd ser. 18: 455–74.

STREET, A. W., 1933, 'The Agricultural Marketing Act', *JRASE* 94: 1–21.

STUBBS, CHARLES WILLIAM, 1885 edn., *The Land and the Labourers: A Record of Facts and Experiments in Cottage Farming and Cooperative Agriculture*, London.

STUBBS, MAYLING, 1982, 'John Beale, philosophical gardener of Herefordshire. Part I, Prelude to the Royal Society (1608–1663)', *Annals of Science*, 39: 463–89; 1989, Part II, 'The improvement of agriculture and trade in the Royal Society (1663–1683)', *Annals of Science*, 46: 323–63.

SUTTON, ARTHUR W., 1897, 'Progress in vegetable cultivation during Queen Victoria's reign', *J. Roy. Hortic. Soc.*, 21/1: 363–93.

SYME, JOHN T. BOSWELL, 1863–86, *English Botany, or Coloured Figures of British Plants*, London.

TALLANT, FRANCIS, 1880, 'Underwood: The planting, growth, conversion and sale thereof', *JRASE* 16: 114–21.

TAWNEY, R. H., and POWER, EILEEN, eds., 1924, *Tudor Economic Documents*, 3 vols., London.

———— *see also* BLAND, BROWN, and TAWNEY.

TAYLOR, A. J., *see* BROWN, COLVIN, and TAYLOR.

TAYLOR, DAVID, 1974, 'The English dairy industry, 1860–1930: The need for a reassessment', *AHR* 22/2: 153–9.

—— 1976, 'The English dairy industry, 1860–1930', *EcHR* 29/4: 585–601.

—— 1987, 'Growth and structural change in the English dairy industry, c.1860–1930', *AHR* 35/1: 47–64.

TAYLOR, H. V., 1929, 'The farm for market-garden crops', *JRASE* 90: 127–40.

TAYLOR, SEDLEY, 1884, *Profit Sharing between Capital and Labour: Six Essays*, London.

TEMPLE, WILLIAM, 1903, *Essays of Sir William Temple*. Selection with an Introduction by J. A. Nicklin, London.

THICK, MALCOLM, 1990a, 'Root crops and the feeding of London's poor in the late sixteenth and seventeenth centuries', in John Chartres and David Hey, eds., 1990, London, 279–96.

—— 1990b, 'Garden seeds in England before the eighteenth century, I. Seed growing; II. The trade in seeds to 1760', *AHR* 38/1 and 2: 58–71, 105–16.

—— 1993, ' "Superior vegetables", greens and roots in London, 1660–1750', in Gerald and Valerie Mars, eds., *Food, Culture, and History*, i, London Food Seminar, 53 Nassington Road, London, NW3.

THIRSK, JOAN, ed., 1967, *The Agrarian History of England and Wales*, iv. *1500–1640*, Cambridge.

—— 1978, *Economic Policy and Projects: The Development of a Consumer Society in Early Modern England*, Oxford.

—— 1980, 'Policies for retrenchment in seventeenth-century Europe: A review article', *Comparative Studies in Society and History*, 22/4: 626–33.

—— 1983, 'Plough and pen: Agricultural writers in the seventeenth century', in T. H. Aston *et al.*, eds., *Social Relations and Ideas*, 295–318.

—— 1984a, 'New crops and their diffusion: Tobacco-growing in seventeenth-century England', in Thirsk, 1984d, 259–85.

—— 1984b, 'Projects for gentlemen, jobs for the poor: Mutual aid in the Vale of Tewkesbury, 1600–30', in Thirsk, 1984d, 287–307.

—— 1984c, 'Horses in early modern England: For service, for pleasure, for power', in Thirsk, 1984d, 375–401.

—— 1984d, *The Rural Economy of England: Collected Essays*, London.

—— 1985, 'Forest, field, and garden: Landscapes and economies in Shakespeare's England', in John Andrewes, ed., *William Shakespeare: His World, his Work, his Influence*, 3 vols., New York, i.

—— 1987, 'Raleigh's England', in H. G. Jones, ed., *Raleigh and Quinn: The Explorer and his Boswell*, Chapel Hill, NC: 35–49.

—— 1990a, 'The fashioning of the Tudor–Stuart gentry', *Bulletin John Rylands University Library of Manchester*, 72/1: 69–85.

—— 1990*b*, *Agricultural Change: Policy and Practice, 1500–1750*, Cambridge.

—— 1991, 'Rural migration in England: The long historical perspective', in J. A. Mollett, ed., *Migrants in Agricultural Development: A Study of Intra-rural Migration*, London, 32–55.

—— 1992*a*, 'Making a fresh start: Sixteenth-century agriculture and the classical inspiration', in Michael Leslie and Timothy Raylor, eds., *Culture and Cultivation in Early Modern England: Writing and the Land*, Leicester and London, 15–34.

—— 1992*b*, 'Agrarian problems and the English Revolution', in Richardson, 1992, 169–97.

—— 1992*c*, 'The Crown as projector on its own estates', in Hoyle, 1992, 297–352.

—— 1992*d*, 'Conference Report: Rural society and the poor. Winter conference, 1991', *AHR* 40/1: 81–2.

—— 1995, Review of Campbell and Overton, *Land, Labour and Livestock, Eng. Hist. Rev.* 110/435: 272–3.

—— *see also* ASTON, COSS, DYER, and THIRSK.

—— and COOPER, J. P., eds., 1972, *Seventeenth-Century Economic Documents*, Oxford.

THOMAS, EDGAR, 1927, *The Economics of Small Holdings: A Study Based on a Survey of Small Scale Farming in Carmarthenshire*, Cambridge.

THOMAS, WILLIAM, 1774, *The Works of William Thomas, Clerk of the Privy Council in the Year 1549*, ed. Abraham d'Aubant, London.

THOMPSON, FLORA, 1939, repr. 1957, *Lark Rise to Candleford*, London.

THOMPSON, F. M. L., 1963, *English Landed Society in the Nineteenth Century*, London.

—— 1968, 'The second agricultural revolution, 1815–80', *EcHR* 2nd ser. 21/1: 62–77.

—— 1991, 'An anatomy of English agriculture, 1870–1914', in B. A. Holderness and M. Turner, eds., *Land, Labour, and Agriculture, 1700–1920: Essays for Gordon Mingay*, London.

THOMPSTONE, STUART, 1992, 'Bab'ye khozyaystvoʹ: Poultry-keeping and its contribution to peasant income in pre-1914 Russia', *AHR* 40/1: 52–63.

THORNTON, CHRISTOPHER, 1991, 'The determinants of land productivity on the Bishop of Winchester's demesne of Rimpton, 1208 to 1403', in Campbell and Overton, 1991, 183–210.

TITOW, J. Z., 1972, *Winchester Yields: A Study in Medieval Agricultural Productivity*, Cambridge.

TITS-DIEUAIDE, M.-J., 1981, 'L'Évolution des techniques agricoles en Flandre et en Brabant du XIVe au XVIe siècle, *Annales ESC* 36/3: 362–81.

TITTENSOR, RUTH and ANDREW, 1986, *The Rabbit Warren at West Dean*, Walberton, Arundel, Sussex.

TODD, NIGEL, 1986, *Roses and Revolutionists: The Story of the Clousden Hill Free Communist and Cooperative Colony, 1894–1902*, London.

TONIOLO, G., *see* O'BRIEN and TONIOLO.

TOPHAM, EDWARD, ed., 1776, *Letters from Edinburgh; written in the Years 1774 and 1775; containing some Observations on the Diversions, Customs, Manners, and Laws of the Scotch Nation during a six Months' Residence in Edinburgh*, London.

TORODE, ANGELIKI, 1966, 'Trends in fruit consumption', in T. C. Barker, J. C. McKenzie, and J. Yudkin, eds., 1966, *Our Changing Fare: Two Hundred Years of British Food Habits*, London, 115-34.

TRIBE, KEITH, 1978, *Land, Labour, and Economic Discourse*, London.

TROWELL, SAMUEL, 1739, *A New Treatise of Husbandry*, London.

TRYON, THOMAS, 1699, *England's Grandeur and Way to get Wealth: or Promotion of Trade made easy and Lands Advanced*, London.

—— 1705, *Some Memoirs of the Life of Mr Thos. Tryon, late of London, Merchant, written by Himself*, London.

UDALE, JAMES, 1904, 'Practical hints on vegetable farming', *JRASE* 65: 67-105.

UNDERWOOD, F. ASHWORTH, 1953, 'Pharmacy and therapeutics in the age of Elizabeth I', *Pharmaceutical Journal*, 170/4764 (4th ser. 116), May: 406-7, 411-15.

UNWIN, GEORGE, ed. R. H. Tawney, 1927, *Studies in Economic History: The Collected Papers of George Unwin*, London.

URRY, J. B., 1930, *The Woad Plant and its Dye*, Oxford.

USA, National Research Council, 1989, *Alternative Agriculture*. Committee on the Role of Alternative Farming Methods in Modern Production Agriculture, Washington.

USA, Dept. of Agriculture, 1966, *Growing Safflower: An Oilseed Crop*, Farmers' Bulletin 2133, Washington.

VALENZE, DEBORAH, 1991, 'Women's work and the dairy industry, *c.*1740-1840', *Past & Present*, 130: 142-69.

VEALE, ELSPETH M., 1957, 'The rabbit in England', *AHR* 5/2: 85-90.

—— 1966, *The English Fur Trade in the Later Middle Ages*, Oxford.

VERNEY, LADY, 1888, *How the Peasant Owner Lives in Parts of France, Germany, Italy, Russia*, London.

VILMORIN, MAURICE L. DE, 1890, 'The vegetable supply of a large town', *JRASE* 3rd ser. 1: 874-6.

VOELCKER, J. AUGUSTUS, 1880, 'Report by Augustus Voelcker on experiments at Woburn on continuous growing of grain', *JRASE* 2nd ser. 16: 130-49 (and in subsequent vols. *passim*).

—— 1896, 'Fruit and vegetable drying at Leicester', *JRASE* 3rd ser. 7: 500-20.

—— 1923, 'The Woburn experimental farm and its work (1876-1921)', *JRASE* 84: 110-66.

WATSON, J. A. SCOTT, 1936, 'Notable farming enterprises: VII, Mr Clyde Higgs's dairy farms', *JRASE* 97: 112-23.

WEATHERS, JOHN, ed., 1913, *Commercial Gardening: A Practical and Scientific Treatise for Market Gardeners, Market Growers, Fruit, Flower and Vegetable Growers, Nurserymen, etc.*, 4 vols., London.

WEBBER, RONALD, 1968, *The Early Horticulturists*, Newton Abbot.

WEBSTER, CHARLES, 1975, *The Great Instauration: Science, Medicine, and Reform, 1626-1660*, London.

[WESTON, SIR RICHARD], 1652, *A Discours of Husbandrie used in Brabant, and Flanders*, 2nd edn., London.

WHELDON, R. W. *et al.*, 1931, 'The making of pasture', *JRASE* 92: 62-125.

WHETHAM, EDITH H., 1964, 'The London milk trade, 1860-1900', *EcHR* 2nd ser. 17/2: 369-80.

—— 1970, *The London Milk Trade, 1900–1930,* Research Paper 3, Institute of Agricultural History, Reading University.

—— 1971, *see* ORWIN and WHETHAM.

—— 1978, *The Agrarian History of England and Wales,* viii. *1914–39,* Cambridge.

WHITE, EILEEN, 1993, 'The measure of the meat: Monastic diet in medieval England', in C. Anne Wilson, ed., *Food for the Community: Special Diets for Special Groups,* 1991, Edinburgh, 5–42.

WHITEHEAD, CHARLES, 1882, 'Hints on vegetable and fruit farming', *JRASE* 2nd ser. 18: 71–104.

—— 1883, 'The progress of fruit farming', *JRASE* 2nd ser. 19: 368–87.

—— 1884, *Profitable Fruit Farming: An Essay Written for Worshipful Company of Fruiterers,* London.

—— 1889, 'Fifty years of fruit farming', *JRASE* 2nd. ser. 25: 156–80.

—— 1890*a,* 'Fifty years of hop farming', *JRASE* 3rd ser. 1: 321–48.

—— 1890*b,* 'Fruit farming for profit', *JRASE* 3rd ser. 1: 197–9.

—— 1892, 'New modes of disposing of fruit and vegetables', *JRASE* 3rd ser. 3: 589–97.

—— 1893, 'Hop cultivation', *JRASE* 3rd ser. 4: 217–62.

—— 1899, 'A sketch of the agriculture of Kent', *JRASE* 3rd ser. 10: 429–85.

—— 1904, 'Practical hints on fruit farming', *JRASE* 65: 26–66.

WILKINS, MRS ROWLAND, *see* JEBB, LOUISA.

WILLIAMS, HOWARD, 1883, *The Ethics of Diet: A Catena of Authorities Deprecatory of the Practice of Flesh-eating,* London.

WILLIAMS, ROBERT, 1987, 'Rural economy and the antique in the English landscape garden', *J. of Garden History: The Journal of the Garden History Society,* 7/1: 73–96.

WILLS, N. T., 1979, *Woad in the Fens,* Long Sutton, Spalding, Lincs.

WILSON, C., 1968, *The Dutch Republic and the Civilisation of the Seventeenth Century,* London.

WILSON, C. ANNE, 1975, 'Burnt wine and cordial waters: The early days of distilling', *Folklife,* 13: 54–65.

—— 1984, 'Philosophers, *Iōsis* and Water of Life', *Proc. Leeds Philosophical and Literary Soc., Literary and Historical Section,* 19/5, 101–219.

WILSON, FRANZESCA, 1991, *Aromatherapy for you at Home,* London.

WILSON, REVD. JOHN M., ed., 1847, *The Rural Cyclopedia or a General Dictionary of Agriculture,* i, Edinburgh.

WINFREY, R., 1906, 'The progress of the small holdings movement', *Economic J.* 16: 222–9.

WINSTANLEY, MICHAEL, 1996, 'Industrialization and the pastoral economy: Family and household production in nineteenth-century Lancashire', *Past & Present,* 152: 157–95.

WISKERKE, C., 1952, 'De Geschiedenis van het meekrapbedrijf in Nederland,' *Economisch-Historisch Jaarboek,* xxxv, The Hague.

WOODCROFT, BENNET, 1854, *Alphabetical Index of Patentees of Inventions, 1617–1852,* repr. 1969, London.

WOOKEY, BARRY, 1987, *Rushall: The Story of an Organic Farm,* Oxford.

WORLIDGE, JOHN, 1675, and 1687 edn., *Systema Agriculturae,* London.

—— 1677, *Systema Horticulturae,* London.

WORLIDGE, JOHN, 1704, *Dictionarium Rusticum et Urbanicum, or a Dictionary of all Sorts of Country Affairs...*, London.

WRIGHT, JOHN, 1886, *Mushrooms for the Million (illustrated) with Supplement: A Practical Treatise on the Cultivation of the Most Profitable Outdoor Crop Known*, 4th edn., London.

—— 1889, *Profitable Fruit Growing: The Worshipful Company of Fruiterers Prize Essay*, London.

—— 1893, *Primer of Horticulture: Ten Lectures delivered for the Surrey County Council*, London.

—— 1920, *Profitable Fruit Growing*, 11th edn., ed. Walter Wright, London.

WRIGHTSON, JOHN, 1890, 'The agricultural lessons of "the Eighties" ', *JRASE* 3rd ser. 1: 275–88.

WRIGLEY, E. A., and SCHOFIELD, R. S., 1981, *The Population History of England, 1541–1871: A Reconstruction*, Cambridge.

YATES, E. M., 1974, 'Enclosure and the rise of grassland farming in Staffordshire', *North Staffs. J. of Field Studies*, 14: 46–60.

YOUNG, ARTHUR, 1813, *General View of the Agriculture of Lincolnshire*, London.

YOUNGS, F. A., 1976, *The Proclamations of the Tudor Queens: Marian and Elizabethan Proclamations*, Cambridge.

INDEX

Names of certain counties are abbreviated thus: Cnw. = Cornwall, Cumbd = Cumberland, Dvn = Devon, Dors. = Dorset, Ldn = London, Mdx = Middlesex, Northd = Northumberland, Rutld = Rutland, Som. = Somerset, Sfk = Suffolk, Surr. = Surrey, Sx = Sussex, Westmd = Westmorland.